Comparative
Administrative Law

Comparative Administrative Law

AN ANALYSIS OF THE ADMINISTRATIVE SYSTEMS
NATIONAL AND LOCAL, OF THE UNITED STATES,
ENGLAND, FRANCE AND GERMANY

By

Frank J. Goodnow, A. M., LL.B.

PROFESSOR OF ADMINISTRATIVE LAW IN THE UNIVERSITY FACULTY OF
POLITICAL SCIENCE, COLUMBIA COLLEGE IN THE CITY OF NEW YORK

In One Combined Volume
Volume-I
Organization

Volume-II
Legal Relations

BeardBooks
Washington, D.C.

New York:

Burt Franklin

Published 1903

Reprinted 2000 by Beard Books, Washington, D.C.

ISBN 1-58798-072-X

Printed in the United States of America

PREFACE.

It will be well perhaps to explain the purpose of the book which is herewith submitted to the public. For it is necessary, in order to do justice to all concerned, that the author apprise his readers at the outset that he has not attempted to treat exhaustively of the entire domain of administrative law. His intention has been rather to set forth, in the first place, the methods of administrative organization adopted in the four countries whose law is considered, namely, the United States, England, France, and Germany, and to state, in the second place, somewhat in detail, the means of holding this organization up to its work, and of preventing it from encroaching on those rights which have been guaranteed to the individual by the constitution or laws. The treatment of this control over the administration has made it necessary to include a summary of the forms and methods of administrative action; for without an understanding of them an adequate conception of the control over the administration would be impossible of attainment. This particular portion of the work is confessedly the least complete, but the author considers this incompleteness a virtue rather than a fault, if he has been able, as he hopes he has, in the few pages devoted to this matter, to make it clear to his readers, in what manner the administration acts, and even to suggest in this or in the other portions of the work the directions of the action of the administration. A detailed consideration of the directions of administrative action, as well as of its methods, is, it is true, a necessity for the practising lawyer. It would, however, be of slight interest if not a positive disadvantage to the beginner in the study of administrative law; while the general reader, for whose use this work is also intended, would probably be deterred by the magnitude of the work presented by such a consideration from entering upon the study of administrative law at all. This study the author naturally considers to be of the greatest importance. The great problems of modern public law are almost exclusively administrative in character. While the age that has passed was one of constitutional, the present age is one of administrative reform. Our modern complex social conditions are making enormous demands of the administrative side of the government, demands which will not be satisfied at all or which will be inadequately met, unless a greater knowledge of administrative law and science is possessed by our legislators and moulders of opinion. This knowledge can be obtained only by study, and by comparison of our own with foreign administrative methods. It is in the hope of pointing out the way to future students in this subject that the following pages have been written. The needs of the legal practitioner have been met elsewhere by excellent treatises on the most important branches of administrative law, such as that of Judge Dillon on *The Law of Municipal Corporations*, that of Judge Cooley on *The Law of Taxation*, and that of Mr. Mechem on *The Law of Officers,* on which the author has placed great reliance. The details of foreign law also may be found in excellent treatises, either French or German, to which continual references have been made in the text. Finally the book has been written with the end in view of supplementing the work done by Professor John W. Burgess in his *Political Science and Comparative Constitutional Law.* For this reason as well as owing to the lack of space, all matters of a distinctively constitutional character have been omitted, and the student has been referred to Professor Burgess' work. It is only where a comprehension of administrative subjects has absolutely required a knowledge of their constitutional foundations that the author has ventured to treat even in the most cursory manner of constitutional questions.

It is only fair to add also that the work was begun by first studying with considerable care books on foreign administrative law. This was necessary, owing to the complete lack of any work in the English language on administrative law as a whole, and was possible and profitable owing to the richness of the literature of foreign administrative law. After a method of treatment had thus been obtained, the attempt was made to apply it to American law. American conditions necessitated numerous and important modifications of this method of treatment, but the author is conscious of the fact that a foreign point of view will often be noticed, a fact for which, however, he does not consider an apology necessary. For in the present stage of the study it is to foreign writers that we must look for all scientific presentations of the subject.

The author deems it necessary to acknowledge how much he is indebted to the published works and personal influence felt in lectures he has heard, of Professor Rudolph von Gneist, of the University of Berlin, Germany. Great reliance has been placed also on the excellent work, contained in the *Introduction to the Local Constitutional History of the United States,* of Professor Howard, of Leland Stanford, Jr., University, California, whose conclusions have been in most cases accepted without question, and re-stated in the text. He desires also to express his indebtedness to the many friends from whom he has received most helpful suggestions, and particularly to Professors John W. Burgess and Edwin R. A. Seligman of Columbia College, and to Doctor Ernst Freund of the New York Bar, who have read either all or parts of what he has written. The author finally desires to call the attention of his readers to the fact that in all of the cross references made in the text, the first volume is to be understood unless the number of the volume is given.

Trusting that an indulgent public will pardon those errors which will creep in, notwithstanding the greatest care, he submits with hesitation a work on a new subject, and hopes that what he has done will at any rate have the effect of inducing others to study what has been of the greatest interest to him and what he believes all interested in social problems should know something about.

Frank J. Goodnow.

Columbia College,
September 1st, 1893.

COMPARATIVE ADMINISTRATIVE LAW.

TABLE OF CONTENTS.

VOLUME I. ORGANIZATION.

BOOK I. THE SEPARATION OF POWERS.

CHAPTER I. ADMINISTRATION.

CHAPTER II. ADMINISTRATIVE LAW.

CHAPTER III. THE THEORY OF THE SEPARATION OF POWERS.

CHAPTER IV. EXCEPTIONS TO THE THEORY OF THE SEPARATION OF POWERS.

CHAPTER V. THE RELATION OF THE EXECUTIVE TO THE OTHER AUTHORITIES.

CHAPTER VI. TERRITORIAL DISTRIBUTION OF ADMINIS-
TRATIVE FUNCTIONS.

BOOK II. CENTRAL ADMINISTRATION.

DIVISION I. THE EXECUTIVE POWER AND THE CHIEF EXECUTIVE AUTHORITY.

CHAPTER I. IN GENERAL.

CHAPTER II. HISTORY OF THE EXECUTIVE AUTHORITY AND POWER IN THE UNITED STATES.

CHAPTER III. THE ORGANIZATION OF THE CHIEF EXECUTIVE AUTHORITY IN THE UNITED STATES.

BOOK III. LOCAL ADMINISTRATION.

CHAPTER I. HISTORY OF RURAL LOCAL ADMINISTRATION IN THE UNITED STATES.

CHAPTER II. RURAL LOCAL ADMINISTRATION IN THE UNITED STATES AT THE PRESENT TIME.

CHAPTER III. MUNICIPAL ORGANIZATION IN THE UNITED STATES.

CHAPTER VII. LOCAL ADMINISTRATION IN PRUSSIA.

TABLE OF CASES CITED.

BOOK I.

THE SEPARATION OF POWERS.

CHAPTER I.

ADMINISTRATION.

I.—Administration as a function of government.

THE word administration is used in several senses. Thus we speak of the administration of an estate, the administration of a business, and of the administration of government.[1] In the following pages the word administration will be used with reference to government. But even when used with reference to government, this word has as many as three meanings. In its widest sense, it is used to indicate the entire activity of the government; again in a narrower sense, the entire activity of the government with the exception of that of the legislature; in a third and narrowest sense, the activity of the government with the exception of the activity of both the legislature and the courts.[2] Administration in this narrowest of senses, which is the proper sense for it as indicative of a function of government, is the activity of the executive officers of

---

[1] Stengel, *Deutsches Verwaltungsrecht*, 1.

[2] Kirchenheim, *Einführung in das Verwaltungsrecht*, 2.

the government. The government administers when it appoints an officer, instructs its diplomatic agents, assesses and collects its taxes, drills its army, investigates a case of the commission of crime, and executes the judgment of a court. Whenever we see the government in action as opposed to deliberation or the rendering of a judicial decision, there we say is administration. Administration is thus to be found in all the manifestations of executive action. The directions in which this action manifests itself depend upon the position of the state and the duties of the government.

In the first place, the state occupies a position among other states; it is a subject of international law, and as such has rights and duties over against other states and must enter into relations with them. The management of these relations calls for certain executive action. This action constitutes a branch of the general function of administration, *viz.*, the Administration of Foreign Relations.

In the second place, the state must have means at its command to repel any attempts which may be made against its existence or power by other states or against its peace and order by its own inhabitants. In other words, it must have an army and in most cases a navy. The executive action made necessary by the existence of a military force constitutes another branch of administration, *viz.*, the Administration of Military Affairs.

In the third place, every government must do something to decide the conflicts which arise between its inhabitants relative to their rights. This duty makes the existence of courts necessary; and they in turn require executive action, which forms a third branch of administration, *viz.*, the Administration of Judicial Affairs.[1]

In the fourth place, in order that the government may perform all its duties, it must have pecuniary means. The management of its financial resources forms another and fourth branch of administration, *viz.*, the Financial Administration or the Administration of Financial Affairs. The theories of some political philosophers would almost confine the action of government to these branches of administration; but no government was ever actually so confined by its constitution ; and every modern state has recognized that it is the duty of the government to further directly the welfare, both physical and intellectual, of its citizens. This it does by the formation and maintenance of a system of means of communication, of an educational system, of a system of public charity, *etc.* How far the action of the government shall extend in this direction ; what it shall do and what it shall leave to the private enterprise of its citizens; are most important political questions, but questions which must be answered by political and social science.[2] The duties performed by the government in furthering the welfare of its citizens may be classed together as internal

---

[1] By this term is meant not the decision by the courts themselves of the controversies which may arise, since by the definition of the term administration which has been adopted this branch of governmental activity has been excluded from the conception of administration ; but the activity of the executive organs of the government to the end that the courts be in existence and in a position to discharge their duties, *i. e.* the appointment, discipline, and distribution of the judges and their subordinate officers. This is a side of what is ordinarily called the administration of justice, which in most countries is easily distinguished from the rendering of judicial decisions.

[2] *Cf.* Burgess, *Political Science and Comparative Constitutional Law*, I., 83.

affairs; and the executive action of the government necessitated by the performance of these duties forms a fifth branch of administration, *viz.*, the Administration of Internal Affairs.

These five branches of administration embrace all the functions which the government is called upon to discharge whatever may be its form of organization. In the fifth branch—the administration of internal affairs—we find the greatest difference between states in the functions discharged by the government—a difference which is dependent upon the political philosophy which obtains.[1]

Such, then, is the meaning which will be given in the following pages to the term administration considered as a function of government. It is the entire activity of the government, exclusive of that of the legislature and the purely judicial work of the courts, in the fivefold direction of foreign, military, judicial, financial, and internal affairs.

II.—The administration as an organization.

The government is, however, simply an ideal conception with no physical existence. In order that it may make itself felt in the world of action it must have agents capable of physical action who are to represent it. These agents must be properly organized for each

[1] Several of the latest continental writers on administration have endeavored to differentiate another branch of administration, which they call the general administration of the country. See Kirchenheim, *op. cit.*, 5 ; Stengel, *Deutsches Verwaltungsrecht*, 5. They classify under this branch such matters as the elections and the relations of the government with the church. This attempted formation of a sixth branch of administration is, however, contrary to general usage and seems unnecessarily to complicate the subject, as all matters may, without doing them great violence, be classed under the appropriate one of the five branches distinguished.

of the five branches of administration which have been distinguished : and further in order to secure unity in their action in these various directions there must also be organized an authority at the head of this administrative personnel—an executive chief. On this account the study of administration is not taken up exclusively with a consideration of the rules of administrative action; but a large part of the time devoted to this study must be given to the subject of administrative organization. Indeed, the importance of the administrative organization is so great that the term administration is often used to indicate the entire administrative organization extending down from the executive chief to the most humble of his subordinates. The word administration thus means, at the same time that it indicates a function of government, the executive organization of the state. Administration is the function of execution ; the administration is the totality of the executive and administrative authorities.

CHAPTER II.

I.—Definition.

In this country and in England, where no serious attempt has been made to classify the law in accordance with the relations which it governs, the term administrative law is almost meaningless. While we speak with perfect propriety of administration as indicative of a function of government, and of the administration as an executive organization, there is hardly an American or English lawyer who would recognize the existence of a branch of law called administrative law. Indeed as eminent a writer as Professor Dicey claims[1] that "in England and in countries which, like the United States, derive their civilization from English sources, the system of administrative law and the very principles on which it rests are unknown." He does not, however, mean by this to deny the existence of an administrative law in the true continental sense, but simply the existence of his conception of the French *droit administratif*, a conception which appears to be quite unwarranted. The general failure in England and the United States to recognize an administrative law is really due, not to the non-existence in these

---

[1] *The Law of the Constitution*, 3rd Ed., 304–306.

6

countries of this branch of the law but rather to the well-known failure of English law writers to classify the law. For not only has there always existed in England, as well as in this country, an administrative law, in the true continental sense of the word, but this law has exercised on Anglo-Saxon political development an influence perhaps greater than that exerted by any other part of the English law. Of late years, with the great awakening on the continent of Europe of interest in administrative subjects, the term administrative law—in reality a simple translation of a French expression—has gradually crept into our legal vocabulary, and at the present time has obtained recognition from some of the most advanced legal thinkers.[1] The use of the term may therefore be regarded as perfectly proper ; though that use must be accompanied by an explanation. Adopting the system of legal classification now generally admitted to be the most desirable, *viz.*, according to relations governed, we find that administrative law is that part of the law which governs the relations of the executive and administrative authorities of the government. It is therefore a part of the public law, but it is only a part. All such rules of law as concern the function of administration, and only such rules of law, belong to administrative law. Further, since the function of administration depends for its discharge upon the existence of administrative authorities, whose totality is called the administration, adminstrative law is concerned not alone with the relations of the administrative authorities but

---

[1] *E. g.* see Holland, *Elements of Jurisprudence,* 4th Edition, 1888, 122, 303, 308–311 ; Lightwood, *The Nature of Positive Law,* 402 ; *The Juridical Review,* II., No. 5, 13 ; Stimson, *American Statute Law,* v.

also with their organization. Administrative law at the same time fixes the offices which shall form part of the administration and determines the relations into which the holders of these offices shall enter.

In so far as it fixes the organization of the administrative authorities, administrative law is the necessary supplement to constitutional law. While constitutional law gives the general plan of governmental organization, administrative law carries out this plan in its minutest details. But administrative law not only supplements constitutional law, in so far as it regulates the administrative organization of the government; it also complements constitutional law, in so far as it determines the rules of law relative to the activity of the administrative authorities. For while constitutional law treats the relations of the government with the individual from the standpoint of the rights of the individual, administrative law treats them from the standpoint of the powers of the government. Constitutional law, it has been said, lays stress upon rights; administrative law emphasizes duties.[1] But while administrative law emphasizes the powers of the government and the duties of the citizen, it is nevertheless to the administrative law that the individual must have recourse when his rights are violated. For just so far as administrative law delimits the sphere of action of the administration it indicates what are the rights of the individual which the administration must respect; and, in order to prevent the administration from violating them, offers to the individual remedies for the violation of these rights.

Administrative law is therefore that part of the public law which fixes the organization and determines

---

[1] Boeuf, *Droit Administratif*, iv.

the competence of the administrative authorities, and indicates to the individual remedies for the violation of his rights.

II.—Necessity for separate treatment.

It may be asked why is it necessary to separate administrative law from the body of the law ? Do the rules of law governing the relations of the administration differ so much from the rules governing the relations of individuals as to necessitate in a logical classification of the law the assignment of a special domain to administrative law ? The question is susceptible of easy answer so far as the first great class of the rules of administrative law are concerned. The rules of law governing the organization of the administration must be quite different from the rules of law governing the relations of individuals, since the whole purpose of such rules is the public rather than the individual welfare. When we come to the second great class of rules it may, however, well be asked, are there or must there be rules of law for the regulation of the action of the administration different from those which regulate the action of individuals ? The government in many cases acts in much the same way as an ordinary individual ; and in these cases, it may be urged, might be subjected to the same rules of law which affect private individuals. Thus the government may carry on railroad enterprises, may offer means of communication by carrying the mails, may own large landed properties. In all of these cases the government has many of the characteristics of a private person, and it might be concluded from this fact, that the ordinary rules of private law might be applied to it, that no special rules of law were necessary. Nevertheless, for the regulation of even these matters, special rules of law are enacted because the government cannot wisely or conveniently be treated as a private person. When it carries a letter the government cannot be regarded as an ordinary carrier of merchandise, because in transacting this business its object is not usually the acquisition of gain but the furtherance of the welfare of the community. This is the great distinction between public and private business.[1] Therefore the government enacts, for the regulation of the relations into which it enters with those persons who entrust letters to it, rules of law which differ from the ordinary rules of law regulating the relations of carriers, in that they are more favorable to the government. We find a special set of laws which we call postal laws. These form part of the administrative law, since they govern the action of the officers of the administration in the performance of this particular duty of the government.

In other, and indeed in most, cases, however, the government has few if any of the characteristics of a private person. It represents the sovereign power of the land. Through its administrative authorities it demands of the persons in its obedience the sacrifice of their property and curtails their freedom of action. It orders the tearing down of a house and the payment of taxes; it requires those who have charge of persons suffering from a contagious disease to notify the administration and enforces a quarantine against the diseased persons themselves. That the administration must do all of these things is now everywhere recognized; but nowhere is it recognized that it may

---

[1] *Cf.* Kirchenheim, *op. cit.*, 21 ; Adams, *Public Debts*, 369.

act in the doing of these things in accordance with its own unlimited discretion.[1] The grant to the administration of such enormous discretionary powers as would be necessary, would prove, indeed has in the past proved, dangerous in the extreme to the maintenance of individual liberty. There has therefore been a continuous attempt on the part of the people to control the discretion of the administration in the exercise of the sovereign powers of the state. This attempt has resulted in the formation of a new body of law which determines and delimits administrative action and discretion; and this body of law is made as a general thing by the legislature, the representative of the people and the supposed protector of individual rights.[2] The administration is thus brought within the law, but it still does not lose its position as the representative of the sovereign power. Therefore, in spite of the great development of popular institutions, at the present time the action of the administration in the most democratic states is easily distinguished in kind from that of private persons.

The result of the position of the administration as the representative of the sovereign is that the law which governs the relations into which it enters as such representative is quite different in many respects from the private law. In this law contract and tort play a very subordinate rôle. While contract and tort lie at the basis of a large part of the private law, in public law and therefore in administrative law there is hardly any room for them, no room for them at all it may be said, except where the government is treated as *fis-*

---

[1] Kirchenheim, *op. cit.*, 21.
[2] *Cf.* Sarwey, *Allgemeines Verwaltungsrecht*, 37.

cus, i. e. as a subject of private law. For the relations
into which the administration enters are not as a rule
contractual relations, but find their sources and their
limitations rather in obligations or powers conferred by
the sovereign power through its representative the legislature ; nor are the injuries which the administration
as administration commits often torts, but are rather
to be classed as *damna absque injuria.* Thus the relations of the administration with the individual resulting from the exercise of the taxing power are almost
never contractual relations ; taxes are not debts but
obligations imposed on the individual by the public
law,[1] and are not governed by the principles of the
private law. Thus also the relations into which the
administration enters with its officers are not governed by the private-law rules affecting the relation
of master and servant. For the official relation is
not a contractual relation but again a relation formed
by the operation of public law.[2] Still again, while the
relations of the government with private corporations
are by the laws of the United States in many cases
governed by contract principles, *i. e.* the clause of the
United States constitution preventing a commonwealth
from passing a law impairing the obligation of a contract (which is supposed to be found in its charter),
the relations of the government with public corporations are governed rather by the rules of public law
and are not much affected by the contract idea.[3]

In some of the cases decided by the courts of this
country the necessity of the separate study and treat-

[1] See Merriwether v. Garrett, 102 U. S., 472 ; and Pierce v. Boston, 3 Metc.
Mass., 520 ; *cf.* Cooley, Taxation 2d. Ed. 17, 18.

[2] Butler v. Penna., 18 How. U. S., 402 ; *infra*, II., p. 3.

[3] See Dartmouth College v. Woodward, 4 Wheaton, 636.

ment of the administrative law as a part of the public law is made particularly apparent. For the result of entrusting the development of the principles of the public law to judges engaged for the most part in the study and application of the principles of the private law, and of the resulting failure on the part of such judges to distinguish public from private relations, has been the application to public relations of the principles of the private law. This is most unfortunate. For in some cases the result of the too great insistence on the idea of contract in these public relations has been to revive in our public law, principles which are characteristic rather of feudal than of democratic states. Thus the decision that a commonwealth which has relinquished its taxing power may forever be precluded from reässuming it because in so doing it impairs the obligation of a contract, results in the formation of a class of persons possessed of privileges of a public and not private character, and privileges which may never be taken from them. This was exactly the feudal idea.[1] Again the decision that a commonwealth, for the same reason, may not amend the charter of a private corporation is another instance of the same tendency. That the public policy of such a decision is bad may be seen from the insertion in the constitutions of most all the commonwealths of a provision which expressly allows charters to be amended in the case of corporations chartered after the putting in force of the constitution. Further the great expansion of the police power by the decisions of the United States Supreme Court is an evidence also of the growing feeling

---

[1] See New Jersey v. Wilson, 7 Cranch, 164 ; Cooley, *Taxation*, 67 ; Burgess, *Political Science, etc.*, I., 238.

that the idea of contract has been applied unjustifiably in the relations of the public law.[1]   The position of the administration thus, both when it acts as the man of business, of society, and when it represents the sovereign, is so peculiar that its legal relations must be set aside for separate treatment in any system of legal classification which has regard for actual conditions.

III.—*Distinction of administrative law from private law.*

While administrative law has a sufficiently distinctive character to justify its assignment to a separate position in a scheme of legal classification, there are many cases in which it is extremely difficult to distinguish it from other branches of the law, many cases also where practical considerations have such weight as to overbalance any desire for logical exactness. This is especially true of some of the points where the domain of administrative law seems to touch upon that of private law.

We find many rules of law which, if we abide by the definition that has been given of administrative law, *viz.*, as that portion of the law which governs the relations of the administration, must be regarded as falling within its borders, but which at the same time have been enacted mainly with the idea of founding or strengthening purely private rights. Such for example are the rules of law governing the registration of legal instruments and the issue of patents. Such rules of law either alter the force of an existing right over against third persons or actually found a new

---

[1] For the distinction between private and public law, see Benson v. Mayor, 10 Barbour, N. Y., 223, 245.

private legal right and are thus private in character. On account of their character the usual practice is, notwithstanding the fact that they at the same time govern the relations of the administration, to regard them as a part of the private law. That is, all rules of law whose immediate purpose is the promotion of the rights of individuals are parts of the private law whether they govern at the same time the relations of the administration or not.[1] This was the rule of the Roman law. Ulpian says : "*Publicum jus est quod ad statum rei Romanæ spectat, privatum quod ad singulorum utilitatem.*"[2]

IV.—*Distinction from other branches of public law.*

The endeavor must also be made to distinguish administrative law from the other branches of public law. The distinction between administrative and constitutional law has already been indicated. While constitutional law defines the general plan of state organization and action, administrative law carries out this plan in its minutest details, supplements, and complements it.[3] The distinction between the two is thus one more of degree than of kind. Both treat to a large extent of the same subjects, the latter more in detail than the former, while the latter devotes itself almost entirely to the consideration of the executive organs of the government, since they are the only ones which actually act and administer. The distinction between administrative and international law also is quite clear. While administrative law lays down the

---

[1] *Cf.* Kirchenheim, *op. cit.*, 22.
[2] *Insts.*, I., sec. 4.
[3] See *supra*, p. 8.

rules which shall guide the officers of the administration in their action as agents of the government, international law consists of that body of usage which it is supposed that a state will follow in its relations with other states. While it is the guide of conduct of a state in its relations with other states, while its observance will conduce to peace and its non-observance may lead to trouble, it still cannot be regarded as binding upon the officers of any government considered in their relation to their own government except in so far as it has been adopted into the administrative law of the state. On this account the German jurist Zorn treats international law as external public law.[1]

The usual method of legal classification assigns to the criminal law a place in the public law. If this method is correct it becomes necessary to distinguish the administrative law from the criminal law. Any attempt to make such a distinction, as indeed to distinguish the criminal law from any of the clearly defined branches of the law, will be found, however, to present almost insurmountable difficulties. The conclusion is irresistible that from the scientific point of view the criminal law does not occupy any well defined position in the legal system separated in kind from the distinct branches of the law. It consists really of a body of penal sanctions which are applied to all the branches of the law.[2] A great many of the rules of all the branches of the law are found to require such sanctions in order to ensure their observance. Thus certain rules of law governing the relations of individuals one with

---

[1] *Das Reichsstaatsrecht*, II., 419; *cf.* Gumplowicz, *Das Oesterreichische Staatsrecht*, 348.

[2] *Cf.* Boeuf, *op. cit.*, iv. ; Lightwood, *The Nature of Positive Law*, 396–402.

another are found to be practicably unenforceable under any system of private actions. The government, therefore, steps in and gives them a penal sanction. The necessities are the same in other branches of the law. Penal sanctions often become necessary. The rules of law imposing these sanctions come to form a system of law, to which the name of criminal or penal law is attached. This law sanctions and protects all branches of the law without itself forming a distinct branch of the law. But while this law of penal sanction may not thus properly be regarded as a distinct portion of the law in the same way that the administrative law is a distinct portion of it, still the application of sufficiently rigorous penalties to enforce obedience to the law and the preservation at the same time of the rights of the individual present problems of such importance as to demand for their solution separate methods of thought and treatment, and to have brought it about that the law which imposes penal sanctions is regarded, and properly regarded, as forming a separate part of legal study. A science of penalties, *viz.*, penology, has also been developed, in accordance with whose theories the criminal law is moulded. It is thus seen that the rules of law which have been protected by a penal sanction may be really administrative in character. If they are of this character the student of administrative law may not, simply because they are thus protected, dismiss them from his consideration on the ground that they are a part of the criminal law. For, indeed, one of the most common and efficient means of enforcing a rule of administrative law is to give it a penal sanction, and the mere affixing of a penalty to

the violation of a rule of administrative law does not
deprive such rule of law of its administrative character.[1]   Nor does the mere imposition of a penalty of
necessity make the rule of law to the violation of which
the penalty is imposed a rule of criminal law in the
sense that it must be strictly construed.[2]   This comes
out particularly clearly in the distinction which is so
often made between crimes and police offences.[3]

[1] See *Infra*, II., p. 106.

[2] See Taylor *et al.* v. U. S., 3 How., 197, 210, where Judge Story says :
" The judge was therefore strictly accurate when he said [in his charge] ' it
must not be understood that every law which imposes a penalty is therefore,
legally speaking, a penal law, that is a law which is to be construed with great
strictness in favor of the defendant.   Laws enacted for the prevention of fraud,
for the suppression of public wrong or to effect a public good, are not, in the
strict sense, penal acts although they may inflict a penalty.'   It is in this light
I view revenue laws, and I would construe them so as most effectually to accomplish the intention of the Legislature in passing them."   See also Cliquot's
Champagne, 3 Wall., 114, 145 ; Smythe v. Fiske, 23 Wall., 374.

[3] See Wharton, *Criminal Law*, 9th Ed., I., secs. 23a and 28 ; also Oshkosh v.
Schwartz, 55 Wisc., 483 ; Commonwealth v. Willard, 22 Pickering, 476 ; U. S.
v. Barrels of Spirits, 2 Abbott's U. S., 305, 314 ; Cooley, *Taxation*, 2d Ed., 270.

CHAPTER III.

It has been shown that administration is to be found in the activity of the government exclusive of that of the legislature and that of the courts, *i. e.* in the activity of the executive organs of the government. The differentiation of three somewhat separate governmental authorities was the result of the political history and experience of Europe and especially of England. Historically it may be shown that all governmental power was at one time expressed in all cases in final instance by a single organ, *viz.*, the early mediæval monarch. Experience proved, however, that certain expressions of it should be made by the state, *i. e.* by the constitution-making power, and not by the government at all. This resulted in the distinction of the state from the government. Experience also showed that in the case where this governmental power should be expressed by the government it is a deliberative body largely independent of any other governmental organ which should act in a series of instances; that in another series it is an executing organ, largely separate from and independent of all other governmental authorities which should act; and that finally in another series of cases duties should be imposed upon a third series of authorities forming the judiciary. These three authorities were called respectively the legislature, the executive, and the judicial authority. This differentiation of governmental authorities was first noticed in modern times by Locke and Montesquieu, the latter of whom based upon this fact his famous theory of the separation or distribution of powers. In his great work on the *Esprit des Lois*, he first distinguished three great powers of government, *viz.*, the legislative, the executive, and the judicial, and then insisted on the importance of entrusting each of the powers to a separate authority distinct from and independent of the others.[1] This theory was very generally adopted by the political science of the time immediately succeeding Montesquieu, and, in a somewhat more extreme form than was probably believed in by Montesquieu himself, came to be regarded as almost a political axiom, which should lie at the basis of the political organization of all civilized states.[2]

Modern political science has, however, generally discarded this theory[3] both because it is incapable of accurate statement, and because it seems to be impossible to apply it with beneficial results in the formation of any concrete political organization. While it is true, says a judge of the supreme court of North Carolina[4] that "the executive, legislative, and supreme judicial powers of the government ought to be forever separate and distinct, it is also true that the science of government is a practical one; therefore, while each should firmly maintain the essential powers belonging to it, it cannot

---

[1] *Esprit des Lois*, book xi., chap. vi.

[2] For example, the Constituent Assembly of France laid it down in 1789 as a rule that a country in which the separation of powers is not determined, does not have a constitution. *Déclaration des droits de l'homme et du citoyen*, art. 16.

[3] Kirchenheim, *op. cit.*, I.

[4] Brown v. Turner, 70 N. C., 93, 102.

be forgotten that the three co-ordinate parts constitute one brotherhood whose common trust requires a mutual toleration of the occupancy of what seems to be a 'common because of vicinage' bordering on the domains of each."[1] The flaw in Montesquieu's reasoning, and in that of his followers, was the assumption that the expressions of the governmental power by different authorities were different powers. Seeing that the most important function of the English Parliament was the making of laws, they assumed that the sole duty of the Parliament was the making of laws, and that it alone possessed that power. This, indeed, as every one knows, was not the fact, but even had it been the fact, all that could be logically deduced from it was that the power of the English legislature consisted in the making of laws, and that this was the function of the Parliament alone. But they went a step farther, and, basing their generalization upon an insufficient induction, concluded that what was true of England, or rather what they supposed was true of England, was true everywhere or should be true everywhere. They stated as a truth of political science what was simply a local phenomenon. For just as English experience was at the basis of the differentiation of powers which Montesquieu supposed he had discovered and which undoubtedly existed in a general way in England, so continental experience is at the basis of a somewhat different differentiation of powers. In no two countries do we find exactly the same sphere of action assigned to any one of the governmental authorities which may be differentiated. In some, for example, the executive authority possesses a large power of control over legis-

[1] *Cf.* Sarwey, *op. cit.*, 26.

lation and over the policy of the government, in others almost none; in some the legislative authority has a large power over the formation of the executive authority, in others almost none.[1] What ought in theory to be the sphere of action of each of the different government authorities and what ought to be the sphere of action of the state, *i. e.* the constitution-making authority, are matters which must very largely be governed by the history and political needs of the particular country, and any attempt to impose on a country any hard and fast rule derived either from *a priori* reasoning or from any inductive generalization, based upon the experience of other countries, is rather more apt to meet with failure than success.

But while Montesquieu's theory is therefore lacking in both scientific and practical foundation, still it must be confessed that he stated a principle which has had an immense effect upon the political systems which have been elaborated since his day. His theory still lies at the basis of most political organizations at the present time. It is, however, subject to many exceptions which exceptions are not the same in different states. This theory may be stated as follows. The action of the legislature, which is commonly called the legislative power, but which is in reality merely an expression of the governmental power by the legislature, consists for the most part in the enactment of general norms of conduct for all persons and authorities within the state; the action of the executive authority, commonly called the executive power, is the application of these norms to concrete cases; and finally the action of the judges or the courts, commonly called

[1] *Cf.* Judge Christiancy's remarks in People v. Hurlburt, 24 Mich., 44, 63.

the judicial power, is the settlement of controversies arising between individuals or between individuals and the governmental authorities as to the application of the laws. It may further be added that experience has shown that in general it is best that these different authorities be confined to the exercise of the powers respectively assigned to them by this theory. There must, however, be important exceptions to any such rule ; and these exceptions are not the same in the different states, nor should they be the same, since the political experience and needs of no two states are the same. So long as the discussion as to the theory of the separation of powers is carried on from the stand-point of merely what ought to be, little difficulty arises, but if once the scientific theory is formulated as a legal rule, if once it is adopted in the positive law, the difficulties that arise are legion and are insoluble—insoluble simply because the theory is incapable of accurate statement; and therefore the decisions of the courts are necessarily very largely the expression of the subjective opinions of the judges making them. Judge Christiancy frankly admits [1] that the various powers which may be differentiated in accordance with the theory of the separation of powers differ in extent in different states, which is simply another way of saying that the opinions of judges and publicists differ. Nevertheless there is the rule of law that the legislative authority shall not exercise any judicial or executive powers, that the executive shall not exercise any legislative or judicial powers, and that the judicial authority shall not exercise any legislative or executive powers [2];

[1]. People v. Hurlburt, 24 Mich., 44, 63.
[2] See the Constitution of Massachusetts, art. xxx., pt. i.

and an infringement of the rule will lead to the inva-
lidity of the act of the authority so disobeying the rule
of the constitution.[1]   The student must therefore examine the constitution of his own state and its interpretation by the courts of that state where they have
the right to interpret the constitution, if he would
know how far the principle of the separation of powers
has any legal effect.   This is particularly true of the
United States both in its national and commonwealth
organizations, the principle of the separation of powers
being regarded in many cases as a fundamental rule in
this country.   But he must not expect that the rule
in the national government can be reconciled with the
rule in the commonwealth governments or that the
rules of any two of the commonwealth governments
must necessarily be the same.   Thus it has been held
in some of the commonwealths that even in the absence of constitutional restriction the legislature may
not grant a divorce, while in other commonwealths
this power has been recognized by the courts as belonging to the legislature.[2]   Again it has been held
that the courts may not act in the incorporation of
municipalities in accordance with the provisions of
general incorporating acts, since they are judicial bodies
and this is an administrative function.[3]   On the other
hand, the courts of other commonwealths have regarded
this action as perfectly proper.[4]

[1] Gordon v. U. S., 2 Wallace, 561.

[2] Cooley, *Constitutional Limitations*, 6th Ed., 128, 133.

[3] People v. Bennet, 29 Mich., 451 ; People v. Nevada, 6 Cal., 143.

[4] Kayser v. Trustees, 16 Mo., 88 ; Galesburg v. Hawkinson, 75 Ill., 152 ;
cf. Dillon, *Municipal Corporations*, 4th Ed. I., 265. See also for the construction of what is judicial power under the national constitution Hayburn's case,
2 Dallas, 408, 409 ; U. S. v. Yale Todd in note to U. S. v. Ferreira, 13 How.,
40, 52 ; Gordon v. U. S., 2 Wallace, 561 ; Miller on *The Constitution*, VII.

CHAPTER IV.

I.—Executive functions of the legislature.

In no constitutional state can the legislature be shut out from all participation in the work of administration. The organic law of all states, even of those which pretend to adopt the theory of the separation of powers, provides that some of the most important administrative or executive acts shall be performed not by the executive but by the legislature. One of these exceptions to the rigid adoption of the principle of the separation of powers is to be found in the usual constitutional provision that the assumption of all obligations by the state shall be made only with the consent of the legislature or upon its initiation.[1] Again we find that the constitutions of most states give to the legislature the power of fixing the budget of the expenses of the government. All such acts performed by the legislature, although they owe their legal force to the fact that they have been performed by the legislature or with its consent, and although they are put into the form of statutes, are nevertheless in fact administrative acts,

---

[1] Sometimes such obligations are to be assumed, not by the government at all, but by the constitution-making power. See *e. g.* New York constitution. art. vii., sections 9–12.

i. e. acts resembling more the acts usually performed by the administration than those usually performed by the legislature. Therefore in those states in which a formal promulgation of purely legislative acts, *i. e.* general rules of conduct, by the executive authority is necessary, neither do such acts need for their validity such a formality, nor is such a promulgation of them made in practice.[1] Still in form such acts are not administrative acts, but are what have been called by some writers, who lay great stress on the theory of the separation of powers, formal though not material statutes.[2]

Other important acts not of a legislative character performed by the legislature, but which are not even put into the form of statutes, result from the participation of the legislature in the determination of the executive personnel. Thus in the United States a branch of the legislative authority is called upon to approve the appointment of almost all the important executive officers or executive officers are elected by the legislature.[3] Further, the legislature very often possesses the power of removing executive officers from office either by the process of impeachment or by declaring its lack of confidence in the executive authorities.

II.—*Legislative functions of the executive authority.*

Just as the legislature cannot be shut out of all participation in the work of administration so the executive authority cannot be deprived of all participation in the work of legislation. The executive cannot be assigned

---

[1] Sarwey, *Allegemeines Verwaltungsrecht*, 26.

[2] *Cf. ibid.*

[3] *Infra*, pp. 103, 135.

to the position of a mere executing officer. Such an application of the theory of the separation of powers has never been accepted in monarchical governments or even in most republics and would lead to most deplorable results.[1] The veto power is one of the most noticeable legislative functions discharged by the executive.[2] It is recognized almost everywhere in the United States as belonging to the executive, at any rate in a limited form.[3] The power of the executive authority to initiate law is also a legislative function. While it is not granted to the executive authority in the United States in either national or commonwealth governments, it is universally recognized as belonging to the executive in France, England, and Germany. The American executive has, however, usually to recommend to the legislature for adoption such measures as he shall deem expedient.[4]

But the executive authority should participate in the work of legislation not only by the power of veto and of initiating law but it also should have the power of issuing orders of more or less general application. The needs of the government make it necessary that many details in the law be fixed less permanently than by statute. No legislature, however wise or far-seeing, can, with due regard for the interests of the people, which differ with the locality and change with the passage of time, regulate all the matters that need the

---

[1] Sarwey, *op. cit.*, 21.

[2] Montesquieu himself recognized the inadvisability of confining the executive to the function of execution and approves expressly of granting to the executive the veto power. *Esprit des Lois, loc. cit.*

[3] United States Const., art. i., section 7, par. 2 ; Stimson, *American Statute Law*, section 305.

[4] *Cf.* U. S. Const., art. ii., sec. 3.

regulation of administrative law. A large discretion must be given to the administrative authorities to adapt many general rules of law to the wants of the people. Even though the organic law of the country may in the main confine the executive authority to the execution of the resolutions of the legislature, it still either recognizes in the chief executive authority the power of legislation to fill up details in the administrative law, or it permits the legislature to delegate such a power to him or his subordinates, where no such constitutional power is recognized as belonging to him.[1]

This power of the executive authority to issue general rules is known as the ordinance power; and the ordinances which are issued as a result of the exercise of this power are of three kinds, *viz.*, independent ordinances, supplementary ordinances, and delegated ordinances.[2]

Independent ordinances are those ordinances which are issued by the chief executive authority as the result of his constitutional power to fill up all those places in the law which have not been touched at all by the legislature. In so far as their content is concerned they relate to those portions of the law which have not been regulated in any way by statute. Such an independent power is found as a rule only in monarchical governments.

Supplementary ordinances, like independent ordinances, are issued by the chief executive as a result of his constitutional power of ordinance. They differ,

---

[1] Sarwey, *op. cit.* 31 *et seq. ; cf.* U. S. v. Eliason, 16 Peters, 291, 301 ; Sampson v. Peaslee, 20 How, 571 ; The Brig Aurora, 7 Cranch, 382, 388 ; Field v. Clark, U. S. Sup. Court, Oct. term, 1891; U. S. v. Barrows, 1 Abbott, U. S. 351.

[2] Gneist, *Das Englische Verwaltungsrecht*, 1884, 127.

however, from independent ordinances in that they do not attempt to regulate subjects that have not been regulated at all by the legislature, but are issued to supplement already existing statutes, and to fill up the places in such statutes which have not been regulated in detail by them, or to make arrangements for their execution. The power to issue this class of ordinances is found only in monarchical governments or in republics where monarchical traditions are strong.

Delegated ordinances are issued by any of the administrative authorities indiscriminately, not as a result of any constitutional power of ordinance in the chief executive, but as a result of a direct delegation by the legislature of its power of legislation. These delegated ordinances, like the supplementary ordinances, affect those subjects which have been already regulated in a general way by the legislature, but all of whose details have not been thus fixed. These ordinances we find in all states and in all branches of the administration. They are really the most important of all the ordinances to be considered, and are by far the most numerous.

III.—*Executive functions of the judicial authorities.*

Although the general rule may be that the courts shall be confined in the main to the decision of controversies between individuals, nevertheless in many instances the needs of government make it seem advisable to entrust the courts with functions somewhat administrative in character. While this may be said of all states, it is especially true of those which have not really striven in their law to reach any clear distinction between judicial and administrative functions.

Thus in the commonwealths of the United States and England where the exceptions to the logical adoption and application of the theory of the separation of powers are numerous, judicial officers from time immemorial have been entrusted with the discharge of executive or administrative functions.[1]

We in the United States are indebted for this confusion to England, which for a long time did not attempt to separate the judicial and administrative authorities. The justices of the peace have been at the same time judicial and highly important administrative officers. As almost all our important local administrative officers originated in the justices of the peace, they have been regarded by the courts as inferior statutory tribunals, subject to the never ceasing interference of the courts ; and this fact has led to the failure in many cases to distinguish at all in our law and political thought between judicial and administrative functions and to there being no opposition to the actual conferring of functions upon the courts which would seem to be administrative in nature. A most noticeable instance of this is found in the power given to the supreme court in New York to approve the acts and determinations of various administrative commissions such as the rapid-transit commission, such acts being of no effect until they have been so approved.[2]

---

[1] In certain cases this has been held to be unconstitutional, *supra*, p. 24.

[2] *E. g.* see New York laws, 1875, chap. 606, section 21 ; New York Constitution, art. iii., section 18.

CHAPTER V.

The principle of the separation of powers not only involves the existence of three somewhat separate authorities, but also insists that each authority shall be independent of the other authorities. But just as it is impossible to distinguish clearly three powers and authorities of government, so is it impossible that any of the three authorities shall be absolutely independent of the other two. As administrative law has to do with the position of the executive it is necessary to examine its relations with the other two authorities.

I.—Relation to the legislature.

1. *The legislature the regulator of the administration.* —In all countries the action of the executive is subject to the control of the legislature. In the first place the legislature has the power to lay down norms in accordance with which the executive is to act. The legislature has been called the regulator of the administration.[1] This does not mean, however, that the executive can act only in the execution of the resolutions of the legislature, and that it possesses no discretion. Even in the United States, where the power of the legislature to regulate the

---

[1] Sarwey, *op. cit.*, 37 ; Gneist, *Der Rechtsstaat*, 181.

action of the administration has been carried as far as anywhere, it is held that there is a sphere in which the administration may move without looking to a statute of the legislature for its authorization. Thus Justice McLean says in an opinion given in the United States Supreme Court.[1]

A practical knowledge of the action of any one of the great departments of the government must convince every person that the head of a department, in the distribution of its duties and responsibilities, is often compelled to use his discretion. He is limited in the exercise of his powers by the law ; but it does not follow that he must show a statutory provision for everything he does. No government could be administered on such principles. To attempt to regulate by law the minute movements of every part of the complicated machinery of government would evince a most unpardonable ignorance on the subject. Whilst the great outlines of its movements may be marked out, and limitations imposed on the exercise of its powers, there are numberless things which must be done that can neither be anticipated nor defined, and which are essential to the proper action of the government. Hence, of necessity, usages have been established in every department of the government, which have become a kind of common law, and regulate the rights and duties of those who act within their respective limits.[2]

Further, it is generally recognized in the United States that there is in the executive authority a latent power of discretionary action which is denominated the war power, and which is, in times of extraordinary danger, capable of great expansion. This was brought out most forcibly in the critical period of our civil war.[3] The same general principle is true in all states.[4]

---

[1] U. S. v. McDaniel, 7 Peters, i., 14.

[2] See also *In re* Neagle, 135 U. S., i., 64–68, which claims somewhat similar powers for the President as a result of his duty to see that the laws are faithfully executed. *Infra*, p. 64.

[3] *Cf.* W. A. Dunning on '' The Constitution in Civil War,'' in the *Pol. Sci. Qu.*, III., 454.   [4] *Cf.* Sarwey, *op. cit.*, 37.

It is seen thus that while the main duty of the executive is to execute the will of the legislature as expressed in statute, still in all countries there is a realm of action in which the executive authority possesses large discretion, and that it looks for its authority not to the legislature but to the constitution.

2. *The control of the legislature.*—Further, besides regulating the action of the administration, the legislature exercises in all countries a direct control over the administration to keep it within the law. The extent of such control varies with the relation in tenure of the executive to the legislature. If, as in England and France, the acting executive is dependent in tenure upon the legislature, the extent of this control will depend entirely upon the attitude which the legislature takes. If, as in France, the legislature makes an immoderate use of its powers of control, the executive authority becomes completely dependent in action upon the legislature; if, as in England, the legislature imposes bounds upon its control over the executive, beyond which it will not go, the executive, though in theory completely dependent in action upon the legislature, still in practice will be largely independent of it. The existence of the power of control will have simply the effect of deterring the administration from illegal action. In the United States and Germany the executive is not dependent upon the legislature in tenure; in Germany, not at all; in the United States, only in such a way that it may be removed in case of absolute corruption and illegal action. The result is that the control of the legislature over the actions of the administration in these countries is very slight.[1]

3   [1] See *infra*, II., p. 262.

II.—*Relation to the courts.*

In all countries the executive authorities are subject
also, to some extent, to the control of the courts.   In
all states many of the acts of the administration may
be reviewed by the courts.   The extent and character
of the control which the courts may exercise over the
administration, depend upon the character of the act
to be controlled.   From the point of view of this control the acts of the administration may be classed
under four heads, *viz.*, political acts, legislative acts,
acts in the nature of contracts, and special administrative acts not of general application.

1. *Political acts.*—By political acts are meant those
acts whether of general or of special application done
by the administration in the discharge of its political
functions, such as the carrying on of the diplomatic relations of the country, the making of treaties, the command and disposition of the military forces of the
government, the conduct of the relations of the executive with the legislature.   The general rule in all countries is that the courts have no control over this class
of acts.   Where the principle of ministerial responsibility to the legislature has been adopted it is believed
that this will be sufficient to insure the impartial and
wise performance of these political acts.   Where the
principle of popular responsibility has been adopted it
is believed that this will be sufficient, and that it is
unwise to allow the courts any control whatever over
the political functions of the executive.[1]

[1] *E. g.* see Nabob of Carnatic v. East India Co., 1 Vesey Jr., 375, 393, 2 *Id.*,
56, 60 ; Penn. v. Lord Baltimore, 1 Vesey, 467 ; Cherokee Nation v. Georgia,
5 Peters, 1, 20 ; Luther v. Borden, 7 Howard U. S., 1 ; and Mississippi v.
Johnson, 4 Wallace, 475.

In France, where the executive is more independent of the courts than in any other country,[1] a much wider interpretation has been given to political acts than is given in other countries. The courts have gone so far as to hold that acts of a very arbitrary character and restrictive of private rights, which were taken to promote the public safety in time of public excitement, were of a political character.[2]

2. *Legislative acts.*—The legislative acts of the administration are to be found in the ordinances which it has the power to issue. The rule as to the control which the courts may exercise over them is in all countries about the same. The courts have the same power over them as the courts of the United States have over the statutes of the legislature, *i. e.* they may interpret them and in most cases declare them void or refuse to enforce them in case they are contrary to the law.[3]

3. *Contractual acts.*—The general tendency at the present time as to the control which the courts possess over the contractual acts of the administration is to admit a pretty full control. England and the United States are the most backward in this respect.[4]

4. *Administrative acts of special application.*—The fourth class of acts distinguished are special administrative acts not of general application. In the United States they are called indiscriminately orders, decisions,

---

[1] See *Code Pénal*, art. 137.

[2] Thus the administrative authorities have, in order to prevent the publication of a journal which, it was claimed, was exciting the passions of the people, wrecked its office, and the courts have held that this was a political act, and not subject to review. *Arrêt du Conseil d'État*, 5 Jan., 1855, *affaire Boule ;* cited in Ducrocq, *Traité du Droit, Administratif*, I., section 64 ; *cf.* Aucoc, *Conférences sur l'administration, etc.*, 441, *et seq.*

[3] *Infra*, p. 74.   [4] See *infra*, II. p. 149.

precepts, and warrants. By the performance of these acts the administrative authorities perform a large part of their duties, and in their performance they are coming into continual conflict with the individuals whom they govern. Some sort of a control over these acts is extremely necessary ; and in the kind and extent of the control provided in different states we find greater differences than exist in the case of the control provided for the three other classes of acts. The four countries whose law is being considered may, from the point of view of the control possessed by the courts over this class of acts, be divided into two classes. In the first are found England and the United States. The rule in these countries is, that when an individual act of the administration is not of a political or a contractual character the courts have a very large control over it. In many cases they may annul it, amend it, interpret it, and prevent the administration from proceeding to execute it.[1] In the second class of countries, in which are to be found France and Germany, the rule is completely different. The French principle of the independence of the administration prevents the courts from exercising any sort of a control over such acts. This principle has been adopted in Germany. But in both countries in order to render justice to the individual there have been established, for the review and control of certain of these special administrative acts, special tribunals known as administrative courts, organized quite differently from the ordinary courts and not forming part of the regular judicial system.[2]

---

[1] *Infra*, II., p. 200.

[2] For the development of this subject in detail, see *infra*, II., pp. 217, 240.

III.—The position of the executive.

It is now possible, after this consideration of the relations of the executive authority, with the legislature and the courts, to see what is the position of the executive authority. In the United States the executive authority is almost entirely independent of the legislature, but its acts not of a political or contractual character are subject in many cases to the control of the courts which are to keep the executive within the limits of the law. In France the executive authority is subject to the control of the legislature as a result of the adoption of the principle of ministerial responsibility to the legislature. Its relation to the courts is one of almost absolute independence. In Germany the executive authority is independent of the legislature, and to a large extent also of the courts. In England the executive authority is subject to the control of both the legislature and the courts. Its only acts which are independent of the courts are its political acts, and certain of its contractual acts.

The result is that the executive authority is, from the administrative point of view, the strongest in Germany and France. In France this strength is somewhat weakened over against the legislature by the existence of the parliamentary responsibility of the important executive organs, but is very great over against the courts. Therefore, on the continent of Europe, administration, the function of the executive authority, will be found to be more important than in the other countries; and it is on this account that the study of this function of administration is pursued there with greater interest than in either the United States or England.

CHAPTER VI.

TERRITORIAL DISTRIBUTION OF ADMINISTRATIVE FUNCTIONS.

I.—Participation of the localities in administration.

The ends of the state which it is the duty of the government to realize may be called public ends in distinction from the ends of individuals. The term public ends does not, however, indicate simply those ends which are to be realized through the instrumentality of the central government. For, though the state is an indivisible union of persons within a given territory, still the people forming the state are, in all countries of any size, organized in a number of local communities which have been called into being through the simple fact that the people living within a defined district have common needs which are peculiar to themselves. If the ends which such people follow in their local organizations are recognized by the state as reaching beyond the interests of the individual then such ends become public ends, just as much as the ends which the state attempts to have realized through the central governmental organization. For the mere fact that such ends may be regarded by the state as public ends does not make it necessary that the government shall act solely or mainly in the attainment of these ends through its central organization. The

38

state everywhere grants, directly or indirectly, to the localities powers to act in the attainment of this class of public ends and provides that its central governmental organization shall step in simply to assist and control the localities. In other words central and local government work together in the attainment of the ends of the state. The state may not, it is true, recognize that there is any actual sphere of local government at all in the sense that the localities have by the constitution powers, with the exercise of which the central government may not interfere. The localities may be left largely at the mercy of the central government. This is very largely true of all countries, though in the United States the largest of the localities, *viz.*, the commonwealths, are protected by the United States constitution against the central government, and there is arising the belief that the divisions of the commonwealths should in like manner be protected by the commonwealth constitutions against the commonwealth governments.[1] In many countries also, notwithstanding the absence of constitutional provisions assuring to the localities a sphere of local government, the people have become so convinced of the necessity of the existence of a degree of local autonomy that the legislature has provided that within certain limits the localities shall act as they see fit, in the pursuit of local public ends. As to what shall be the sphere of local autonomy, whether it be fixed by the constitution or by legislation, it is impossible to lay down many general principles of universal application. It may, however, be said that the localities in a state may not with due regard to the unity of the state be

[1] Burgess, "The American Commonwealth," *Pol. Sci. Qu.*, I., 32.

permitted to exercise powers of legislation with regard to private relations. Of the four important countries only one has seen fit to grant by its constitution to the localities such a legislative power. This is the United States, and the evils resulting from the consequent diversity of the private law are so great that in more than one instance the demand is being made either for national regulation of private relations or for the devising of some method by which the law may be made uniform.[1]

In the second place it may be said also that, for the same reasons, the localities should possess no powers with regard to the administration of justice, that the judicial system should not be subject to local regulation. Here again the United States is the only one of the four countries which permits its localities to organize courts that are to decide the controversies arising among its citizens relative to their private rights. When, however, we come to the function of administration the demand for harmony and uniformity is not so imperious. Even in France, the home of centralized government, it is recognized that, while the country can be governed from the centre better than from the localities, it can be administered better in the localities than from the centre. But while this principle may be accepted as generally true, it must also be admitted that there are certain branches of administration in which the localities can in the nature of things not act at all. Thus the localities can have no duties to perform in the administration of foreign relations.

---

[1] See Munroe Smith on "State Statute and Common Law" in *Pol. Sci. Qu.*, III., 147, 148. The recent appointment by the various commonwealth legislatures of commissioners for harmonizing the law in important matters is an evidence of the evils of diversity.

Further, in certain other administrative branches, the demand for uniformity in administrative methods is so imperious, that if the localities are permitted to act at all within them, they must act subject to the control of the central government. This is true of the administration of military, judicial, and financial affairs. In these branches the localities cannot be permitted to have any powers of independent action, but must be regarded as agents of the central government and subject to its control. The result of this process of exclusion is that the sphere of local administrative autonomy, if recognized at all, is to be found in that branch of administration known as internal affairs. Even in this branch, as in the others just mentioned, in many cases the localities must, on account of the necessity of administrative uniformity, be subjected to the control of the central government. Thus the administration of the public health and the public charity and the preservation of the peace cannot be left altogether to the localities independent of all central control. What shall be the spheres of central and local administrative action in a given state, and what shall be the kind and extent of central control exercised over the localities where they are regarded as the agents of the central government, are matters to be determined by the positive law of the particular state; and the determinations reached by different states differ considerably one from the other, and are based upon the differing social and political conditions obtaining therein.[1]

II.—English method.

Two general methods of providing for the participation of the localities in the work of administration

[1] *Cf.* Stengel, *Organisation der Preussischen Verwaltung*, 11 *et seq.*

have been adopted. By the one all the duties to be performed by the localities, both as agents of the central government and as local governmental organizations, are fixed in detail by the legislature of the central government.[1] Where this system of enumeration by the legislature of the powers of the localities is adopted, as is the case in England and the United States, no sphere of independent local action is assigned to the localities. They may, it is true, be regarded as local corporations with the power of owning property and of suing and being sued, but they have no sphere of action of their own. They are regarded simply as districts of the central government of the state or commonwealth, and their officers are simply agents of that central government acting in the local divisions. This is the case in the smaller localities of the United States. This idea is well brought out in the case of *Hamilton Co. v. Mighels*,[2] where the court says that the county is merely a division for the purposes of general commonwealth administration, and in the case of *Lorillard v. The Town of Monroe*,[3] where it is held that "town officers," such as assessors, collectors, etc., are public commonwealth officers, and not officers of the town corporation for whose action the town is responsible. Full municipal corporations are, from this point of view in about the same position as these *quasi* corporations, as the towns and counties are called.

---

[1] In case the legislative power as to administrative matters is, as in Germany and in the United States, given to the largest divisions of the state, *viz.*, the commonwealths ; the legislatures of these divisions have the power to arrange the administrative system as they see fit within the boundaries of the commonwealth.

[2] 7 Ohio St., 109.

[3] 11 N. Y., 392.

Their powers are all enumerated, and it cannot be said that they have by the constitutions or the statutes many powers of independent local action.[2] Under such a system of legislative enumeration the needs of uniform administration are, it is thought, satisfied by the exercise by the legislature of its power to change the duties and increase or decrease the powers of the localities. The continual interference of the legislature resulting from the exercise of this power has had such evil results in the United States that the attempt has in many cases been made to limit in the commonwealth constitution the power of special and local legislation possessed by the legislature. But as the general acts with regard to local administration usually follow the same method of enumerating in detail the powers and duties of the local authorities, they have in some cases, on account of the rigidity and inflexibility of their provisions and of their inadaptability to local needs, proved almost as unsatisfactory as the habit of special and local legislation. This method of regarding the localities as in all cases the agents of the central government, and of enumerating in detail their duties and powers, makes unnecessary any further central control over the administration in the localities. The control over localities and over local officers is by this system a legislative control.

III.—Continental method.

The other method of permitting localities to participate in the work of administration depends upon clearly distinguishing between that administrative work which

---

[2] See U. S. v. B. & O. R.R. Co., 17 Wall., 322 ; *cf.* Dillon, *Municipal Corporations*, 4th edition, I., 145.

needs central regulation and that which can with advantage be entrusted to the localities. The delimitation of a sphere of local action is accomplished by the determination of those matters which need for their efficient treatment uniformity in administrative action, and which should therefore be attended to by the central administration. What is left after the subtraction of these matters from the whole sphere of administration constitutes the sphere of local administrative action. The regulation of the matters falling within this sphere of local action is then given by general grant to the local corporations and their officers. By this method the local corporations are not authorities of enumerated powers but may exercise any power which has not been expressly denied to them, or has not been expressly given to the central administration. This is the method very generally adopted on the continent of Europe.[1] Now if the localities were permitted to determine in concrete cases their competence there would be danger of disintegration through their attempts to usurp functions not recognized as local. Therefore, where such a system of distributing administrative powers has been adopted, the power is given to the central administrative authorities to step in and prevent the local corporations or authorities from making such usurpation. Further, as all administration demands pecuniary resources and as the exercise of the taxing power by the localities may result in the disorganization of the general financial system of the state, the central legislature usually fixes what kinds of taxes the localities may raise, and permits the central administrative officers to exercise a general control over the

[1] *Infra,* p. 266.

administration of the local finances in order that in this way extravagance may be prevented. Finally, while it may be recognized that the local corporations have a sphere of action of their own in which they act subject to the central administrative control, at the same time the central government may under this system recognize that the localities are also in certain branches agents of the central government. So far as this is the case the localities must be subjected to some sort of central control; and this control is usually as in the other cases an administrative control.

IV.—Sphere of central administration.

But, as has been indicated, there are certain branches of administration where, in the nature of things, the localities cannot act at all or cannot act to the same advantage as the central administration. For these branches the central government forms a series of officers unconnected in any way with the local corporations. The tendency in the United States has of late years been to increase the number of such administrative services attended to by the central government. Thus the customs and the indirect taxes, formerly often attended to by local officers,[1] are now entrusted to officers of the central government.[2] In the commonwealths all such matters as factory inspection, railroad supervision, the control of pauper lunatics in some cases, and

[1] Cf. *The History of Tariff Administration in the United States*, by John D. Goss in the series of *Studies in History, Economics, and Public Law*, edited by the University Faculty of Political Science of Columbia College, I., No. 2, pp. 12, 15.

[2] In Germany customs and indirect taxes are attended to by the commonwealths under the supervision of the imperial government. Imperial Constitution, arts. 35 and 38; *cf*. Meyer, *Lehrbuch des Deutschen Verwaltungsrecht*, II., 310 *et seq* ; 335.

a whole series of matters are attended to by commonwealth officials unconnected in any way with the local corporations. In all countries these central officers, if we may so call them, are subject to quite a strict central administrative control.

As a result of these arrangements which we find in all countries, the details offering considerable variety, we conclude that not only is the function of administration largely separated from the functions of legislation and the rendering of judicial decision, and entrusted in most cases to special authorities, but also that these special administrative authorities are in all states of two kinds, *viz.*, central and local, while in some states the local authorities may further be subdivided into commonwealth and local authorities. As the law in the United States distributes what are usually regarded in a unified government as central powers between the national and the commonwealth governments, this order will be so changed in the following pages as to consider as central authorities both federal and commonwealth authorities, and as local only those subordinate commonwealth authorities having a territorial competence within the limits of a commonwealth.

Of these two classes of authorities the central authorities have to attend to those matters which by the law of the land have been recognized as general in character, and where the central control over the localities is an administrative one, have to exercise that control. The local authorities on the other hand act as agents of the central government, and are local corporations with, in some states, their own sphere of independent local action; and in all cases are subject to a central control which in accordance with the method of distributing administrative duties among the localities is either a legislative or an administrative control.

BOOK II.

CENTRAL ADMINISTRATION.

Division 1.—The Executive Power and the Chief Executive Authority.

CHAPTER I.

THE EXECUTIVE POWER AND THE EXECUTIVE AUTHORITY IN GENERAL.

THE organization of a chief executive authority, and the definition of the executive power which should be entrusted to it, are problems which have always been difficult of solution for both political scientists and constitution makers. The first difficulty which presents itself is the organization of the chief executive authority. Shall it be a board or one man? A board ensures deliberation, and by many has been supposed to be a preventive of executive tyranny; the one-headed form is more liable to produce quick and energetic action. The desire to produce this result has in almost all cases been so great that the one-headed form of the executive authority is now almost universally recognized as the proper form. The next great difficulty has been found in the determination of the

extent and character of the power which shall be entrusted to the chief executive authority. Both practical men and students have always had great difficulty
in obtaining a clear conception and an adequate
expression in their governmental organization of their
conception of the power to be given to their chief
executive authority. The cause of this difficulty is
twofold. The first cause of difficulty has come from
the theory of the separation of powers. This theory
insists that the executive authority should both have.
in his hands all of what is regarded as the executive
power and be confined to the exercise of the executive
power. The experience of the world, however, goes to
prove that, if such an attempt is made, the executive
authority tends to become either tyrannical or incapable : tyrannical, if it have the entire executive
power; incapable, if it have no other than the executive
power. Men have therefore been compelled to abandon
the realm of theory and to allow themselves to be
governed in their determination of the power to be given
to the executive authority by the history and needs of
the country for which they were forming a constitution,
with the natural result that the conceptions of the
character and extent of the executive power which
the constitutions of existing states present are quite
different the one from the other.

The second cause of the difficulty of determining
what shall be the power entrusted to the chief executive authority is to be found in the failure, which is so
often made, to recognize that what is called the executive power really consists of two functions. These are
the political or " governmental " function, as the French
call it, and the administrative function. These two

4

functions it is somewhat difficult to distinguish, but the distinction does exist, and is capable of perception. A noted French writer on administration has, as clearly as any one, brought out this distinction, which is more pronounced in France than elsewhere, and has an important influence on the French law. This is M. Aucoc, who says [1]:

When we distinguish government from administration we mean to put into a special category the direction of all affairs which are regarded as political, that is to say the relations of the chief executive authority with the great powers of the government : the summoning of electors for the election of senators and representatives, the closing of the session, the convocation of the chamber of deputies and of the senate, the closing of their session, the dissolution of the chamber of deputies ; the carrying on of diplomatic relations with foreign powers, the disposition of the military forces, the exercise of the right of pardon, the granting of titles of nobility.

He adds :

The administrative authority has a mission altogether different. It is charged with providing for the collective needs of the citizens which the initiative of individuals or associations of individuals could not adequately satisfy ; it must gather together the resources of society both in men and money in order that society may continue to exist and make progress ; it must play the part of the man of business of society, in its management of the various public services, as for example in the matter of public works ; it must take measures of supervision and must through the exercise of foresight preserve the property destined for the use of the public, must maintain order and further the general prosperity.

Some constitution makers and political scientists have regarded the executive power as composed of only the first of these powers ; others, while recognizing

[1] *Conférences sur l'Administration, etc.,* I., 78.

the existence of both, have laid such emphasis on the political side of the executive power as almost to ignore the necessity of the possession by the chief executive authority of any administrative power ; while, finally, others have seen that an efficient executive must be an administrator as well as a statesman. The different ideas that men have had of the part of the executive power which should be given the greatest prominence have thus led to great differences in the determination of the power to be given to the chief executive authority. In some governments we find the executive authority is simply a political chief.[1] This is the position which has been assigned to the executive authority in the commonwealths in the United States. In other governments the political power has been brought largely under the control of the legislature. The position of the chief executive as an administrator is much more important than his position as a political authority. This is very largely true of France and to a certain extent of England. Finally, in other governments the chief executive authority has been recognized as both a political authority and chief of the administration. This is the case in the United States national government and in Germany. In those states which recognize the chief executive as merely a political officer, the administrative power is given to another series of officers quite distinct from the chief executive authority and very largely independent of him,[2] and in many instances is exercised by judicial bodies.

[1] Even as a political chief the powers of the executive authority will vary greatly. In some it will thus have the veto power, in others not ; in some it will have a large power of ordinance, in others, almost none at all except such as is delegated to it by the legislature which may be very chary of its delegations.

[2] *Infra*, p. 136.

CHAPTER II.

The office of chief executive was naturally the most difficult to organize in the United States government. The form of the office gave the framers of the national constitution little trouble. They were substantially agreed upon the one-headed form though the board form was considered.[1] In their decision as to the powers to give to their executive chief they were, even more than in their decision as to the form of the office, guided by the models with which they were acquainted. These models were the office of colonial governor and the English King as they understood his position.[2] It has often been said that they modelled their President on the English King, but careful consideration would seem to show that the influence of English institutions was less strong than is usually believed, and that the framers of the national constitution introduced into their new government the American governor rather than the English King.[3] What now were the powers of the

[1] Elliot's *Debates*, Philadelphia, 1876, v. *passim ;* Rüttiman, *Das Nord-Amerikanische Bundesstaatsrecht*, I., 232 ; see also J. H. Robinson on " Original Features in the United States Constitution," in *Annals of American Academy of Political and Social Science*, I., 222.

[2] Elliot's *Debates, loc. cit. ; Annals, etc., loc. cit.*

[3] The author is glad to see that the result of his own study is corroborated by Prof. James Bryce, *American Commonwealth*, I., 36.

commonwealth governors at the time the national constitution was framed ? This question may be answered by a study of the position of the governor in the three most important commonwealths of the time, *viz.*, New York, Massachusetts, and Virginia.

I.— The executive power in New York at the time of the framing of the national constitution.

By the first two charters or patents relating to the territory embracing what is now the commonwealth of New York the entire governmental power was given to the Duke of York. This power he transferred to a governor whom he appointed.[1] In 1685, James, Duke of York, became King of England. The character of the colony changed. It had been proprietary ; it now became provincial. The character of its institutions remained, however, the same. The commission and instructions issued to the governor, in which his powers are to be found since New York was not a charter colony, still gave to the governor under the King the entire governmental power and limited the exercise of that power only by requiring for the validity of certain of his acts the consent of a council whose members were chosen by the King.[2] After the great revolution of 1688, another limitation was placed upon the exercise of the powers of the governor, in that provision was made in the commission and instructions for the summoning of a popular assembly whose consent was to be necessary for all laws and ordinances.[3] The

---

[1] Poore's *Charters and Constitutions*, I., 785, 786 ; *Documents Relating to the Colonial History of New York*, III., 215 *et seq.*, 331.

[2] Documents, *etc.*, III., 377.

[3] An assembly was summoned in 1683, but it had little influence.

governor had the power to adjourn, prorogue, and dissolve this assembly. His other powers enumerated in the commission and instructions were to appoint all officers necessary for the administration of justice and the execution of the laws ; with the consent of the council and in accordance with royal order, to organize courts of justice and with the council to act as the court of appeals in civil cases. The governor had also the pardoning power and an extensive military power.[1] Such was the legal position of the governor. The assembly in course of time, however, began to encroach on the power of the governor, and practically introduced important modifications into the governmental system. We find the letters of the governors to the English Board of Trade, which had a supervision over the affairs of the colonies, full of complaints of the refractory character of the assemblies.[2]

The points on which the colonists laid the greatest stress in their struggles with the governors were, as might be supposed, first, the control of the finances,

[1] Documents, *etc.*, II., 623 and 685.

[2] See Documents, *etc.*, VI., 456, 460, 472, 533, 543, 550, 554, 597, 752, and 764. In one of these letters the governor says : "By his majesty's commission as well as instructions to his governors of this province all publick money is to be issued by warrant from the governor with the advice and consent of the council. By every act granting money to the king for several years past great part of the money is issued without such warrant and sometimes by warrant of the speaker of the assembly only."

In another letter dated March 19, 1749, and written to the Duke of Bedford, the governor says : " I must beg further to observe to your Grace that the first encroachments on the royal prerogative began under the administration of Mr. Hunter, that the assembly took advantage of the necessities the administration was then under (by the war with France and an expedition then set on foot in America against Canada), to claim a right of appointing their own treasurer and refused to support the government unless this was yielded to them."

He then adds that Mr. Hunter struggled against them for four years and was then forced to yield. *Cf.* Gitterman, " The Council of Appointment in New York," *Pol. Sci. Qu.*, VII., 80.

and, second the right of appointing officers as being
the most important powers which the governors possessed. After the wasteful administration of Lord
Cornbury they insisted on specifying the purposes for
which the money which they granted should be spent,
and, after they had secured the recognition of this power,
during the administration of Governor Clinton they
made use of this power of appropriation to grant their
salaries to the officers of the government by name, thus
assuming to themselves a large portion of the appointing power. The result of the constitutional development during the colonial period in New York was
that the legislature had at the time when New York
became independent almost absolute control over the
finances, granting the money, making the appropriations,
and controlling the officer on whose warrant it was
issued, and participated quite largely in the exercise of
the appointing power. When New York became independent it was only natural that the framers of the
new constitution which was adopted should incorporate
into their new instrument of government the principles
for whose recognition they had for so long a time been
struggling with the colonial governors; and we find
that the constitution of 1777 differed from the previously existing polity of New York only in that these
principles were now given the sanction of written law
and in that the whole political system was somewhat
leavened by the prevailing political philosophy, especially by the two principles of popular sovereignty
and the separation of powers. Thus by the new constitution the finances for whose control the people had
been struggling were put into the hands of the legislature. Taxes could be levied and money appropriated

only by the legislature.[1] The treasurer on whose warrant all money was to be issued was to be elected by the legislature by an act to originate in the assembly.[2] The governor's power of appointment, which had also been a point at issue in former times, was subjected to a legislative control in that the consent of a council of appointment, to be composed of members of the legislature and elected by the legislature, was made necessary for the valid appointment of all officers appointed by the governor.[3] The principle of the separation of powers made itself felt in that the new constitution attempted to define the so-called different powers of government,[4] and allowed the governor almost no control over legislation[5] and absolutely none over the rendering of justice. This resulted from the failure to enumerate among his powers any judicial powers other than the power of pardon[6] and the express formation of a system of courts which were to decide all controversies. The principle of popular sovereignty made itself felt in that the governor was to be elected by the people and was reduced to the position of an officer who was simply to execute the laws with little discretion.[7] There could no longer be any authority to issue instructions to him since the power of the English King was no longer recognized.

II.— The executive power in Massachusetts.

The history of the province of Massachusetts begins with the year 1691. The provincial charter which

---

[1] Art. ix. The system was thus in this respect the same as in the colonial period.

[2] Art. xxii.   [3] Art. xxiii.   [4] Arts. ii., xvii., xxxii.

[5] Art. iii.   [6] Art. xviii.   [7] *Cf.* Art. i.

was then given to the colony united the two formerly
existing colonies of Massachusetts Bay and Plymouth.[1]
This charter formed by the side of the governor a
legislative body, the General Court, which consisted of
the governor's council, chosen by the General Court,
and of representatives chosen by the freeholders of the
colony. The governor had the power to adjourn, prorogue, and dissolve the General Court; could, with the
consent of the council, appoint a great many officers,
mostly local in character, though the general appointing power, where there was no special provision in
the charter, belonged to the General Court; had a veto
power over all the acts of the General Court; had
very limited judicial powers—only the probate of wills
and the granting of administrations; and finally had
extensive military powers, some of which could be
exercised only with the consent of the council.

It will be noticed from this enumeration that the
legislature had under the charter of 1691 almost all
the powers which the New York assembly tried for so
long a time to get. It had the general appointing
power, and through this a large control over the finances, since it could appoint its own treasurer. We find
therefore that the Massachusetts legislature did not
encroach seriously upon the powers of the governor;
and that on the adoption of a constitution in 1780 no
very great changes were made in the form of the government. Of course the substitution of the doctrine
of popular sovereignty for that of royal sovereignty,
as well as the adoption of the principle of the separation of powers which was very forcibly announced,[2]
made some changes, but these are about all. Thus the

---

[1] Poore, *op. cit.*, I., 949.   [2] See Const., Art. xxx., part i.

constitution of the new commonwealth provided that
the governor was to be elected by the people. The
governor lost his control over the legislature; his veto
power was limited and his judicial powers disappeared.
His military powers were about the same as before, and
as before he could appoint most of the judicial and
local officers, but all the important central officers of
the commonwealth were to be appointed by the General Court.

III.—*The executive power in Virginia.*

Virginia, like New York, had no colonial charter.
Recourse must therefore be had to the commission and
instructions issued to the governor to find what was
the extent of the executive power. In Beverly's
History of Virginia, published about the year 1705,
is found a tolerably complete description of the civil
polity of the colony based on this commission.[1] We
find a governor appointed by the King and subject to
his instructions, with the power to adjourn, prorogue,
and dissolve the assembly and to veto all their acts.
The governor's power of appointment extended, as a
rule, only to the local officers; he had large military
powers, but the appointment of the most important
officers of the colonial financial administration belonged
to the assembly whose speaker acted as treasurer.[2]

It will be noticed that, as in Massachusetts, the
legislature had as early as 1705 what the assembly in
New York struggled so long to get, *viz.*, the control of
the finances. Therefore we find few attempts on the
part of the legislature to encroach upon the powers of

[1] Book iv., part i.
[2] Campbell, *History of Virginia*, 535 *et seq.*

the governor; and that when the colonists came to form their commonwealth government at the time of the declaration of independence they did not find it necessary to make many changes beyond those which the prevalent political philosophy made it probable they would adopt.

Thus the principle of the sovereignty of the people is seen in the fact that the governor was to be elected by the people's representatives, the legislature. In accordance with the principle of the separation of powers he lost his control over the legislature, by the abolition of the power of dissolution and prorogation and the veto power. He had still the same appointing power as before—that is, for local officers,—but subject to the consent of the council. He had also to exercise with the advice of the same body the military power and the power of pardon. The important central officers, including the treasurer, were to be appointed by the legislature.

IV.—The American conception of the executive power in 1787.

The American conception of the executive power prevailing at the time of the adoption of the common-wealth and national constitutions, as evidenced by the examples which have been adduced, corresponded with that part of the executive power which has been called the political or governmental power. The great exception to this was that the carrying on of foreign relations was not included in the governor's powers. This does not, however, prove that this power was not considered a part of the executive power. The omission of this power was due entirely to the peculiar

position of the colonies, and later of the commonwealths. The care of the foreign relations was not in
the governor's hands simply because, during the colonial period, the mother country, and during the existence
of the commonwealths as separate states the continental
congress had attended to this matter.

To a similar reason is due the fact that the governor
did not have very extensive administrative powers.
Administrative matters, outside of those connected
with the military powers of the governor, had not been
attended to by the central colonial government, but, in
accordance with the English principles of local government, by officers in the various localities, and mainly
judicial in character. Thus in the case of the administrative matters connected with justice, almost the only
matters attended to by the governor were embraced in
the powers of appointment and removal. The every-
day matters of court administration were attended to
either by the courts themselves, or by the officers in
the localities in which the courts had jurisdiction.
The facts were the same in the branch of the administration known as internal affairs. Here the central
colonial government had little to do except to appoint
certain of the officers, the justices of the peace and
sheriffs, who, after their appointment, attended to those
matters in their own discretion. Further, this branch
of administration was a very small one, embracing
practically only such matters as the preservation of the
peace, the care of the poor and of highways and local
finances. There was thus left only one branch of
administration in which the central colonial government had any powers to exercise. This was the
administration of the central finances; and here, on

account of the importance of this branch of administration, we find that in all the three colonies the question was definitely settled before the revolution that the legislature should exercise a very important control over the finances, if it did not take them into its absolute administration. It claimed, and obtained the power to vote all the supplies that the government could obtain, to specify in its appropriation acts for what purposes the money it had raised should be expended, and to designate the officer who was to have charge of its collection and disbursement. The power of appointment, which is an administrative power that is to be found in all the branches of administration, was treated differently in different commonwealths, but the conception that it belonged to the governor in the case of other than judicial and local officers was not very clear. In New York alone it can be said that the general power of appointment was regarded as one of the governor's powers, and even here it was subjected to a legislative control. One fact further deserves mention. That is, that the governor possessed neither in the colony nor in the commonwealth any general ordinance power, even to supplement existing law. As Roger Sherman said: "The executive is not to execute his own will, but the will of the legislature declared by laws." [1]

The only purely administrative branch attended to by the central colonial and commonwealth government was, then, the financial administration, which was almost entirely attended to by the legislature. This formed the model which the framers of the new national government tried to copy when they came to

[1] Quoted in Conkling's *Executive Power*, 1882, pp. 62 *et seq.*

build up a great administrative system, but which their successors were forced by circumstances to abandon.

V.— The history of the executive power in the early national government.

1. *Original position of the President.*—The national constitution provided for a President, in whom the executive power should be vested.[1] What the meaning of those words was in 1787 has just been shown. It was that the President was to have a military and political power rather than an administrative power. The meaning of these words is further explained by the enumeration of the specific powers which were granted to the President by the constitution. These are the same powers possessed by the governors of the commonwealths. They are the power of military command, the diplomatic power, the limited veto power, the power of pardon, the power to call an extra session of Congress, to adjourn it in case of a disagreement between the houses, and the power to send a message to the Congress. The general grant of the executive power to the President means little except that the President was to be the authority in the government that was to exercise the powers afterwards enumerated as his. The only other enumerated power is an administrative power, and is also the only purely administrative power that is mentioned clearly in the constitution. This is the power of appointment.[2]

---

[1] Art. ii., section 1.

[2] Art. ii., sec. 2, par. 2, provides that "the President shall nominate, and by and with the advice and consent of the senate shall appoint, ambassadors, other public ministers and consuls, judges of the Supreme Court, and all other officers of

Finally it is to be noted that, in accordance with the American conception of the executive power, the President did not have any power to issue general ordinances, even to supplement existing law, which would bind the citizen. The only ordinance power which the President had at the beginning of our history, and indeed has now, is the power to issue ordinances when the legislature has specifically delegated to him the power to regulate a given subject. The only possible exception to this rule is that in times of war the war power which is generally recognized as belonging to the President is susceptible of very great extension and may be construed, indeed in the past has been construed, as giving to the President quite an ordinance power.[1]

It will be seen from this enumeration of the powers given to the President by the national constitution that the conception of the executive power held by the framers of the national constitution was the same as that to be found expressed in the constitutions of the three commonwealths whose constitutional history has been examined. The President had the political power and one administrative power, *viz.,* the power of appointment. Beyond the power of appointment he had, so far as the express provisions of the consti-

the United States whose appointments are not otherwise provided for, and which shall be established by law. But the Congress may, by law, vest the appointment of such inferior officers as they may think proper in the President alone, in the courts of law, or in the heads of departments." Paragraph 3 adds : " The President shall have power to fill all vacancies that may happen during the recess of the senate by granting commissions which shall expire at the end of their next session." Further, section 3 gives to the President the power of commissioning all the officers of the United States.

[1] See *supra*, p. 32 ; and Fisher, " Suspension of Habeas Corpus " in *Pol. Sci. Qu.*, III., 163.

tution were concerned, no control over the administration at all.

2. *Change due to the power of removal.*—But American development has completely changed this conception of the power possessed by the President. In the first place the duty imposed upon him by the constitution, to see that the laws be faithfully executed,[1] has been construed by the Congress as giving it the power of imposing duties and conferring powers upon the President by statute, and has led to the passage of almost innumerable laws which have greatly increased the importance of the President's position, and have given him powers and duties relative to the details of many administrative branches of the national government.[2] In the case of *In re Neagle* it is said that under this power the President is not limited to the enforcement of acts of Congress according to their express terms. This power includes rights and obligations growing out of the constitution itself. As a result of it the President may protect an officer of the United States in the discharge of his duties.[3]

The second cause of the change in the position of the President is to be found in the interpretation of the constitution made by the first Congress relative to the power of removal. The constitution gave the power of removal to no authority expressly. The question came up before the first Congress in the discussion of the act organizing the department of foreign affairs. Although there was a difference of opinion in the Congress as to who under the constitution possessed

[1] Art. ii., sec. 3.
[2] Elmes, *Executive Departments*, 13, 14.
[3] 135 U. S., 1., 64, 68.

this power, it was finally decided by a very small majority that the power of removal was a part of the executive power and therefore belonged to the President. This was the recognized construction of the constitution for a great number of years, although it did not meet with the approval of some of the most eminent statesmen.[1] After more than three quarters of a century Congress deliberately reversed this decision and by the tenure-of-office acts of 1867–9 (later incorporated in the Revised Statutes as sections 1767–1769) decided that the constitution had not impliedly or expressly settled this point, and that Congress was therefore the body to decide who possessed the power of removal. Congress then decided that the power of removal of senate appointments belonged to the President and the senate.[2] For twenty years this was the law of the land though no one was able to explain exactly what the tenure-of-office acts meant, on account of the obscurity of their wording; but finally in 1887 Congress repealed them. The result is that the early interpretation of the constitution must be regarded as the correct one at the present time. That is, the President alone has the power of removal of even senate appointments. Though the tenure-of-office acts had the effect of temporarily weakening the power of the President, the complete power of removal had existed so long as to determine the position of the President in the national government and has been of incalculable advantage in producing an efficient and harmonious national administration. The benefits which

---

[1] This construction was approved by the United States Courts in United States v. Avery, Deady, 204.

[2] This was constitutional, United States v. Avery, Deady, 204.

followed the interpretation of the first Congress on this question were unquestionably the reason why the tenure-of-office acts were finally repealed. From this power of removal has been evolved the President's power of direction and supervision over the· entire national administration. To it is due the recognition of the possession by the President of the administrative power.

3. *Power of direction.*—The power of direction and control over the administration through which the President has become the chief of administration is hardly recognized in the constitution. The only provision from which it might be derived is that which permits him to "require the opinion in writing of the principal officer in each of the executive departments upon any subject relating to the duties of their respective offices."[1] But perusal of the early acts of Congress organizing the administrative system will show that the first Congress did not have the idea that the President had any power of direction over any matters not political in character, while the conception of the executive power possessed by the statesmen of the time, as seen from the examples which have been adduced, goes to corroborate this position. The acts of Congress organizing the departments of foreign affairs and war did, it is true, expressly give the President the power of directing the principal officers of these departments how they should perform their duties, but these were departments which were of a political character. But the act organizing the treasury department[2] contains no reference to any presidential power of direction. It simply says that the secretary of the treasury shall

---

[1] Art. ii., sec. ii., p. 1.　　　　　　　　[2] Sept. 2, 1789.

generally perform all such services relative to the finances as he shall be directed to perform; and the context shows that reference is made to the direction of Congress and not to that of the President. The debates in Congress substantiate this view. Further, the fact that the secretary of the treasury, different from the other secretaries, was to make his annual report, not to the President, but to Congress, shows that Congress intended, after the manner of the time, to keep the finances under its own supervision. The administration of the finances which, as has been shown, was really almost the only non-political branch attended to by the central government of the commonwealths served the men of those times as a model for the other purely administrative branches. Thus the post-office was organized at first in such a way as to remove it completely from the control of the President. The appointment of all officers in the post-office was given to the postmaster-general, while the law which finally organized the department in 1825 had nothing whatever to say about presidential control or direction. The original absence of this power of direction is commented upon by one of the United States courts. The court says [1]:

The legislature may prescribe the duties of the office at the time of its creation or from time to time, as circumstances may require. If these duties are absolute and specific, and not by law made subject to the control or discretion of any superior officer who is by law especially authorized to direct how those duties are to be performed, the officer whose duties are thus prescribed by law is bound to execute them according to his own judgment. That judgment cannot lawfully be controlled by any other

[1] United States v. Kendall, 5 Cranch, C. C., 163, 272.

person . . . As the head of an executive department he is bound, when required by the President, to give his opinion in writing upon any subject relating to the duties of his office. The President, in the execution of his duties to see that the laws be faithfully executed, is bound to see that the Postmaster-General discharges 'faithfully' the duties assigned by law ; but this does not authorize the President to direct him how he shall discharge them.

The court admits, however, that the President might remove the postmaster-general from office, and it is from this power of removal that we must derive any power that the President has to direct and control the acts of officials in those departments where the law has not expressly provided for the direction and control of the President. So much force did this power of removal have that in 1855, only twenty years after the decision that has been cited was made, we find in an opinion of Mr. Cushing, the attorney-general, the following recognition of the power of direction of the President.[1]

I think . . . the general rule to be . . . that the head of department is subject to the direction of the President. [This was said in relation to duties imposed by statute upon a head of department.] I hold that no head of a department can lawfully perform an official act against the will of the President ; and that will is by the constitution to govern the performance of all such acts. If it were not thus, Congress might by statute so divide and transfer the executive power as utterly to subvert the government and change it into a parliamentary despotism like that of Venice or Great Britain, with a nominal executive chief or President utterly powerless—whether under the name of Doge or King or President would then be of little account so far as regards the question of the maintenance of the constitution.

[1] 7 Opinions of the Attorneys-General, 453, 470.

This is, of course, an extreme view, and it is probably not meant by it that the President has any dispensing power by which he might relieve an officer from
obeying a positive direction of law, since the law, when
constitutional, is always above any executive order.[1] But
it indicates, at any rate, the drift of public opinion as
to what was the position of the President. Indeed, by
this time it was pretty well recognized that the President
had a power of direction over all of the departments
regardless of the fact whether the law organizing the
department had made mention of such a power or not.
This may be seen from the celebrated United States
bank episode when Andrew Jackson made use of the
power of direction, together with the power of removal
on which it is necessarily based, to force the secretary
of the treasury, notwithstanding the semi-independent
position in which the first Congress attempted to place
him, to withdraw the national deposit from the bank.
This was done in spite of the disapproval of Congress,
and no serious attempt was made to condemn his action.[2]
The effect of giving to the President these powers of
removal and direction has been to give him the administrative power, and to make him the chief of administration. The result of our national development has
been a great enlargement of the American conception
of the executive power as exemplified in the office of
the President. The executive power in the United
States, so far as the national government is concerned,
embraces both the powers of which it may in theory

---

[1] Kendall v. U. S., 12 Peters, 524.

[2] See Rüttiman, *op. cit.*, I., 170. For a modern illustration of the presidential
power of direction see F. P. Powers on the Guilford Miller case in an article
on "Railroad Indemnity-Lands" in the *Pol. Sci. Qu.*, IV., 452, 456.

be composed, and the chief executive authority is at the same time the political and the administrative chief of the government, and has under his direction and control the actions of all the officers of the national government.

CHAPTER III.

I.—The President.

It may be said that the executive power possessed
by the President of the United States embraces first,
the political power, which is sometimes exercised by
and with the advice and consent of the senate acting
as an administrative council, and second, the administrative power, which is of especial interest to the
student of administrative law. This administrative
power consists of two classes of minor powers; first, of
the powers which relate to the personnel of the administration. These have been discussed in the historical treatment of the President's power. At the present
time they are complete, and the President is therefore
the head of the national administration, with power
to appoint (with consent of the senate for most important officers), remove, and direct all the subordinates. In the second place, the President has powers
relative to the administrative services themselves,
material rather than personal powers. That is, the
President has the right himself to perform a series of
acts in the different branches of the national administration.

1. *Administrative powers.*—These powers are to be found in the various acts of Congress relative to the different services by which Congress has conferred powers and imposed duties upon the President, which he is obliged to exercise and perform as a result of his constitutional duty to see that the laws be faithfully executed.[1] Principal among them is the ordinance power which in numerous instances Congress has delegated to the President, and which the President may exercise only as a result of such a delegation. In the exercise of these powers it is not necessary that the President act personally even in the case of duties whose performance has been expressly required of him by law.[2]

The acts by means of which the President performs his duties are either of a general or a special character. Those of a general character are either regulations or instructions, the difference between them being that the former bind both the officials of the government and the citizens as a result of the fact that Congress has delegated to the President the power to issue them, while the latter bind only the officials of the government, and are issued by the President as a result of his power of direction and control over the entire administration. Some of the most important of the general regulations issued by the President are the consular regulations and the civil-service rules. But the most important of the executive regulations are issued, not

---

[1] See also *In re* Neagle 135, U. S., i, 64, 68 ; *supra*, p. 64.

[2] Williamson v. The United States, 1 How, 290 ; 17 Peters, 144. This case decided that an act prohibiting the advance of money to disbursing officers except under the special direction of the President did not require of the President the performance of this direction in every instance under his own hand. For political and judicial acts the courts seem to require the personal action of the President. See Runkle v. U. S., 122 U.S., 543, 557 ; U. S. v. Page, 137 U. S., 673, 678 ; *Ex parte* Field, 5 Blatchford, 63.

by the President, but by the different heads of departments, though the President is regarded as responsible for them all and to have acted through the heads of departments.[1]

The other class of the President's acts are of special and not general application, and are directions or orders issued to a single head of a department and decisions in those few cases where it is recognized that the President has the power of deciding appeals from the decisions of his subordinates. The latter power of decision on appeal is not generally recognized as belonging to the President. Indeed it has been laid down as the general rule that the President has no power to correct by his own official act the errors of judgment of incompetent or unfaithful subordinates[2]; and that the individual has no right of appeal from the decision of a head of a department to the President[3]; and that where an appeal lies it can go no further than to the head of a department.[4]

The only case where an appeal lies to the President is where the question to be decided is as to the jurisdiction of the officer whose decision is appealed from. Here the appeal seems to be permitted.[5]

2. *Remedies against the action of the President.*— There are, it may be said, almost no remedies against the action of the President. The President is neither

---

[1] Wilcox v. Jackson, 13 Peters, 498, 513 ; U. S. v. Eliason, 16 *Id.*, 291 ; Confiscation Cases, 20 Wall. 92, 109 ; U. S. v. Farden, 99 U. S., 10, 19 ; Wolsey v. Chapman, 101 U. S., 755.

[2] 4 Opinions of the Attorneys-General, 515; but see the Guilford Miller case. *Supra*, p. 69.

[3] 9 Opinions, 462.   [4] 10 *Ibid.*, 526.

[5] 15 *Ibid.*, 94, 100. This opinion was given in 1876, and is very valuable, as in it are collected and reviewed all the opinions of the attorneys-general on this point.

civilly nor criminally responsible to the courts.[1] Nor can the courts review his acts where the attempt will bring them in direct conflict with him.[2] The only cases where the courts can exercise any control over the President are those in which a regulation or order of the President comes up before them for execution when, if they regard it as an act in excess of the President's powers, they may refuse to enforce and declare it null and void.[3] But even in these cases where the action of the President is regarded as political in its nature the courts will refuse to interfere.[4]

II.—The commonwealth governor.

1. *The governor a political officer.*—The originally political character of the governor[5] has tended to become more prominent, largely on account of the grant to him of the limited veto power. His political powers consist in the first place of military powers, which are always exercised subject to the limitations contained in the United States constitution. This provides that the militia of the several commonwealths shall be under the command of the President when in the actual service of the United States.[6] These military powers consist for the most part of the commandership of the commonwealth militia and include also the military administration as there is no commonwealth secretary of war.[7] This fact is due probably to the possession

---

[1] Durand v. Hollis, 4 Blatchford, 451, which also claims irresponsibility for his subordinates when executing orders issued in the discretion of the President.

[2] *Infra*, II., p. 208; Miss. v. Johnson, 4 Wall, 475.

[3] The Schooner Orono, I. Gallison C. C., 137 ; *Ex parte* Merryman, 9 American Law Register, 524.

[4] *Supra*, p. 34.　　[6] Const., art. ii., sec. 2, par. 1.

[5] *Supra*, p. 59.　　[7] Stimson, *American Statute Law*, p. 41, sec. 202.

by the English crown, at the time the office of governor was established, of the military administration which was considered a part of the royal prerogative. In several of the commonwealths the governor may not act personally in the field unless advised so to do by a resolution of the legislature.[1] As commander-in-chief he has very commonly the power to call out the militia in case of insurrection, invasion, or resistance to the execution of the laws.[2] In some cases here again this right is subject to passage of a resolution to that effect by the legislature. This is so in New Hampshire, Massachusetts, and Tennessee in case of insurrection and in Texas in case of invasion.[3]

The second class of powers possessed by the governor are to be found in the powers he possesses over the actions of the legislature. Thus the governor very generally has the veto power. This includes in many cases the power to veto items in appropriation-bills and usually consists in the power to demand from the legislature a reconsideration of the objectionable bill. On the reconsideration, the bill may be passed usually by a two-thirds vote, in some cases a three-fifths, and finally in some by a simple majority.[4] The governor also has the power to adjourn the legislature in case the two houses disagree as to the time of adjournment[5]; the power to call extra sessions of the legislature[6]; and the power and duty to send to the legislature messages in which he is to give the legislature such information as to the condition of the commonwealth, and

---

[1] Alabama, Kentucky, Maryland, and Missouri. Stimson, *op. cit.* sec. 297.
[2] Stimson, *op. cit.* sec. 298.
[3] *Ibid.*
[4] *Ibid.*, sec. 305, C.
[5] *Ibid.*, sec. 278.
[6] *Ibid.*, sec. 277.

to recommend such measures as he deems proper.[1]   In
the third place the governor has very generally the
power to grant pardons, reprieves, and commutations
of sentences and may remit fines and forfeitures.[2]   In
some instances treason and conviction on impeachment
are excepted from his pardoning power,[3] while in certain
of the States the power in all cases is conditioned
upon obtaining the consent of the council (Massachusetts, Maine, and New Hampshire), or the senate
(Rhode Island), or that of the judges of the supreme
court and the attorney-general or a majority of them
(Nevada and Florida), or of a board of pardons consisting of " state officers "[4] (Pennsylvania).   Finally the
governor has in some cases the power to proclaim in
accordance with the law the time of general elections.
This power is often possessed by the secretary of state.[5]

2. *Power of appointment.*—While the political
powers of the governor have increased, his administrative powers have decreased.   First among these is the
power of appointment.   This power was originally
rather greater in New York than elsewhere.   Here the
governor had the power to appoint most officers in the
commonwealth, but was subject in the exercise of the
power to the necessity of obtaining the consent of the
council of appointment formed of members of the senate elected by the assembly.[6]   In 1801, however, the
power was given to each member of the council to
nominate for appointment.[7]   The diffusion of responsibility resulting from this amendment at a time when
the patronage of the central government of the com-

---

[1] *Ibid.*, sec. 280.
[2] *Ibid.*, secs. 160, 163, 164.
[3] *Ibid.*, sec. 161.
[4] *Ibid.*, sec. 160.
[5] See Nebraska Compiled Statutes, 1889, p. 453.
[6] *Supra*, p. 56.
[7] Amendment V. to the first constitution.

monwealth was very large [1] resulted in great evils; and
the demand began to be made that the patronage of
the central government of the commonwealth be lessened. This was done by the constitution of 1821,
which abolished the council of appointment and provided that the heads of the executive departments
should be appointed by the legislature as had been the
rule from the beginning in Massachusetts and Virginia. Most of the officers of the commonwealth in
the localities were made elective, and in the few cases
in which the power of appointment was left with the
governor its exercise was conditioned by the necessity
of obtaining the consent of the senate. The constitution of 1846 still further lessened the power of the
governor to appoint officers; but since that time there
has been a reaction in favor of increasing this power.
Amendments to the constitution and statutes, have
provided new officers unknown to the original constitution, and these officers are for the most part appointed
by the governor and senate. Finally, the general power
has been given to the governor to appoint to any
position for which no other method of appointment or
election has been provided,[2] and to fill vacancies except
in the principal " state offices," which are filled by
the legislature.[3] The same development has been going
on in the other commonwealths with the result that
the governor's power of appointment at the present
time is as follows:

The governor has the power with the consent of the
council or senate to appoint the less important " state

---

[1] In 1821 the number of civil appointees was 7,000, that of military appointees, 8,000. See schedule in Clark's *Debates of the Convention of 1821.*

[2] N. Y. L. 1892, c. 681, sec. 6.

[3] *Ibid.,* secs. 30, 31.

officers " [1] and almost never any of the local officers;
to fill many vacancies until the expiration of the term
or the next election, and to fill all offices for which
some other method of filling is not provided. This
power of appointment is generally based on statute, and
therefore may be decreased at any time by the legislature. But in some cases it is based on the constitution,[2]
when of course the legislature would have no such power.
In a few commonwealths it is provided that the term
of the officers to be appointed by the governor and of
those to be elected by the people shall expire at the
same time that the term of the governor expires, so
that the new governor may fill the offices to his
satisfaction at the beginning of the term, and so that
there will be harmony in general policy between the
governor and the elected officers, who it is supposed
will belong to the same party as the governor.[3] But
this is quite rare.

3. *Power of removal.*—In New York, where the administrative powers of the governor were rather greater
than elsewhere, it was provided by the first constitution that the governor had, subject to the necessity of
obtaining the consent of the council of appointment,
the power to remove almost every important officer in
the commonwealth government not judicial in character
and not purely local.[4] It is said that " use was made
of this power to produce an entire change of officers
throughout the state from the highest to the lowest,
at any rate in all those cases where the immediate pre-
decessors of the council [of appointment] had made an

---

[1] But see Florida where he appoints almost all. See Const. 1881, art. v.,
sec. 17.

[2] See Stimson, *op. cit.*, sec. 202, B.

[3] See Kentucky, General Statutes, secs. 2, 25, 28 ; Constitution of Nebraska,
v., sec. 1 ; Florida Const. 1881, v., sec. 17.   [4] Const., art. xxvii.

appointment." [1] This gross misuse of the power of removal was one of the reasons why the council of appointment was abolished in 1821. With its abolition the governor's power of removal was greatly diminished. At first the governor lost practically all power of removal, but later a certain power of removal was restored to him ; and at the present time the power of removal of the commonwealth governor is as follows :

This power is as a rule confined to the officers whom the governor appoints, though in New York he is permitted to remove all the important " state officers " [2]; and local officers are seldom removable by the governor except in New York where the power to remove local officers is quite large. [3] In almost all cases, however, the exercise of this power is conditioned upon obtaining the consent of the council or senate and upon the finding of cause for removal, which cause is usually either malfeasance in office or neglect of duty, but in a few cases may consist in incompetency. [4] Where cause is the ground of removal, in accordance with the general principles of the administrative law of the United States the person to be removed must be given a hearing. [5] Sometimes pending the removal proceedings the governor has by statute the right to suspend the officer. [6] As in the case of the power of appointment the power of removal is based sometimes on the constitution, indeed generally so, but also in some cases on the statutes when the legislature may take it away.

4. *Power of direction.*—The governor's powers of

---

[1] Hammond, *History of Political Parties in the State of New York*, I., 289.

[2] Const., art. v., secs. 3, 4 ; art. x., secs. 1, 3, and 10 ; L., 1892, c. 681, secs. 22, 23 ; *cf.* Stimson, *op. cit.*, sec. 266.

[3] L., 1892, c. 681, sec. 23.

[4] *Ibid.*, secs. 22 and 23 ; Stimson, *op. cit.*, sec. 266.

[5] *Infra*, II., p. 99.　　　　[6] See Indiana Rev. Stats., 1881, sec. 5643.

direction and control over the administrative officers are very small and must of necessity be so, so long as the power of removal is so weak. Further, the statutes seldom give him expressly any such power. The only general exception to this rule seems to be in the case of the attorney-general who is regarded as the legal adviser of the governor and as such subject to his direction.[1] Further, it is very generally provided that the governor may demand information from the various officers, who must also report to him.[2]

5. *The governor's power over the administrative services.*—In addition to these rather limited powers over the personnel of the commonwealth administration the governor has also a few but rather unimportant powers relative to the administrative services. As a general thing, however, these services are managed by the various " state officers " independently of the governor. Among the governor's powers of this character may be mentioned the ordinance power. This, like the ordinance power of the President, is a delegated ordinance power; but different from the national Congress, the commonwealth legislature has not often delegated to the governor any ordinance power. Further, the governor has in several of the commonwealths comparatively extended financial powers. Thus in seven of the commonwealths[3] he is to draw up estimates of the amount of money to be raised by taxation for the purposes of the government; in several commonwealths also all money is to be paid out of the treasury on his order[4];

---

[1] See, *e. g.*, California Political Code, sec. 380, paragraphs 5, 6, and 7 ; Georgia Code, sec. 367 ; Indiana Rev. Stats., sec. 5659.

[2] Stimson, *op. cit.*, sec. 281.

[3] Illinois, Nebraska, West Virginia, Missouri, Texas, Colorado, and Alabama. Stimson, *op. cit.*, sec. 280.

[4] *E. g.* see Code of Georgia, 1882, sec. 76.

and finally in a number he is to examine the accounts of financial officers at stated times and sometimes unexpectedly.[1]

6. *General position of the governor.* — It will be noticed from this description of the governor's powers how different his position in the commonwealth administration is from that of the President in the national administration. Originally occupying about the same relative position, the governor has been stripped of his administrative powers, and has been more and more confined to the exercise of political powers, while the President has been gaining more and more administrative power, until at the present time he makes or unmakes the administration of the United States. It has been impossible for the governor to become the head of the commonwealth administration, because the people of the commonwealth have decided that the governor shall be in the main a political officer. They have lessened his power of appointment, they have all but destroyed his power of removal. He has thus been unable to develop any power of direction. The governor's office has been deprived of all means of administrative development.[2] He is now more than he ever was a political officer. His political powers indeed have tended to increase. This is especially true of the veto power, which now extends to items of bills appropriating money. But because the governor has thus been confined to the

[1] See Virginia Code, sec. 238 ; Colorado General Statutes, 1883, sec. 1361 ; Iowa, McLain's Annotated Statutes, 1882, secs. 759, 763 ; Kansas, Dassler's Compiled Laws, sec. 5964.

[2] The remark of one of the commonwealth governors that all the power he had was " to pardon criminals and appoint notaries " is indicative of the governor's position at the present time.

exercise of political powers his influence upon the welfare of the commonwealth must not be underestimated. He is still a very important officer. His veto power gives him a vast power over legislation, while the little power of removal which he possesses often enables him to punish summarily any gross malconduct on the part of many of the important administrative officers of the commonwealth both at the centre and in the localities.

7. *Remedies against his action.*—The remedies against the acts of the governor are about the same as the remedies provided against the action of the President, though perhaps a little more effectual on account of the fact that the courts are not so careful of avoiding conflict with the commonwealth executive. Thus, while the better rule would seem to be that the courts will not attempt to control his action by attempting to exercise a direct restraint over him,[1] still there are cases in which they have not hesitated to issue direct commands to him, whose disobedience would, in accordance with the usual rules of law, result in his commitment for contempt of court; and they have had little compunction about declaring an act of the governor, in which it would appear that he had considerable discretion, null and void.[2]

[1] High, *Extraordinary Legal Remedies*, 2d Ed., secs. 118, 136; People v. Hill, 13 N. Y. Supplement, 186; *N. Y. Law Journal*, April 13, 1891; affirmed, but on different grounds, in 126 N. Y., 497.

[2] People v. Curtis, 50 N. Y., 321, where it was decided that a warrant of extradition made by the governor in pursuance of an unconstitutional law was void; People v. Lawrence, 56 N. Y., 182, where the court went back of a warrant of extradition issued by the governor, and decided that the affidavits on which the warrant was issued were not sufficient to justify the inference that a legal crime had been committed; People v. Platt, 50 Hun., 454, where the court decided that the act of the governor appointing an officer was without jurisdiction, on the ground that the person appointed was not qualified. See also Dullam v. Willson, 53 Mich., 392.

CHAPTER IV.

THE EXECUTIVE POWER AND AUTHORITY IN FRANCE.

I.—General position.

The office of the chief executive is filled in France by the President, who is elected by the legislature acting in national assembly. His position is, from the administrative point of view, similar to that of the President of the United States, but somewhat more influential, on account of the existence in France of many monarchical traditions and on account of the existence also for so long a time of a hierarchically organized administration, at whose head it is well recognized that the President stands. While from the administrative point of view his position is somewhat more important, from the political point of view his position is considerably less important than that of the President of the United States, particularly on account of the absence of any veto power and on account of the adoption of the principle of the responsibility of his ministers to the legislature.

II.—Administrative powers.

1. *Power of appointment.*—His administrative powers relative to the personnel of the official service are to be found in the first place in a wide power of

appointment. He appoints without any limitations whatever to most of the important positions in the administration, the only exception to this rule being that his ministers must have the confidence of the legislature, which by precedent has come to mean the confidence of the chamber of deputies.[1] The President has the power of appointing not only the agents of the central administration, but also most of the officers acting in the localities, such as the prefects in the departments, the under-prefects in the districts, and the treasurers of the departments. Really the only important administrative officer in the localities not appointed by the President is the mayor in the commune, who since 1882 has been appointed by the municipal council.[2] Formerly the power of appointment of the chief executive was much greater than now, the members of all the deliberating bodies in the localities being designated by the central government. These are now elected by the people of the respective localities. In addition to appointing the officers of the active administration, the President also appoints the members of the administrative councils and courts, *viz.*, the council of state,[3] and the council of the prefecture,[4] and the members of all the ordinary courts.[5]

2. *Powers of removal and direction.*—In the second place the President has in the case of purely administrative officers an unlimited power of removal which is even more extensive than his power of appointment since he may remove not only all officers whom he has

---

[1] L., Feb. 25, 1875, art. 3, Burgess, *op. cit.*, I., 302.
[2] L., March 28, 1882.
[3] L., Feb. 25, 1875.
[4] L., June 21, 1875.
[5] L., Feb. 25, 1875.

appointed,[1] but also may remove the mayors of the communes,[2] and may dissolve the local deliberative and legislative bodies, such as the general council of the department and the municipal councils of the communes.[3] In the third place, the President's power of direction is as great as his powers of appointment and removal. It is, however, the result of tradition rather than of positive law. The administration has been so long hierarchically organized that the idea that the President is the head of the administration, subject always to the principle of ministerial responsibility to the legislature, is universally recognized. Further, the power of removal is so great that the power of direction has the greatest possible administrative sanction.

3. *The ordinance power.*—Among the President's powers which relate not so much to the personnel of the service as to the actual conduct of the administrative business of the government may be mentioned the ordinance power. It is a well recognized principle of French law that the President has a general power to supplement the law by means of ordinances, even where the legislature has not expressly delegated any such power to him. The ordinances are known to the French law as decrees. This power of supplementary ordinance results from the constitutional law,[4] which imposes upon the President the duty of watching over and securing the execution of the laws.[5] The reason why such an interpretation should be put upon this clause, when in the United States a similar clause has

[1] Aucoc, *op. cit.*, I., p. 106.

[2] L., April 5, 1884, arts. 85, 86.

[3] L., August 10, 1871, art. 35 ; L., April 5, 1884, art. 43.

[4] L., February 25, 1875.

[5] Aucoc, *op. cit.*, I., 108 ; Ducrocq, *op. cit.*, I., 57 ; Boeuf, *op. cit.*, 14

received such a different interpretation, is to be found in the monarchical traditions of the country. It results from the old idea that the residuary governmental power of the land is vested in the chief executive, who may therefore issue ordinances, which supplement existing laws, and do not conflict with either their letter or their spirit. But besides this power of supplementary ordinance many statutes have expressly delegated to the President the power to issue decrees which regulate in detail such points as the legislature has not seen fit to regulate itself. All decrees issued in either of these ways have the same characteristics as the laws which they supplement. They are binding upon individuals who in case they violate them may be subjected to the penalties provided by law.[1] Certain of these decrees are called decrees of public administration, *viz.*, those which the President issues as a result of a delegation of the ordinance power of the legislature. In the issue of these decrees of public administration the President has, as a rule, wider powers than in the case of the supplementary ordinances. For this reason it is a general principle of the French law that the President shall before issuing them ask the advice of the council of state.[2] Wherever the law requires such a formality, its non-observance would make the decree void, though at the same time it is to be noticed that the President is never bound to act in accordance with the advice which has been given by the council of state. This is a peculiarity which is characteristic of the entire French administrative law. The purpose of the provision is to ensure sufficient

[1] See Art. 471, No. 15 of the *Penal Code.*
[2] L., May 24, 1872, arts. 8 and 13 ; Ducrocq, *op. cit.*, I., 57.

deliberation on important subjects, and at the same time a concentrated responsibility for the action taken, which is always regarded as the action of the officer issuing the decree and not that of the council whose advice is asked. To act is the function of one, to deliberate that of several, is the fundamental principle of French administration.

Besides the general acts or ordinances which the President has the power to issue, he has often the power to issue a decree which affects only some one particular individual case. Thus he opens by means of a decree supplementary appropriations,[1] declares that certain public works are of public utility, which means that the right of eminent domain may be exercised[2]; exercises by special decree the administrative control which is given to the central government over the actions of certain local corporations. This power is not nearly so large now as it formerly was.[3] The President also grants by special decree certain charters and concessions, *e. g.*, for railways of minor importance and for mines.[4] The President must always exercise these powers through one of his ministers, who must countersign his act and thus becomes responsible for it to the legislature.[5]

4. *Remedies against his action.*—The remedies open to the individual against the acts of the President are much greater than under the American system. The control of the courts over his penal ordinances is the same as in the United States. That is, if any one is

---

[1] L., September 16, 1871, arts. 31 and 32.
[2] L., July 27, 1870.
[3] *Infra*, p. 271.
[4] Boeuf, *op. cit.*, 15.
[5] L., February 25, 1875, art. 3.

prosecuted before the courts for the violation of an ordinance or decree of the President, the courts may refuse to convict on the ground that the decree is not legally made, since the penal code gives the courts the power to punish violations of only ordinances which are legally made.[1] Further, any one may appeal from any act of the President, not of a political character, directly to the council of state, which may annul it if it has been done in excess of the powers possessed by the President or in violation of the law, and may amend and modify it so as to render justice in case it violates an individual right. Finally, any one who deems himself aggrieved by an act of the President may petition the legislature which may hold the minister responsible who has countersigned it.[2]

[1] *Penal Code*, Art. 471, No. 15 ; Boeuf, *op cit.*, 17.
[2] Aucoc, *op. cit.*, I., 113.

CHAPTER V.

I.— The prince.

1. *An authority of general powers.*—In Germany, as in France and for the same reason, the conception of the executive power and of the position of the chief executive authority, as exemplified in the prince, is much broader than it is in the United States. Consequently, the chief executive authority is more important, certainly from the administrative point of view, than in the United States. Monarchical traditions have led to the adoption of the theory that the entire governmental power of the land is vested in the prince who is quite irresponsible.[1] But in order that such a theory may not lead in its application to absolute government, a corollary of the principle adds, that the prince may act only in a certain way, and that in order that he act even in that way some one shall be responsible for each one of his acts.[2] The constitution therefore places important limitations on his action, but where no such limitation exists the prince is recognized as having the governmental power. The prince is, different from the American President and governor, not an authority

---

[1] Schulze, *Deutsches Staatsrecht*, I., 187.
[2] *Ibid.*, Meyer, *Deutsches Staatsrecht*, 186, *et seq.*

of enumerated powers, but is the possessor of the residuum of governmental power in the partition of the governmental power made by the constitution. He may therefore exercise the governmental power in such instances and in such ways as best suit him, provided that the constitution has not given the exercise of the power to some other authority and has not designated the way in which the power shall be exercised. The express limitations upon the power of the prince become thus of the same importance as the enumerated powers of the United States President, and the prince possesses, even in the absence of special grant, provided that the constitution has not taken such power from him, both the political and the administrative powers.

2. *Limitations of his power.*—The constitutional limitations of the power of the prince belong, it is true, rather to the domain of constitutional than to that of administrative law, but they must be considered briefly in order to reach a clear understanding of the position in the administrative system of the German prince.

In the first place, by the princely constitutions the consent of the legislative body is necessary for the validity of all legislative acts affecting the freedom of the person and property [1]; for the fixing of the budget of the expenses and receipts and the levying of taxes.[2] The judicial power, *i. e.*, the decision of controversies in regard to the private and criminal law, has been given to courts over whose actions the prince can exercise no influence whatever.[3] Finally every official act of the

---

[1] Meyer, *Staatsrecht*, 408 ; Schulze, *op. cit.*, I., 190.

[2] Meyer, *op. cit.*, 204, 205.

[3] Schulze, *op. cit.* I., 190.

prince, whatever be its nature, must be countersigned by some one of the ministers who assumes the responsibility for it either to the legislature or to the criminal courts, generally to the latter.[1]

In the second place, the imperial constitution has seriously limited the political powers of the prince although it has not changed the legal theory that the prince possesses all the governmental powers not granted specifically to some other authority. Thus the princes have lost for the most part their diplomatic and military powers[2]; a certain part of their legislative power, indeed almost all their legislative power over the relations regulated by the private law, while certain branches of administration which were formerly attended to by the princes have been transferred to the imperial government.[3]

3. *His administrative powers.*—As a result of these principles and of these limitations the German prince at the present time has the following administrative powers:

a. A wide power of appointment which extends to many of the officers in the localities and is not in any case limited by any principle of ministerial responsibility to the legislature. The prince is not obliged to keep or obtain the confidence of the legislature in the selection of his advisers and agents.[4]

b. The prince has a wide power of removal even of local officers—a power which in some cases may result in the actual dismissal from office of an objectionable officer, in other and most cases may result simply in

---

[1] Meyer, *op. cit.*, 186 ; Schulze, *op. cit.*, I., 191, 298.

[2] Const., art. 11.

[3] For the details see the Const., art, 4 ; Meyer, *Staatsrecht*, 176 *et. seq.*

[4] Schulze, *op. cit.* I., 299, 320.

retiring the officer from active participation in the work of administration. In such cases the retired officer is still regarded as an officer with most of the privileges and duties which are attached to the official relation.[1] This power is also unlimited by the necessity of obtaining or keeping the confidence of the legislature.[2]

c. The prince has a wide power of direction to be exercised, however, in all cases through ministers who become criminally responsible and sometimes responsible to the legislature for all the acts by means of which the power of direction is exercised.[3]

d. The prince has a large ordinance power over all matters which have not been regulated in detail by the legislature.[4] There is somewhat of a conflict among the commentators as to how large this ordinance power is, but the better opinion would seem to be that where the constitution has not assigned limits to the ordinance power, and where the statutes of the legislature have not regulated a given subject, the prince may regulate any matter by ordinance.[5] In accordance with custom based upon this theory many things are in Germany regulated by ordinance, both independent and supplementary ordinance, which in the United States are regulated by statute. This ordinance power must, however, be exercised through some one of the ministers, who must countersign the ordinance and becomes responsible as in the other cases for his acts.

From the juristic point of view the acts of the prince

---

[1] See *infra*, pp. 94, 118 ; II., 100.

[2] Schulze, *op. cit.*, I., 341.

[3] *Ibid.*, 298 ; Bornhak *Preussisches Staatsrecht*, I., 144.

[4] Schulze, *op. cit.*, I., 528 *et. seq.*

[5] Gneist, *Verwaltung, Justiz und Rechtsweg*, sec. 74 ; Bornhak, *op. cit.*, I., 436.

are in almost all cases the acts of the ministers. The remedies offered to the individual against the acts of the prince must therefore be found in the remedies offered against the acts of the ministers.[1]

II.—*The Emperor.*

1. *General position.* The German Emperor, who is the chief executive authority in the imperial government, occupies quite a different position from that of the prince in the separate members of the empire. While the prince possesses all the governmental powers which have not been given to some other authority, the Emperor is an authority of enumerated powers. He thus occupies, from the administrative point of view, about the same position which is occupied by the United States President.[2]

The constitution[3] declares that the King of Prussia shall be German Emperor. The provisions of the Prussian constitution relative to the King are of value therefore as to the tenure of the Emperor, but the questions arising therefrom, as well as all questions arising in regard to the political powers of the Emperor, belong to constitutional law and will not be treated here.[4]

2. *Powers relative to the official service.*—The administrative powers of the Emperor relate, in the first place, to the official service of the empire. Among this class of powers may be mentioned a power of appointment. A general power of appointment is given by

---

[1] For these see *infra*, p. 158 ; II., pp. 177, 188.

[2] One of the best of the German commentators on this account regards the governmental form of the empire as a republic. Zorn, *op. cit.*, I., 162.

[3] Art. 11.

[4] See Burgess, *op. cit.*, II., 264 *et seq.*

the constitution to the Emperor. [1] This clause is somewhat modified by other provisions, as well as by certain statutes whose result is somewhat to limit the broad power of appointment, by requiring either the presentation or the confirmation of the person to be appointed, by the Federal Council, or a committee thereof. [2] In addition to this general power of appointment, the constitution further gives to the Emperor the sole power of appointing the imperial chancellor,[3] who is the only responsible minister in the imperial administration.[4] The only limitation of this power is to be found in the requirement that the chancellor must be a member of the Federal Council. But this does not amount to much, inasmuch as the Emperor as King of Prussia has the right of appointing several members of the Federal Council. Further a power of removal is to be mentioned.[5] This power of removal is not, however, an arbitrary one. For in accordance with the principles which have been all but universally adopted in the German administrative system, discharge from office may take place only as the result of the conviction by a criminal or a disciplinary court of the commission of a crime, or the violation of official duty.[6] In order, however, to permit the Emperor to secure a harmonious administration, he is permitted to retire most of the officers who occupy places involving the exercise of large discretion. The official relation is not, however, broken by such retirement, but the officer receives a portion, three quarters, of his pay, and is subject to all the duties and enjoys all the privileges

[1] Art. 18, sec. 1.
[2] See *infra*, p. 118.
[3] Art. 15.

[4] Zorn, *op. cit.*, I. 195 *et seq.*
[5] Const., art. 18.
[6] *Cf.* L., March 31, 1873.

connected with the office, with the exception of that of performing official acts.[1]

The power of direction is recognized as existing in the Emperor in accordance with the general principles of a hierarchically organized service, of which the Emperor is the head. This power of direction is, however, exercised under the responsibility of the chancellor, who must countersign all the acts by means of which it is exercised.[2] Exactly what the responsibility of the chancellor is, no one seems to be able to say. All that it practically amounts to, on account of the fact that legislation has never elaborated it, is that the chancellor may be called upon to defend his policy before the Federal Council.

3. *Ordinance power.*—The Emperor is further recognized by the constitution[3] as the head of the administration, and as such has powers and duties affecting the administrative services. He is to execute the imperial laws,[4] and is to represent the empire.[5] He does not, as a result of this position, have any ordinance power except such as may be expressly mentioned in the constitution, or may be delegated to him by the legislature.[6] The constitution has given him the ordinance power in one or two instances, but has not given to him any general power even of supplementary ordinance.[7] In the exercise of this ordinance power it is often necessary that the Emperor get the consent of the Federal Council[8]; and all his ordinances

---

[1] *Ibid.*, Meyer, *Staatsrecht*, 393.
[2] Const., art. 17.
[3] Arts. 12–19.
[4] Art. 17.
[5] Art. 11.
[6] Zorn, *op. cit.*, I., 132.
[7] Arts. 50 and 63, respectively, give the Emperor the power of supplementary ordinance relative to the posts and telegraphs and the army.
[8] Zorn, *op. cit.*, I., 132.

must be countersigned by the chancellor, who assumes responsibility therefor.[1]   In some cases, finally, his ordinances must be submitted to the imperial diet for its approval.[2]   In this limited power of ordinance is to be found almost all of the power of the Emperor over the administrative services, all the details being worked out by the chancellor and his assistants.

As the Emperor is irresponsible, there are strictly speaking no remedies against his action, except such as are to be found against the action of the chancellor.[3]

[1] Const., art. 17.
[2] Zorn, *op. cit.*, I., 133.
[3] For these see *infra*, p. 158 ; II., pp. 177, 188.

CHAPTER VI.

THE EXECUTIVE POWER AND AUTHORITY IN ENGLAND.

I.—General power of the Crown.

The theory which governs the distribution of powers in the English government is in principle the same as that which governs the distribution of powers in the princely governments of Germany. The Crown has the residuum of governmental power. All the governmental powers which have not been expressly granted to some other authority belong to the Crown; and the Crown may act in the exercise of its powers as it sees fit, so far as no express limitations have been put upon its action. The only difference between the English and the German systems is to be found in the fact that in Germany the distribution of governmental powers and the limitations on the exercise of the powers of the executive are to be found in a written constitution, while in England it is the Parliament ultimately which decides what powers shall be exercised by the Crown and how it shall exercise them.[1] This position of the English Crown results from the absolute character of the government established by the early Norman Kings. "The Norman idea of royalty," says Dr. Stubbs,[2] "was very comprehensive . . . It combined all the powers of national sovereighty, as they had been exercised by Edgar and

[1] Burgess, *op. cit.*, II., 198, 199.
[2] *Constitutional History of England*, I., 338.

Canute, with those of the feudal theory of monarchy, which was exemplified at the time in France and the Empire." The King was thus both the chosen head of the nation and the feudal lord of the whole land. Further, the Norman idea of the kingship discarded the limitations which had been placed on either the continental or Anglo-Saxon monarchs—in England, the constitutional action of the witan, and on the continent, the extorted immunities and usurpations of the feudatories.[1] At first the Crown was not hereditary, but later it became so; and its power grew to be absolutely despotic.[2] Soon, however, this despotic power became limited by the necessity of the concurrence of the action of Parliament, which we find well developed by the latter part of the thirteenth century, and whose consent was necessary for the imposition of taxes, and also for the enactment of all rules of law which affected the ordinary relations of individuals. For whatever had once been enacted by Parliament became a part of the *lex terræ* and therefore, in accordance with the old Teutonic principle, could not then be changed without the consent of the people as expressed by Parliament, its representative.[3] Later on, Parliament assumed to itself the right to initiate as well as to approve law; and finally the Crown lost through misuse its original power to refuse its consent to what Parliament does.[4]

[1] *Ibid.*

[2] *Cf.* Gneist, *Das Englische Verwaltungsrecht*, 1884, p. 214 and *passim.* Anson, *The Law and Custom of the Constitution*, II., 56 *et seq.*

[3] See Gneist, *op. cit.*, 207.

[4] Though the general opinion seems to be that the veto power of the Crown has become obsolete, Mr. Todd thought that this power though dormant might be revived. See *Parliamentary Government in England*, 2d edition, II., 390-392 ; *cf.* also Burgess, *op. cit.*, II., 201.

II.—Limitations on the power of the Crown.

The result of this development is that Parliament has assumed most of the legislative power, since it has by statute regulated most important subjects. The Crown may still, however, regulate any matters which have not been regulated by Parliament and has thus quite a large ordinance power both independent and supplementary.[1] Parliament has also assumed the exercise of the taxing power and has in several cases forbidden the Crown to levy taxes without its consent.[2] The Crown has further lost almost all its judicial power.[3] But it has retained in large part its old executive powers together with the power of ordinance which has already been alluded to. In the exercise of these powers the Crown has, however, been seriously limited in its action. For at the same time that Parliament was developing there was also developing another body by which the action of the Crown has always been more or less controlled. This was the Privy Council.[4] The consent of this body has become necessary for the valid exercise of the ordinance power.[5] Finally, every act of the Crown must be performed under the responsibility of one of the members of the Privy Council who alone are the responsible advisers of the Crown.[6] The adoption of this principle was necessary because the legal theory of the English government assigns to the Crown a position of absolute irresponsibility. The king can do no wrong is one of the fundamental English maxims.[7]

---

[1] *Cf.* Burgess, *op. cit.*, II., 199.

[2] *E. g.* see Petition of Right, 3 Car. I., c. 1. X. ; and Bill of Rights, I. William and Mary, 2d Session, c. 2.

[3] Bill of Rights and the Act of Settlement, 11 and 12 William III., c. 11.

[4] For its history see *infra.* p. 122.   [6] *Ibid.*, I., 116, 266.

[5] Todd, *op. cit.*, II. 80.   [7] Anson, *op. cit.*, II., 41.

But with these limitations of the power of the Crown, the Crown may do anything. In certain cases the Crown "acts in Parliament," as the expression is, in others in council, or some privy councillor is responsible for its acts. The English Crown is not therefore an authority of enumerated powers but may do anything which it has not been forbidden to do. The limitations on the power of the Crown become as important in England as the enumerated powers of the President in the United States. What these limitations are has already been shown. As a result of them and of the general theory, the Crown has the administrative[1] as well as the political power. The Crown has the power to create offices, to appoint in many cases their incumbents except in the case of local administrative officers who are usually elected, to remove them except as above, and to direct them how to act. The Crown is therefore the chief of the administration as well as the political head of the government. The position of the Crown is, however, greatly modified by the adoption of the principle that the advisers of the Crown, without whom the Crown cannot act, must possess the confidence of the party in the majority in the lower house of Parliament, must practically be its nominees.[2] This principle of parliamentary responsibility plays the same rôle in England as in France which borrowed it from England. It puts the Crown in the position of reigning but not governing. But, just as in France, the theory of the distribution of powers has a great influence on the action of the administration; for the advisers of the Crown may with the consent of the Crown do everything which this theory permits the

[1] Anson, *op. cit.*, II., 53.   [2] Todd, *op. cit.*, II., 134 and 142.

Crown to do. So long as the Crown and its ministers have the confidence of the lower house of Parliament they have most extensive executive powers, greater perhaps than in any other country. Thus the Crown in council may declare war and make treaties of peace [1] which in all other countries can only be done with the consent of the legislature, or that of one of the houses of the legislature as in Germany. It is only when the Crown and its ministers lose the confidence of the lower house of Parliament that the principle of the freedom of action of the Crown in the exercise of the powers left to it by Parliament is susceptible of limitation. And in such cases it must be remembered that the result of the lack of confidence is not that Parliament proceeds to take action itself but that the Crown has to choose new ministers who will have the confidence of Parliament or dissolves Parliament in the hope that the new house will have confidence in the existing ministers. In all cases it is the Crown and not Parliament which administers.

As the Crown is in theory irresponsible there is no remedy against its acts except such as is to be found against the ministers who may have countersigned the acts of the Crown, thereby assuming responsibility therefor.[2] But, as in the United States and France, the courts may refuse to enforce the ordinances of the Crown in case they regard them as illegal.[3]

[1] *Ibid.*, I., 351 *et seq.*

[2] For the remedies against the acts of the ministers see *infra* p. 158.

[3] Todd, *op. cit.*, I., 461, citing Attorney-General v. Bishop of Manchester, L., R. 3, Eq. 436.

Division 2.— Executive Councils.

CHAPTER I.

THE EXECUTIVE COUNCIL IN THE UNITED STATES.

I.—General position.

By the side of the executive authority there is often placed a council to which is given some sort of a control over executive action. In almost every one of the American colonies there was a body known as the council of the governor, the members of which were appointed by the King, and whose consent was necessary for the validity of certain of the acts of the governor. With the governor it formed one branch of the colonial legislature.[1] When the colonies became independent, in several of them this institution was retained and exists at the present time. Thus in the commonwealths of Maine, Massachusetts, and New Hampshire we find still a governor's council whose consent is necessary for the governor's appointments.[2] In others, the council as such has disappeared, and the powers which it possessed have been transferred to the upper house of the legislature.[3] This is the general rule at the present time and is true of the national government and of the commonwealth of New York.[4]

[1] So in New York, see *supra*, pp. 53, 57.
[2] See Stimson, *op. cit.*, sec. 210, B.
[3] *Ibid.*, sec. 210, C.
[4] *Supra*, p. 77.

The powers which these councils or the senates as executive councils possess at the present are somewhat different in the national and commonwealth governments.

II.—*In the national government.*

In the national government the only power which the Senate possesses over the administrative acts of the President is the power to refuse its consent to the most important of his appointments. For a time it had also the power to prevent the President from removing those officers for whose appointment its consent was necessary ; but with the repeal of the tenure-of-office acts[1] this power was lost.[2] In addition to this control over the purely administrative acts of the President, the Senate also has the power to control one of his political powers. All treaties negotiated by the President must, to be binding upon the government, receive the approval of the Senate to be expressed by a two-thirds vote.[3] These powers which the Senate possesses over the acts of the President must not be classed among its legislative powers. For, though the Senate is an important legislative body, it is at the same time an executive council and the only executive council in the national government ; and when acting as such, acts separately and apart from the other legislative body, the House of Representatives. When so acting it is said to be in executive session and may sit at a time when the house of representatives is not in

[1] *Supra*, p. 65.

[2] The Senate has such a power only in those cases in which the statutes of Congress expressly recognize it as *e. g.* in the case of the postmaster-general. United States Revised Statutes, secs. 388 and 389.

[3] Const., art. ii., sec. 2, par. 2.

session, which may not be the case when it is acting as a part of the legislature. Nothing is more common than to see the Senate summoned for a special session when Congress has adjourned or is not in session. Further, the Senate as an executive council may be distinguished from the Senate as a part of Congress by the difference in procedure which is followed in the two cases. When it acts as an executive council its sessions are as a rule secret, while its sessions as a part of the legislature are open to the public. The reason of this rule is to be found in the delicate character of the business which comes before it when acting as an executive council.

III.—In the commonwealths.

While the United States Senate has a control over certain of both the political and the administrative acts of the President, the commonwealth Senate, acting as an executive council, and the governor's council, which is elected by the legislature in Maine,[1] but elsewhere elected by the people,[2] has control over only the administrative acts of the governor. Its control over these administrative acts is, however, more extended than the similar control of the Senate over the acts of the President. For the rule in the various commonwealths is, that the consent of the executive council is necessary not only for appointments but also for removals.[3] What has been said with regard to the separate session of the national Senate when acting as an executive council, may be repeated here.

[1] Maine Constitution, art. 5, 22.

[2] Stimson, *op. cit.*, sec. 202, B.

[3] For New York see *supra*, p. 79.   See also Maine Constitution, art. 9, sec. 6 ; Stimson, sec. 210 ; *cf.*, Bryce, *American Commonwealth*, I., 468.

IV.—*Comparison.*

It will be seen from this description of the executive council in the United States that its most important function is to control one of the administrative powers of the chief executive and that this control is exercised especially over his relations with his subordinates. Through it the power has been taken away from the chief executive to constitute the official personnel as he sees fit. This limitation of his power naturally involves a lessening of his responsibility. The evil effects of such a plan may be avoided only through the moderate use by the Senate of its powers of control. In the national government this has fortunately been the policy of the Senate almost from the beginning of our administrative history. It may be laid down as one of the customary rules of our constitutional law that the Senate should permit the President complete freedom in the filling of the most important administrative positions.[1] Almost the only cases in which the Senate habitually exercises any control over the President's power of appointment are the judicial appointments. The Senate has, however, not been so careful to leave the President free hand in the exercise of his political powers. There are not a few cases in our history where treaties negotiated by the President have not obtained the confirmation of the Senate. One reason for the distinction which is thus made is undoubtedly to be found in the fact that the approval of treaties requires a two-thirds vote of the Senate; but another is as undoubtedly to be found in the fact that while the Senate has felt that its control over the President's power of

[1] *Cf.* Rüttiman, *op. cit.*, I., 276, and authorities cited.

appointment should be made use of only in such a way as not to hamper the action and limit the responsibility of the President, it may properly interfere to prevent the conclusion of a treaty which in its opinion is not for the best interest of the country. In administration the President is to be supreme in order that the government may be efficient and harmonious ; in his political relations the President is to be subject to some control.

The commonwealth executive council has unfortunately not always adopted this conservative rule, but has frequently made an immoderate use of its power of control over the administrative powers of the governor with the result that the governor's responsibility for appointments has been all but destroyed. Nothing is more common in the commonwealth than to see the Senate reject the governor's appointees for no other reason apparently than that it does not think the appointments conducive to the interests of the political party in control of that body, or in order to force the governor to take some action approved by it.

CHAPTER II.

I.—History.

The executive council in France has always played a much more important rôle than has been assigned to it in the United States. At one time it was much more important even than now. In its intelligence and fairness were found almost the only guaranty of a good and impartial government.[1] The most important executive council was originally the great council of the king, which at one time discharged almost all the functions of government. From this was developed the Parliament of Paris, the first purely judicial body that France possessed, and the royal council which assumed the administrative powers of the great council.[2] In the reign of Louis XIV the royal council was divided into five sections, each of which attended to certain branches of the administration. The section which corresponded most nearly with our ideas of an executive council was known as the council of despatches.[3] This organization lasted almost unchanged up to the time of the revolution, when the constituent assembly re-organized the government of France and abolished the executive

---

[1] Aucoc, *op. cit.*, I., 126. [2] *Ibid.*, 127.

[3] *Ibid.*, 128.

council.[1] With the advent of Napoleon, the executive council was revived, a new council, called the Council of State, being established. Under the direction of Napoleon it accomplished an enormous amount of work. Indeed, this was the most brilliant period of the executive council in France. Its duties were largely legislative in character, and it decided all difficulties that arose in the course of the administration of the government.[2] The Council of State was so closely associated with the glories of the empire, that the attempt was made under the government of the restoration to do away with it, but this failed and the council resumed its place in the government. During the government of the restoration, as well as under the July monarchy, the Council of State was regarded as an executive council exclusively, a legislature having been formed in the meantime which relieved it of its legislative duties; but with the republic of 1848 the council was made use of by the legislature to control the acts of the executive authority.[3] During the second empire the legislative functions of the council were very much increased, and it was again almost the only guaranty of impartial government. When the present republic was formed, with a legislative body of great power, the council was again relegated to the position of an advisory executive council, which position it occupies at the present time.

II.—*Organization.*

The organization of the present Council of State is governed by the laws of May 24, 1872, and July 13, 1879. In accordance with these laws it is composed of thirty-two councillors of state in what is known as

[1] *Ibid.*, 131. [2] *Ibid.*, 132. [3] *Ibid.*, 133.

ordinary service, eighteen councillors of state in what is known as extraordinary service, thirty commissioners (*maîtres des requêtes*), and finally of thirty-six auditors, twelve of whom are of the first class, and twenty-four of the second class. The ministers have the right to attend the deliberations of the general assembly of the council, and to vote on matters affecting their departments, when the council is not acting as a court. The Council of State is, when not acting as a court, presided over by the Keeper of the Seals, minister of justice, and in his absence by a vice-president appointed by the President of the republic from among the councillors of state in ordinary service. The method of appointment for the different classes of the members differs. Thus the councillors of state in ordinary service are appointed and dismissed by the President of the republic after hearing, but not necessarily taking, the advice of the council of ministers.[1] The councillors of state in extraordinary service are chosen by the President of the republic from among the members of the administration, whose advice it is considered desirable to have in important administrative matters. They receive no pay, as do the other councillors of state, and have no vote when the council is acting as a court. The commissioners are appointed by the President of the republic on the presentation of the vice-president of the council and the presidents of the different sections into which the council is divided, and are dismissed after hearing the opinion of these officers. The auditors are appointed as the result of a competitive examination, the auditors of the first class being chosen from those of the second class.

[1] L., Feb. 25, 1875, art. 4.

For all these different classes of officers there are conditions of age whose intention is to secure only those persons from whom the government can hope to obtain the best work. These conditions of age vary from not less than twenty-one and not more than twenty-five years for the auditors of the second class to not less than thirty years for the councillors of state. While the President is not limited in his choice of councillors of state in ordinary service, who are the most important of the members, the intention of the law is to facilitate the choice of such officers from among the commissioners who in their turn will be chosen from among the auditors of the first class. As the subjects for the competitive examination for the position of auditor are law, politics, and political economy the Council of State will ordinarily consist of a body of experts in political and administrative matters whose advice must, in the nature of things, be of the greatest value both to the administration and to the legislature.

The Council of State is divided into four administrative sections and one judicial section. Each of the administrative sections has a certain number of administrative departments to advise ; while the judicial section is occupied altogether as an administrative court.[1] The council acts in section, in sections united, and in general assembly. Only the most important matters are attended to in the general assembly, to which they go after examination by one of the sections or by two or more sections united. What affairs are to go to the general assembly is decided by the laws of the country and the by-laws of the council ; and where it is provided that any matter shall go to the general

---

[1] Boeuf, *op. cit.*, citing Decree Aug. 2, 1879.

assembly, where the examination is much more thorough than in the sections, this is an absolutely necessary pre-requisite to the validity of the action subsequently taken.[1]

III.—Functions.

The functions of this council are both legislative and administrative. The legislative functions are much less important now than formerly. Its intervention in legislative matters is now altogether optional with the legislature which may send any bill which is before it to the council for its advice. The executive which, it will be remembered, may initiate law, may also send any bill which it is proposed to submit to the legisla-ture to the council for its advice and may by decree designate any of the councillors of state to support any of its bills before the legislature. Its administrative functions are, however, very important. In the first place the advice of the council must be asked for all ordinances of public administration or decrees in the form of ordinances of public administration.[2] When it is remembered that it is the habit of the French legislature to incorporate into the statutes only very general principles and expressly to delegate to the ex-ecutive the power to regulate details by an ordinance of public administration it will be seen what an impor-tant function the Council of State discharges in work-ing out, as it does, the details of almost all statutes. Finally the traditions of the French government lead the President and the ministers to submit to the council all questions which are valuable as offering precedents for future action.[3] This custom alone makes the work

---

[1] Aucoc, *op. cit.*, I., 144 and 145, citing several decisions of the council.
[2] *Supra*, p. 86.   [3] Aucoc, *op. cit.*, L., 143.

of the council very large. Its advice is nearly always asked as to the exercise of the central control which the executive authority possesses over the actions of the localities, and over the recognized religious denominations ; as to the grant of charters ; and as to many acts in the financial administration. Indeed it may be said that what in this country and in England is done by means of special and local legislation is in France done by the decrees of the President or orders of the ministers issued after hearing the advice of the Council of State.[1] An idea of the extent of the work of the Council of State may be obtained from the fact that from 1861 to 1866, 88,888 matters were submitted to the council.[2] It should be added that the character of the questions which are submitted to the Council of State is almost altogether legal and political. Technical questions are submitted to other councils attached to each of the administrative departments such as the general council of public works and of mines, the committees of infantry, of cavalry, and fortifications, *etc.,* *etc.*[3]

While it is necessary in many cases that the advice of the council must be asked in order that an act of the government be legal it is to be noticed that, in accordance with the principle of French administration that to act is the function of one, which has already been alluded to,[4] the government is never bound by the advice of the council but may reject it if it sees fit.

---

[1] De Franqueville, *Le Gouvernement et le Parlement Britanniques*, III., 119–228 ; *cf.* Dicey, *The Law of the Constitution*, 3d Ed. 50.

[2] Aucoc, *op. cit.*, I., 144 citing *Moniteur Universel* March 30, 1862 and Sept. 11, 1868.

[3] Aucoc, *op. cit.*, I., 146.

[4] *Supra*, p. 86.

The French executive council thus differs radically not only in composition but also in functions to be discharged from the American executive council. It is composed of experts in administration while the American executive council is merely a part of the legislature. While the main duty of the American executive council is to control the action of the executive authority in the exercise of the one function, which, in order to secure an efficient and harmonious administration, he should discharge on his own responsibility and subject only to the control which the people may exercise on election day; the duty of the French executive council is to advise the executive in the discharge of the important function of issuing ordinances and to fill up those details of the law which it is the policy of the French that the legislature shall not regulate but shall be regulated by a body of specialists. Even in such matters the French are so afraid of a diffusion of responsibility that they do not permit the executive to be bound by the advice which his council may give him. To permit the Council of State to control the President's power to choose his subordinates would be regarded as a gross violation of the fundamental principles of good administration.

8

CHAPTER III.

I.—In the princely governments.

As in France, so in the separate members of the German empire, the executive council was for a time, *i. e.* after the disappearance of the feudal estates, almost the only organ through which the absolute monarchy was at all limited. During this period of its history it was known as the Privy Council.[1] Later the Privy Council became known as the Council of State.[2] In Prussia under Stein and Hardenburg it did an immense work—work mostly of a legislative character inasmuch as there was no legislature in Prussia at the time. In this Council of State were drawn up most of the great laws which did so much towards the reorganization of Prussia at the beginning of this century.[3] It was only natural that, when the revolution of 1848 brought with it the creation of a legislature, the council should retire into the background although it was not formally abolished.[4] In 1852 the attempt was made to revive the institution with which so much that was good was associated, but failed. It is said that from 1848 to 1883

[1] Stengel, *Organisation der Preussischen Verwaltung*, 55 ; Meyer, *Deutsches Staatsrecht*, 258 and 259.

[2] Stengel, *Organisation, etc.*, 60.

[3] *Ibid.*, 67.

[4] Loening, *Deutsches Verwaltungsrecht*, 70.

the council met but twice.[1]   Again in 1883 the attempt
to revive it was repeated and of late it seems to be
acting once more.   The reason for this second attempt
was to obtain a body to which the government might
have recourse for advice as to bills which it was intended to submit to the legislature.   But its composition is not such as to secure a body similar to the
French council, as it is to be composed of prominent
personages appointed by the King as he sees fit.[2]

In addition to this council which has not as yet attained to any great importance there is in Prussia a
council of a somewhat special character, formed by
ordinance of November 17, 1880, and called the Council for Economical Affairs.   It is composed of seventy-
five members, chosen for the most part from men
engaged in the pursuit of commerce, manufacturing
industry, and agriculture.   It is divided into three
sections, each of which represents one of these three
pursuits, and is presided over by the competent
minister.   The duties of the council are to give its
opinion in regard to all projects of law or ordinances
which affect the most important economical interests,
and to consider what shall be the vote of Prussia in
the Federal Council on these matters.   As a rule, the
government is under no obligation to consult this
council.[3]

In some of the other members of the empire, notably
in Bavaria and Würtemberg, a council of state is to be
found, but as in Prussia it is of little importance as an
executive council.[4]

[1] *Ibid.*   [2] *Cf.* Bornhak, *Preussisches Staatsrecht*, II., 396.
[3] Bornhak, *op. cit.*, II., 396 ; Loening, *Deutsches Verwaltungsrecht*, 70.
[4] *Cf.* Stengel, *Wörterbuch des Deutschen Verwaltungsrecht*, art. *Staatsrat.*

II.—*In the empire.*

1. *Organization.*—In the empire the Federal Council, which is also the upper house of the legislature, has, as an executive council, a series of executive functions to discharge. While resembling those discharged by the United States Senate when acting in a similar capacity, these functions are of much greater importance. So important indeed are the executive functions of the Federal Council that some of the German commentators regard the Federal Council as the chief executive, and relegate the Emperor to the position of its subordinate, who is to carry out its decisions.[1] This body is composed of representatives sent from the twenty-five members of the empire,[2] each of which has a number of votes varying with its importance. All the votes of each member must be cast in the same way and in accordance with instructions which have been issued to its representatives in the council by each of the members of the empire, but the council is not called upon to examine into the correspondence of the vote with the instructions given.[3] The council meets periodically and as an executive council may meet when the other house of the legislature is not in session.[4] It is presided over by the imperial chancellor,[5] and acts either in general assembly or in committees of which four are provided for by the constitution, and three additional by subsequent legislation.[6] The general principles that govern the formation of these committees, exclusive of

---

[1] *Cf.* Zorn, *op. cit.*, I., 136 to 142.   [2] *Constitution*, art. 6.

[3] *Ibid.*, arts. 6 and 7 ; Meyer, *Staatsrecht*, 318 ; Zorn, *op. cit.*, I., 146.

[4] Constitution, arts. 12 and 13.   [5] *Ibid.*, art. 15.

[6] *Ibid.*, art. 8 ; Zorn, *op. cit.*, I., 148 *et seq.*

that on foreign affairs, are that four members of the empire shall be represented on each committee besides Prussia, which presides. The members of most of the committees are designated by the council, though in a few cases the constitution assures to particular members a permanent seat, and also provides in other cases that the Emperor may appoint the members which are to be represented. The committee on foreign affairs occupies a peculiar position. It was formed to flatter the *amour propre* of Bavaria, Würtemberg, and Saxony. Therefore Prussia is not represented upon it, and it is composed of representatives of these districts and two other members of the empire, to be elected by the council.[1] It is said that this committee has not met once in the history of the empire; so its importance as a controlling factor in the diplomacy of the empire is not very great.[2]

2. *Functions.*—The Federal Council occupies a very peculiar position. It may be regarded as a branch of the legislature and as an executive council for the control of the action of the Emperor, and finally it must be admitted that it is an executive authority which may take action irrespective of the Emperor. Its main function is, however, the control of the action of the Emperor.

Like the United States Senate the Federal Council has a control, in certain respects more, in certain respects less, extended, over the relations of the executive, *i. e.* the Emperor, with the federal official service, *i. e.,* over the personnel of the service. Thus it participates either in general assembly or in committee in

---

[1] Meyer, *Staatsrecht,* 322, citing the rules of the council.
[2] Zorn, *op. cit.,* I., 151.

the appointment of certain of the imperial officers. The appointment itself is made in theory by the Emperor, but the Emperor in making the appointment is either limited to the names presented by the council or else must consult with it or with one of its committees. The officers appointed in one or the other of these ways are the imperial commissioners to supervise the collection of the customs and the indirect taxes, which are collected by the governments of the separate members of the empire; the judges of the imperial court at Leipsic; the members of the imperial poor-law board, of the imperial disciplinary court and chambers, of the invalid fund commission, and of the directory of the imperial bank.[1] The council further participates in the disciplinary power exercised over the officers of the empire and in the settling of the amount of their pensions.[2] It will be remembered that the Emperor has not the arbitrary power of removal, but that the official relation can be terminated against the will of the officer only by conviction of a crime or by the judgment of a disciplinary court, which may also inflict penalties less severe than discharge from the service.[3] The supreme disciplinary court is composed of five members of the imperial court at Leipsic chosen by the Federal Council and of four members of the Federal Council chosen by it.

The Federal Council further participates in the actual administration of the empire. It is the principal organ for the issue of ordinances and has the supplementary ordinance power.[4] In general a simple major-

---

[1] Const., art. 36 ; Zorn, *op. cit.*, I., 156, and authorities cited.
[2] *Ibid.*, 158.   [3] *Supra*, p. 94.
[4] Const., art. 7, secs. 2 and 3 ; Zorn, *op. cit.*, I., 129.

ity vote is all that is necessary for the validity of an ordinance of the Federal Council. In case of a tie vote, the vote of the presiding state, Prussia, decides,[1] but in certain cases (in the main tax and military matters) the presiding state has the power of unconditionally vetoing a proposition aiming to change existing law.[2] While the Federal Council has the ordinance power in case the constitution has not expressly given it to any other authority, the constitution itself in several cases gives the ordinance power to some other authority and also provides that an imperial statute may give some other authority the power to issue ordinances in particular cases.[3] Finally, it is to be noticed that in several cases, where the constitution or the statutes permit the Emperor to issue ordinances, provision is made at the same time that such ordinances to be valid must have received the approval of the Federal Council.

The Federal Council has also quite a control over the financial administration of the empire. Thus it examines by means of one of its committees the quarterly accounts of the separate members of the empire relative to the customs and indirect taxes collected by them, and in general assembly fixes the amount each member shall pay into the imperial treasury as a matricular contribution.[4] It is also to act as the highest instance of control over the customs and indirect tax administration and has the power to remedy any defect that may appear in the system of collection.[5] The Federal Council is also to examine the accounts of the imperial chancellor so as to see whether he has made

---

[1] Const., art. 7.
[2] *Ibid.*, arts. 35 and 37.
[3] *Ibid.*, art. 7, sec. 2 ; Zorn, *op. cit.*, I., 131.
[4] Const., art. 39.
[5] Zorn, *op. cit.*, I., 157.

proper use of the imperial revenue and, in case everything is in order, is formally to relieve him from all responsibility therefor.[1] It exercises a control over the imperial debt and the imperial bank in that it appoints a certain number of the members of the commissions which attend to these matters.[2] Its consent is necessary to all the Emperor's ordinances relative to the war-treasure.[3]

Finally the Federal Council exercises a control over certain of the political acts of the Emperor. Thus its consent is necessary for the declaration of war, for the making of certain treaties,[4] and it is to decide when what is known as federal execution shall be decreed against any member of the empire for neglect or refusal to discharge its duties to the empire.[5] This is a power peculiar to the German imperial system. Though more properly treated in works on constitutional than in those on administrative law, its administrative aspects are so important that it deserves special mention in this connection. Different from the United States constitution the German imperial constitution recognizes expressly in the imperial government the right to enforce by the army if necessary the performance of the constitutional duties of any member of the empire. It is needless to say that up to the present time there has been no occasion for the exercise of this power, but there may be a time when the express mention of such a power will be of great advantage to the imperial government as the existence of such a provision would

[1] Const., art. 72.
[2] L., June 19, 1868, sec. 4 ; L., March 14, 1875, sec. 5.
[3] L., Nov. 11, 1871, secs. 1 and 5.
[4] Const., art. 11.
[5] *Ibid.*, art. 19.

have been to the United States national government at the beginning of the civil war.[1]

3. *Remedies against its action.*—There are no remedies against the acts of the Federal Council except what are to be found in the power of the courts to declare its ordinances invalid in case it attempts to issue an ordinance in excess of its powers. It would seem that, in accordance with the general principles of German law, the courts have the right to refuse to enforce an unconstitutional ordinance though, it must be said, there appears to be no case in which the courts have so refused. The decisions, however, show a tendency on the part of the imperial court to claim such a power.[2]

---

[1] As to the difficulty which the national government had in finding some theory upon which could be based its right to put down the rebellion in 1861, see Dunning, " The Constitution in Civil War," in the *Pol. Sci. Qu.*, I., 163.

[2] See Stengel, *Deutsches Verwaltungsrecht*, 180 ; *Entscheidungen des Reichsgerichts in Strafsachen*, xii., 40 ; xiii., 321.

CHAPTER IV.

THE ENGLISH PRIVY COUNCIL.

I.—History.

In the discussion of the powers of the English Crown it was shown that at the time the Parliament was developing its legislative powers there was being developed a council which was to control the Crown in the exercise of its executive prerogatives. This council arose out of the old *curia regis.* While the Parliament from the first tried to exercise a control over the taxing and legislative power of the Crown the council was originally formed more to aid the Crown in the performance of its administrative and judicial duties than to control its actions.[1] What its relation to the national council or Parliament was is really unknown.[2] We find, however, in the reign of Henry I a judicial organization called the *curia regis*, which, organized separately as the exchequer, attended also to the financial administration.[3] It was not, however, till the minority of Henry III that a really important council can be spoken of.[4] At that time its existence is clear and its action is traceable in every department of work, and it becomes permanent and continuous.

[1] Stubbs, *Constitutional History of England,* I., 343.
[2] *Ibid.*, 376.
[3] *Ibid.*, 377, 387, and 601.   [4] *Ibid.*, II., 255.

From that time on it contained the officers of state, and of the household, the whole judicial staff, a number of bishops and barons and other members simply called councillors. What the qualifications of the members were is unknown. Its functions were of a varied character, but its distinguishing characteristic was its permanent employment as a court.[1] It had also administrative and executive duties to perform. Thus originated what was soon afterwards and now is called the Privy Council, which from the time of Henry III constantly increased its powers and multiplied its functions, retiring somewhat into the background under strong kings, coming forward under weak or unpopular kings, but always growing in power until it came to be recognized as a power almost co-ordinate with the Crown. It aided the Crown in the performance of its duties and also came finally to exercise a control over its actions.[2] Since the development of the Privy Council in its modern form it has lost a great many of its powers. Most of its judicial functions were taken from it at the time of the abolition of the Star Chamber.[3] Parliament has robbed it of its most important legislative functions, while an informal body known as the cabinet has taken from it actually, though not legally, most of its powers as the adviser of the Crown in the work of administration.

II.—*Organization.*

At present the Privy Council is composed of about two hundred persons appointed by the Crown. Every English subject is eligible to appointment.[4] The ele-

[1] *Ibid.*, II., 256.
[2] *Ibid.*, III., 247.
[3] 16 Car., I., c. 10.
[4] 7 and 8 Vict., c. 66, secs. 1 and 2.

ments of which it is formed are at present the same as during the middle ages. These are the chiefs of the various departments, and, as the appointment is practically for life, the chiefs of departments under former administrations, certain judicial officers, and other important officers, such as the Speaker of the House of Commons, the Commander-in-Chief, and a large representation of the secular and ecclesiastical peerage. Legally the position of privy councillor is only for the life of the reigning monarch and six months thereafter, but re-appointment, on the coming to the throne of his successor, is made as a matter of course. Discharge is very infrequent.[1]

This council meets once in three or four weeks at the residence of the Crown, and no member is expected to be present who has not received a special invitation. The quorum is fixed at six with the clerk, whose signature is authentication of its deliberations.[2]

III.—*Functions.*

The main duty that the council, as council, now has is to advise the Crown as to the issue of ordinances, which are known on that account to the English law as orders in council. Its approval of proposals of ordinances seems to be necessary, since no ordinance not issued in council is valid.[3] This power is really a very important one, since many matters are regulated by orders in council which in this country are attended to by the legislature. Further, as the result of the development within this century of a central adminis-

---

[1] Gneist, *Das Englische Verwaltungsrecht*, 1884, 103 ; *cf.* Anson, *op. cit.*, II., 135.

[2] Gneist, *op. cit.*, 194.   [3] *Supra*, p. 99.

trative control, the duty is imposed upon the council
of examining a series of ordinances issued by the local
authorities whose validity is made to depend upon its
approval.[1] Finally its members are the only constitutional advisers of the Crown, and it is only as members of the Privy Council that the various ministers
are permitted to advise the Crown.[2] As each member
of the cabinet must thus be a privy councillor, it follows
that the action and advice of the Privy Council are controlled by the cabinet, so that the existence of the
Privy Council does not in any way weaken that responsibility of the ministers for the action of the
Crown, which plays such an important rôle in the
English governmental system. Out of this Privy
Council have been developed several boards, which
are really executive departments. Some of these, like
the board of trade and the board of agriculture, are
now completely separated from the council,[3] while
others have not yet attained a similar independence,
but the president of the council is regarded as responsible for their action. Such is, *e. g.*, the committee of
council for education, commonly known as the education department.[4] Finally we find the judicial committee of the Privy Council, which is a court of appeals
for ecclesiastical and colonial cases.[5]

Mention has been made of a cabinet which practically controls the action of the Privy Council. This
body was developed largely for the reason that the
Privy Council was too large a body to attend effectually to the work of administration. Therefore it was

[1] *Infra*, p. 260.   [3] Anson, *op. cit.*, II., 179 *et seq.*, 186.
[2] *Cf.* Anson, *op. cit.*, II., 134.   [4] *Ibid.*, 187.
                            [5] Gneist, *op. cit.*, 189.

the habit of the king to choose a certain number of its members in whom he had special confidence and from whom he asked advice. These met together in an inner room or cabinet of the palace, and from this circumstance the name of cabinet was given to the body of ministers whom the king chose to advise him.[1] This practice, after the Restoration, was regarded as a dangerous one, but the cabinet grew more and more in power until at length it drew to itself the chief executive powers in the government, and is now regarded as an essential feature of the English polity. Yet it is altogether unknown to the law; the names of the persons of which it is composed are never officially announced to the public[2]; no record is kept of its proceedings,[3] and it is only as a result of its identity with the controlling factors of the Privy Council that it has any powers.[4]

[1] Todd, *Parliamentary Government in England*, 2nd Ed. II., 92.
[2] *Ibid.*, 181.
[3] *Ibid.*, 178 ; Macaulay, *History of England*, IV., 435, 437.
[4] For the history of the development of the cabinet, *cf.* Anson, *op. cit.*, 100.

Division 3.—Heads of Departments.

CHAPTER I.

DISTRIBUTION OF BUSINESS AND METHOD OF ORGANI-
ZATION.

I.—Method of distributing business.

In all countries, whether the chief executive authority be the head of the administration or simply the
political head of the government, there are officers who
are to attend to the details of the administration. The
name usually given to such officers is that of ministers,
since they are generally regarded as the servants of the
chief executive authority and since it is through them
alone that he can act. They are regarded as the constitutional organs of the executive for the discharge of
his powers, and generally have to countersign every
one of his acts for which they assume the responsibility. In addition to this they have in all states almost
always the position of chiefs of particular administrative departments whose affairs they are to direct. This
is true even in those countries, of which the United
States is an example, where they are not responsible
for the acts of the executive. On this account the
American law has chosen for these officers the title of

heads of executive departments. Since the following pages are devoted to a consideration of their administrative functions, their political functions where they exist being relegated for detailed treatment to constitutional law, these officers will be considered under the title of heads of departments.

It has been shown that in all countries there are five well developed branches of administration, *viz.*, foreign, military, judicial, financial, and internal affairs. All the different matters requiring attention from the administration will fall under one of these five branches. It has come to be well recognized, that the best arrangement of administrative business is to place some one authority at the head of each of these branches, and where it is found by experience to be necessary to make a further specialization, to take out of one of these five departments thus formed some particular matter or matters and form a separate department for its or their management. Thus we generally find that the matter of naval affairs is taken out of the department of military affairs and put in charge of a special department.

Again we find that the care of public works is often given to a separate department. Often also the question of education becomes so important as to demand a separate authority for its management. So also in some states with agriculture and with commerce. In all these cases it will be noticed that the principle of the distribution of administrative business among the

---

[1] In the United States naval affairs were originally in charge of the war department, but were soon put in a special department, where they have ever since remained. See Guggenheimer on " The Development of Executive Departments" in Jameson, *Essays in the Constitutional History of the United States*, 179. This is an excellent historical sketch of the departments.

departments is the division of the work according to its nature; and to us of the present age any other method of distribution seems preposterous. But this method has not always been followed. In most of the European states all administrative matters were originally attended to by one organ, generally a board or council of some sort. In this body the distribution of business was made according to geographical lines rather than according to the nature of the business to be transacted.[1] Indeed such a system of geographical division was in force in one of the English departments up to quite a late date. Up to 1782 the secretariat of state was divided into the northern and the southern departments, and each division attended to all matters whether internal or external to be attended to in its territorial district. But in 1782 the secretariat was divided into a foreign and a home office.[2] At the present time even, there are a few instances of this system of geographical division. In England there are a secretary for India,[3] one for Scotland,[4] and an Irish secretary.[5] In Germany there is an office for the imperial territory of Alsace-Lorraine,[6] while in the Austro-Hungarian empire there are several instances of such an arrangement.[7]

II.—*Power of organization.*

An important question connected with the subject of the departments is who shall organize them? Shall it be the executive or the legislative authority

---

[1] *Cf.* Schulze, *op. cit.*, I., 291.

[2] Cox, *Institutions of the English Government*, 666.

[3] 21 and 22 Vict., c. 106.

[4] 48 and 49 Vict., c. 61.

[5] Todd, *op. cit.*, II., 848.

[6] Zorn, *op. cit.*, I., 428.

[7] Gumplowicz, *Das Oesterreichische Staatsrecht*, 161.

that shall have the organizing power ?   In the United States it is the legislature alone which possesses the organizing power.   The national constitution has not expressly provided for this matter.   Indeed, the constitution does not expressly provide for the organization of executive departments, although it impliedly recognizes their existence in two places.[1] It permits the President to require the opinion in writing of the heads of the executive departments, and allows Congress to vest the power of appointing inferior officers in the heads of such departments.   The last clause cited speaks of " offices established by law," and has been interpreted in our constitutional practice as giving to the legislature the organizing power.   Indeed, it has been the rule from the foundation of the government that the executive departments and offices generally may be established by Congress only.[2]   Further, not only are the departments themselves organized by Congress, but also their internal arrangements, and the powers and duties of their heads and of the heads of the various divisions into which they may be divided are often regulated in detail by statute, generally by the statute organizing the department.   In some cases it is true Congress will declare that the head of this or that department shall do certain things, and then will leave to him the organization of the particular division which it is necessary to form in order to perform the duty thus placed upon him.   But this is now rarely the case, and then only where the most unimportant divisions of the departments are con-

[1] Art. ii., sec. 2, pp. 1 and 2.
[2] Cf. Rüttiman, op. cit., I., 274, citing Benton, Thirty Years' View, II., 678.

cerned. It was in this way, however, that some of our present administrative departments were developed.

In the separate commonwealths there are seldom to be found in the constitution any express provisions as to the organizing power. The only ones relating at all to the departments are those which themselves organize the executive departments. These are very common and sometimes forbid the establishment of new offices.[1] The result of such provisions is that the constitution-making authority is the organizing power, and not the commonwealth government or any branch thereof. Where, however, the constitution has not made provision, in accordance with the usual rule of interpreting the constitution, it is the legislature and not the executive which has the organizing power. For while the executive is an authority of enumerated powers, the legislature has all governmental power not given to some other authority, if the constitution has not expressly limited its powers.[2] Where the commonwealth legislature acts, however, it does not, as a rule, descend into the same detail as does Congress. The commonwealth statutes are usually absolutely silent as to the divisions which shall exist within a given department. They simply provide for a certain department, and the legislature each year or every two years grants in its appropriation acts a sum of money to the head of the department, leaving him perfect freedom as to its distribution. At the same time it must be noticed that the departments in the common-

---

[1] See Nebraska Constitution, art. v., sec. 26 ; *In re* R. R. Commissioners, 15 Neb., 682.

[2] Bank of Chenango v. Brown, 26 N. Y., 469 ; People v. Dayton, 55 N. Y., 380.

wealth administration are much more special than the national departments, so that in reality the facts are about the same in the commonwealth and the national administration. In the United States, both in the national and the commonwealth government, then, it is the legislature which possesses the organizing power, and in practice it exercises its power in such a way as to regulate in detail the organization of the departments.

In France the rule is not the same.   There, with very few exceptions, it has always been recognized that the organizing power belongs to the chief executive authority,[1] subject, however, to the necessity of going to the legislature in case any re-arrangement of offices or the establishment of new offices makes necessary a greater expenditure of money.

In Germany the rule is the same as in France. Of course in both countries the legislature may act if it sees fit when it would be impossible for the executive to make any changes, since a statute is always of greater force than an executive decree or ordinance.[2]

In England the theory seems to be about the same as upon the continent.[3] The only practical difference is to be found in the fact that Parliament has in most of the recent cases of the establishment of an office or a department exercised an organizing power, with the result that most of the departments of any importance owe their existence to a statute and therefore cannot be modified by executive ordinance.

[1] Boeuf, *op. cit.*, 21.

[2] In some instances in Germany the departments are, as in the American commonwealths, fixed by the constitution. *Cf.*, for the organizing power in Germany, Loening, *op. cit.*, 55–57 ; Schulze, *op. cit.*, I., 297.

[3] Todd, *op. cit.*, I., 609–660.

The method of organization by the executive would seem the preferable one, inasmuch as the executive is in a better position to know the needs of the administration than is the legislature, and is responsible for the actions of the administration. Further it can act more quickly than can the legislature. What the administration gains in stability from the fact of its being organized by the legislature it loses in flexibility. The control which the legislature has over the finances is sufficient to prevent the administration from incurring too great expense in any change that it may wish to make. Indeed the danger of extravagance on the part of the administration is not in modern times so great as it is on the part of the legislature. We have a good instance of this fact and of the disadvantages of giving to the legislature the organizing power in the conditions of the United States customs service. It is the opinion of several of the secretaries of the treasury expressed in their annual reports that there is an unnecessary number of customs collection districts; and the secretaries have repeatedly recommended to Congress the abolition of the less important ones, with of course the mustering out of the service of the officers now assigned to them. But Congress has uniformly refused to follow the suggestions of the secretaries ; it has been thought because of the loss which would accrue to the members of Congress as distributors of Federal patronage. If the power of organizing the official service had been recognized in our system as belonging to the President we might hope for some reform in the direction indicated, but so long as it is possessed by Congress it seems almost hopeless to expect that this much needed reform will be accomplished.

CHAPTER II.

The relations of the heads of departments with the chief executive authority are of the greatest importance, for on their nature depends whether there is to be a harmonious administration following out some general plan or whether the head of each department is to be a law unto himself and is to be able to conduct the affairs of his department in such manner as he sees fit regardless of the needs of other departments and of the wishes of the chief executive. These relations of the heads of departments with the chief executive are governed by two things almost entirely, *viz.*, the term and the tenure of office of the heads of departments.

I.—*In the United States.*

The constitution of the United States and the constitutions of the commonwealths differ considerably in this respect.[1] The former instrument as interpreted gives to the chief executive the power to appoint, remove, and direct all the heads of departments. The commonwealths, however, have pursued a different plan. In most of the original commonwealths the chief

---

[1] *Supra*, pp. 62–82.

134

executive did not have the absolute power of appointing the heads of the commonwealth departments. The
tendency was to fill these offices at first by appointment by the legislature, as was the rule originally in
some of the commonwealths, then by election by the
people, which is the rule at present. It is said [1] that
" all the executive officers are, as a general rule in all
the states, elected by the people at a general election."
There are of course a few exceptions to this rule, as, in
New York, the superintendents of public works and
prisons, who are appointed by the governor and senate.[2]
Finally there are still instances of the appointment of
heads of departments by the legislature. Thus in New
York the superintendent of public instruction is appointed at the present time in this way.[3] As far as the
continuance of the term of office is concerned, the
methods adopted in the commonwealths differ as much
as the methods of filling the offices. But in most cases
the term of office of the heads of departments is fixed
either by the constitution or the statutes at a certain
number of years. The term is not generally the same for
all offices, nor does it always coincide with that of the
governor.[4] The result is that it is not necessarily the
case that all the officers who are to conduct the commonwealth government belong to the same political
party or that they share the same views as to the way
in which the commonwealth administration shall be

---

[1] Stimson, *op. cit.*, p. 42, art. 20 B.

[2] Const., art. v., secs. 3 and 4 ; *cf.* Stimson, *loc. cit.*

[3] L.,1864, c. 555, sec.1; *cf.* Stimson, *loc. cit.* In some of the commonwealths
such a power is regarded as unconstitutional, as being in violation of the principle of the separation of powers. *Supra*, p. 24 ; State v. Kennon, 7 Ohio St.,
560.

[4] *Supra*, p. 78.

conducted. Further the governor cannot usually in case of conflict produce a uniformity in views by the removal of the head of a department.[1]

What now are the relations existing between the chief executive authority and the heads of departments in the American system of administration which result from this state of facts? In the national administration the heads of the departments are completely subordinate to and dependent upon the chief executive authority as a result of the precariousness of their tenure and will be in harmony one with the other and with the President on account of the fact that they have been chosen by him to fill their respective positions as a result of his knowledge of their opinions. We find therefore in the national administration complete guaranties for an efficient and harmonious administration under the direction of the President.

In the commonwealths, however, the case is quite different. Each head of a department has, so long as he is not corrupt, the right to conduct the affairs of his department just about as he sees fit; and is practically independent of the governor who has little or no influence over affairs of administration. The constitutions of some of the commonwealths have been honest enough to recognize what is the real position of the governor and what is that of the heads of the departments, and devote an article to the consideration of the " administrative " officers of the commonwealth, among whom the governor is not included.[2] But whether the constitution recognizes this or not, the fact is the same, that the governor is not the head of the administration

[1] *Supra*, p. 79.
[2] See Florida Constitution, 1881, art. 5, sec. 17.

in the commonwealths of the American Union. American administrative law has added to the famous trinity of Montesquieu a fourth department, *viz.*, the administrative department, which is almost entirely independent of the chief executive and which, as far as the central administration is concerned, is assigned to a number of officers not only independent of the governor but also independent of each other. This independence which each of the heads of departments in the American commonwealths may claim under the law has resulted in there being little attempt made to secure uniformity in administrative action. While in the national government every President tries to surround himself with advisers who have the same general views as to the conduct of the government and calls regular meetings of his heads of departments, popularly termed cabinet meetings, when these heads of departments may exchange opinions on the important questions which come up before them for settlement; in the commonwealths we seldom hear of any such thing as a meeting of the heads of the departments.[1] Such a meeting would be of little use as there resides nowhere the power to compel a head of department to change his opinion so as to suit that of the governor or that of his colleagues. In a word, in the commonwealth administration there are seldom any guaranties for efficient and harmonious action on account of the independent position of the heads of departments not only over against the governor, but also over against each other. This is not merely a theoretical objection to the commonwealth system of administration. For the jealousies and prejudices of the various heads of

[1] But see Florida Const., art. 5, sec. 17, and Iowa Code, 1888, p. 32.

departments and their conflict with the governor do in practice not infrequently lead to an absolute cessation of the work of administration.

II.—*In France.*

In France, as in the United States national administration, the term and tenure of the heads of departments are such as to place them in a relation of apparently complete dependence upon the President. But French political history has assigned to the ministers a much more important rôle to play. In one of the constitutional laws now in force is contained the provision that the ministers as a body are responsible to the legislature.[1] This means that they must command the confidence of the majority in the chamber of deputies. One of the results of this law has been to make the relation of the ministers, as a body, to the President one of great independence. If no further steps were taken there would be little guaranty for a harmonious and efficient administration under the direction of one person. For each minister is the legal equal of the others. But the French parliamentary system has, in fact, taken another step. It has gradually come to recognize in the president of the council of ministers a superior of the other ministers. He it is who is politically the person exercising the powers which the President has lost over his ministers as a result of the adoption of the principle of the parliamentary responsibility of the ministers. He is actually, though not legally, the chief of the administration. Now in the case of the formation of a new ministry the President " sends for " some prominent statesman,

[1] L., Feb. 25, 1875, art. 6.

who will command temporarily at least the confidence of the Chamber of Deputies, and appoints him president of the council of ministers. As president of such council he has legally no greater powers than his colleagues whom he causes the President to appoint, but actually he it is who is the chief of the French government; and all the other ministers are subordinate to him. He has the power of forcing them out of office in case he is dissatisfied with their actions. For he has the confidence of the President of the republic who has the legal powers of removal and direction. The presidency of the council of ministers is often held by the minister of foreign affairs.

Such is the actual condition of affairs in the French republic. Owing to the possession by the President of the republic of the powers of both chief of government and chief of administration, and to the fact of their exercise by the president of the council of ministers subject to keeping the confidence of the chamber of deputies, there exist still guaranties for the harmonious conduct of the administration, notwithstanding the real weakness of the apparently powerful position of the President of the republic, through the adoption of the principle of the parliamentary responsibility of his ministers.

III.—In Germany.

In Germany the high position of the Emperor and the princes in their respective governments, as the actual as well as the legal chiefs of government and administration, ensures the carrying on of the government harmoniously. The parliamentary system has never taken root in Germany.[1]   In the empire the chancellor is the only responsible minister.[2]   All the other heads of departments are simply his subordinates, and are appointed and dismissed by the Emperor on his recommendation.[3]   They are merely secretaries of state and must follow the directions of the chancellor. As the chancellor is appointed and dismissed by the Emperor, the heads of the imperial departments are completely dependent upon the Emperor, and sufficient guaranties exist for a harmonious administration.

In the separate members of the empire the conditions are not, however, exactly the same.   While the parliamentary system has not taken root in Germany the constitutional system has.   This demands that the legally irresponsible prince shall exercise his powers through responsible ministers—ministers responsible at any rate before the criminal courts.   For this reason each minister must countersign all important acts of the prince which bear upon his particular department, and thereby assumes the responsibility therefor.   The tendency of such a system is of course to break up somewhat the uniformity and harmony of the administration.   For a minister might block the action of the prince, although it might be approved by his colleagues, by refusing his counter-signature, or might by his single advice commit the prince to actions which were not approved by his colleagues.   Of course much of the danger of such a thing is obviated by the existence in the prince of the power to dismiss a minister who refused to countersign an act which the prince

---

[1] Schulze, *op. cit.*, I., 299 ; Meyer, *Staatsrecht*, 184.
[2] Const., art. 17.
[3] Zorn, *op. cit.*, I., 201, citing L., March 17, 1878.

thought was within his powers.[1] But there is provided a further guaranty of harmonious administration in the "state ministry," as it is called. This is
composed of all the heads of departments who meet in
common session, as a rule under the presidency of the
prince, or of one of the ministers designated by the
prince and having the title of minister-president.[2] His
position is not at all like that of the French president
of the council of ministers or the imperial chancellor.
On the contrary, though the title of minister-president
may bring with it additional dignity, he has no greater
legal powers than any of the other ministers, with the
exception of presiding over the meetings of the ministry in the absence of the prince.[3] The main function
of the state ministry is to preserve harmony and uniformity in the policy of the administration. On this
account it is generally settled by law or ordinance
what matters shall be decided by it, while further the
prince may generally send any matter to it for decision.
Among the matters which by law or ordinance are to
come before it are all government bills and drafts of
general ordinances, the appointment of all the higher
administrative officers, and generally all matters which
do not come entirely within the competence of one
minister. Further, whenever the views of one of the
ministers do not coincide with that of the prince the
matter is to be submitted to the state ministry.[4] In all
of these matters, however, the state ministry acts sim-

---

[1] *Cf.* Loening, *op. cit.*, 62.

[2] *Ibid.*, 66.

[3] Bornhak, *Preussisches Staatsrecht*, II., 389. In Prussia an ordinance of
1852 has, however, provided that in most matters the ministers shall communi-
cate with the king through the minister-president.

[4] Loening, *op. cit.*, 67.

ply as an advisory body and simply lays before the
prince the result of its deliberations and then he decides
the matter.   Its decisions of themselves have no legal
force whatever; and never bind any one of the ministers who does not think that they are right.   This, it is
believed, would interfere with the principle of the
responsibility of the ministers for the acts of the irresponsible prince.   But if a minister cannot conscien-
tiously carry out a decision of the state ministry he is
at liberty to resign, while, if he does not so resign, the
prince has the right to remove him from active participation in the administration.[1]   Such are the means
adopted in the princely governments of Germany to
secure a harmonious administration.   The position of
the prince as the head of the administration is so well
recognized and his right to appoint, dismiss, and direct
his agents is so well recognized that theoretically it
might be said that the state ministry was a useless institution.   It does, however, perform a useful function
if it does nothing more than make the advice, which is
given to the prince by the heads of departments, uniform.   For it is only through the action of the ministers that the action of the prince has any political
effects.

IV.—In England.

In England the heads of departments are chosen
somewhat in the same way as in France.   That is, the
Crown, on the occasion of the resignation of a ministry,
sends for some eminent statesman who is a recognized
leader in one or the other houses of Parliament and who

[1] *Ibid.*, Schulze, *op. cit.*, I., 303.

has the confidence of the party which is in majority in the House of Commons and asks him to form a ministry.[1] If the person so selected accepts the trust, he himself is to select his colleagues.[2] All of the persons whom he selects are ministers though all are not necessarily members of that informal board, the cabinet, which, it has been shown, controls the action of the Privy Council and the Crown. Each is also a privy councillor, and it is in this capacity alone that the ministers may advise the Crown. For a long time it was doubtful whether the cabinet was to act as a board or whether it was to be governed by the wishes of the one member of it who was distinguished from the rest as the prime-minister or premier. Some of the ministers claimed that after their appointment they were responsible to the Crown alone and were in a position of independence over against the prime-minister at whose request they had agreed to act as ministers. This claim led to a conflict between Lord Palmerston who was foreign secretary and Lord John Russell who had been entrusted by the Queen with the duty of forming a ministry and who had chosen Lord Palmerston for the portfolio of foreign affairs. Lord Palmerston sent off certain despatches which had not received the approval of Lord John Russell. The latter officer obtained a note from the Queen in which it was distinctly said that the Queen did not wish any despatches to be sent before they had received her approval. Lord Palmerston disobeyed the order contained in this letter and was dismissed from office.[3] This precedent has finally settled that the

---

[1] Todd, *op. cit.*, I., 330., II., 183.   [2] *Ibid.*, I., 332.
[3] For a full history of this episode see Todd, *op. cit.*, II., 265 *et seq.* *Cf.* also Anson, *op. cit.*, II., 116 *et seq.*

prime-minister is to direct the policy of the government and has a control over the actions of all the other
ministers and members of the cabinet—that their relation to the prime-minister is one of dependence. The
position of prime-minister is nearly always associated
with that of first lord of the treasury. The reason
why the first lord of the treasury is generally prime-
minister is that the first lord has no portfolio and
may devote himself entirely to the consideration of
questions of general policy. Further there is associated
with this office a much wider power of appointment
than is possessed by any other office in the government.
It is now generally recognized that the first lord has
a control over all appointments which may have an
important influence on the general policy of the government. Thus he controls the appointment of all important ambassadors and ministers, certain colonial
governors among whom is the governor-general of
India, the commanders of the army and navy, the
bishops, and the presiding justices of the courts at
Westminster, and has the presentation to all the Crown
benefices.[1]

From what has been said it will be seen that the
acting executive in England is the prime-minister. He
controls the actions of the members of the cabinet and
the ministers, who are quite dependent upon him and
who in their turn control the action of the Crown and
the Privy Council and are themselves controlled by
the necessity of keeping the confidence of the party in
majority in the House of Commons. By this method
of developing the principle of parliamentary responsibility there are as in France sufficient guaranties for a

[1] Gneist, *Das Englische Verwaltungsrecht, etc.*, 1884, 218, 219.

harmonious administration notwithstanding that in legal theory the position of each of the ministers is of equal importance with that of any of the others.

V.—*Comparison.*

This review of the relations of the heads of departments with the acting chief executive shows that the almost universal rule is, that the heads of departments are dependent upon the chief executive; and that, if dependence is not absolutely secured, provision of some sort is made to secure harmony in the action of the administration. The only country which does not make some such provision is the United States. Here though, as a result of the development of the office of President, the national administration has been centralized under his direction, in the separate commonwealths seldom does it seem to be considered necessary to have an administration so formed as either to shut out the possibility of conflict or to settle such conflicts as may arise. The experience of the world is against the administrative arrangements in the commonwealths, and our own experience has shown us that such an arrangement leads to conflicts in the administration which not only diminish its efficiency but in some cases have absolutely caused a cessation of administrative work.

CHAPTER III.

Notwithstanding the general subordination of the heads of departments to the control and direction of the chief executive authority, still in all countries they have a series of duties, generally administrative in character, which they may perform largely independently of the action of the chief executive, in so far as they have not received positive directions from him. This is so even in monarchical governments.[1] More than this is true in the commonwealths of the United States, where the heads of departments often have functions to discharge with which the chief executive has little if any thing to do. First to be mentioned among their powers are those which affect the personnel of the official service.

I.—The power of appointment.

In all the countries under consideration the law grants to each head of department the power to appoint at least the subordinate officers of the department. In the United States national government the constitution provides that Congress may grant to the heads of departments the power to appoint

---

[1] Loening, *op. cit.*, 62.

to inferior offices.[1] Numerous laws have granted to the heads of departments such a power, so that now the great mass of the officers of the United States national government are appointed by the heads of the departments. Several laws have, however, limited this power in permitting the President to issue rules regulating the mode of appointment. Notable among them is the civil-service law of 1883. Most of the important subordinates of the heads of departments are, however, appointed by the President or the President and Senate.[2]

In the commonwealths the rule is the same. Thus, in New York the Public Officers Law[3] declares that all subordinate officers, whose appointment is not otherwise provided for by law, shall be appointed by their principal officer. It is expressly provided by law that many of the agents of the central government in the localities shall be elected by the people. In some of the commonwealths the power of appointment of the heads of departments is limited in the same way as in the national government. This is so in New York and Massachusetts.[4]

In France the rule is that the heads of departments shall appoint all but their most important subordinates who are appointed by the President. Very few of the subordinates of the departments who are acting in the localities are elected by the people thereof. It is, however, to be noted that many of the subordinate officers of the departments as, *e. g.*, the less important postmasters, are appointed by the representative of the central

---

[1] Art. ii., sec. 2, p. 2.
[2] See United States Revised Statutes, *passim.*
[3] L., 1892, c. 681, sec. 9.   [4] *Infra*, II., p. 35.

government in the localities, *viz.*, the prefect. He appoints many officers who in this country would be appointed by the heads of departments.[1] Where the heads of the departments have the power of appointment, they must be guided in their exercise of the power by the rules laid down in the decrees of the President relative to the method of appointment, which, like our civil-service rules, require often that the appointment shall be the result of a competitive examination open to all persons having the necessary qualifications.[2]

In Germany the rule is very much the same as in France. The law permits the Emperor or the prince, in whom the constitution vests the power of appointment, to delegate the exercise of this power to his subordinates.[3] But laws and ordinances lay down in great detail the qualifications of appointment, which are more severe than in any other country, especially for the higher positions. Finally many of the subordinates of the imperial administration are appointed by the commonwealth governments and not by the heads of the imperial departments,[4] while a few of the subordinates of the princely governments in the localities are elected indirectly by the people.[5]

In England, too, the rule is almost the same.[6] The first lord of the treasury has a greater power of appointment than the heads of the other departments,

---

[1] Aucoc, *op. cit.*, 119, sec. 62 ; Block, *Dictionnaire de l'administration française*, 753.

[2] *Infra*, II., p. 47.

[3] Imperial Constitution, art. 18 ; Meyer, *Staatsrecht*, 363.

[4] Loening, *op. cit.*, 120 ; Schulze, *op. cit.*, 332.

[5] *Infra*, pp. 303, 307, 315.

[6] Todd, *op. cit.*, II., 532.

having the appointment of all officers who have an important influence on the government.[1]   Here, as elsewhere, the heads of departments must be guided in the exercise of their powers of appointment by the rules issued by the Crown relative to the method of appointment, which for the purely subordinate positions is usually as the result of a competitive examination.[2]   In England quite a number of the subordinates of the departments in the localities are elected by the people of the localities.   This is true of the poor-law and sanitary administration.[3]

II.—The power of removal.

In the United States national government it was early laid down by the courts that the power of removal was incident to the power of appointment.[4] Therefore whenever the heads of departments have the appointing power, they have, in the absence of express statutory provisions to the contrary, the power of removal also.   The same rule is true in the commonwealth government.[5]   In not a few cases, however, especially in the case of the representatives of the central commonwealth government in the localities, the duration of the office is fixed by statute.   Removal in these cases is made only for cause, and then by the governor and not by the heads of departments.[6]   Neither in the national nor in the commonwealth government have

---

[1] Gneist, *Das Englische Verwaltungsrecht*, 1884, pp. 218, 219.

[2] In England these rules are issued by the civil-service commission as a result of the delegation to it of the power by an order in council.   *Infra*, II., p. 53.

[3] *Infra*, p. 248.   [4] *Ex parte* Hennen, 13 Peters, 230.

[5] People *ex rel.* Sims *v.* Fire Commissioners, 73 N. Y. 437 ; *cf.* Mechem, *Law of Officers*, sec. 445.

[6] *E. g.* see N. Y. L., 1892, c. 681, sec. 23.

the civil-service laws attempted to limit directly the power of removal of the heads of departments.

In France the power of removal of the heads of departments over their subordinates is practically complete. Whatever officers they may appoint they may also remove.[1] The same is true in England, where the power is exercised in theory by the Crown on the advice of responsible ministers.[2] The power of removal of the head of one of the departments is very much greater than in the matter of appointment. The Local Government Board in London has the right and the sole right to dismiss the subordinate officers of the various boards of poor-law guardians—whose appointment is made by the guardians subject simply to the approval of the local government board.[3]

In Germany, however, the power of removal of the heads of departments is not nearly so great as their power of appointment. As has already been said, the German law generally recognizes office as a vested right which cannot be taken away from its possessor except as the result of conviction of crime, or of a judgment before a regular disciplinary court.[4] In compensation for the absence of this power the heads of departments have the right to impose lighter disciplinary punishments, such as fines, for dereliction of duty.[5]

III.—*The power of direction and supervision.*

While the different countries differ very little in the matters of the powers of appointment and removal of the heads of departments we find a difference in the

[1] Aucoc, *op. cit.*, I., 119, sec. 62.　　[3] 34 and 35 Vict., c. 70.
[2] Todd, *op. cit.*, I., 629, 636.　　[4] *Supra*, p. 94.
[5] *Infra*, II., p. 87.

extent of the power of direction. The four countries may be divided into two classes.

1. *United States and England.*—In the one class composed of the United States and England the original conception of the head of a department was that of an officer stationed at the centre of the government who might have, it is true, in many cases the powers of appointment and removal but who was not supposed to direct the actions of the subordinates of his department. This was particularly true of the branch of administration which has been designated the administration of internal affairs, where it may be said that almost everything was attended to in the localities and subject to almost no central supervision. The need of central instruction and supervision was not felt for the reason that the statutes of the legislature descended into the most minute details as to the duties and powers of the officers. The conception indeed of a hierarchy of subordinate and superior officers was very dim, if it existed at all. This is seen in our national administration in the position originally occupied by the collectors of the customs. Though nominally perhaps the subordinates of the secretary of the treasury, the law never recognized that they were subject to his instructions and directions, nor was it the practice to regulate the administrative details by means of central instructions.[1] No one, further, thought in our early history of appealing from the decision of a collector to the secretary of the treasury. In the commonwealths the system was very much the same.

---

[1] *Cf. Report of the Secretary of the Treasury on the Collection of Duties,* 1885, p. xxxvii; see Eliot v. Swartout, 10 Peters, 37 ; Tracy v. Swartout, 10 *Id.,* 80.

Almost all the administrative matters affecting the commonwealth were attended to by officers in the localities who were really quite independent, after they had assumed office, of all central instruction, notwithstanding the fact that the most important of them were originally appointed by the central government of the commonwealth. It was not the habit of the central government to send to these officers in the localities instructions as to how they should act in the execution of the law whatever might have been the actual power of the heads of departments. In the commonwealths the system has remained almost unchanged so far as the officers attending to the affairs of the commonwealth in the localities are concerned. Indeed their independence of the heads of the departments of the central commonwealth government is even greater now than it originally was, on account of the fact that they are for the most part elected by the people of the localities in which they act.[1] In some cases the law does recognize a right in a head of a department in the commonwealth to send instructions to the officers in the localities as to how certain branches of administrative work shall be attended to.[2] These cases are extremely rare. But certain matters which were either formerly not attended to at all by the commonwealth administration or which were attended to by the officers in the localities are now attended to directly by the heads of the commonwealth departments and their subordinates who are under central control. Such matters in New York are: prisons, pauper lunatics in most cases, factory inspection, edu-

---

[1] *Infra*, p. 178.

[2] *E. g.*, the comptroller in New York is authorized by statute to make regulations and issue directions in regard to the transmission to the treasury of public money. L., 1843, c. 44.

cation, railway supervision, *etc., etc.* As to these matters the heads of the commonwealth departments have a large power of direction sanctioned by the power of removal. What has been the exception in the commonwealth administration has been the rule in the national administration. The century of national development has produced perhaps more change in this respect than in any other. The result of this development has been the recognition of an official hierarchy in the national administration with the power in the heads of the departments to reverse or modify, on appeal of persons interested, the decisions of the inferior officers and to direct them how to act.[1] Here again the treasury department offers a good example. Now the collectors of the customs would hardly think of attempting to apply the law in a doubtful case without first receiving instructions from the secretary of the treasury ;[2] and the law makes an appeal from the collector of internal revenue to the treasury necessary before the aggrieved party has any standing in court. He must exhaust his administrative remedy before he may resort to his judicial remedy.[3] The same thing is true in many cases in the department of the interior.[4] Finally it has been held that the head of a department may change the erroneous decision of a subordinate officer.[5]

---

[1] See, *e. g.*, United States Revised Statutes, sec. 251 ; Butterworth v. U. S., 112 U. S., 50.

[2] *Cf.* U. S. R. S., sec. 2652.

[3] U. S. R. S., sec. 3226 ; this was the case also in the customs administration until the passage of the late administrative bill, which has taken away the administrative remedy of appeal to the secretary and has provided an appeal to the appraisers. *Cf.* Goss, "History of Tariff Administration in the United States," in *Studies in History, Economics, and Public Law*, I., 155.

[4] *Ibid.*, sec. 2273.   [5] U. S. v. Cobb, 11 Fed. Rep., 76.

In England the development that is to be noticed in this country has also taken place, but even to a greater extent. The reform of the system of local government since 1834[1] has made the English administrative system one of the most centralized in existence. The new department of the interior, *i. e.* the local government board, and also the treasury have the most extended right of direction and control over the numerous local boards which attend to affairs in the localities. This has not failed to have its influence on the other departments, and at the present time the best authority on English administrative law, Professor Gneist, lays it down as a rule[2] that the English heads of departments have a very wide power of issuing instructions and directions to their subordinates throughout the land and thus of guiding the action of inferior administrative officers.

2. *In France and Germany.*—In France and Germany, contrary to the original rule in England and the United States, the officers of the central government have always had the right to issue instructions to their subordinates, among whom were many officers who in England and the United States would be considered local officers, since the central government has had almost from the beginning many representatives in the localities, who were regarded as distinctively central officers.[3] The long existence of such a system has naturally given to the instructions and directions of the heads of departments a much greater importance than they have ever had in this country or in

---

[1] *Infra*, p. 236.

[2] *Das Englische Verwaltungsrecht*, I., 354 *et seq.*

[3] Aucoc, *op. cit.*, I., 89, 119 ; Stengel, *Deutsches Verwaltungsrecht*, 163, 164.

England. The laws have never gone into such detail as with us in regard to the duties of the officers, but have left these to be filled out by ordinance and instructions.[1] Indeed it would be almost impossible to understand much of the administrative law without a reference to these ministerial circulars of instructions and directions. Germany and France have thus from the beginning possessed a most centralized system of administration. Now while the tendency in the United States and England has been towards administrative centralization, the tendency in France and Germany has been towards administrative decentralization. Within the last twenty years many matters which formerly were regulated by the instructions of the heads of departments have been put into the hands of the officers of the localities to be attended to in their own discretion, subject, it is true, at times to the supervision of the heads of the departments.[2]

The heads of departments in the four countries have thus the power of direction. The only exception is the case of the heads of departments in the commonwealths in the United States, who do not, as a general thing, have any power of directing their subordinates in the localities how they shall execute the laws.

The heads of departments, like the chief executive authority, have a class of material as well as personal powers—that is, they have direct powers in connection with the administrative services attended to by the government. Among these may be mentioned:

[1] *Cf.* Dicey, *The Law of the Constitution*, 3d. Ed., 50.
[2] Boeuf, *op. cit.*, 118 ; De Grais, *Handbuch der Verfassung und Verwaltung*, 1883, p. 54.

IV.—*The ordinance power.*

In all countries the heads of departments have a delegated but only a delegated ordinance power. This is true even in the United States where very few matters comparatively are regulated by ordinance. In the national government in many cases, Congress has delegated to the heads of departments the power to regulate by general orders the details of the administrative law; and when such a delegation has been made the regulations issued as a result of it have a force even upon individuals equal to that of statute.[1] Where such regulations are not clearly based on some legal provision giving the power to issue them the courts do not hesitate to declare them void when they come before them for enforcement.[2] In the separate commonwealths of the United States the ordinance power of the heads of departments is not a large one because the legislature has not seen fit to grant to them this power. In foreign countries also the rule seems to be the same with perhaps the exception of England, where matters are often regulated by the head of a department which on the continent would be regulated by executive ordinance. But even in our national government the administrative regulations, which are issued by the heads of departments as a result of their possession of the delegated ordinance power, are regarded by the courts as the acts of the President, who is supposed to have acted through the heads of departments.[3] These ordinances are to be

[1] *E. g.* U. S. R. S., sec. 251 ; United States v. Barrows, I. Abbott, U. S., 351, *Ex parte* Reed, 100 U. S., 13, 23 ; citing Gratiot v. U. S., 4 How., 80.

[2] Little v. Barreme, 2 Cranch, 170 ; *Ex parte* Field, 5 Blatchford, 63 ; Campbell v. U. S., 107 U. S., 592.

[3] Willcox v. Jackson, 13 Peters, 498 ; *supra*, p. 73.

distinguished from ministerial circulars or instructions, which, while general in character like the ordinances, are not like the ordinances binding upon the individual but only upon the officers subjected to the power of direction of the head of the department. Such instructions are based on this power of direction.[1] In Europe the distinction between these two kinds of acts is much clearer than in this country, but even in the United States the United States Supreme Court has held that regulations of departments for the transaction of their business are subject, if they are unjust, to revision by the courts at the instance of individuals who, it would seem, are not in such a case bound by them.[2]

V.—*Special acts of individual application.*

In addition to these general acts, the heads of departments must, in order to discharge the functions given to them, perform many special acts. They have to make most of the contracts which are made by the government; they must issue orders affecting only one case; they must make decisions either of their own motion or on the appeal of interested parties. The position of the heads of departments is in this respect essentially the same in all countries. In both the continental countries it has for a long time been recognized that any individual who deems himself aggrieved by a decision of a subordinate officer may appeal to the head of the department to have the objectionable decision reversed. This appeal is always allowed even

[1] Boeuf, *op. cit.*, 28.
[2] U. S. v., Cadwalader, Gilp., 563, 577.

where the law has not specifically authorized the taking of such an appeal.[1] The reason of the existence of this right in the individual is to be found in the hierarchical character of the administrative system with the monarch originally at the head, to whom as fountain of justice the individual always had the right to present a petition for justice.   In this country, also, although the administration was not hierarchically organized originally, it would seem that the head of a department possesses the power to hear appeals from subordinates' decisions.   This power has been given by statute in numerous instances in the national administration but not often in the commonwealth administration, and it is held that the power of direction and control gives the power to hear appeals and correct mistakes.[2]

VI.—Remedies.

In only one of the four countries is there recognized a direct remedy against the general acts of the heads of departments.   That country is France where any one may appeal to the council of state to have an objectionable ordinance quashed on the ground that it has been issued by the head of a department in excess of his powers.   In all the other countries, as well as in France also, the courts have the right collaterally to declare an ordinance void which has been issued in excess of powers.[3]   In almost all the countries, in fact all except

---

[1] Boeuf, *op. cit.*, 28 ; Loening, *op. cit.*, 794.

[2] Butterworth v. U. S., 112 U. S., 50, 57, which discusses the appellate power of the secretary of the interior in patent matters.   Here, it is said, that " the official duty of direction and supervision implies a correlative right of appeal . . . in every case of complaint although no such appeal is expressly given." See also Bell v. Hearne, 19 How., 252.

[3] For American cases see *supra*, p. 74.   See also Stengel, *Deutsches Verwaltungsrecht*, 180 ; French *Code Pénal*, art. 471, sec. 15.

Germany, there is a remedy against the special acts of the heads of departments. In England and the United States this remedy is to be found in an appeal in the proper form to the courts to overturn or modify the act complained of.[1] In France the appeal goes to the council of state acting as an administrative court.[2]

VII.—Local subordinates of the executive departments.

In all countries certain of the executive departments have scattered about the country in the districts, into which it has for this purpose been divided, subordinate officers who act under the direction and control of the heads of departments. Thus in the United States national administration the treasury department has its collectors, naval officers, surveyors, inspectors, measurers, weighers, and gaugers in the customs and internal-revenue districts; the department of the interior, its land receivers and registers and Indian agents, *etc., etc.* The national administration is highly centralized, rarely making use of the officers of the commonwealth or of the various local corporations within the commonwealths, such as the counties and the towns. While this is also true of certain branches of administration in the commonwealths of the United States[3] and foreign countries,[4] still in many cases the central government, if the government is a federal one as in Germany, makes use of commonwealth officers,[5] or it imposes a series of duties upon officers who are at the same time

[1] *Infra*, II., p. 209.

[2] *Infra*, II., pp. 229, 238.

[3] As, *e. g.*, in New York, the factory inspectors of the labor commissioner, and the various agents of the department of public works.

[4] For France see Aucoc, *op. cit.*, I., 182.

[5] As, *e. g.*, in the case of the customs and the internal indirect taxes.

officers of the local corporations or even upon such local corporations themselves.   Thus in the commonwealths of the United States the commonwealth central government often uses county and town officers and the counties and towns themselves—these bodies are indeed primarily administrative districts for the purposes of the general commonwealth administration [1]—as its agents for a series of purposes.   For example, in most of the commonwealths the counties and the towns attend to the financial administration of the commonwealth as a whole, defray most of the expenses of the judicial administration, take care of the poor, *etc.*, *etc.*, while the county authority is not uncommonly made the board of canvassers for general elections.   The only great difference between the English and American system on the one hand and the continental system on the other, is that the control which the central executive departments have over such local corporations and their officers, both when acting as the agents of the central administration and when acting as the agents of the local corporations, is much less extensive in the former than in the latter.   In the United States and England most of the local corporations elect their own officers, who, even when acting as they so often do as agents of the central administration, are quite independent of the heads of the central executive departments [2]; while on the continent such officers are often appointed by the central government and act in all cases more or less under its control.[3]   Though not so centralized usually as the United States national administration, the continental system is much more centralized than either the English or the United States commonwealth sys-

[1] *Infra*, p. 173.   [2] *Infra*, p. 228.   [3] *Infra*, pp. 272, 315.

tem. It must, however, be said that the tendency in England is to put the local corporations and their officers under a strict central control, especially when they are acting as the agents of the central government [1]; while the latest steps taken in Germany tend greatly to relax the formerly strong central control.

[1] *Infra*, p. 259.

11

BOOK III.

LOCAL ADMINISTRATION.

CHAPTER I.

I.—History of rural local administration in England to the eighteenth century.

1. *The sheriff.*—The character of the English system of local government was fixed by the Norman kings. The absolutism of the Norman government reduced all classes of the inhabitants to complete submission to the Crown.[1] On account of the race conflict between Norman and Saxon, the Crown was obliged to establish some system of government by means of which the peace might be preserved and the King might act as the impartial arbiter between the conflicting race elements of the nation.[2] The King therefore districted the kingdom, using in the main the old divisions, *i. e.*, shires which had come down from Anglo-Saxon times, and placed in each district an officer on

---

[1] Stubbs, *op. cit.*, I., 257, 259, note 1 ; 260, 338 ; *cf.* Goodnow, "Local Government in England" in *Pol. Sci. Qu.*, II., 638.

[2] Gneist, *Selfgovernment, Communalverfassung und Verwaltungsgerichte*, 14.

whom he could rely to carry out his plans and enforce his orders. Such districts were not considered to be public corporations. They had no affairs of their own to attend to, but all administrative business was attended to by royal officers placed within them, to wit, the sheriffs or *vice-comites.*[1] The sheriff was always an unpopular officer; he was therefore gradually stripped of his powers and a system of administration established which was more popular in character. But before this was done the strong centralized administration of the Normans had consolidated the people of England into a nation. This was accomplished in England much sooner than on the continent. As a result of the centralization, autonomous communities had no opportunity to develop, and though the administrative system later became really quite decentralized, the same general principles remained true, *i. e.,* the localities remained simply administrative districts without juristic personality and with no affairs of their own to attend to, districts in which royal officers attended to all administrative business. The prefectoral administration of the sheriffs lasted from the time of the conquest to about the reign of Richard II, when changes were made which reduced the sheriff to the position of a ministerial officer of the royal courts, which had sprung up in the meantime, a returning officer for elections and a conservator of the peace.[2] These changes are to be found in the establishment of the office of the justice of the peace,[3] and the subsequent enlargement of its powers.

---

[1] Stubbs, *op. cit.,* I., 276 ; *cf. Pol. Sci. Qu.,* II., 639.

[2] See Anson, *op. cit.,* II., 236.

[3] 34 Edward III, c. I. ; *cf. Pol. Sci. Qu.,* II., 644, and authorities cited.

2. *The justice of the peace.*—To the justices of the peace were given most of the powers of the sheriff. They further gained control of the parish administration which sprang up in the times of the Tudors in connection with the church, and in their courts of quarter sessions acted as the county authority. They were finally by far the most important officers in the localities, discharging both administrative and judicial functions, and having under their direction almost all other officers in the localities. The system whose whole tone was given by the justices of the peace was much more decentralized than the prefectoral system of the sheriffs. All the officers were chosen in the localities in which they acted. Most of them, it is true, were appointed directly or indirectly by the central government, and could be removed by it. But the fact that they received no salary, although service as a rule was obligatory and arduous, and that they were chosen from the well-to-do classes made the personnel of the service after all very independent, and kept it from falling into bureaucratic ways. For the threat of dismissal from office had little terror for a justice of the peace. Dismissal meant relief from arduous service and not the loss of a means of livelihood. The system thus really secured a high degree of local self-government. The independence of the justices brought it about that the control over their actions, which could be exercised by the central administration, amounted to almost nothing finally. To provide for some sort of central control the statutes of Parliament, regulating the powers and duties of the justices, had to descend into the most minute details. That the justices acted in accordance with these de-

tailed statutes was ensured by the control given to the royal courts over their action, by means of which the courts might, on the application of any person aggrieved by the action of the justices, force them to act as the law required or else quash their illegal action.[1]

II.—*The development of the system in the United States.*

1. *The three original forms of local administration.* —The justice of the peace system was in full force at the time of the colonization of North America. It is only natural that its main features should characterize the original system of American local administration. We find, however, three pretty distinct forms of it in the different colonies, one in the New England colonies, one in the middle colonies, and a third in the southern colonies. The main distinction between these three forms is to be found in the relative position which was assigned to the areas adopted for the purpose of administration. In New England while the county was recognized [2] it was not nearly so important as the town which was the other area. The town may be taken as the American type of the English parish but it cannot be regarded as the legal successor of the parish. It is really the creation of American statute law, and thus the principles of the common law applicable to the English parish may not be applied to the American town.[3] The town resembles the Anglo-Saxon tunscipe, indeed more than the English parish. This resemblance

---

[1] *Pol. Sci. Qu.,* II., 648 ; *infra,* II., p. 200.

[2] Howard in his *Local Constitutional History of the United States,* I., 320, says that the county was formed in Rhode Island in 1703, but was comparatively unimportant. In Massachusetts, however, it is found as early as 1635. See 9 Gray, 512 note.

[3] Morey v. Town of Newfane, 8 Barb. N. Y., 645, 648.

to its old Teutonic prototype would seem to be due more to the fact that the American colonists had to face conditions similar to those before their German forefathers than to any conscious imitation on their part of Saxon institutions.

In the middle colonies also we find both the town and the county. But the functions of administration were quite equally distributed between them or else the town was less important than the county. The latter was especially true of Pennsylvania, where the town was not established until the latter part of the eighteenth century and after its establishment was much less important than the New England town.[1]

In the south social conditions were such as to necessitate the existence of the county alone and to prevent the development during the colonial period of any lesser administrative area at all.

2. *The early American county.*— The county was found in all the American colonies with the exception perhaps of some of the New England colonies where, if it existed at all as an administrative district, it existed in a very rudimentary form. Wherever the county did exist as an administrative district the county authority was, as in England, the court of sessions of the justices of the peace who were appointed by the governor of the colony.[2] By the side of the justices of the peace was the sheriff occupying a position similar to that of the English sheriff of the same period. That is, he was a conservator of the peace, the returning officer for elections, and the ministerial officer of the

[1] Howard, *op. cit.*, I., 385.
[2] For New York see *Documents Relating to the Colonial History of New York*, IV., 25 ; *cf.* Howard, I., 406.

courts. He was appointed also by the governor.[1] In the court of sessions were centred about all the administrative duties relating to the county. In this court the justices appointed some person to be county treasurer, attended to the county finances and supervised the administration of the poor-law. Acting separately they had charge of police and highway matters and directed the actions of a great number of subordinates who had duties relative to these matters.

The first change to be noticed in the county organization is the substitution of officers elected by the people of the county for these appointed justices. This begins in New York certainly as early as 1691, and probably as early as 1683.[2] In 1691 an officer called a supervisor was to be elected in each town. His name comes from the fact that when these officers from each of the towns in the county were assembled together they formed the county board, and were to "supervise and examine the publick and necessary charge of each county."[3] The motive for this change was probably to provide for the co-existence of local representation with local taxation, since the main duties of the first board of supervisors were relative to the

[1] See Brodhead, *History of New York*, I., 63, and authorities cited.

[2] See Laws of 1691, c. vi. There is in the office of the secretary of state of New York a manuscript law of the date of November 2, 1683, which provides that there should be elected in each town persons "for the superviseing of the publique affaires and charge of each respective towne and county." But as the assembly in New York previous to 1691 was an almost extra legal-body, it is safer to set the introduction of the elective principle in the county organization at 1691.

[3] This system was abolished ten years later by Laws, 1701, c. 96, but was reintroduced by Law of June 19, 1703. This accounts for the mistake which is so commonly made of assigning 1703 as the date of the introduction of the supervisor system in New York.

fiscal administration of the county.[1] The justices still
retained important functions in other administrative
branches, such as highways.[2] A little later the elective
system was introduced into Pennsylvania but in a
somewhat different form, the towns not being represented on the county board, probably on account of
their unimportance. In 1724 provision was made for
the election by the people of the county of three commissioners who were to manage the fiscal affairs of the
county.[3] Sheriffs were also elected by the people in
Pennsylvania from an early time.[4] This change in the
county organization was destined to have a profound
influence on the subsequent development of local administration in the United States. As Professor
Howard well says[5]: "To New York first, and next to
Pennsylvania belongs the honor of predetermining the
character of local government in the west. But if
New York was first to return to the ancient practice
of township representation in the county court it was
in Pennsylvania that the capabilities of the independent county were first tested. Here the principle of
election to county offices was carried farther than it
was ever carried in England.[6] New York is the parent
of the supervisor system. On the other hand Penn-

[1] See New York Law of November 1, 1722, where it says : " Whereas by that
means," *i. e.* the method of voting provided by the act of 1703, "the inhabitants of several manors, Liberties and Precincts which bear a considerable share
of the county rate have not the liberty of chusing their own Supervisors, be it
enacted" that they may vote in the town adjoining the manor, *etc.*

[2] *Cf.* Howard, I., 362.

[3] *Ibid.*, I., 382.

[4] *Ibid.*, I., 384, and authorities cited.

[5] *Ibid.*, I., 387.

[6] It is, however, to be noted that the New York law of 1683, above referred
to, provided that the county treasurer should be elected by the voters of the
county.

sylvania is the originator of the commissioner system." The elective system thus introduced into New York and Pennsylvania has been adopted in almost every commonwealth, and has been extended to almost all county offices at the present time, not only the original county offices but also those which the increase of the work of administration has caused to be provided.

3. *The early American town.*—While we find in the early American county an organization similar to that of the English county of the seventeenth and eighteenth centuries, in the early American town we do not find an organization which resembles very closely the English parish of the same period. The town is, as has been said, an American creation and its development has been quite different in different sections. In New England it is older than the county.[1] In the middle colonies it seems to be a later creation.[2] The town originated either in legislation[3] or in an executive act of the early colonial government,[4] while in some cases it seems to have originated in the settlement of lands bought for this purpose from the Indians by companies of persons who then formed a sort of social compact for their government.[5] Towns formed in this last manner seem at first to have had about all of the attributes of government, but were later absorbed into the colonies and lost in this way all rights but the ordinary rights of self-administration.

---

[1] We find it in this section as early as 1630, 9 Gray, Mass., 511.

[2] *E. g.*, Pennsylvania, *supra*, p. 166.

[3] As, *e. g.*, in New England, Howard, I., 56.

[4] *E. g.*, in New York where the town of Hempstead, on Long Island, was created by a patent given by Director General Kieft in 1644, Brodhead *op. cit.*, I., 388, and authorities cited.

[5] Wood, *History of Long Island*, 19 *et seq.*

From the very beginning the principle of election by the voters of the town seems to have been the method of filling all the town offices; and in this principle is to be found the great point of difference between American town organization and the English parish organization, and between the positions of the American and English justices of the peace. For in the English parish the justices of the peace appointed ultimately almost all of the parish officers and directed them how to act. The powers of the American justices of the peace over the affairs of the towns were much less extensive. In the New England town the town officers were elected by the town meeting, *i. e.*, the assembly of the political people of the town. The principal officers were the selectmen. They had a general supervision of town affairs, and were to execute the resolutions of the town meeting which was the deliberative body in the town.[1] In addition to the selectmen there was also an almost innumerable list of officers, each of whom attended to some particular matter affecting the welfare of the town. Some of these minor officers were elected at the town meeting, some were appointed by the selectmen.[2] The existence of such a number of officers was necessary because salaries were not paid, and because service was, as a rule, obligatory; for no man could be expected, without compensation, to give up a large share of his time to the performance of public duties. In New York the principal officers of the town after 1691 were the supervisor, two assessors, a constable, a collector, a clerk, highway commissioners or surveyors, and overseers of the poor. They were for the most part

[1] Howard, I., 78.   [2] *Ibid.*, 88, 96.

elected, as in Massachusetts, by the town meeting, which in New York had functions to discharge similar to those discharged by the Massachusetts town meeting with the difference that its sphere of action was not so extended. For the county did a great deal of the work in New York that was attended to by the town in New England.[1] In Pennsylvania we find in the town after its establishment, two overseers of the poor appointed by the justices and two supervisors of highways elected by the people of the town. As the county was much more important in Pennsylvania even than in New York there was very little for the town to do. It was more in the nature of an administrative division of the county than a local organization with its own duties to perform. Therefore the town meeting was not present in the original Pennsylvania plan of local administration.[2]

III.—Corporate capacity of the localities.

1. *Original absence of corporate capacity.*—When the elective principle was made the rule for the filling of offices in the local administrative system the whole local organization became quite popular in character and at the same time quite independent of the central administration, since all possible administrative sanction for instructions issued to the officers in the localities from the central administrative authorities was destroyed. But for a considerable time after this decentralizing of the administrative system the various areas for the purposes of administration, in which these independent officers acted, were, no more than the cor-

[1] See N. Y. L., June 19, 1703.   [2] Howard, I., 385.

responding English areas,[1] regarded as juristic persons.[2] They had no services of their own to attend to apart from the sphere set aside to them by the statutes of the central legislature, which regarded them as agents of the central administration of the commonwealth, nor could they even hold property or sue or be sued.[3] One result of the non-corporate character of towns is to be found in the fact that by common law the property of an inhabitant of a New England town may be taken upon execution on a judgment against the town.[4] The first step in New York towards recognizing that the areas of administration possessed any juristic personality was taken in the case of *North Hempstead v. Hempstead,*[5] which held that a town had a certain corporate capacity though what that corporate capacity was, was not clearly defined. The undoubted corporate capacity of the old Dutch towns, due to the influence of the Roman law and the continental idea of the territorial distribution of administrative functions,[6] seems to have influenced the court in its decision of this case.[7] In 1801 the legislature expressly made the county a capable grantee of lands[8] and finally the

---

[1] Russell v. The Men of Devon, 2 T. R., 672, A. D. 1788.

[2] Ward v. Co. of Hartford, 12 Conn., 406.

[3] See for New York, which may be taken as typical, the cases of Jackson v. Hartwell, 8 Johnson, 422 ; Jackson v. Cory, *Ibid.*, 385 ; Hornbeck v. Westbrook, 9 Johnson, 73 ; and Jackson v. Schoonmaker, 2 Johnson, 230.

[4] See Bloomfield v. Charter Oak Bank, 121 U. S., 121, 129 ; Hill v. Boston, 122 Mass., 344, 349.

[5] 2 Wendell, N. Y., 109. In Massachusetts, however, towns were authorized to grant lands in 1635, to sue and be sued in 1694 ; and were expressly incorporated in 1785. See 9 Gray, Mass., 511, note, which gives a history of the legislation as to towns.

[6] *Supra*, p. 44.

[7] See Denton v. Jackson, 2 Johnson, ch. 320, 355.

[8] I Kent & Radcliff's Laws, 561.

New York Revised Statutes of 1829 expressly declared each county and town to be a body corporate with certain specified powers, to wit, the power to hold property and to sue and be sued.[1] The principle established in Massachusetts and New York has been adopted in most of the other commonwealths of the United States so that it may be said that the American county and town are, where they have any administrative importance, at the present time bodies corporate with these specified powers.[2]

2. *Present corporate capacity.*—But while the result of American development has been the recognition of the local areas as public corporations the further step has not been taken of recognizing that such corporations possess any sphere of local action of their own. The duties attended to by them or by the officers acting within them are regarded as essentially matters of central concern, and the officers, though elected by the people of the localities, are not regarded as local officers in the sense that they are agents of the local corporations. They are simply central officers who are, in accordance with the method adopted in the United States of filling these positions, elected by the people resident in the local areas. The position of the town is well stated in the case of *Lorillard v. the Town of Monroe.*[3]

The several towns of the state, says Judge Denio, are corporations for special and very limited purposes, or to speak more

[1] The chapter devoted to the towns is explained by the original reports of the revisers to the legislature in 1827 in which it is said that " this article is wholly new in its present form."

[2] *Cf.* Dillon, *Municipal Corporations,* 4th edition, I., chapter ii. ; Levy Court v. Coroner, 2 Wallace, 501, 507.

[3] 11 N. Y., 392, 393.

accurately, they have a certain limited corporate capacity. They may purchase and hold lands within their own limits for the use of their inhabitants. They may as a corporation make such contracts and hold such personal property as may be necessary to the exercise of their corporate or administrative powers, and they may regulate and manage their corporate property and as a necessary incident sue and be sued where the assertion of their corporate rights or the enforcement of their corporate liabilities shall require such proceedings. In all other respects, for instance in everything which concerns the administration of civil or criminal justice, the preservation of the public health or morals, the conservation of highways, roads, and bridges, the relief of the poor, and the assessment and collection of taxes, the several towns are political divisions, organized for the convenient exercise of portions of the political power of the state ; and are no more corporations than the judicial or assembly districts. The functions and the duties of the several town officers respecting these subjects are not in any sense corporate functions or duties.

The judge goes on to say it is convenient to have the officers chosen in the towns, but they are, when chosen, public and not corporate officers just as much as the highest official functionaries of the state; they are not therefore in any legal sense the servants or agents of the towns.[1] The position of the county, which is quite similar to that of the town is well stated in the case of *Hamilton Co. v. Mighels*.[2] The court says here:

A county is at most but a local organization which for purposes of civil administration is invested with a few functions characteristic of a corporate existence. . . . A county organization is created almost exclusively with a view to the policy of the state at large, for purposes of political organization and civil administration, in matters of finance, of education, of provision for the

[1] See also Town of Gallatin v. Loucks, 21 Barbour, N. Y., 578 ; City of Rochester v. Town of Rush, 80 N. Y., 302 ; Sikes v. Hatfield, 13 Gray, Mass., 347 ; and particularly Hill v. Boston, 122 Mass., 344.

[2] 7 Ohio St., 109, 115.

poor, of military organization, of the means of travel and transport, and especially for the general administration of justice. With scarcely an exception all the powers and functions of the county organization have a direct and exclusive reference to the general policy of the state, and are in fact but a branch of the general administration of that policy.

Again in *Talbot Co. v. Queen Anne's Co.,*[1] the court says :

A county is one of the public territorial divisions of the state created and organized for public political purposes connected with the administration of the state government, and especially charged with the superintendence and administration of the local affairs of the community.[2]

It will be seen what a slight recognition there has been, notwithstanding the corporate capacity of the local areas, of the possession by them of any sphere of action of their own as distinguished from their sphere of action as the mere agents of the commonwealth government. Their corporate capacity is made a mere incident to their public governmental capacity and is of value to them only in that through it it is possible for them to own lands and property. But even this property is subject to the regulation of the legislature, which may take it away from them and provide at any time that it may be made use of for some purpose other than that for which it was purchased.[3] Outside of this problematical advantage of holding property which is really more the property of the commonwealth than of the local areas, their corporate capacity is as much a disadvantage as an advantage to them, since

[1] 50 Md., 245, 259.

[2] See also Scales, v. The Ordinary, 41 Ga., 225, 227, 229 ; *cf.* Dillon, *Municipal Corporations*, 4th edition, I., chap. ii.

[3] See *infra*, p. 202.

while they are able through it to bring suits they are also liable to be sued. This corporate capacity has indeed been so narrowly construed by the courts that it gives the localities no other powers than those already mentioned of owning property, of suing, and of being sued. The courts have held that as a result of it they have no borrowing power[1] and practically that from it there can be derived no principle of *respondeat superior* for the acts of the officers of these local areas. The last point was distinctly held in the cases of *Lorillard v. the Town of Monroe* and *Sikes v. Hatfield*, to which reference has been made. It is true, however, that either general or special statutes have conferred upon the local areas the power to borrow money for a series of specified purposes, the most common of which are to erect county or town buildings, which serve at the same time as the offices of the administrative services of the commonwealth attended to in the county or town ; and to aid means of transportation, such as railroads which are being constructed and operated by private companies. But no general sphere of action in which the localities have any independent powers has been derived from the corporate capacity which they possess.

Thus, notwithstanding the great decentralization of the administrative system which has resulted from the development of American local institutions, and notwithstanding the recognition of the juristic personality of the local areas, it cannot be said that the course of American local administrative history has given to the localities any sphere of independent local action. They are, as their English prototypes were after the Norman

---

[1] Starin v. Town of Genoa, 23 N. Y., 441, 447.

conquest, simply agents of the central administration with, however, a corporate capacity which is to be made use of more for the benefit of the common-wealth as a whole than for the benefit of the particular areas themselves.

12

CHAPTER II.

I.—The compromise system.

1. *The county.*—The three general types of the
English local administrative system which were formed
in America at the time of its settlement or which were
developed soon after its settlement are still to be found.
That developed in New York and Pennsylvania, which
provided at a very early period for popular representation in the county authority and which distributed
administrative affairs somewhat equally among the two
important areas, has had the greatest influence, is at
the present time the most widely adopted, and seems
destined to become the prevailing type of local administration in the United States.   One of the principles
on which it was based has been all but universally
adopted, *i. e.*, the election of the county authority by
the people of the county, who are now defined in accordance with the principles of universal manhood
suffrage.   This principle has in most cases been extended, in accordance with the Pennsylvania idea, to
other officers besides the county authority proper, so
that now the usual rule is that all important officers in
the county are elected by the people of the county.

For example, the sheriff, the county clerk, the county treasurer, the register or recorder of deeds, the district attorney, and the county superintendent of the poor, where that officer is to be found, are generally elected by the people, and not appointed by the central administration of the commonwealth or by the county authority, as was the case in the original English and American system. In many cases their election by the people is prescribed by the constitution of the commonwealth.[1]

This system of local administration, in accordance with which administrative duties are about equally distributed among the counties and the towns, is called the compromise system, inasmuch as it adopts the extremes of neither the New England nor the southern system. It is found in the middle commonwealths, and in those of the west and northwest. It has even invaded the domain of the southern system in that it has been partially adopted in Virginia, and the domain of the New England system in that it has been partially adopted in Massachusetts and Maine. The compromise system itself, however, presents two quite distinct varieties, to wit, that of New York by which representation on the county authority is given to each of the towns of which the county is composed; and that of Pennsylvania in which the county authority consists of three commissioners elected by the people of the county as a whole. The first is called the New York or supervisor plan, the second is called the Pennsylvania or commissioner plan. The supervisor plan has the advantage of lessening the danger of local discrimination by the county authority, since each locality

---

[1] See Stimson, *op. cit.*. p. 47, sec. 210 B.

is represented on the county authority; the second or commissioner plan is to be preferred as ensuring a more energetic and efficient administration since there are not so many minds to be made up in the county authority. The supervisor form of the compromise system is to be found in New York, Michigan, Illinois, Wisconsin, Nebraska, and, to a certain extent, in Virginia [1]; the commissioner form of the compromise system is to be found in Pennsylvania, Ohio, Indiana, Iowa, Kansas, and Missouri, and, to a certain extent, in Maine, Massachusetts, Minnesota, and the Dakotas, and has very generally been adopted as the form for the county authority in the commonwealths of the south, where there are in the county generally no lesser districts to be represented.[2] In the compromise system the county authority is then either a board of supervisors, one of whom is elected by the people of each town within the county; or it consists of three commissioners elected sometimes by the people of the county as a whole, sometimes it being necessary that each of the three commissioners shall be elected by one of three election districts into which the county is for this purpose divided. This authority has the general management of the administrative affairs attended to within the limits of the county. In case the commissioner system has been adopted somewhat wider powers appear as a rule to be granted to the county authority.[3] The powers are, however, essentially the same whatever be the method of constituting the authority. They relate to the bridges and roads, the support of the poor and the care of the finances [4];

[1] Howard, I., 439, 453, 465.
[2] *Ibid.*, I., 439.
[3] Howard, I., 442.
[4] *Cf.* Howard, I., 446.

and in many cases include powers which only very indirectly affect the affairs of the county, but are of most interest to the commonwealth as a whole. Thus the county authority has often to publish the laws and election notices for commonwealth elections, acts often as the county board of election canvassers, draws up in some cases the lists of grand jurors, and discharges duties mainly of a financial character in relation to the commonwealth military forces.[1] But the characteristic and most important powers of the county authority are those relating to the county finances. For the expenses of many matters affecting the commonwealth as a whole and not the county, are devolved by law upon the county. Such, for example, are many expenses connected with the administration of justice which, though the courts are recognized now as commonwealth rather than local agencies, are generally borne by the counties. This is in accordance with the old English idea of devolving the expense of almost every administrative service upon the counties or the parishes. We do, however, find certain differences in the different commonwealths in the powers of the county authority relative to the officers acting within the county. While the usual rule would appear to be that the county authority may not be regarded as responsible for the actions of the other officers in the county who are elected by the people of the county, and in some instances, as in New York, may be removed only by the governor and then only for misconduct in office[2]; in one commonwealth at least the administration of affairs in the county is a good deal

---

[1] See Morehouse's *Supervisors' Manual*, 115, 347, 352, 355, 363.
[2] *Supra*, p. 79.

concentrated in the county authority which has quite a disciplinary power over the other officers in the county. This is Nebraska, where the county authority may hear complaints against any county officer and may remove him for official misdemeanors which are defined in the statutes and are, as in New York, simply misconduct in office. It may remove for this cause a county officer whether he has been elected by the people or appointed by the county authority.[1] If the county board refuses to move upon a complaint made to it on the behavior of a county officer it may be forced to take action by the courts.[2] Again there is a difference in the relations of the county authority to the lesser areas of administration, *viz.*, the towns. While the usual rule would seem to be that the county authority has no control over the administration of the towns, in some of the commonwealths which have adopted the New York form of administration the county authority has considerable supervisory power over the administration of the towns. Thus in this form the towns do not possess the taxing power, but all the town taxes are to be voted by the county authority.[3] Up to 1892 the board of supervisors had in New York another power, which gave it considerable control over the town administration. This was the power to refuse its approval of the incurring of certain expenses by the town, without which approval, such expense would not be a valid charge upon the town; or to direct how town business shall

---

[1] Compiled Statutes of Nebraska, 1889, p. 369 ; *cf.* Howard, I., 445.

[2] The State v. Saline Co., 18 Neb., 428.

[3] *E. g.*, New York L. 1892. c. 686, sec. 12 ; L. 1892, c. 569 ; L. 1890, c., 568, sec. 139.

be transacted.[1] This power seems to have been taken away by the laws of 1892.[2]

2. *The town.*—The town organization in the compromise system varies considerably more in the different commonwealths than that of the county. In the New York form there is in the first place a town meeting,[3] which is to decide most matters affecting the interests of the town, always in accordance with the statutes giving the town power and, where the county authority has power of supervision over the actions of the town, subject to the approval of the county authority. This town meeting does not however exist in the pure Pennsylvania form,[4] but does in a very rudimentary form in Minnesota and the Dakotas where it may enact by-laws and elect officers.[5] In the pure Pennsylvania plan the functions of the town are discharged by a corps of officers elected by the people of the town.[6]

In the second place the principal town officers differ considerably. In some of the commonwealths, mostly those which have followed the New York form, an officer called by different names, but similar to the supervisor is elected by the town. He is the general executive of the town as a local corporation, has charge of its property, represents it over against third persons, and has a series of duties to perform in various administrative branches, such as public education and public charity.[7] In some cases, however, such officer is not a member of the county board as in the pure New York

---

[1] *Cf.* Morehouse, *op. cit.*, 303, 344, citing L. 1869, c. 855 ; L. 1886, c. 355.
[2] N. Y. L. 1892, c. 686. Schedule of laws repealed.
[3] See N. Y. L., 1892, c. 569, Article II.
[4] Howard, I., 157.   [6] *Ibid.*, 157.
[5] *Ibid.*, 158.   [7] For New York see L. 1892, c. 569, sec. 80.

plan. This is the case with the town trustee who is elected by the people of the town in Indiana, Missouri, and Kansas, and with the town chairman who is elected in a similar way in Wisconsin.[1] Generally the actions of such officer are controlled by a town board which in other cases is the only real authority.[2] In some cases the supervisor or similar officer performs other duties, such as those of the assessor,[3] or those of the overseer of the poor.[4] In Michigan he is also census enumerator and registrar of births and deaths.[5] The town board to which reference has been made is variously formed, but generally of the supervisor or similar officer and other minor town officers such as the town clerk, and the justices of the peace who thus still retain certain administrative functions, or the assessors.[6] Besides controlling the action of the supervisor or similar officer, or itself conducting the affairs of the town, the town board has to audit all claims against the town and the accounts of town officers.[7] In New York of late years the attempt has been made to form a separate board of town audit though the old method is still followed in a good many of the towns.[8] In some cases this town board may levy taxes as in Michigan and Ohio.[9] There are quite a number of other town officers

---

[1] Howard, I., 168, and authorities cited.

[2] The town board is the real authority in Ohio, Pennsylvania, Iowa, Minnesota, and the Dakotas. *Ibid.*, 168–169.

[3] As in Michigan, *Ibid.*, 170.

[4] As in Nebraska and Michigan, *Ibid.*, 170; Cocker, *Civil Government in Michigan*, 26.

[5] Cocker, *op. cit.*, 26.

[6] Howard, I., 172.

[7] *Ibid.*, 172.

[8] See New York Laws of 1840, c. 305 ; 1860, c. 58 ; 1863, c. 172 ; 1866, c. 832 ; 1875, c. 180, now incorporated in L. 1892, c. 569, secs. 172 *et seq.*

[9] Howard, I., 173.

who attend each to some special branch of administration, such as the town clerk, collector, assessor, overseer of the poor, highway commissioners, and overseers and constables, but these are for the most part officers of the central administration acting within the limits of the town, and cannot be regarded as agents of the town corporation, though they are generally elected by the people of the town.[1] It should be noted that in the compromise system the town is not usually entrusted with the care of the schools, which are attended to by separately organized school districts.[2] Finally, in the compromise system the officers in the town are usually elected by the people of the town; if there is a town meeting, then in the town meeting as in New York,[3] if not, then at a town election, as in Pennsylvania.[4]

II.— *The New England system.*

1. *The county.*—The characteristic of the New England system of local administration is that the county is almost ignored. Almost all important local administrative functions are centred in the town, even where the existence of the county as a district for certain purposes of administration is recognized. In Rhode Island the county is to be found, but only in an extremely rudimentary form. Here the county is simply a district for the purposes of judicial administration, but seems to have no juristic personality. Officers in the county, like the sheriff and the clerks of certain courts, are elected by the general assembly of the commonwealth.[5] In Vermont also, all real local power is centred in the

---

[1] *Cf*, Lorillard v. Town of Monroe, 11 N. Y., 392.

[2] Howard, I., 235; Cocker, *op. cit.*, 92.   [4] *Supra*, p. 171.

[3] See statutes cited above.   [5] Public Statutes, 39 and 74.

town ; the only administrative business which is given
to officers in the county consisting first, of the powers
possessed by the sheriff as conservator of the peace and
as ministerial officer of the courts and of the powers
given to an elected county commissioner to supervise
the execution of the laws prohibiting the sale of liquors,
which are really enforced by the town agents [1] ; second,
of the powers given to the assistant judges of the county
courts to control the financial administration of the
county, appoint the county treasurer, and hear appeals
in highway matters [2]; and third, of the powers given
to a county equalizing convention, composed of delegates appointed by the town listers or assessors from
among their own number, to make quadrennially an
equalization of the assessments of the various towns for
the purposes of taxation. [3] In Vermont there is no
county administrative authority like the board of supervisors or the county commissioners in the compromise
system, but all matters affecting the county, not attended to by the special officers mentioned, especially
those affecting the financial administration of the
county, are attended to by the assistant judges of the
county court.

In Connecticut the general assembly of the commonwealth appoints periodically three commissioners in
each county, who have the care of the county property
and the oversight of the county jail, supervise the county
workhouses and levy taxes within certain limits for the
repair of the court house and the jail. The fiscal
administration of the county, so far as there is any, is
attended to by a joint assembly of the senators and
representatives for the county in the commonwealth

---

[1] Revised Laws, 732, 733.   [2] *Ibid.*, 517, 573.   [3] *Ibid.*, 124, 125.

legislature, who are to meet biennially at the capital of the commonwealth, make appropriations for county expenditure, estimate and apportion the county taxes, and examine the accounts of the county officers. The county treasurer is appointed by the commissioners, the coroner by the supreme court, but the sheriffs are elected by the people of the county.[1]

In New Hampshire there are three commissioners elected by the people of the county, who have, however, little independent power, and are subject to the control of a county convention composed of the representatives to the legislature of the towns of the county. This convention meets biennially, when it may levy taxes, may authorize the commissioners to issue bonds and to repair the county buildings, such authorization being necessary whenever the amount of the repairs exceeds $1,000. The commissioners are to attend to the care of the county paupers and county property, and may lay out highways and establish houses of correction; and, when authorized so to do, purchase and convey real estate. Besides the commissioners, the people of the county elect every two years a sheriff, treasurer, solicitor, a registrar of deeds, and a registrar of probate.[2]

It will be seen from this slight sketch of the county organization in the New England commonwealths that the New England county is in the process of becoming of some importance in administrative matters. It has already in several instances become a body corporate, but as yet it has not succeeded in obtaining a county

---

[1] General Statutes 1888, 429–32, 434, 740, 748.

[2] General Laws 1878, 80–94. On the general subject of the county administration in New England see Howard, *op. cit.*, I., 459, 464.

authority of any great independence, which is separated from the other departments of the commonwealth government. Thus in Connecticut and New Hampshire, it is under the control of the representatives of the towns in the county to the legislature, while in Vermont the most important administrative functions in the county are discharged by the assistant judges of the ordinary county court. In so far as a county authority has been developed, as *e. g.* the commissioners, who are found in Connecticut and New Hampshire, and it may be added in Massachusetts, where they have larger powers than in any other of the New England commonwealths, the Pennsylvania rather than the New York form is the model that is being copied. The rule as to the filling of the other offices in the county is not at all uniform, in some cases the people of the county electing such officers, in others some other authority having the right to appoint them.

2. *The New England town.*—What the New England county loses in importance the town gains. In the New England towns are centred most of the administrative functions discharged in the localities. In all the towns we find the town meeting similar to the New York town meeting, but generally possessed of greater powers. Thus the town meeting may not only pass by-laws but may also levy taxes, makes all necessary appropriations and decides all town matters, such as the making of contracts[1]; and its action is not subject to the control of any county authority. The town officers are, however, differently organized in New England. The chief officers are still the selectmen.[2]

---

[1] See Bloomfield v. Charter Oak Bank, 121 U. S., 121 ; *cf.* for duties and powers of towns, Dillon, *op. cit.*, I., 47, note.

[2] Howard, *op. cit.*, I., 227.

In Rhode Island, however, the town authority is to be found in a council of from three to seven members elected by the town meeting.[1] This body resembles somewhat the town board, which is to be found in some of the western commonwealths, and by which, it will be remembered, most of the business of the town is to be discharged. Often in New England the select-men, who, like the town council of Rhode Island, are elected by the town meeting, have the right to appoint some of the other town officers, though the rule would seem to be that they also are elected by the town meeting. Everywhere the selectmen have the right to fill vacancies in town offices. The selectmen also dis-charge many functions which, in the New York form, are attended to by separate officers. Thus in Massa-chusetts the selectmen act as overseers of the poor while the constable very generally acts as collector of taxes.[2] In New England generally the town is the school district, though there are separate officers to attend to the school administration.[3]

III.—*The southern system.*

The third type of local administration in the United States is to be found in the southern commonwealths. The main characteristics of this system is that nearly all administrative business, not absolutely municipal in character for which the municipal corporation has been formed, and not affecting education, for which the school district has been formed,[4] is centred in the

---

[1] *Ibid. ;* see also Public Statutes 1882, pp. 109–119.

[2] Howard, I., 227.

[3] *Ibid.*, 235.

[4] As, *e. g.*, in Virginia, Kentucky, Texas, and Tennessee. Howard, *op. cit.*, I., 237.

county and its officers.   In some of the commonwealths, however, even school matters are attended to
by county officers.[1] In Alabama the district for the
purpose of school administration is called the township.[2] It is believed that the introduction of the
school district is causing a disintegration of the county
and the establishment of a smaller local area.[3]

The county authority in the south presents quite a
variety in the forms of its organization.   But it may
safely be said that the tendency has been to adopt the
principle of popular election for not only the county
authority but for most of the officers in the county.[4]
North Carolina and Tennessee seem to be the farthest
behind in this respect.   Here the justices of the peace
appointed by the general assembly of the commonwealth have large administrative powers, and the
sheriff, who is, it is true, elected by the people of the
county, has still very many of the fiscal powers of the
old Norman sheriff.   Thus he is still the collector of
taxes and may be the treasurer of the county.[5]   It
may be further said of the southern system that the
Pennsylvania or commissioner form is the one generally adopted.[6]   That is, the county authority usually
consists of three commissioners elected by the people
of the county.   There are, however, exceptions to this
rule.   Thus the New York form of the county authority has been adopted in Virginia.   There we find
a board of supervisors, each member of which is

---

[1] *E. g.*, South and North Carolina and Georgia, *Ibid.*

[2] *Ibid.*, citing Code of Alabama, 1886, I., **221, 222.**

[3] Howard, I., 237.

[4] *Ibid.*, 468.

[5] *Ibid.*, 469, 470, citing Code of North Carolina, 1883, pp. **287, 312.**

[6] Howard, I., 468.

elected in one of the magisterial districts into which the county is divided. The attempt of northern men under the leadership of a New York man to introduce the New York town failed. The magisterial district established in 1874 has taken the place of the town which existed only for a few years. In this district a supervisor, constable, and overseer of the poor are elected by the people. There is, however, nothing like the town meeting.[1] Further the board of supervisors is not as independent as in New York, appeals going in many cases from its decisions to the county court, not only in points of law, but also on points of fact and questions of expediency. Powers in highway matters also are about equally divided between the board of supervisors and the county court. Assessments for the purposes of taxation are made by another popular authority, *viz.*, the commissioners of revenue, elected by popular vote.[2] The matter of education is under the control of the central government of the commonwealth, and quite a number of officers in the local administrative system are appointed either by the central government of the commonwealth or by the county court. This latter body has quite a wide range of administrative powers, among which are the powers to revise assessments, to determine election contests, *etc.*, *etc.*, and finally the most extraordinary power of removing county officers.[3] Another exception to the rule that the county authority in the south is a board of three commissioners is to be found in Georgia, where the ordinary, an officer who corresponds to the surrogate of the middle states, or the

[1] *Ibid.*, 231.   [2] *Ibid.*, 465–7, citing Code of Virginia, 1887.
[3] Howard, I., 466, 467.

probate judge of New England, and who is elected by the people of the county, is the most important county officer. In important matters he must act with the grand jury. The justices of the peace in Georgia also still have important duties to perform.[1]

In some of the southern commonwealths there is an area lower than the county which is sometimes called the town.[2] But it is not generally a corporation but simply an administrative district of the county, in which there is no town meeting. In it are elected by the people certain officers like commissioners of high-ways and constables, though generally such officers are appointed for such district by the county authority.

[1] Const., art. v., sec. 5, p. 2 ; Code, 1882, part I., title vi., chap. ii. ; title v., chap. viii.

[2] See *supra*, p. 190, in relation to Alabama.

CHAPTER III.

MUNICIPAL ORGANIZATION IN THE UNITED STATES.

I.—History of the English municipality to the seventeenth and eighteenth centuries.[1]

1. *Origin of the borough.*—According to the English method of permitting the localities to participate in the work of administration the more thickly populated districts have always had a somewhat peculiar organization. The origin of this peculiar organization is to be found in the grant to districts with a greater than average population of a series of privileges for the exercise of which there was gradually formed a series of authorities differing in many respects from the authorities in the rural districts. These privileges were known as the *firma burgi* and the court leet.

The *firma burgi* was the lease of the town by the Crown to the inhabitants. From the very beginning of the Norman period the inhabitants of the towns, as well as of the rural districts, owed certain payments or services to the Crown. As a rule these payments were to be collected by the sheriff, as the fiscal representative of the Crown in the localities. In order to permit of the more easy collection of such payments, the Crown made contracts with the inhabitants of the town, in accordance with which they paid it a fixed sum, which they were permitted to raise among themselves

[1] See Gneist, *Selfgovernment, etc.*, 580–592.

in such manner as they saw fit. For the collection of this town *quota* there was provided an officer called the fermor or provost or mayor, who was to be selected as a rule by the inhabitants of the town, their selection being subject to the approval of the Norman exchequer, and who was to act under its supervision.

The court leet was a privilege granted to the inhabitants of special districts or to the lord of a given manor to hold a special police and judicial court when the inhabitants of the district were exempted from the jurisdiction of the ordinary court, to wit, the sheriff's tourn. This privilege was granted by the Crown generally, in the case of the towns, in return for a sum of money. Like the *firma burgi,* it soon came to be regarded as a right. The union of these two privileges constituted a municipal borough. The townsmen, meeting in court leet, found it a natural and easy matter to assume such other functions as were necessitated by the presence of a large number of persons in a small district. They established rules as to participation in the court leet and as to the election of the mayor or provost. The general rule was that no one should participate in the court leet who did not pay taxes, was not a householder, and was not in the eyes of the law capable of participating in the administration of justice. In the quaint language of the period, only those could be members of the court leet who were freemen householders, paying scot and bearing lot; and the formal criterion of the existence of these qualities in a given person was the fact that he had been sworn and enrolled in the court leet. This body had thus the ultimate decision as to the qualifications of municipal citizenship.

2. *Development of the municipal council.*—This originally simple and equitable organization was later completely changed through the acquisition by a large
number of the boroughs of the right of representation
in Parliament, which was formed in the time of Edward
I (1295). The amount of the *quota* of the town was
after the formation of Parliament fixed by that body,
so that all that remained to be done by the town in
the financial administration was to assess the *quota*
assigned to it by Parliament. This business could be
transacted better by a small committee of the townsmen than by the entire court leet or municipal assembly. At the same time that this influence was at work
the whole judicial system was being completely changed
by the introduction of judges learned in the law, by the
formation of royal courts, and by the establishment of
the office of justice of the peace, which was introduced
into the urban as well as the rural districts. Through
the formation of these authorities the court leet lost
almost all its judicial functions, and was reduced to the
position of a jury for the determination of the questions
of fact rather than of law. This business could also
be more easily attended to by a committee than by the
entire court leet. The result was the formation of a
committee of the original court leet or assembly of the
municipal citizens for the transaction of both financial
and judicial business. This committee gradually assumed the performance of all municipal business which
had sprung up, such as the management of the property of the municipality, and finally was composed of
the larger tax-payers—the most important men of the
town, who often at the same time were granted by the
Crown a commission of the peace, as a result of which

they became justices of the peace with the usual powers. In the larger boroughs they had not only the commission of the peace but also the right to hold a court of quarter sessions for the city with the usual powers. The larger tax-payers got these extensive powers simply as a result of the fact that the smaller tax-payers did not avail themselves of their privileges. The old basis of municipal rights, *i. e.*, the paying scot and bearing lot was undermined, and was replaced by different principles, varying in accordance with the social and economical conditions of the various boroughs. In those boroughs or cities which, like London, had great commercial and manufacturing interests membership in one of the guilds or mercantile companies became the basis of the right to discharge municipal functions. Thus was formed the town council or leet jury or capital burgesses, as the new municipal authority composed of the important men of the town was called, which, whatever the name that was given to it, was generally renewed by co-optation. The result was that in the fifteenth century in the towns as well as in the open country the government was administered by the gentry, the gentry in the towns being composed of the persons who had become rich in commerce and trade.

3. *Period of incorporation.*—Soon after this definite form of municipal organization was reached, in accordance with which the town was controlled by a council of rich men chosen by co-optation, the period of municipal charters begins and the charters incorporated not the inhabitants of the town, but the council which controlled the affairs of the town. The only purpose of these charters was to give to these districts the right to hold property and to sue and be sued.   They had

no special political significance, they did not grant any new governmental powers to the town authorities. The desire of the Crown to control, through the representation in Parliament granted to the municipal boroughs, the composition of Parliament led the Crown to make most improvident grants of municipal charters carrying with them parliamentary representation, with the result that the municipal population had for a long time more than its fair share of representation in Parliament. As the grant of such charters would not have served the purpose of the king if he were not able to control the municipal elections, the king strove so far as he could to put all municipal powers into a few hands. The courts, therefore, which were dependent upon the Crown, held that any custom which provided for the control of the municipal administration by the narrow town council was in accordance with public policy and valid.[1] Further, in the early part of the reigns of the Stuarts the *quo warranto* was issued in many cases (81) to municipal corporations in order to forfeit their charters for irregularities and illegal actions, and on the adverse decision of the courts, new and less liberal charters were granted. Many corporations, alarmed at the action of the Crown and the courts, surrendered their charters and received new charters of a much less liberal character. All this was done to enable the Crown to control the action of the boroughs in their election of members of Parliament.[2] The result was that the municipal organization was so formed

[1] See the case of corporations decided in the time of Elizabeth, Dillon, *op. cit.*, I., 18 ; and Ireland v. Free Borough, 12, Co., 120.

[2] See Dillon, *op. cit.*, I., 18 ; Allinson and Penrose, *Philadelphia*, 10 ; Rex v. London, 8 How. St. Tr., 1039, 1340.

and its powers so prostituted as almost entirely to destroy its usefulness for administrative purposes. When, after the revolution of 1688, the nobles and gentry got the control of the government the case was the same, the only difference being that the nobles instead of the Crown made use of the municipal organization in order to control the composition of Parliament. Not only was the condition of the municipalities an extremely bad one, but all hopes of reform were vain so long as either the Crown or the nobles controlled the government. For the composition of Parliament was too valuable a power to be given up voluntarily by its holders.

So long as the municipal organization was so defective, it was useless to expect that the new functions of municipal administration, the adoption of which was necessitated by the increase of population in the cities, would be put into the hands of notoriously corrupt and unrepresentative municipal authorities. When the parish administration grew up in the time of the Tudors it was therefore extended into the cities as well as into the rural districts. In this way the poor-law was administered not by the borough council but by the parish authorities which acted under the continual supervision of the justices of the peace. As it became necessary to make some provision for the lighting and paving of the streets, the course adopted for the satisfaction of these needs was the same. Either these matters were entrusted to the parishes or special trusts or commissions were formed for their care by local and special legislation in particular cities, and the inhabitants were forced to contribute to the expenses of these branches.[1]

---

[1] Gneist, *Selfgovernment, etc.*, 595.

Such was the condition of the English municipality at the time that America was colonized. The strictly municipal affairs, which were mainly such matters as the care of the city property, the issue of local police ordinances and a certain power in the administration of justice,[1] were attended to by the municipal council or by its members in their capacity as justices of the peace ; and this council was chosen generally by co-optation. This body did not attend to all matters affecting the welfare of the city since many of these were entrusted to the parishes and other special authorities and had almost no functions to discharge which related to the general administration of the country. The form of the municipal council was the same as it had been during the middle ages. It was composed generally of the mayor, recorder, aldermen, and councilmen.

II.—*History of the American municipality.*

1. *The original American municipality.*—Just as the English system of rural local government was made the model on which the original system of American rural local administration was formed, so the form of the municipal administration, as it existed in England in the seventeenth century, was made the model of the original system of American municipal administration.

In the first place a special organization was provided from the beginning for most of the cities in the colonies. Only one city, to wit, Boston, was ever governed in the same way as the rural towns.[2] New York and Philadelphia have, from the beginning

---

[1] On account of the fact that in most cases a special commission of the peace was issued to the cities.

[2] *Johns Hopkins University Studies in Historical and Political Science*, V., 79.

of their history as English possessions, had charters or
forms of organization which differed considerably from
the organization of the surrounding rural districts.
The original form granted by these charters also re-
sembled very closely the English municipal organization
of the same period.[1] The city authority was the town
council, composed of the mayor, recorder, aldermen,
and assistants or councilmen. In this body was
centred the entire municipal business. The administrative powers were not, however, so large as
they are now. Like the English municipal corporation, the original American municipal corporation
was mainly an organization for the satisfaction of
purely local needs, *i. e.* for the management of the
local property and finances and the issue of local
police ordinances. Certain of the officers of the
corporation, however, discharged a series of judicial
and police functions as was the case in the English
municipality. Thus in both New York and Philadelphia, the mayor, recorder, and aldermen were the
municipal justices of the peace and judges.[2] The affairs of the general administration of the colony were
attended to in the municipality by officers similar to
the regular officers in the counties and rural districts.[3]

[1] For New York, see the Dongan Charter of 1686 and the Montgomerie
Charter of 1730, to be found in Kent's *Commentary on the City Charter* and Ash,
Consolidated Act; for Philadelphia, see Penn's Charter, J. H. U. S., V., 15.

[2] For New York, Charter of 1730, secs. 23, 26, 27, and 31. All the present
local courts in New York City with the exception, of course, of the supreme
court, are simply outgrowths of the original judicial powers of the mayor,
recorder, and aldermen. The recorder has also become an almost exclusively
judicial officer. For Philadelphia, J. H. U. S., V., 19 and 29.

[3] *E. g.*, for the administration of the poor-law there were the regular overseers
of the poor elected in the wards of the city and the expenses of this branch of
administration were defrayed by the church parishes. See Black, " The History
of the Municipal Ownership of Land on Manhattan Island," in *Studies in History*,
etc., edited by the University Faculty of Political Science of Columbia College.

One of the results of this purely local character of the American municipality was that the town council had no power to tax in order to provide for the expenses of the local services. It was not regarded as a sufficiently governmental authority to be endowed with this attribute of sovereignty.[1] A New York law of 1787 (chapter 62) provided that the mayor, recorder, and aldermen, as the board of supervisors of the county of New York, were to levy the taxes demanded by the central government of the commonwealth of the inhabitants of the city as inhabitants of the commonwealth, the principle of the *firma burgi* having long ago been forgotten. The city council in New York, with the exception of the mayor and recorder, who were appointed by the governor and council, were by the charter to be elected by the freemen of the city, being inhabitants and the freeholders of each of the wards into which the city for the purposes of administration was divided. The freedom of the city was given by the mayor and four or more aldermen in common council, generally in return for the payment of money ; and, besides giving in the proper cases the right to vote, was the only authorization to pursue certain trades within the confines of the city.[2] In Philadelphia the council was, as was so common in England at the time, elected by co-optation.[3] Finally the city corporation was, as in England, regarded as consisting of the city officers, *i. e.* the council, or the council and the freemen.[4]

I., 182 ; also J. H. U. S., V., 27. For the collection of the central colonial tax the New York Charter provided for the election of assessors similar to the town assessors. See Charter of 1730, sec. 3.

[1] See Black, *op. cit.*, 181 ; J. H. U. S., V., 22.

[2] See Kent's Charter, note 35.   [3] See Allinson and Penrose, *op. cit.*, 9.

[4] So in Philadelphia. See Allinson and Penrose, *loc. cit.*

Such was the original position and organization of the American municipality.   Since the beginning of its history the American municipality has
developed in two directions.   In the first place
the position of the municipality and the duties to
be attended to by its officers have greatly changed.

2. *Change in the position of the municipality.*—The
legislature of the commonwealth has, to a large extent,
lost sight of the original purpose of the municipality
and has come to regard it as an organ of the central
government for the purposes of the general commonwealth administration, making little distinction between
central and municipal matters, and exercising over it
much the same control which it exercises over counties
and towns.   Some of the cases in the courts claim for
the legislature practically the same powers over the
city and its property as the legislature possesses over
the counties and towns which, as has been shown, are
regarded as mere administrative districts for the purposes of general commonwealth administration.[1]   Practically the only point where it is generally recognized
that the legislative control over municipalities is not so
great as over the *quasi* municipal corporations, such as
counties and towns, is in the case of the private property
of the municipality, of which, it has sometimes been
held, the legislature may not deprive the municipality
as it may deprive it of its public property.[2]   One
result of the more public character which is assigned
to the municipalities by the American law and development is that the corporation is no longer regarded as

[1] See Darlington v. New York, 31 N. Y., 164 ; U. S. v. B. & O. R. R. Co.,
17 Wallace, 322.

[2] Dillon, *op. cit.*, I., 110 *et seq.*, and cases cited.

consisting of the officers, but consists of all the people residing within the municipal district, while municipal suffrage is in most cases the same as commonwealth suffrage.[1] Further, the commonwealth makes use very frequently of the municipality or its officers as agents for the purposes of commonwealth administration. Thus in financial matters, the city, when of large size, is often made the agent of the commonwealth administration for the assessment and collection of taxes; indeed the city itself is often practically the tax-payer of certain of the commonwealth taxes, *e. g.*, the general property tax,[2] which it is then to collect of the owners of property. Further in many cases, where the city has not been made directly the agent of the central commonwealth administration, in that it itself through its officers is to attend to certain matters of general interest, the expense of a long series of matters is often devolved upon the city. This is particularly true of the matter of education.[3] The board of education, which has control of the educational administration within the limits of the city, and which is usually regarded as a separate *quasi* municipal corporation, is usually elected by the people residing within the district. In some cases, however, this body is appointed by the municipal authorities, as *e. g.* in New York and Brooklyn[4]; in others it is appointed by the legislature, as in Baltimore.[5] Finally municipal officers are often made use of for the purposes of general com-

---

[1] *Ibid.*, 70.

[2] It is to be noted, however, that the city has very generally been granted the local taxing power. *Ibid.*, 69. It is no longer compelled to defray its municipal expenses from the revenue of its property.

[3] *Cf.* Bryce, *American Commonwealth*, I., 599.

[4] N. Y. L. 1882, c. 410, sec. 1022; N. Y. L. 1888, ch. 5, title xvii., sec. 1.

[5] Bryce, *op. cit.*, I., 596, 599.

monwealth administration. Thus in most of the large
cities municipal officers, either elected by the people of
the city or appointed by the municipal authorities, are
entrusted with the care of the public health and the
support of the poor, attend to election matters, and have
a series of duties to perform relative to the administration of judicial affairs, such as the making up of the
jury lists.

In certain cases duties, which were in old times entrusted to the municipalities or their officers, have been
assumed by the central commonwealth administration.
Thus the preservation of the peace has in several of the
large cities been put into the hands of a commission
appointed by the central government of the commonwealth.[1] Further the courts of several of the commonwealths have held that the preservation of the peace is
not a municipal function.[2]

What is true in exceptional cases of the preservation
of the peace is almost universally true of the administration of justice, which is no longer regarded as a
matter of local concern, but as a matter which should
be attended to in accordance with a uniform system
throughout the commonwealth. The courts which act
at the present time in the various municipalities are
not municipal but commonwealth courts. Their expenses may, it is true, be paid in large part by the

---

[1] This is so in Boston, where the care of the police is given to a board of
police, appointed by the governor and council of the commonwealth. Mass.
L. of 1885, c. 323. In Nebraska the boards of police and fire commissioners
in cities of over 80,000 inhabitants are appointed by the governor. Compiled
Statutes 1889, pp. 147,148. See for St. Louis, J. H. U. S., VII., 186. In Baltimore the board of police is appointed by the legislature of the commonwealth.
See Allinson and Penrose, *Philadelphia*, 329.

[2] People v. Draper, 15 N. Y., 532 ; Baltimore v. Board of Police, 15. Md.,
376. ; People v. Mahaney, 13 Mich., 481. ; *cf.* Dillon, *op. cit.*, I., 102.

municipalities in which they act, but the judges and their subordinate officers are not regarded as municipal officers.[1] An exception to this rule may be found in the case of the local tribunals called by different names, such as the mayor's court, the recorder's court, and the like.[2] These may be regarded as municipal courts when the judges who form them are elected by municipal electors or appointed by the municipal authorities, and when they have jurisdiction over municipal ordinances only. In some cities the aldermen still discharge judicial functions.

Further, the cities themselves have largely lost the power of regulating their own purely municipal affairs. For the central government of the commonwealth has decided, in many instances, to exercise its undoubted legal right to regulate even purely local affairs. Further, while at one time city charters were seldom changed or amended by the legislature without the consent of the city authorities or that of the people within the city, at the present time changes are made therein continually without even asking the opinion of the city. Many bills affecting the welfare of the cities are rushed through the legislature on the suggestion of the local member, who does not in all cases represent the desires or the true interests of the city. The American idea at the present time seems to be that the city does not any more than the county have the right to regulate its own local affairs; that the

---

[1] Dillon, *op. cit.*, I., 99, and cases cited. The action of the Civil-Service Commission in New York in classifying the officers in the courts as commonwealth rather than municipal officers shows what is the general opinion as to the character of the function of administering justice.—*Sixth Report of the New York Civil-Service Commission*, 448.

[2] Dillon, *op. cit.*, I., 492.

municipal authorities are largely the agents of the
central commonwealth government, indeed that the
city itself is simply an administrative district possessing, it is true, corporate powers, but possessing no
sphere of action of its own in which it should
decide for itself what it shall do and what it shall not
do.[1] Few are the constitutional provisions which protect a city against the interference of the commonwealth legislature; and the legislatures of some of the
commonwealths are too prone to take advantage of the
unprotected position of the municipalities to interfere
in matters which might be much better regulated by
the municipalities themselves. The true sphere of the
municipality as an organ for the satisfaction of local
needs in accordance with the wishes of the inhabitants[2]
is being in many cases overlooked, and the city is
coming to be regarded, very much as the county, as
simply an agency of the central commonwealth government.

3. *Change in the organization of the municipality.*—
In the second place the old plan of consolidating all
the administrative functions of the city corporation in
the town council has been abandoned. There has
very generally been made a clear distinction between
the function of deliberation and the function of execution, the former being possessed by the council from

[1] See the case of U. S. v. The Baltimore and Ohio R.R. Co., 17 Wallace,
322, where the court says : " A municipal corporation . . . is a representative
not only of the state, but is a portion of its governmental power. It is one of
its creatures made for a specific purpose, to exercise within a limited sphere the
powers of the state. The state may govern . . . the local territory as it governs
the state at large. It may enlarge or contract its powers or destroy its existence."

[2] Dillon, *op. cit.,* I., 38.

which the mayor has been excluded, the latter being granted to the mayor and the various executive depart-ments which have in the course of time been estab-lished.[1] This separation of the function of deliberation from that of execution was made in Philadelphia in 1789[2] and in New York in 1830.[3] The first charter of Boston, granted in 1822, however, permitted the mayor to be a member of the council.[4] Since 1830 most city charters have provided for this separation of the deliberative and executive functions.[5]

III.—The present organization of the American municipality.

1. *The mayor and the executive departments.*—When the mayor was first excluded from the council he was to be elected by the council.[6] In Philadelphia the mayor was elected by the council as late as 1839,[7] but in Boston by the very first charter the mayor was elected by the people of the city.[8] This seems to be the rule at the present time.[9] His term of office

---

[1] The recorder, it is to be noted, has become an almost exclusively judicial officer, though in some cases his functions show traces of his original position as a member of the council ; *e. g.*, in the city of New York at the present time the recorder is a member of the sinking-fund commission, the reason being that he was a member of that commission before his position as a judicial officer had been determined. See Consolidation Act of 1882, c. 410, sec. 170.

[2] J. H. U. S., V., 34.

[3] L. 1830, c. 122, sec. 15.

[4] J. H. U. S., V., 96.

[5] See outline of the ordinary municipal charter in the United States given in Dillon, *op. cit.*, I., 68. In Chicago and San Francisco, however, the mayor at the present time sits in the council. Bryce, *American Commonwealth*, I., 595, note 5 ; Dillon says, *op. cit.*, I., 291, that "the mayor is frequently declared to be a member of the council."

[6] *E. g.*, see N. Y. Const. of 1821, art. 4, sec. 10.

[7] J. H. U. S., V., 34.

[8] *Ibid.*, 96.

[9] In New York this was provided in 1834 ; L. 1834, c. 23 ; in Philadelphia in 1839, J. H. U. S., V., 35 ; *cf.* Dillon, *op. cit.*, I., 69 ; Bryce, *op. cit.*, I., 594.

varies from one year in Boston to four years in Philadelphia.[1]

The ordinary charter provides that the mayor shall
be the chief executive of the city. But this really
means nothing more than the same phrase with reference to the President or the governor. That is, few if
any powers are to be assumed as existing in the mayor
as the result of the existence of such a provision in the
charter. The only power which can be derived from
it is that the mayor is to execute the laws within the
city, which in its turn really means little more than
that he is to "provide for the public peace, quell riots,
and if necessary call out the militia,"[2] though this duty
is primarily that of the sheriff as the chief conservator
of the peace of the county.

While originally, and even after the grant to the
mayor of the executive functions in the city government, the mayor had little power of appointing the
various city officers, the whole tendency of American
municipal development has been to increase this power
of appointment. Originally there were no city executive departments such as are now to be found in
such numbers in all large American cities, but the administrative matters of the cities were attended to in
their details by committees of the council, which itself had the appointment of most of the subordinate
officers, and could arrange and distribute the municipal
business as it saw fit. Later the council formed, often
by ordinance, separate executive departments. Thus,
in New York, the charter of 1830 provided that the
executive business should be attended to by depart-

---

[1] J. H. U. S., V., 117 ; Pa. Law, June 1st, 1885, art. 1, sec. 1.
[2] Bryce, *op. cit.*, I., 595.

ments which were to be organized, and whose heads were to be appointed by the common council.[1] The same power was possessed by the council of Philadelphia, and that of Boston.[2] But soon after the council lost the power of electing the mayor, it lost also in many cases the power of organizing the city executive departments and of designating their heads.[3]

Where the organizing power has been lost, it has been lost through the fact that many departments have been organized by statutes of the legislature. For the general rule of law is that what has been fixed by statute cannot be changed by ordinance.[4] In certain cases it would seem that the council still possesses the organizing power.[5] The taking away from the council of the power of designating the heads of the executive departments seems to have been a result of the movement which resulted so generally in the election of the mayor by the people of the city and of the heads of the commonwealth executive departments by the people of the commonwealth. This spirit of democratic government which was so strong at the middle of the century resulted also in the election of most of the heads of executive departments in the

[1] See also the Corporation Ordinances, revised 1845.

[2] J. H. U. S., V., 36 and 97.

[3] See, *e. g.*, N. Y. L., 1849, c. 187, sec. 20.

[4] *Cf.* Kearney v. Andrews, 2 Stockton, N. J., 70 ; White v. Tallman, 2 Dutch, N. J. 67.

[5] Thus in Boston, to a certain extent, J. H. U. S., V., 116 *et seq.;* St. Louis, *Ibid.*, 154 ; New Orleans, *Ibid.*, VII., 173. In New York the board of aldermen have still the power to make by ordinance, regulations other than those specially authorized by law "for fuller organization, perfecting, and carrying out the powers and duties prescribed to any department." Consolidated Act of 1882, c. 410, sec. 85. By common law finally the council has the right to create offices as incidental to its express powers. See Dillon, *op. cit.*, I., 290, and cases cited.

14

municipalities by the people of the municipality. This was the case in New York in 1846, and for quite a time thereafter, and is to a certain extent the case at the present time in the cities of Boston,[1] of St. Louis,[2] and of New Orleans.[3]   Lately, however, there has been a reaction against this tendency.   It has been believed of late that the mayor's powers should be increased, and that he should be in reality as well as in name the chief executive officer in the city government, and should have a large power of determining who shall be his subordinates.   Therefore almost all the later charters have granted to the mayor a very large power of appointment.   The only general exception to this rule that the heads of departments are appointed by the mayor is to be found in the case of the officer who has charge of the municipal finances, who is almost universally elected even now by the people of the city. This officer is called the comptroller or treasurer.[4]   A further exception to the rule that the mayor appoints the heads of departments is often to be found in the case of the head of the department of public works, and in some instances in the case of the heads of other departments.[5]   But though the tendency of the later charters is, as said, towards increasing the power of appointment of the mayor, still there are many city

[1] J. H. U. S., V., 116 *et seq.*

[2] *Ibid.*, 106, 171.

[3] *Ibid.*, VII., 173.

[4] For New York see L. 1884, c. 73 ; Philadelphia and St. Louis, J. H. U. S., V., 68, 171 ; New Orleans, *Ibid.*, VII., 173 ; Brooklyn and Chicago, Allinson and Penrose, *Philadelphia*, 298, 331.   This is not, however, the case in Boston and Baltimore, where the mayor appoints the treasurer or comptroller. *Ibid.*, 329 ; J. H. U. S., V., 114, 123.

[5] This is especially true of Boston, St. Louis, and New Orleans, J. H. U. S., V., 118 *et seq. ;* 170 *et seq. ;* VII., 173.

charters which provide for the election by the people
of the city of the heads of the executive departments.
Where the mayor possesses the power of appointing
the heads of executive departments, the general rule
is that his appointments, to be valid, must receive
the approval of the whole city council or one of its
branches. Here, however, again the tendency of the
later charters is to throw the entire responsibility for
filling the office of head of executive department upon
the mayor, who is not obliged to get his appointment
confirmed by the city council. This is true in New
York, Brooklyn, and Philadelphia.[1]

This increase in the power of appointment of the
mayor has in some cases been accompanied by the
grant to him of the power of removal. Of the larger
cities Philadelphia and Boston give to the mayor
absolute power of removing officers whom he appoints[2];
but in most of the cities the removal of an officer is
conditioned upon obtaining the consent of the common
council or a branch thereof.[3] A peculiar rule has been
adopted in New York and Brooklyn. In New York
the mayor may remove the heads of the executive
departments, but only for cause, and subject to the
confirmation of the governor of the commonwealth.[4] In
Brooklyn the heads of departments are removed for
cause by the courts on the application of the mayor.[5]
It should be noticed, however, that in many cases

---

[1] N. Y. L. 1884, c. 43; N. Y. L. 1888, c. 583; Allinson and Penrose, *op. cit.*, 298, 329, 331. For Boston and St. Louis which require the confirmation of the council or a branch thereof, see J. H. U. S., V., 120 *et seq.*

[2] Pa. Law, June 1, 1885, art. 1, sec. 1; J. H. U. S., V., 117.

[3] St. Louis, where the same rule applies to the elected officers also, J. H. U. S., V., 156; Chicago, Allinson and Penrose, *op. cit.*, 331.

[4] N. Y. L. 1882, c. 410, sec. 108.

[5] N. Y. L. 1888, c. 583.

the terms of the heads of departments are not the same as that of the mayor, so that if he does not possess the power of removal, he may not, on coming into office, fill these positions as he may wish.[1] The charter of Brooklyn, however, recognizes that the coincidence of the terms of the heads of executive departments with that of the mayor is an important means of securing administrative harmony and efficiency.[2] As a general thing the city charters do not recognize in the mayor any power to direct the actions of the heads of departments, but where he possesses the absolute power of removal he must perforce practically possess such a power. As this power of removal is very slight in most cases, it cannot be said that the mayor possesses any large powers of directing the heads of departments how they shall perform their duties. Generally, however, the later charters do provide that the mayor may call on the heads of departments for reports as to the workings of their departments, and in several instances give the mayor the right to examine their accounts.[3]

In addition to these powers over the *personnel* of the city official service, the mayor often has powers relating to the several administrative services of a material rather than a personal character. Thus the mayor has, as a usual thing, the power to veto all the ordinances of the common council and in the case of ordinances making appropriations to veto the specific items which seem to him improper. This veto may be

---

[1] *E. g.* see St. Louis, Boston, J. H. U. S., V., 121–3, 156 ; New York, N. Y. L. 1882, c. 410, secs. 34–45.

[2] N. Y. L. 1888, c. 583 ; *cf.* Allinson and Penrose, *op. cit.*, 289.

[3] Phila., Pa., L. June 1, 1885, art. 1 ; N. Y. L. 1882, c. 410, secs. 110, 164.

overridden by a two-thirds vote of the council.[1] Finally
in many cases the mayor is an *ex-officio* member of
certain special boards which have been established to
attend to certain matters affecting the city welfare.[2]

2. *The municipal council.*—The same lack of confidence in the council which has led to its disintegration and to the establishment of the mayor separate
and apart from it with an increasingly greater number
of powers over the executive official service of the city,
has led in certain instances to a great decrease in the
powers, regarded as distinctively deliberative in character, which, at the time of the attempted separation
of the executive and deliberative functions, were reserved to the council. By the original charters and by
the common law it was recognized that the city council,
as the representative of the city corporation had a wide
power of police ordinance.[3] This formerly wide-reaching ordinance power has been curtailed quite generally
either by the fact that the legislature has itself fixed
in detail the sanitary or other police regulations which
shall be observed by the inhabitants of the city,[4] or
has granted the ordinance power to the heads of the
various executive departments of the city administration.[5]

Further the attempt has been made in some of the

[1] So in Boston, J. H. U. S., V., 117 ; St. Louis, *Ibid.*, 157 ; Philadelphia,
Pa., Law, June 1, 1885 ; *cf.* Bryce, *op. cit.*, I., 595.

[2] See, *e. g.*, Philadelphia, Pa., Law, June 1, 1885, art. 1.

[3] See as to Boston, J. H. U. S., V., 119 ; as to Philadelphia and the Pennsylvania corporations, Wartman v. City, 33 Pa. St., 202, 209 ; Dillon, *op. cit.*,
I., 392.

[4] *E. g.* see the case of New York City L. 1882, c. 410, secs. 86, 310, 330,
393, 440 *et passim*.

[5] *E. g.* take the cases of Boston, J. H. U. S., V., 121, 122, and St. Louis,
Ibid., 167.

larger cities of the commonwealth of New York to curtail very largely the power of the council over the finances of the city. While the original city corporation did not possess the taxing power for local matters, the devolution of the expenses of so many matters of central concern upon the cities, as well as the necessary assumption by the city corporation of so many new branches of administration, made necessary by the greater complexity of modern municipal life, has made it necessary to give to the city corporation the taxing power.[1] That is, the legislature designates the kind of taxes which the city may raise and leaves to the city authorities the fixing of their amount, in some cases, as *e. g.* in Boston, limiting the rate which may be levied.[2] The municipal authority which originally received the taxing power was the city council. This seems to be the rule at the present. But in New York and Brooklyn this did not seem to work satisfactorily, and the scheme has been devised of really limiting the amount of taxes which may be raised by the council by taking away from it the power of making the appropriations, for the purpose of paying which, resort has to be had to taxes. In these two cities the power of making the appropriations has been given to a board of executive officers, of whom the mayor is one, differently constituted in the different cities. In Brooklyn the council has the right to cut down but not to raise the appropriations made by this board; in New York the board of aldermen may not change them in any way.[3] In general, however, it is the council which

---

[1] Dillon, *op. cit.*, I., 69.

[2] J. H. U. S., V., 114.

[3] N. Y. L. 1888, c. 583, title ii., 18.   N. Y. L. 1882, c. 410, sec. 189.   See also Allinson and Penrose, *op. cit.*, 300.

has the power of making the appropriations necessary
to carry on the city government. But it must be remembered that the tendency in all the commonwealths
is for the legislature to enumerate in detail the objects
for which municipal expenditure may be incurred.
Sometimes this tendency is carried so far as to enumerate in statutes the salaries of many of the officers
of the city government. Nothing is more common in
some of the commonwealths than for the legislature to
interfere to raise the salaries of certain of the city
officers who have political "influence" without con-
sulting the city authorities in any way.[1] Where the
legislature has thus fixed in detail the work of the city
and the salaries of its officers the power of appropriating money loses almost altogether its discretionary
character and becomes little more than an arithmetical
process, a purely ministerial act whose performance
may be enforced by the courts on the application of
any person interested in having the particular appropriation made.[2] An extreme example of this tendency
to fix in detail the work of the city and the salaries
of its officers by legislative enactment is to be found
in the city of New York.[3] In Philadelphia, however
the councils seem to have quite a large power over the
appropriations,[4] and in all cities the authority for
making the appropriations, generally the council, may
provide for certain, though not for many, optional expenses whose amount also it has the power to fix.

[1] *Cf.* Pres. Seth Low in his chapter on "Municipal Government" in Bryce,
American Commonwealth, I., 630.

[2] People *ex rel.* Wright v. Common Council of Buffalo, 16 Abbott's New
Cases affirmed in 38 Hun N. Y., 637.

[3] See L. of 1882, c. 410, sec. 52 *et passim.*

[4] See an ordinance of the councils of date Dec. 30, 1886, cited in Allinson
and Penrose, *op. cit.,* 359.

The form of the city council has been subjected to considerable change. In some cases it is formed, as originally, of a single body, as *e. g.* in New York, Brooklyn, and Chicago[1]; in others, of two chambers, as *e. g.* in Boston, Baltimore, St. Louis, and Philadelphia.[2] The members of the council, whether it consists of a single body or of two chambers, are elected by the people of the city, which is often differently districted for each chamber where the two-chamber system has been adopted. In one case, St. Louis, the members of the smaller chamber are elected on a general ticket.[3] In Brooklyn also a certain number of the aldermen are called aldermen at large and are elected by general ticket, though, when elected, they form part of the single chamber of which the council is composed.[4] In no instance do we find an instance of a self-perpetuating council, though this was the case in Philadelphia as under the old English system.[5] In one case we find minority representation. This is Chicago.[6] The term of office of the members of the council varies

---

[1] N. Y. L. 1882, c. 410, sec. 29 ; Allinson and Penrose, *op. cit.*, 331.

[2] J. H. U. S., V., 118, 157 ; Allinson and Penrose, *op. cit.*, 331.

[3] J. H. U. S., V., 157.

[4] N. Y. L. 1888, c. 583, title ii., 3.

[5] J. H. U. S., V., 15 *et seq.*

[6] Allinson and Penrose, *op. cit.*, 331. The authors of this book adduce New York as a place where the principle of minority representation has been adopted in the board of aldermen. This is a mistake, but a natural one. For the consolidated act provides for minority representation (sec. 29). This provision was taken from L. 1873, c. 335, sec. 4, as amended by L. 1878, c. 400, but is to be read in connection with Laws of 1882, c. 403, which provides for representation of the majority alone. The fact that the consolidated act bears a later date than that of the chapter of the laws of 1882 providing for majority representation does not affect the validity of chapter 403 of the laws of 1882, since the last section of the consolidated act provides that it shall be regarded as passed on January 1, 1882. Section 29 of the consolidated act is therefore amended by chapter 403 of the laws of 1882.

from one year as in New York,[1] to four years as in St. Louis.[2] Where the bicameral system has been adopted for the council the term of the members of the smaller chamber is often longer than that of the members of the larger chamber.[3] Generally the council is totally renewed at one time. But in some cases, as *e. g.* St. Louis,[4] one half only retire on the occasion of a council election.

As a general rule all the officers of the United States municipality are salaried, with the exception, in some cases, of the members of the council, and service is as a rule voluntary, though this was not originally the rule.[5] For the higher positions even, no special technical qualifications for office are provided as a general thing, but for the lower, especially in the case of the clerical service, the appointment is made often as a result of competitive examinations.[6] This is so in the commonwealths of New York and Massachusetts and the city of Philadelphia.[7]

The elections by which so many of the positions in the city service are filled are generally by universal suffrage. The only important exception to this rule is to be found in the case of those commonwealths which have made provision for registration laws. Such laws really provide an unlimited lodger suffrage with, however, a very short term of residence within the city,

---

[1] L. 1882, c. 410, sec. 29.

[2] J. H. U. S., V., 157.

[3] See, *e. g.*, the charter of St. Louis where the term of office of the members of the " council," as the smaller branch is called, is four years and that of the house of delegates is only two years. J. H. U. S., V., 157, 158.

[4] J. H. U. S., V., 85.

[5] *E. g.* see the early New York charters.

[6] See the proposal made by Pres. Eliot in *The Forum*, October, 1891.

[7] See *infra*, II., p. 35.

sometimes as low as one month, and seldom longer than six months. In one city, however, *viz.*, Philadelphia it is said that most of the voters are freeholders or rent payers. This would seem to be the result of the peculiar social conditions of the city.[1] The conditions of eligibility are generally the same as those for electors, though in one or two instances in order to be qualified for office it is necessary for the elector to be assessed at a certain amount for the purposes of taxation.[2]

IV.—The village or borough.

1. *General position.*—The city is not, however, the only municipality known to the American law. In many cases the needs of a locality, which may be a portion of one town or may lie in two towns, demand a different form of government from that offered in the ordinary town organization, while at the same time they do not demand so compact an organization as that to be found in a city. For the purpose of satisfying these demands the village or borough organization has been provided. In New England, where the people have been able to satisfy the demands made by thickly populated districts through the ordinary instrumentalities of the town, this embryonic municipal organization is said to be comparatively rare, though it is still to be

---

[1] See Allinson and Penrose, *op. cit.*, 297 ; Bryce, *op. cit.*, II., 360, note 2.

[2] Thus in Baltimore the members of the council must be assessed for at least $300. They must further be residents of the city for at least three years, and must be citizens of the United States. This last is so in Brooklyn also, N. Y. L. 1888, c. 583, title II., 3. Those of the smaller branch of the Baltimore council must be assessed at $500, be resident for four years, and be twenty-five years of age. Similar qualifications are required of the mayor. Allinson and Penrose, *op. cit.*, 329. In St. Louis every member of the council must be thirty years of age, a citizen of the commonwealth for five years, and a resident and freeholder in the city for one year. J. H. U. S., V., 157.

found, as *e. g.* in Connecticut and Vermont, which have probably been influenced by their nearness to New York. But in the middle commonwealths, and in the west and northwest, the village or borough organization is very common, so common indeed as very seriously to encroach upon the sphere of town government. For in almost all cases where the social conditions are such as to permit the adoption of the village organization (*i. e.*, where a comparatively large number of people live within a small area) we find that it is as a matter of fact adopted. Thus in New York the general law for the incorporation of villages provides that the village organization may be adopted where three hundred resident inhabitants are to found in a district of less than one square mile in extent.[1] The main difference between the town and the village is that, while the town is governed by the town meeting, *i. e.* the meeting of the political people of the town, the village is governed by a select body, to wit, the board of trustees or burgesses. Further, while the town is a *quasi* municipal corporation, the village or borough is a municipal corporation proper,[2] since it is formed primarily for the satisfaction of local needs. But, like the city, the village, though formed primarily for local needs, may be made use of by the commonwealth for the purposes of general administration. On the other hand, the village may practically be distinguished from the city from the fact that, on account of its small size, it is seldom as a matter of fact made an agent of general administration. About the only branch of general administration which is entrusted to the village is the preservation of the peace.

[1] See N. Y. L. 1870, c. 291, sec. 1.   [2] Dillon, *op. cit.*, I., 45.

2. *The village organization.*—The organization pro-vided by the New York law for the incorporation of villages, to which reference has already been made, may be taken as an example of the village organization in the United States.

By this the village authority is a board of three or more trustees and a president who is a member of the board. By the side of the trustees are a treasurer, a clerk, a collector, and a street commissioner. The trus-tees, the president, the treasurer, and the collector are elected by the electors in the village. The trustees serve for two years, one half or the major part of the number retiring each year, while the other elected offi-cers serve for one year. Residence in the village is a necessary qualification of eligibility for all offices, and the ownership of property to be assessed for the taxes made necessary by the expenditures of the village, is an additional qualification for the positions of president and trustee. The other officers are to be appointed annually by the board of trustees, who may also ap-point fire and police officers and a sealer of weights and measures. None of the offices is obligatory; and the offices of president and trustee are unpaid.

The board of trustees has large powers relative to the official service of the village, having the powers to remove for misconduct and after a hearing, any officer whom they appoint (the shortness of the term of office makes a larger disciplinary power unnecessary), and, by regulation, to fix the powers and duties of all the village officers so far as this has not been done by the law, which is the case for the offices of president and treasurer and one or two others. Most of their other powers are economical in character relating to the finances and local services of the village. They have the care of the village property, make contracts for the village, and audit all claims against it. In their management of the finances they are subjected to a popular control. For this purpose the expenditures of the village are divided into ordinary and extraordinary expenditures, the latter consisting generally of all expenditures of over $500 for any one specific object. The estimates for ordinary expenditures for the ensuing year are to be presented to the people at the annual election, who may then judge of the wisdom of the trustees' action before casting their votes, though they take no direct action upon the estimates. The extraordinary expenditures must, however, be voted by those electors who are liable to be assessed for the tax to defray them in their own right or in that of their wives. To pay the expenses of the village administration power is given to the trustees to levy a general property tax in about the usual way, and a poll tax of $1 on each male inhabitant between the ages of twenty-one and sixty years. No debts of a permanent character may be contracted with the exception that debts of not more than ten *per cent.* of the assessed value of taxable property in the village, may be incurred for the purpose of supplying the village with water.[1] The power to borrow money is, however, often granted by special and local legislation. Besides these powers of a financial character the trustees have quite an extensive power to issue local police ordinances which they may sanction with a penalty not exceeding $100 ; have care of the public health and have the ordinary powers of the town highway commissioners for the village district

---

[1] N. Y. L. 1875, c. 181.

which is taken out of the jurisdiction of the town high-way commissioners.　A later law [1] allows the trustees to provide for the election by the people in the larger villages of police justices with the same criminal juris-diction, as that possessed by the town justices of the peace who are not to have jurisdiction within the vil-lage district.　These police justices have also jurisdic-tion over violations of village ordinances, and in case of the non-payment of the penalty, which is to be sued for in an action for debt, may commit the violator to the county jail.

[1] N. Y. L. 1875, c. 514.

CHAPTER IV.

GENERAL CHARACTERISTICS OF LOCAL ADMINISTRATION IN THE UNITED STATES.

I.—Statutory enumeration of powers.

One of the most noticeable characteristics of the system of local administration in the United States is to be found in the fact that all matters relative to the organization of the local administrative system, all the powers of the various local districts considered as municipal corporations, and the duties of the officers acting within these districts are fixed in their most minute details by statute.[1] As no administration can long be carried on on the same general rules, and as the needs of different districts differ very much one from the other, it is necessary to give to some authority the power to change in its details the general plan of administration so as to suit changed conditions and varying needs. But as these minute details have been fixed by statute they can be changed only by statute. Therefore, the statute-making authority is being called upon all the time to act, in order that the administration of local affairs may be carried on to advantage. The general system is continually suffering modifications, and the various districts have, as a result of the intervention of the legislature, quite different powers.

---

[1] *Cf.* Dillon, *op. cit.*, I., 145.

Being accustomed to this continual interference by means of special and local legislation in the affairs of the localities, the legislature comes to think that these local affairs may best be regulated from the centre of the commonwealth, and often acts where it has not been asked to act by the local authorities or by the inhabitants of the localities. It often imposes burdens upon the localities which are unwise, and not infrequently allows itself to be made use of by unscrupulous persons or some political clique to forward their interests at the expense of the true interests of the locality directly concerned.[1] How far this habit of special and local legislation is carried is seen on examining the session laws of New York for the year 1886, a year which has been chosen simply at random. Of the 681 acts passed that year by the legislature, 280, *i. e.* between one third and one half of the entire work of the legislature, interfered directly with the affairs of some particular county, city, village, or town which was mentioned by name in the act. The results of this custom of special and local legislation are:

1. *The centralization of local matters in the hands of an irresponsible central authority.*—So few matters relating to the localities are fixed by the constitution that the power of the legislature over the localities is supreme. Almost the only thing which the legislature cannot do is to take away from the localities their privilege of electing their own officers. This is provided for in the constitutions of several of the commonwealths and is therefore beyond the power

---

[1] President Seth Low says in his chapter on Municipal Government contained in Bryce, *American Commonwealth*, I., 630, that in the commonwealth of New York "the habit of interference in city action has become to the legislature almost a second nature."

of the legislature.[1] The force of such provisions is often, however, destroyed by the interpretation put upon them by the courts. Thus in New York the court of appeals decided in the case of *People v. Draper*[2] that the appointment of police commissioners by the governor and senate in accordance with a statute of the legislature was not in conflict with the constitution, because such officers were not local but commonwealth officers.[3] The same court held later[4] that fire and health officers might also be appointed by the governor because these officers were not only public commonwealth officers, but were also new officers, *i. e.* were not in existence at the time of the adoption of the constitution, and were therefore not subject to its provisions. This distinction between old and new officers first made in these cases was carried to the bounds of the absurd in the case of *Astor v. The Mayor*,[5] which permitted the transfer of old functions, performed by old municipal officers, to new officers who might constitutionally be regarded as public and not local officers, and might be appointed by the governor. The result of this line of decisions has been to deprive the cities of New York, and particularly the city of New York, of the right of local self-administration which, it was supposed, was guaranteed by the constitution of the commonwealth. Thus at one time there was to be seen in the city of New York, attend-

---

[1] *E. g.* see constitution of New York, art. 10, sec. 2. *Cf.* Dillon, *op. cit.*, I., 100.

[2] 15 N. Y., 532.

[3] See *supra*, p. 204 for other decisions of a similar tenor.

[4] People v. Pinckney, 32 N. Y., 377, and Metropolitan Board of Health v. Heister, 37 N. Y., 661.

[5] 62 N. Y., 567.

ing to a work which has been held by the highest
court of the commonwealth to be a purely municipal undertaking,[1] *viz.* the aqueduct, a commission
whose members were for the most part appointed by
the central government of the commonwealth and not
by the authorities of the city which alone is interested.[2] On this commission provision was made[3] for
only one representative of the city which was paying
for the work, and which was primarily if not alone interested therein, to wit, the municipal commissioner of
public works. This same legislative interference in
municipal matters has been characteristic of the action
of the legislature with regard to the providing of
means of rapid transit for the city. The court of appeals in one of its decisions gives evidence of its belief in
the dangers resulting from this line of decisions. This
is the case of *People v. Albertson*,[4] where it distinctly
says that the purpose of article 10, section 2, of the
New York constitution was to secure the right of local
government to the civil divisions of the commonwealth
and that this right could not be taken away from them
by the legislature. But the majority of its decisions
would seem to be in the direction of permitting the
legislature to centralize as much as it saw fit the administration of the commonwealth. That these decisions are impolitic and unwise no one will deny. That
legally they were in some cases unnecessary is to be
seen when they are compared with the decisions of the
courts of other commonwealths. Thus in Michigan

[1] Bailey v. The Mayor, 3 Hill, 531 ; People v. Civil-Service Boards, 103
N. Y., 657.

[2] N. Y. L. of 1883, c. 490 ; N. Y. L. of 1886, c. 337.

[3] N. Y. L. 1886, c. 337.

[4] 55 N. Y., 50.

and Indiana a similar constitutional provision has been interpreted as preventing the legislature from granting to the governor the power to appoint municipal commissioners of public works,[1] or itself to appoint park commissioners and force the city to provide a park.[2]

This tendency towards a legislative centralization, which is to be seen also in commonwealths other than New York, has led in some of them to the insertion in the constitution of provisions which aim at giving the local areas a greater independence of the legislature, at fixing by the law in the constitution of many matters of local administration, or at assuring to the localities the right to regulate within the law their own affairs free from all legislative interference.[3]

2. *Local variations.*—A further result of this habit of special and local legislation is a great lack of uniformity in the administrative system of even a single commonwealth, especially in a commonwealth like New York, where the constitutional provisions ensuring the independence of the local corporations are of comparatively little importance. Such a lack of uniformity is not of course a serious defect; indeed it has the advantage of not sacrificing local interests to the fetish of uniformity and symmetry. It does of course add very greatly to the difficulties of both the student and the practising lawyer since search for special statutes must always be made to find out what are the actual powers of any particular district, it being unsafe to place much dependence on general statutes. This

---

[1] People v. Hurlburt, 24 Mich., 44 ; *Cf.* State v. Denny, 118 Indiana, 449 ; Evansville v. State, *Ibid.*, 426.

[2] People v. Detroit, 28 Mich., 228.

[3] *Cf.* Stimson, *American Statute Law*, pp. 94, 95.

local and special legislation is apt to result in conflicting legislation also.

3. *No local independence.*—The possession by the legislature of this right of control over the affairs of the local areas and the readiness which the legislature has ever shown to exercise this right have brought it about finally, that it is almost impossible to distinguish the sphere of central from the sphere of local action. The officers acting in the local areas and elected by the people of the localities are for the most part, notwithstanding the juristic personality which has been recognized as belonging to the localities, mere agents of the central administration of the commonwealth, and the entire administrative system in the localities may be changed at will by the legislature.[1]

II.—Administrative independence of the local authorities.

1. *Absence of central administrative control.*—The second general characteristic of the American system of local administration is to be found in the great number of the authorities and their independence both of each other and of the central administration of the commonwealth. The great number of the authorities is due to the fact that the administration is not professional in character.[2] Their independence is due to the decentralized character of the administrative system adopted in the commonwealths. The rule is, that, notwithstanding most of the authorities in the local areas attend to a great deal of work which interests the commonwealth as a whole, they shall still be elected by the people of the localities in which they act, and when

[1] *Cf.* Lorillard v. Town of Monroe, 11 N. Y., 392 ; United States v. the Baltimore and Ohio R. R. Co., 17 Wallace, 322.

[2] *Infra*, II., p. 7.

elected shall act free from almost all central administrative control. Seldom do we find that any administrative authority has the power to direct them how they shall perform their duties or to quash or amend their action or to exercise any disciplinary power over them. In a few instances, however, where the action of the authorities in the localities may have a disastrous effect upon the general administration of the commonwealth in matters where it is particularly desirable that the administration shall be conducted in accordance with a uniform plan and where local action may produce inequalities in the burden of commonwealth taxation, resort has been had to a central administrative control which, however, up to the present time has not been thoroughly worked out. Thus in New York the governor has disciplinary powers of a limited character over a number of officers acting in the localities among whom may be mentioned the sheriff, the district attorney, and the superintendent of the poor.[1] The county treasurer who is the fiscal agent both of the county and of the commonwealth was formerly removable in the same way. Such powers seem, however, to be exceptional. In New York also in the sanitary administration the state board of health has a series of supervisory powers over the actions of the local boards of health.[2] In the administration of public education the commonwealth superintendent of public instruction has similar and even larger powers of administrative supervision over everything connected with the common schools.[3] Such a central administra-

---

[1] *Supra*, p. 79.
[2] Public Health Act of 1885, c. 270, secs. 3, 5, and 8.
[3] School Law of 1864,. Title I., sec. 18 ; Title XII.

tive control in educational matters seems to be quite common. Finally in the tax administration provision is often made for the equalization of assessment valuations both for the county and for the commonwealth, in order to prevent the assessors in one town or county from assessing the property subject to taxation in that town or county at such a low rate of valuation as to throw part of the town's share of commonwealth or county taxation upon the other towns.[1] But these instances of the administrative control are quite rare.

2. *Decentralized character of the local organizations.* —Not only is the central administrative control over the actions of the officers in the localities very weak, but the administration in any given district is not at all concentrated. Seldom do we find any authority which has administrative supervision of any extent over the actions of the other authorities in the locality. A reference to the powers of the county authority, *i. e.* the supervisors or the commissioners, will show how few are their powers of administrative control.[2] The only possible exception to this general independence of the local authorities from the other local authorities is to be found in the case of the municipal administration, where the organization is considerably more concentrated. It has been pointed out that the tendency of modern American municipal development is to concentrate the municipal administration still more and to increase very largely the powers of the mayor.[3] But as a general thing even now the various municipal officers are comparatively independent of the mayor,

[1] See Cooley on *Taxation*, 2d Ed., 421–423, 747–749.
[2] *Supra*, pp. 178–192.
[3] *Supra*, p. 210.

though they are somewhat more dependent upon the mayor and the city council acting together. The general characteristic of the American system of local administration is that it is from the administrative point of view extremely decentralized. The administrative control, both central and local, is believed to be unnecessary because of the detailed enumeration in the statutes of all the powers of the local corporations, and of the officers in the local areas. Everything is so fully regulated by the legislature that there is little room left for administrative instructions to be sent either by the central authorities of the commonwealth or any superior local authority. In order to ensure that officers will perform the duties imposed upon them by the statutes resort has been had to the sanctions of the criminal law. To the violation of almost every official duty is attached a criminal penalty which is to be enforced by the ordinary criminal courts. Detailed enumeration of official duties in the statutes and punishment of the violation of official duties by the criminal courts are thought to be sufficient to ensure efficient and impartial administration and to obviate the necessity of forming any strong administrative control.[1]

III.—Non-professional character of the system.

The third general characteristic of the American system of local administration, as indeed of the entire American system of administration, is to be found in the non-professional character of the officers. We find almost no professional officers. Almost all are non-professional in character. That is, as a rule the officers receive no salary but only *per diem* allowances,

[1] *Infra*, II., pp. 80, 88.

which are seldom greater than the wages received by a skilled laborer, serve for short terms of office, and, after filling their term of office, return again to the ranks of society from which they came. Having no opportunity to develop professional habits they thus do not form a special class in the community. The result of such a system of official organization is that society governs itself, whence the name that is given to the system, *viz.*, that of self-government, which means a system of government and administration in which society governs itself through the organization of the state. In such a system the state delegates certain specific powers to officers appointed by society in its local organizations—officers who on account of the shortness of their terms of office do not cease to have all the feelings of society. The only exception to this rule of the non-professional character of the officers in the local administrative system is to be found in the cities, where the necessities of municipal administration seem to call for quite a number of professional officers, who are generally salaried and serve for longer terms.

Service as officer is not only unpaid but it is often obligatory. There are at the present time more exceptions to this rule of the obligatory character of the service than in former years, and indeed the obligation itself seems to be disappearing. By the original English system, however, service as administrative officer was really obligatory in almost all cases, just as much as service on a jury or in the army, but at the present time the tendency would seem to be towards voluntary-ism. In New York many of the local offices were until recently obligatory, refusal to serve being punishable with a fine of $50. This was true of most of the town offices, *e. g.* supervisor, town clerk, assessor, commissioner of highways, and overseer of the poor,[1] but the obligation to serve seems to have been omitted in the revision of the law made in 1890.[2]

[1] See New York Revised Statutes, Part I., Chap. XI., Title III., art. 2d., sections 25 and 26 ; *cf.* State v. Ferguson, 31 N. J. L., 107.

[2] L. 1890, c. 569.

CHAPTER V.

I.—History from the seventeenth century to the present time.

1. *Defects of the old system.*—The history of the
English system of local administration up to the beginning of the seventeenth century has already been
traced.[1] It has been shown how the original prefectoral administration of the sheriffs was gradually replaced by the administration of the justices of the
peace, who practically had within their hands the entire
control of administrative matters in the localities and
from whom were recruited to a large extent the members of Parliament. This system, it has been pointed
out, was really one of great local self-government. It
was not, however, in the modern sense representative
in character; and when, in 1830, its financial side became more important on account of the great increase
in the amount of local taxes through the increase of
the poor-rates, it was thought that some voice as to the
amount of these local taxes should be given to the tax-
payers. The change in feeling was due in large part
also to social changes. The application of steam power
to manufactures and the very general introduction of
machinery revolutionized industrial methods, massed

---

[1] *Supra*, pp. 162–165.

large populations in the cities, and gave to the posses-
sors of personal property, that is the commercial and
industrial classes, an importance they never had before.
This change in the relative importance and power of
the property-owning classes led first to a change in
the representation in Parliament—a change which was
brought about by the celebrated reform bill of 1832.
By this act the balance of political power was taken
away from the nobility and gentry and given to the
middle classes. As the system of local administration
of that time gave most of the power in the localities to
the nobility and the gentry, it was only natural that
the new political masters should seek to discover and
adopt some plan of administering local affairs by
means of which their local influence might be increased.

Another reason for the change which soon followed
was the necessity of wide-reaching reforms. The deplorable condition of the municipal administration has
already been alluded to.[1] The power exercised at first
by the Crown and later by the nobility over the municipal elections, in order thereby to control the representation in Parliament, had been used in such a way that
the municipal organization and institutions were utterly
incapable of any sort of even passable administration.
Further the poor-rates had increased to such an enormous sum in the years immediately preceding 1832
and the anxiety of the local authorities everywhere to
throw the burden of supporting the poor on some
other locality than their own had led to a complicated
law of settlement which was totally at variance with
the needs of an advancing industrial society. But

[1] *Supra*, p. 198.

the necessary reforms could only be realized by
the establishment of a uniform system of administration. This implied a central control such as had
not before existed. In theory the justices of the
peace were subject to the guidance of the central
government, and the central government could in
theory dismiss them from office if they disobeyed
its instructions. But the high social and political
position of the justices made it a delicate matter for
the central government to send instructions to them;
and even if such instructions were sent it was extremely difficult to enforce them. The threat of dismissal
from office had no terrors for the average justice of the
peace. Dismissal meant relief from arduous service,
and involved no pecuniary loss, since the justices
received no pay. Hence the dismissal of a justice of
the peace is rarely met with in later English history;
and the power to send the justices instructions became
finally an empty prerogative.[1]

2. *The reforms of 1834 and 1835.*—For these
reasons some of the first resolutions passed by the new
Parliament, formed as a result of the reform bill, provided for a thorough investigation of the administration of the poor-law and of municipal government. In
1833 the celebrated poor-law commission was appointed
and began its work. The result of this work was
published in 1834, and has been described as " perhaps
the most remarkable and startling document to be
found in the whole range of English, perhaps, indeed,

---

[1] The last attempt to coerce justices of the peace through the power of dismissal from office was made in the reign of William III by Lord Somers and
created such a storm that no subsequent ministry has dared to repeat it. Gneist,
Das Englische Verwaltungsrecht, 1884, p. 389

of all, social history." [1]   The plans of reform advocated
in this report and finally adopted in the Poor-Law
Amendment Act of 1834 involved the formation of a
system of local administration which should be representative of the local tax-payers, and at the same time subject to central administrative control.   The parishes on
which had been devolved the burden of supporting the
poor under the old system were grouped into unions.
In each union there was formed a board of poor-law
guardians, to be elected by the inhabitants of the
union.   Service as guardian was not obligatory as had
been service in most of the positions under the old
system.   This board confined itself practically to deciding the amount of money to be spent while the
actual detailed administrative work, formerly attended
to by the unpaid overseers of the poor and the justices
of the peace, was now to be attended to by salaried
subordinates devoting their whole time to the work.
That is the actual poor-relief was to be distributed
mainly by a salaried relieving officer.   This board and
all its officers were subject to a most strict central administrative control exercised by the central poor-law
board at London.   There were several reasons for the
introduction of this control.   In the first place it was
felt that some method must be devised to restrain the
local selfishness which had been one of the greatest
evils of the old system.   If under the new system a
locality showed a desire to escape any of the burdens
that were imposed upon it by the law, the central control could hold it up to the performance of its duties.
In the second place the new system did not offer the
same guaranties as the old for the integrity and intel-

---

[1] Fowle, *The Poor-Law*, 1881, p. 75.

ligence of its officers.   Under the old system as a rule,
the justices of the peace—the most prominent men in
the county—either did the work themselves, or had it
done under their personal direction ; under the new
system the detailed administrative work was to be
attended to by salaried subordinates of the boards of
guardians.   A central control was necessary finally because of the necessity of uniform administration.

As the needs of English society have increased, new
administrative agencies have been demanded and devised for their satisfaction ; and these new agencies
have been organized on the same lines as the organs
for the poor-law administration.   Finally the county
has been reorganized on somewhat the same plan.   At
about the same time that the poor-law administration
was being investigated the municipal administration
also was being studied with the purpose of devising
some plan of reform which should do away with existing defects and make the municipal organization an
efficient instrument for municipal administration.   The
result of the report of the commission appointed for
this purpose was the Municipal Corporations Act of
1835, which introduced a uniform law for the organization of the municipal corporations of the kingdom and
abolished most of the abuses of the previously existing
charters.   The form of organization adopted for the
municipal boroughs has since been adopted for the
county organization by the Local-Government Act of
1888.

As a result of these changes the justices of the
peace have lost much of their importance.   Most of
their administrative functions have been taken from
them, and given to special administrative officers

established by the reform legislation. They have, however, retained most of their judicial functions, which have really, somewhat as in the United States, been increased.

3. *Present position of the justices of the peace.*—The long-continued failure of the English law to make any clear distinction between justice and administration has brought it about that, notwithstanding the recent attempts to separate these two classes of functions, the justices of the peace still have under the present system, as indeed they also have in the United States, a series of duties which are, from the continental point of view at any rate, administrative in character.[1] They are thus still conservators of the peace and as such have the right to bind over all disorderly persons to keep the peace. They act as the preliminary investigators of all crimes, even of felonies. Acting either singly or in petty or special sessions they convict of petty offences, commonly without a jury.[2] In the courts of quarter sessions, when all the justices of the peace of the county meet together, they form when acting with a jury the lowest criminal court, and without a jury an administrative court of appeal from the orders and convictions of the justices acting singly or in petty and special sessions.[3] Certain of these functions have at the same time the characteristics of judicial and administrative action, that is the matters dealt with are frequently administrative in character, while it may be impossible to distinguish them in form from judicial acts. For

---

[1] *Cf.* Wigram, *The Justices' Note-Book*, Chap. I.; Anson, *op. cit.*, II., 237.

[2] Stone, *Practice of Justices of the Peace at Petty and Special Sessions*, 9th edition, Part I.

[3] Smith, *Practice at Quarter Sessions* 1882, p. 4; *infra*, II., p. 214.

English administrative law is highly specialized; its rules are put into the form of direct commands to the people to do or not to do particular things. These commands are sanctioned by criminal penalties, and the imposition of these penalties is entrusted to the justices of the peace acting as police judges.[1] The result of this specialization of the English law has been an enormous extension of the police powers of the justices of the peace even under the present system. In the cities, however, the tendency is for the justices, both in England and in the United States, to give way to stipendiary magistrates and salaried recorders.[2]

Besides these cases in which the action of the justices of the peace is judicial in form but often administrative in effect, there is a further class of cases in which their action is more obviously administrative. Not all the laws whose execution is entrusted to the justices of the peace can be reduced to the form of simple commands addressed to the people at large. Certain matters have to be left to the discretion of the justices. Thus it has been left to them to decide the questions of law and fact that arise in connection with removals under the poor and sanitary legislation, the assessment of local taxes, *etc.*, *etc.* In these cases the justices act otherwise than in the foregoing cases. Their decision takes on the form, not of the conviction of a violation of the law accompanied by the imposition of the proper penalty, but rather of an order commanding that what is proper be done. Here it will be seen that the justice acts as an administrative rather than as a judicial officer.

---

[1] For further explanation see *infra*, II., p. 107.

[2] Wigram, *op. cit.*, 6; Probyn, *Local Government and Taxation in the United Kingdom*, 31, 32.

His action is administrative in form as well as in effect. He does not decide a controversy but orders something to be done which it is necessary shall be done in order that the government shall be carried on.[1] This is largely true of the United States also.

Finally the justices of the peace have in their courts of special and petty sessions to appoint a few unimportant officers in the localities, *e. g.* the overseers of the poor not *ex-officio* overseers and the unsalaried constables; they also have a series of powers relating to the various branches of the administration of internal affairs attended to in the localities. Thus they have even now considerable power relative to the highways though the new county council has robbed them of the most important of this class of powers.[2] They still revise and allow the list of persons liable to serve on the juries.[3] They grant licences for the sale of liquor.[4] Finally the Local-Government Act of 1888 gives the justices a large power over the administration of the police force.[5]

II.—*The county.*

1. *Organization of the county council.*—The English Local-Government Act of 1888, which is the last of the series of acts relating to the present system of local administration, provides that in each of the administrative counties into which England is divided[6] there shall be a county council elected, speaking broadly, by the citizens of the county who are occupiers of land

---

[1] Stone, *op. cit.* Part II.; *cf. infra,* II., p. 109.

[2] See 25 and 26 Vict., c. 61, and 27 and 28 Vict., c. 101.

[3] 9 Geo. IV., c. 50.

[4] 9 Geo. IV., c. 61 ; 35 and 36 Vict., c. 94.

[5] *Infra,* p. 243. [6] Except the new county of London.

of a clear yearly value of ten pounds and upwards, or are occupiers of buildings of any value.[1] This county council is composed of councillors, aldermen, and a chairman, being modelled on the town council established by the Municipal Corporations Act of 1835.[2] All fit persons may be elected county councillors who are county electors, parliamentary electors, or who being non-residents still reside within fifteen miles of the county, and are occupiers of property in the county of a certain annual value, or pay a certain amount in rates for the support of the poor.[3] The term of office is three years and all the county councillors retire from office at the same time.[4] The county aldermen are one third in number of the councillors. Any person qualified to be county councillor may be county alderman, but the practice will probably be the same as it has been in the case of the municipal boroughs that only councillors will be made aldermen. The term of office of county alderman is six years, one half the number of the aldermen retiring every third year. The aldermen are elected by the council.[5]

The county chairman, who in the county takes a position similar to that of the mayor in the municipal borough, is elected in the same way by the county council from among those persons qualified to be county councillors, but if, as is probable, the practice will prevail which has been adopted in the municipal

---

[1] 51 Vict., c. 10 ; Herbert and Jenkin, *The Councillor's Handbook*, 2.

[2] 51 and 52 Vict., c. 41, sec. 1.

[3] Property of an annual value of from £500 to £1,000, or rates of from £15 to £30.

[4] 51 and 52 Vict., c. 41, sec. 2 ; Stephen and Miller, *The County Council Compendium*, 24, with authorities.

[5] 51 and 52 Vict., c. 41, sec. 75, and 45 and 46 Vict., c. 50, sec. 14.

boroughs, the chairman will be selected from among the aldermen.[1] His term of office is one year and he is *ex-officio* justice of the peace.[2] The chairman is the only member of the county council who may receive any remuneration.[3] His remuneration is to be fixed by the county council. Service as member of the county council does not seem to be obligatory.[4]

2. *Powers of the county council.*—The powers and duties of the county council relate first to the official service of the county and second to the administrative services of the county. The council has a large power over the organization of the county official service, though some of the offices, such as that of county treasurer, are provided for by statute. The council also appoints most of the officers of the county, may dismiss them from office, direct them how to act, and fix the amount of their salaries. The great exception to this rule is to be found in the administration of the police force of the county, which is to be attended to by a joint committee composed of an equal number of members of the council designated by it, and of an equal number of justices of the peace appointed by the court of quarter sessions. The powers of the council relating to the administrative services attended to in the county affect in the first place the general administration of the kingdom, *i. e.* are central in character. A series of acts had provided that certain matters of general concern should be attended to in the localities by various local authorities. The local-

---

[1] 51 and 52 Vict., c. 41, sec. 75 ; 45 and 46 Vict., c. 50, sec. 15.
[2] 51 and 52 Vict., c. 41, sec. 2.
[3] 51 and 52 Vict., c. 41, sec. 75 ; 45 and 46 Vict., c. 50, sec. 15.
[4] 51 and 52 Vict., c. 41, sec. 75, sub. sec. 16.

government act has very generally taken away from the various local authorities mentioned in these acts the power to act, and has given such power to the county council. The only important exception to this rule is that all municipal boroughs of over 10,000 inhabitants have, even since the passage of the local-government act, the same powers of this character which they possessed before. The result of this arrangement is that, for the purpose of executing these acts of general concern, the local authority is either the county council or the town council of a municipal borough which has more than 10,000 inhabitants.[1]

In the second place the county council is the authority to attend to all business which may affect the county as a corporation. As such county authority it has the power to issue a series of by-laws or ordinances of a police character, has the general supervision of all highways and the actual administration of the main roads, and finally and most important of all, has charge of the county financial administration with the power to make appropriations for certain specified objects, to levy taxes, to acquire property and to borrow money when the purpose of the loan is justified by the law. It must, however, be remembered that the principle of law governing the powers of the county council is the same as that adopted for the powers of the county authority in the United States, *viz.*, that its powers are enumerated in the acts of Parliament and that it may not exercise any power which is not thus based on statute. Parliament has not granted to the county council the general power to attend to the affairs of the county as it sees fit, with the power to

---

[1] For a list of these matters see Herbert and Jenkin, *op. cit.*, 41 *et seq.*

establish and maintain such institutions as it may believe are of advantage to the county. No distinction is made between general and local matters, but the powers of the county council in either of these spheres of action are alike enumerated in the statutes.

In the third place the county council has a series of powers which affect mainly the actions of the local authorities and districts beneath the county. It has already been shown that the general tendency of English development during this century has been in the direction of an administrative centralization by the formation of a strict central control over the actions of the localities and local officers. The result in 1888 was that the acts of almost all the local authorities in the lesser administrative districts were directed and controlled by the central authorities at London. This centralization was deprecated by many persons and was generally felt to have had a bad influence. Therefore the Local-Government Act of 1888 provided that the local-government board at London,[1] which was the most important central supervisory authority, may by provisional order, to be confirmed by Parliament, transfer to the county councils all powers of control possessed by it or by any other central authority over the various local authorities.[2] The Local-Government Act of 1888 also gave to the county council the power to adjust local boundaries which were in a very confused state.

[1] Formed in 1871 out of the union of the poor-law with the public health board.

[2] The probable changes that will be made as a result of the exercise of this power by the local-government board are indicated in Stephen and Miller, *The County Council Compendium*, 54. For the county generally see Anson, *op. cit.*, II., 235–238.

III.—Rural subdivisions of counties.

1. *Local chaos.*—Below the county all is confusion.
The parish was at one time the only rural division below the county, but with the growth of new needs
there have been formed new divisions, and in these
divisions new authorities, for the satisfaction of these
needs. While the parish has, as a rule, been taken as
the basis of these new divisions, the relation of the
parish to the county has from the beginning been so
peculiar that the new divisions at the present time
bear little territorial relation to the county. The
parish in the first place was not always contained within one unbroken fence line. In 1873 there were in one
county more than seventy divided parishes, while one
parish alone had ten outlying portions.[1] When the
union was formed in 1834 it was formed on the basis
of the parish, *i. e.* it was to be composed of a certain
number of parishes. As the parishes often crossed
county lines, the necessary result is that the union
often crosses county lines.[2] The rural sanitary district
which was formed about 1848 was, as a rule, to be the
same in territorial extent as the union. The sanitary
districts were classed as urban and rural sanitary districts. The first were formed out of the second as the
needs of the inhabitants demanded. That is, any aggre-
gation of inhabitants might be formed into an urban
sanitary district, which might thus embrace parts of
two unions and parts of several parishes. After these
urban sanitary districts had been formed all that was
left of any union was denominated a rural sanitary district. Then the rural guardians of the poor were organ-

---

[1] Chalmers, *Local Government,* 33.

[2] One hundred and eighty one out of about six hundred and fifty unions do
so. *Ibid.,* 51.

ized as the rural sanitary authority for such rural sanitary district.[1] Later came the education act, which formed all parishes or parts of parishes which were not within the limits of any municipal borough (for the parish ran through the municipal borough as well as through the county) into school districts. The municipal boroughs themselves also formed school districts. Besides these districts there are highway districts, which may be either parishes or combinations of parishes or unions or municipal boroughs, burial districts, and watching and lighting districts, which, since the establishment of the county police, are simply lighting districts, and are usually the same as the rural parishes. All these parishes may overlap, with the single exception that the poor-law parish forms an integral part of the union. On account of the non-coincidence of their areas it has been impossible to transfer all the administrative functions which are discharged within them to any one well organized authority, though the attempt has been made, as has been indicated, to consolidate several of the most important of these functions in the hands of the boards of poor-law guardians. The result of this condition of things is, in the words of Mr. Wright, that—

the inhabitant of a rural parish lives in a parish, in a union, in a county, and probably in a highway district. He is or may be governed by a vestry, by a school board, a burial board, a highway board, the guardians and the justices. [Now the county council must be added to this formidable list]. There are a multitude of minor matters in respect of which the districts, authorities, and rates are or may be additionally multiplied and complicated in all the above cases.[2]

[1] *Ibid.*, 101.
[2] *Wright's Memorandum*, No. 1, p. 33, cited in Chalmers, *Local Government*, 21.

Nearly every one of these authorities has the power of levying taxes and very often each one has its own machinery for the collection of taxes. Mr. Goschen said in one of his speeches that he "received in one year 87 demand notes on an aggregate valuation of about £1100. One parish alone," he said, "sent me eight rate papers for an aggregate amount of 12s. 4d."[1] The system of areas and authorities has become simply a chaos; "a chaos," in the words of Mr. Goschen again, "as regards authorities, a chaos as regards rates, and a worse chaos as regards areas."

But with regard to this chaos we may lay down the following general principles which, it is hoped, will give an adequate idea of the local government which England possesses at the present time.

2. *The union.*—By the act of 1834, the poor-law parishes, which are not, however, always identical with the ecclesiastical parishes, though they generally are, are grouped into unions for the support of the poor. At the head of each union is placed a board of guardians, composed partly of *ex-officio* members, partly of members elected by the people possessing the local suffrage in the parishes.[2] The *ex-officio* members are the justices of the peace residing in the union. It is said, however, that the justices of the peace participate rarely in the administration of the affairs of the union.[3] The elected members of the board come from the various parishes within the union. Each parish at the time the union is formed is allotted a certain number of elected members whose number is determined largely

---

[1] Probyn, *Local Government and Taxation in the United Kingdom*, 127.

[2] Gneist, *Selfgovernment, etc.*, 727.

[3] Chalmers, *op. cit.*, 55.

by its importance. Such elected members are elected
by the owners of property and rate-payers in the
parish according to a system of plural voting. A ratable value of less than £50 gives one vote; a ratable
value of £50 or more, and less than £100, gives two
votes, and so on up to a ratable value of £250 or
over, which gives six votes. A voter may vote both
as owner and occupier with the result that one person
may cast twelve votes but no more.[1] The guardians
appoint, subject to the approval of the local-government board at London, all the necessary subordinate
officers, but cannot remove them from office.[2] This
power is entrusted to the local-government board,
which thus has a very large administrative control
over the administration of the boards of guardians.
While the boards of guardians were originally established for the purpose of attending to the administration
of the poor-law, since the time of their establishment
they have been called upon to attend to other branches
of administration. Thus in the rural sanitary districts
the boards of guardians are the sanitary authorities,
i. e. the guardians who come from the rural portions of
the union act as the sanitary authority for that part of
the union which forms a rural sanitary district. They
also in many cases act as the rural highway authority.[3]
The parishes, which were the original highway districts,
have in many cases been grouped into larger highway
districts and, as far as may be, the highway districts
so formed have been coterminous with the unions.
Where this has been done the boards of guardians

---

[1] Gneist, *Selfgovernment, etc.*, 723.

[2] *Ibid.*, 730 ; Chalmers, *op. cit.*, 54.

[3] Chalmers, *op. cit.*, 59, 109, 136.

have been given the power of attending to the highways. The actual detailed work of administration connected with the branches which have been put into the hands of the guardians is, as a rule, attended to by the officers appointed by them. The boards of guardians have in the course of time become almost entirely deliberative bodies, and their main function is to raise the money necessary to do the work which has been devolved upon them. The subordinate officers, who do almost all the detailed work, are largely under the control of the local-government board at London and, being salaried, form quite a professional service, which presents a strong contrast to the formerly decentralized non-professional administration of the justices of the peace.[1] The funds from which the expenses of the administration of the boards of guardians are paid, are obtained from local taxation —the poor-, sanitary, and highway rates—which falls upon the divisions of which the union is composed, *i. e.* the parishes, and from subsidies granted by the county council from taxes which, while collected by the central government, are paid over to the county councils for distribution among the unions and other local divisions according to rules laid down in various statutes and on receipt of the certificate of the central government that the standard of efficiency required by the central government has been maintained.[2]

3. *The parish.*—Below the union is the parish. This area, owing to the establishment of the union, has lost much of its importance. At the present time it is little more than a tax and election district for the purposes

---

[1] Gneist, *Selfgovernment, etc.*, 731 *et seq.*
[2] Local Government Act of 1888.

of local government. As a municipal corporation it also has the power to put in operation a series of permissive acts which have peculiar reference to the well-being of its own inhabitants. Such are for example the baths and wash-houses acts, the burial acts, the lighting and watching acts which affect at the present time only the lighting of the parishes, the public libraries acts, and the public improvement acts.[1] These acts when adopted by the parishes are carried out and executed by inspectors and boards of commissioners appointed by the parishes. The general organization of the parishes is as follows. The deliberative authority, *i. e.* the authority which decides as to the adoption of these acts and such other matters as are in the control of the parish, is the vestry. This consists of the rate-payers of the parish in vestry assembled or of a select vestry which is simply a representative body of the rate-payers. The rate-payers, where the select vestry has not been adopted, vote in somewhat the same manner as in the case of the union elections. That is each rate-payer paying on a ratable value of less than £50 has one vote, on one of between £50 and £75 two votes, and so on up to £125, so that one man have as many as six votes, but in this case no more than six votes, as no one is allowed to vote both as owner and occupier.[2] In each parish there are further two overseers of the poor who are appointed by the justices of the peace.[3] In parishes which are at the same time ecclesiastical parishes the two churchwardens, who are elected by the vestry, are *ex-officio* overseers of the poor.[4] The main duty of the overseers of the poor is no longer the administration of

---

[1] Chalmers, *op. cit.*, 42 and 43 ; Herbert and Jenkin, *The Councillor's Handbook*, 5.   [2] Chalmers, *op. cit.*, 42.   [3] *Ibid.*, 43.   [4] *Ibid.*

the poor-relief which has gone into the hands of the guardians of the poor and their subordinate force. The main duty of the overseers of the poor at the present time is the collection of the rates which are to be paid by the rate-payers of the parish for the purpose of supporting the various branches of administration whose expense has been devolved upon the parish; and as most of the rates are tacked to the poor-rate or else the expenses of the administrative branches are actually defrayed out of the poor-rate the overseers of the poor are really the local tax collectors. In certain cases provision is made for paid assistant overseers of the poor and paid collectors of rates.[1] It must be noted that the parish organization extends through the urban as well as the rural districts, though it is rather more important in the rural than in the urban districts.[2] Finally the rural parishes are all school districts,[3] and have, where there are any public schools in the American sense of the word, a school board organized on somewhat the same plan as the board of guardians but with provision for minority representation in order to make the public schools more satisfactory to the various ecclesiastical minorities which are so common in England.[4] There is a bill before the present Parliament (1893) whose intention is to give to the parish a more representative government by the formation of an elective parish council. If it passes, the stronger parish organization resulting from it will undoubtedly lead to an increase of the functions of the parish and to a greater simplicity in the local-government institutions.

[1] *Ibid.*, 43 and 44.

[2] Since in the rural districts the parish more frequently puts into operation the permissive acts to which allusion has been made.

[3] Chalmers, *op. cit.*, 126.   [4] *Ibid.*, 127.

This bill also substitutes district councils for boards of guardians, and abolishes plural voting.[1]

IV.—*Urban subdivisions of counties.*

The municipalities in England are of two classes, *viz.* the boroughs or cities and the urban sanitary districts or improvement act districts. The larger boroughs or cities are exempted for almost all purposes of administration from the jurisdiction of the county authority and form counties by themselves in which the municipal authority acts as the county authority.[2]

1. *The municipal borough.*—The old borough organization has been completely remodelled and made uniform for the entire country by the Municipal Corporations Act of 1835. This act was passed after a most thorough investigation had been made of the conditions of municipal boroughs and provided a form of organization which was imposed upon all localities desiring to become municipal boroughs. At the present time the Crown may, by order in council at the request of the voters of any place, confer upon them the privileges which attach to the municipal organization. The old principle remains the same, that is, that the borough is a corporation of quite limited powers— powers which generally relate simply to local affairs. The borough organization is hardly ever made use of by the central administration as an agency for the purposes of general administration. Thus the whole care of the city poor remains in the hands of the guardians of the poor and is not attended to by the municipal

---

[1] *Review of Reviews*, May, 1893, 404.
[2] Local-Government Act of 1888, sec. 31, Third Schedule.

council. The same is true of the school administration. Where there are any public schools they are administered by the school board, which is elected in the school district, formed by the municipal borough, in the same way in which the school board is elected in the rural parishes. The work of the borough organization is therefore confined almost altogether to the administration of its property and to the execution of the various special powers which Parliament may have conferred upon the borough as the result of either special acts or of general acts conferring particular powers upon all boroughs. These acts cover such a wide field that the work of the municipal borough, notwithstanding that its powers are enumerated in the statutes, is very large in the domain of purely local matters—larger indeed than that of American municipal corporations.

The law of 1835 and the various laws which have been passed since that year relating to the boroughs have been, for the most part, consolidated in the Consolidated Municipal Corporations Act of 1882, which now governs the relations of the municipal boroughs. This act of 1882 simply continues the form of organization adopted by the act of 1835. The borough authority provided by the act of 1835 was the council, the same authority that had been developed in the preceding history of the English municipality. The council was then made to consist of the mayor, aldermen, and councillors. The councillors are elected by the burgesses, *i. e.* the municipal members who possess the municipal franchise. This is obtained by the paying of rates, and as rates are paid by occupiers as well as owners, every householder who has resided a certain time, to wit six months, within the municipality may vote. The decisions of the courts as to the meaning of householder or occupier are, however, such as to shut out mere lodgers from the franchise.[1] The result is, that no one who has not a real permanent interest in the municipality is allowed to vote. Every municipal citizen is eligible for the position of councillor, as are also all persons non-resident who reside within fifteen miles and own property within the borough limits or pay a certain amount of rates.[2] The term of office of municipal councillors is three years, one third of the councillors retiring every year.[3] Municipal elections are conducted on the principle of the Australian ballot act, *i. e.* the ballot act of 1872, and voters must be registered.[4] The aldermen are one third in number of the councillors and are elected by the councillors, as a matter of fact, from their own number though this does not seem to be required by the law.[5] Their term of office is longer, being for six years, one half their number retiring every third year.[6] The mayor is elected by the town council, in fact though not necessarily by law from among the aldermen, and serves for the term of one year.[7] The mayor and the retiring mayor are *ex-officio* justices of the peace.[8] The mayor, who is merely a member of the council is the only member of the council who may receive any remuneration,[9] notwithstanding that service as municipal officer

---

[1] Arnold, *Municipal Corporations*, 3d edition, 83, citing L. R., 8 Q. B. D., 195 ; 46 L. T. R. (N. S.), 253 ; *cf.* Albert Shaw on " Municipal Government in Great Britain," in *Pol. Sci. Qu.*, IV., 199 *et seq.*

[2] Municipal Corporations Act 1882, sec. 11.

[3] *Ibid.*, sec. 13.

[4] *Ibid.*, secs. 50 *et seq.*

[5] *Ibid.*, sec. 14 ; Arnold, *op. cit.*, 70.

[6] Municipal Corporations Act 1882, sec. 14.

[7] *Ibid.*, sec. 15.

[8] *Ibid.*, sec. 155.

[9] *Ibid.*, sec. 15.

is obligatory in that quite a heavy fine is imposed upon refusal to serve.[1] Where the mayor is remunerated his remuneration is fixed in amount by the council.

The borough council has entire charge of the whole of the municipal civil service. With hardly an exception it appoints, directs, and removes all officers of the borough, and may establish such new offices as it thinks best to establish and fixes the salaries that are attached to them.[2] Further it has complete control over the strictly municipal administration, decides within the limits of the law what branches of administration shall be attended to by the borough (*e. g.* may decide to establish and maintain municipal gas-works, or means of communication within the limits of the borough such as tramways), fixes the amount of rates that are to be levied in order to support the municipal administration, and has the entire charge of the financial administration of the borough.[3] With the large grants of power affecting purely local matters there has been formed at the same time quite an extensive administrative control which is exercised by the central authorities at London over the borough officers and authorities. This administrative control is exercised for the most part by the treasury and the local-government board.[4] It will be seen from this description of the position of the town council that there has been no attempt made to distinguish between the deliberative and the purely executive or administrative

[1] *Ibid.*, secs. 34 and 35.

[2] *Ibid.*, secs. 17–21.

[3] *Local Government and Taxation in the United Kingdom*, edited by J. Probyn, 280, 281. Most of these powers have been conferred by other acts than the act of 1882.

[4] *Ibid.*, 282 and 283.

functions discharged in the borough, but that all functions of purely local administration are attended to by the one authority, the borough council. There are no executive departments like those of the American city. In order more carefully to supervise the work of detailed administrative work the council usually divides itself into committees each of which has one or more of the administrative branches to attend to.[1] Thus we find in all boroughs which still have charge of the police, the watch committee, which attends to the administration of the borough police.[2] Under each of these committees there is a subordinate officer who is to carry out the commands and directions of the council or its proper committee. Thus in the administration of the police there is a superintendent of police.[3]

Finally in addition to being the strictly borough authority the borough council is made by the public-health act of 1875 the sanitary authority and as such has the usual functions to discharge.[4] The borough is also the school district, and where there are public schools in the borough, which is often the case, there is established a school board which is separate and apart from the council and elected in the way provided for all school elections, *i. e.* by the rate-payers, provision being made for minority representation in order to allow of the representation of an ecclesiastical minority. Where, however, there are no public schools supported by the district, there is what is called a school-attendance committee of the borough council, which is to see that the compulsory-education act is

[1] Municipal Corporations Act 1882, sec. 22.

[2] *Ibid.*, secs. 190–195.

[3] Probyn, *Local Government and Taxation, etc.*, 279.

[4] *Ibid.*

17

enforced.   This school-attendance committee is appointed in school districts, which are not at the same time municipal boroughs, by the guardians or by the local authority of an urban sanitary district.[1]

2. *The local-government district.*—England was by an act of 1872 divided into sanitary districts which are now governed by the consolidated public-health act of 1875.[2]   Provision was made for rural sanitary districts and for urban sanitary districts.   The former consist of such portions of the poor-law unions as have not been formed into urban sanitary districts; the latter are found in the boroughs and in all aggregations of inhabitants which have been declared by the local-government board at London to be urban sanitary districts or local-government districts.   Further various special acts have also formed into urban sanitary districts, under particular organizations, other portions of the country which are then called improvement act districts.[3]   As these are governed by charters peculiar to them, and as the borough has already been considered, it only remains to speak of the local-government district under the consolidated public-health act of 1875.   Each of these local-government or urban sanitary districts is governed by a local board of health elected by the rate-payers and owners of property according to the general system of plural voting which has been described in what was said in connection with the union.[4]   The term of office of member of the board is three years, one third of the members retiring every year.   Retiring members are, however, re-eligible.   Such a board has very much the same

[1] Craik, *The State and Education*, 113.
[2] Chalmers, *op. cit.*, 108.
[3] *Ibid.*, 109.
[4] *Ibid.*, 111.

powers over the district that the borough council has over the borough. In the first place the board has almost complete control over the entire subordinate personnel of the service of the district; in the second place it has to decide all matters of interest to the district, but does not in any case have charge of the police within the district, who are simply a part of the county police and under the charge of the county police authority. Like the municipal borough, the local-government district has competence only in really local matters. It has nothing to do with the general administration of the country except in so far as the sanitary administration may be considered a part of the general administration. Thus it has nothing to do with the administration of public charity which in the districts is, as in all other places, in the hands of the guardians of the poor, or with the administration of the public board schools, which are attended to by the parish organized as a school district. Its main powers have to do with the care of the streets, the beautifying of the town, and the preservation of the public health, which is its duty *par excellence*. Like the borough, the local-government district is often subject to a central administrative control. This, as in the case of the borough, affects the important acts connected with the financial administration and is so formed that, through its exercise, extravagance and unwisdom may be prevented.

V.—*Central administrative control.*

The central administrative control to which allusion has so often been made and which has resulted from the increase within recent years of local powers is exercised in the following ways:

1. *Necessity of central approval of local action.*—In order that certain of the acts of the local authorities may be of force it is necessary that they be approved by the central government. Thus, while the local authorities very generally have the power of issuing ordinances of a police character for the regulation of certain local matters and of sanctioning them within certain limits, as a general thing such ordinances must be approved either by the privy council, the treasury, or the local-government board before they may be enforced. The same is true of several of the most important acts connected with the local financial administration. Thus as a general thing all local loans need the approval of the treasury or the local-government board, and where a borough is permitted by such acts as the artisans' dwelling-houses acts to enter into a large scheme of local improvements the confirmation of their decision to put the acts into operation is generally necessary. In this case, as in some other instances, the confirmation is to be made by the local-government board, but has no force until it has in its turn been approved by Parliament.[1]

2. *Central audit of accounts.*—In almost all cases except that of the boroughs the accounts of the various local authorities are subject to a central audit and must for this purpose be sent in to the local-government board at London. For the purpose of auditing these accounts the local-government board has divided the country into auditing districts to each of which there is attached a district auditor under the control of the local-government board who has the right, subject to an appeal to the local-government board, to refuse

---

[1] Chalmers, *op. cit.*, 156.

to allow to the officer who has been spending money an allowance for money which in his opinion has been spent contrary to the provisions of the laws.[1] Accounts in the boroughs, are not, however, subject to this central audit, but are audited by the borough auditors, two of whom are elected by the municipal citizens and one of whom is appointed by the mayor and is known as the mayor's auditor.[2]

3. *Powers of compulsion.*—One of the reasons for the reform which has been made in the local-government system since 1834, was the desire to prevent any locality from escaping the burdens which were imposed upon it by the law, as the agent of the central administration, and from so neglecting such matters as were of vital interest to the people of the localities as to endanger their welfare. One of the characteristics of the central administrative control which was introduced as a result of the reform was therefore the grant of the power to the central administration to step in and force a negligent locality to perform the duties which were imposed upon it by the laws. This control is particularly strong in the poor-law administration, in the sanitary administration, and in the administration of public instruction. In the poor-law administration the local-government board has the power to lay down general rules of management which the boards of poor-law guardians are bound to observe, and to force the guardians to provide the necessary accommodation for the poor. In the sanitary administration the same body has the power to force the localities to do what it considers necessary for the preservation of the public

---

[1] *Ibid.*, 156 and 157.
[2] Municipal Corporations Act 1882, secs. 25 and 26.

health and in case of the refusal of the locality to obey, the local-government board has the right to appoint a temporary commission to do what is necessary and to raise the money expended by such commission by means of a rate to be levied on the rate-payers of the locality.[1] So in the matter of education. If the education department, *i. e.* the committee of the privy council for education, believes that there is not sufficient accommodation for the children of a given locality in the private schools which come up to the government requirements, it has the right to order the election of a school board, which then has the right to levy taxes and borrow money for the support of the public schools, or board schools as they are called, which are established by such school board. If the locality refuses to take the necessary action, the education department has the right to proceed as in the case of bad sanitary conditions.[2] As the borough organization proper does not, as has been said, attend to the poor-law or educational administration, and as in the case of the sanitary administration the borough council is the local authority, subject, like all local health boards, to the control of the local-government board at London, the central administration has through these powers of compulsion a pretty complete power over the administration of those matters which affect the general welfare, whether attended to in the urban or rural districts.

4. *Disciplinary powers over the local civil service.*— Besides the powers relating directly to the conduct of the administration which have been mentioned, the local-government board at London has also the

---

[1] Chalmers, *op. cit.*, 121.
[2] *Ibid.*, 151–154.

power of confirmation of almost all the appointments
to subordinate positions in the civil service of the
boards of poor-law guardians, and has the sole right
to remove such subordinate officers. It was considered
necessary to give to the central supervisory authority
of the poor-law administration such strong powers of
central control if it was to be hoped that any sort of
order was to be got out of the chaos which had been
the result of the uncontrolled exercise of the local
powers possessed by the overseers of the poor and the
justices of the peace under the old system.[1]

5. *Grants in aid and central inspection.*—In several
cases the law provides for grants of money made either
by the central government or by the county councils
to the various local authorities in aid of an administrative service, *e. g.* the police. As these grants are made
only after the particular service has been inspected by
the central government, and certified by it to have attained the standard required by the law, the central
administration may, by appealing to the self-interest
of the localities, exercise a large control over them in
the interest of administrative efficiency and uniformity.

VI.—*General characteristics.*

The general characteristics of the English system
are the same as those of the system obtaining in the
United States. That is the legislature enumerates the
powers of the localities and itself exercises a great control over their actions. One important difference is,
however, to be found in the way in which this control
is exercised. While in the United States all local
legislation is subject to about the same rules of proce-

[1] *Ibid.*

dure as are in force for all legislation, *i. e.* local bills are submitted to the proper committees which may or may not, as they see fit, give a hearing to parties interested, and are subjected to the regular number of readings, *viz.*, three; in England the absolute impossibility of the exercise by the legislature of any effective control over private and local legislation through the procedure adopted for ordinary legislation has led the English Parliament to develop a special procedure which must be followed in all cases of local legislation and to the insistence through the adoption of certain acts known as " clauses acts " upon the insertion in all special and local bills of certain important conditions. Further the rules of procedure adopted require that all parties interested in the passage of such bills shall have notice of them and that all the bills themselves shall be examined most thoroughly before particular committees, on which examination counsel are heard and witnesses examined. Finally in many cases local bills have to be approved by the local-government board at London or some other central authority. The development of this system has led to the formation of a special class in the legal profession who are known as parliamentary barristers, and whose sole occupation is the representation of parties before the parliamentary committees appointed for the purpose of examining local and private bills.[1]

The only other points in which the English system differs essentially from that adopted in the United States are : the more concentrated character of the local organization (*e. g.* in the county and borough);

[1] For a good description of the methods pursued see De Franqueville, *Le Parlement et le Gouvernement Britanniques*, vol. III., chap. xxxviii.

the greater strength of the central administrative control which has been rendered necessary by the possession by the localities of rather larger powers than those possessed by the United States localities, though it must be remembered that the same principle of the enumeration in the statutes of local powers, which is in force in the United States, is in force in England; and the greater number and more confused condition of the local areas. While in America the attempt has been made, and with generally great success, to confer almost all powers of local administration upon the county and town or some division of the town such as the school district, in England there is little coincidence of areas. Almost each branch of administration has its own area and in many cases its own administrative organization. The tendency is, however, towards a simplification of these conditions.

It is to be noticed that the system whose outline has been given, does not apply to the new county of London established by the act of 1888, whose organization differs considerably in details from that possessed by the ordinary English county; nor to the City of London, which is formally governed now very much as it was during the middle ages, and in such a peculiar way that little profit may be derived from a study of its institutions.

CHAPTER VI.

I.— The continental method in general.

The continental method of providing for the participation of the localities in the work of administration is quite different from the English method. In the first place the whole work of administration is divided into central administrative work which is to be attended to in the local districts by officers regarded as central officers, and into local administrative work imposed upon the local municipal corporations and attended to by them largely in accordance with their own ideas and through their own officers, who are in many cases separate and distinct from the representatives of the central administration in the local districts, although largely subject to the control of the central officers. In this system local power is given by the legislature by general grant, but its exercise is subject to central administrative control. The legislature has never attempted to enumerate the duties of the local corporations with the same minuteness as in England and in the United States. The statutes simply lay down the general principles of local administration, leaving to the local corporations to carry them out in their details. The legislature simply says that the local cor-

porations are to attend to local affairs or that the principal authority in a given district, which is at the same
time a corporation, is to control by its decisions the
affairs of the particular locality. What " local affairs "
means is to be derived from a perusal of the laws with
the object of finding what the legislature has said
shall be attended to by the central administration.
All that in the nature of things may be called administration and can be attended to by the localities and
has not been put into the hands of one of the central
authorities is then regarded as local in character. The
local municipal corporations are not therefore, as in
the United States, authorities of enumerated powers,
but have the right to exercise all such powers as they
wish to exercise, and in the manner they see fit to
adopt, provided they do not violate the letter or the
spirit of the law. But they are subject to a central
administrative control which is to prevent them from
encroaching upon the competence of the central government and in many cases from acting extravagantly
or unwisely.

In accordance with pure theory such a system of
territorial distribution of administrative functions
necessitates the existence of two separate sets of
authorities, one for the central administrative and one
for the local administrative work. The administrative
districts for the purposes of central administration
may or may not be the same as the districts of the
municipal corporations. Seldom, however, do we find
the pure theory carried to its logical results. Central
authorities are often, both in France and Germany,
called upon to attend to local matters at the same time
that they are attending to central matters and *vice*

versa. But in almost all cases there is a clear distinction between the two spheres of local and central action even when one authority acts in both spheres. The central control over such an authority will differ according as it is attending to central or local business.

The origin of this general system is found in the feudal system which was adopted more completely on the continent than in England and in accordance with which local autonomy received the fullest recognition.[1]

II.—History of the French system of local administration.

1. *Up to the revolution.*—The territorial unity of the French state was attained many years ago. The great vassals, who under a weak monarchy might have developed into independent princes, and whose domains might then have formed separate commonwealths, were suppressed by the kings and their lands became provinces of the kingdom of France. Most matters of administration, which during the feudal régime had been attended to by the vassals, became a part of the royal administration and were attended to by the royal officers who were subject to a strong central control. These were the intendants, who date from the time of Richelieu and Louis XIII, and whose work was performed in the provinces or generalities as they were sometimes called,[2] and the council of the king at the centre which directed all their actions and heard appeals, taken by individuals aggrieved, from their decisions.[3] The great centralization of govern-

---

[1] *Cf.* Stengel, *Organisation der Preussischen Verwaltung,* 18 and 19.

[2] Aucoc, *op. cit.,* I., 150, 151 ; Déthan, *L'Organisation des Conseils Généraux,* 4.

[3] Aucoc, I., 127.

ment under the absolute monarchy left little room for
any important local authorities; though we do find
even in the times of the most extreme centralization
that there were in certain of the provinces, called *pays
d'états* and occupying a privileged position, local assemblies having more or less control over the actions
of the intendants; and also that in some of the largest
of the cities the people had more or less well-defined
rights to elect their municipal officers, rights, however,
of which the king was endeavoring in the interest of
centralized government to deprive them.[1] The attempt made by the government of Louis XVI just
before the revolution to introduce into all parts of the
kingdom provincial assemblies modelled on the assemblies of the *pays d'états* failed;[2] and when
the revolution came in 1789 it found a most highly
centralized system of administration—a system which
hardly recognized the local districts as anything more
than administrative circumscriptions, possessing few
if any corporate powers. In these districts most
matters of administration were attended to by officers
either appointed and removed by the king in his
pleasure, or else subject to a strict central control.
The system which the revolution received as a legacy
from the absolute monarchy it made few radical
changes in.

2. *The revolution.*—The aim of the revolution was
social and political rather than administrative reform.
The revolution destroyed the social system on which
the absolute monarchy rested and introduced the
political principle that the people should have a larger

---

[1] Dareste de la Chavanne, *Histoire de l'Administration en France*, Chap. VI.

[2] Déthan, *op. cit.*, 6 *et seq.*

influence in the management of the government, but it did little more in the way of permanent administrative reform than to make the system more symmetrical than it had been before. The reason why no greater change was made in the general character of the administrative system was that the revolution really aimed at the same end that had been before the eyes of the absolute monarchy. This end was the crushing out of feudalism, the taking away from the privileged classes those semi-political and social privileges and exemptions which had been the cause of so many of the miseries of the absolute monarchy, but for which the absolute monarchy was responsible only in so far as it had allowed them to continue to exist, after the duties which had been originally associated with them had been assumed by the Crown, and after the expenses which their performance necessitated had been imposed upon the tax-payers. The cause of the dissatisfaction of the people with the absolute monarchy is to be found not so much in the character of the government which it gave the people as in the fact that its progress in the desired direction of abolition of feudal privileges seemed almost to have ceased. Therefore we find that the chief reforms of the revolution were social and, to a degree, political but not administrative. The celebrated night of the fourth of August, 1789, saw the abolition at one time of about all that was left of the feudal régime, while the exemption of the privileged classes from taxation was done away with by the new and proportional system of taxation formulated and enacted by the revolutionary leaders in the constituent assembly. After the constituent assembly had thus cleared away the débris of the feudal system it would have been suicidal for it to estab-

lish any system of administration in which large
rights of local government were given to the people of
the localities. For the people, as a whole, were so
utterly incapacitated for political work, through long
administrative and governmental tutelage, that it is im-
probable that they could have succeeded in governing
themselves well. At first it is true there was a slight
attempt in the direction of decentralization, but this,
as might have been expected, was unsuccessful and led
to disorganization and inefficient government, as indeed
did all attempts at reorganization until the government
of the directory when Napoleon came into power.[1]

3. *The Napoleonic legislation.*—Napoleon is to France
what the Norman kings are to England. He moulded
the form of her local institutions. The laws and decrees which were passed during the period of his control
of the government have, it is true, received during this
century most important modifications, but the main
principles of the present system of local administration
are even now to be found in them. Napoleon was
satisfied that the social principles of the revolution
could be adhered to only through the establishment of
a most centralized system of administration and government, by means of which the impulse to action should
come from the centre and which should be controlled
by those who were in sympathy with the new order of
things. Since Napoleon's time, however, there has
been great progress in the direction of decentralization.
This began with the government of the restoration and
reached its climax in the communes act of 1884[2]; and

---

[1] Aucoc, I., 151–3 ; Déthan, 16 *et seq.*

[2] *Cf.* Ducrocq, *Droit Administratif*, 95 *et seq.* The laws which did most in
the way of decentralization are those of June 22, 1833; March 21, 1831; July 18,
1866; August 10, 1871; April 5, 1884; and the decrees of March 25, 1852; and
April 13, 1861.

has consisted in the recognition of the possession by the localities, or at least the most important of the localities, of juristic personality and that there belongs to them a sphere of action of their own in which the central administration is to interfere but little. But notwithstanding the decentralization which has been going on, the French system of administration retains even at the present time quite enough of the old Napoleonic principles to make it, as compared with our own, a system which from the administrative point of view is quite centralized.

III.—*The department.*

The entire country is divided into departments, each of which is an administrative district for many matters of central concern and is at the same time a municipal corporation with its own affairs to attend to and its own officers to attend to many of these affairs.[1]

1. *The prefect.*—In each of these departments is placed an officer called the prefect, who is appointed and removed by the President of the republic on the proposition of the minister of the interior.[2] He receives a large salary, and, from the nature of his position, is obliged to devote his entire time to his work.[3] The prefect is thus a professional officer in that his work is his profession, but the laws do not require any special qualifications, the position being regarded as a purely political one, in the filling of which the President shall be allowed a wide discretion.[4] The prefect is at the

[1] Aucoc, I., 205.

[2] L. 28 *pluviôse, an* VIII, art. 2. This is the great Napoleonic administrative code.

[3] *Cf.* Decree Dec. 23, 1872.

[4] Block, *Dictionnaire, etc.,* 975, sec. 23.

same time the representative in the department of the central government and the executive officer of the purely local administration of the department.[1] That is he is a central and a local officer. As a central officer he is the subordinate of all the ministers of the central departments at Paris. He is to see that all the laws and decrees and central instructions sent out by the ministers are put into operation.[2] He appoints and dismisses a vast number of officers employed in the administrative services of the central government which need attention in the department. Among these officers are many who in the United States would be appointed directly by the heads of departments, *e. g.* he has to appoint all the wardens of the prisons, the less important postmasters and the letter carriers, the less important police officers, supernumeraries in the telegraph service which is a part of the post office, similar officers in the service of the direct and indirect taxes, highway overseers, teachers in the primary schools, *etc., etc.*[3] He has also a wide power of direction and control over the acts of all these officers and may remove them from office.[4] He has a large police ordinance power where the matters to be regulated are of such a character as to need uniform regulation for the entire department or for several communes therein.[5] This power of ordinance is, however, the delegated ordinance power, as his ordinances must always be based upon some statutory provision in order to have any force.[6] The prefect also represents the central government in the courts whenever it sues or is sued.[7]

[1] Aucoc, I., 155.
[2] Aucoc, I., 157.
[3] Block, *Dictionnaire*, 753, sec. 20.
[4] *Ibid.*, sec. 15 and authorities cited.
[5] L. April 5, 1884, art. 99.
[6] Aucoc, I., 159.
[7] L. 28 *pluviôse, an* VIII, art. 4.

Finally, as agent of the central government, the prefect exercises a large control over the local administration of the communes within the department.[1]

In the second place the prefect is a local officer. He is the executive officer of the local administration of the department. He appoints all the officers in the departmental service.[2] He has charge of the financial administration of the department, issuing all orders of payment on the department treasury.[3] He directs the execution of all departmental public works.[4] He draws up the departmental budget or estimate of expenses and receipts and represents the department before the courts.[5] As executive of the departmental municipal corporation the prefect is to execute the decisions and resolutions of the general council which finally determines how the affairs of the department shall be managed. As representative of the central government, however, the prefect is subject to the direction and control of the central departments at Paris.

2. *The council of the prefecture.*—By the side of the prefect is placed a council called the council of the prefecture whose members are appointed and dismissed by the President of the republic, are salaried, and may not follow any other occupation.[6] They are thus professional in character. This body is at the same time an administrative council and an administrative court. As an administrative council the council of the prefecture is called upon in many instances to advise the prefect. But while the prefect is thus bound in many

---

[1] Block, *Dictionnaire*, 756, art. 45.
[2] Aucoc, I., 158, 254.
[3] L. Aug. 10, 1871, art. 65.
[4] Aucoc, I., 254.
[5] L. Aug. 10, 1871.
[6] L. June 21, 1865, arts. 2 and 3.

cases to ask the advice of the council, he is never obliged to act in accordance with the advice so obtained.[1] This is in accordance with the French principle, which has already been alluded to, by which it is hoped to obtain a concentrated responsibility for every administrative act and at the same time to make it certain that the most important acts will not be performed except after proper deliberation. In addition to acting as a council of advice the council of the prefecture is in one or two cases to act independently of the prefect. Thus the commune may not undertake a lawsuit without first obtaining the consent of the council of the prefecture.[2]

3. *Departmental commission.*—Up to 1871 the prefect acted in his capacity as executive of the departmental municipal corporation subject to no permanent local control. He had, it is true, to execute the decisions of the general council of the department, but as this met usually only twice a year his actions as departmental executive were not subject to any effective control on the part of the departmental authorities. The law of August 10, 1871, which is to a large extent a code for the administration of the department, formed an authority of a more permanent character than the general council, which was not only to control the prefect in his administration of departmental affairs, but was also to perform some of the local duties of the prefect. The institution was modelled on a similar one in Belgium.[3] This is the departmental commission. This body is composed of from four to seven members and on it all sections of the depart-

[1] Aucoc, I., 163.   [2] *Ibid.*
[3] Déthan, *op. cit.*, ch. I., p. 51.

ment shall, as far as possible, be represented.[1]   Its
members are elected by the general council of the department,[2] receive no salary, and may follow other
occupations.[3]   It is thus a distinctively popular authority.   It meets once a month regularly and may
meet as often as is necessary.[4]   Its main duty is to
control the administration of departmental interests
by the prefect.   Thus it presents to the general council its views of the prefect's estimates for departmental
expenses.[5]   It also examines the accounts of the prefect who has to lay before it every month all his orders
of payment and his vouchers; and it makes such ob-
servations on them as it sees fit.[6]   It makes an inven-
tory of the property of the department.   Its consent is
necessary to the making of all important contracts
for the department by the prefect and to the bringing
and defending of suits to which the department is a
party.[7]   This control over the administration of departmental affairs by the prefect is its most important
duty, but in addition thereto it has in several cases an
actual power of decision in administrative matters
most of which were, before the law of 1871, decided
by the prefect.   Thus it determines the order of prior-
ity of departmental public works, and fixes the manner
of placing departmental loans when these matters have
not been attended to by the departmental general
council.[8]   It has a series of duties to perform relative
to the highways, aids in the assessment of the land tax,
and appoints the members of commissions attending
to works of a semi-public character which have been

[1] L. Aug. 10, 1871, arts. 69, 70.
[2] *Ibid.*
[3] *Ibid.*, art. 75.
[4] *Ibid.*, art. 73.
[5] *Ibid.*, art. 79, sec. 2.
[6] *Ibid.*, art. 78.
[7] *Ibid.*, art. 54.
[8] *Ibid.*, art. 81.

subsidized by the department.[1] Finally the general council may delegate its powers to the departmental commission.[2]

These are the executive officers in the department, and, so far as the purely departmental administration is concerned, they act mainly by executing the resolutions and decisions of the general council which really determines the character of the departmental administration.

4. *The general council.*—The general council is composed of members elected by the people of the department, one member being elected in each canton of the department.[3] The canton is little more than a judicial and election district. The general council is elected by universal suffrage.[4] All electors twenty-five years of age are eligible who have resided in a commune of the department six months.[5] One quarter of the members of the council may be non-resident provided they have an interest in the department which is evidenced by the fact of paying direct taxes or the possession of landed property therein.[6] Generally all professional officers of the government are ineligible.[7] Finally no one may be a member of two general councils.[8] The term of office is six years, one half of the members of the council retiring every third year.[9] The President of the republic may however, dissolve the general council by special decree.[10] In case he does so he must notify the legislature and must provide for an election for the fourth Sunday after the issue of the decree.[11]

[1] L. Aug. 10, 1871 *passim.*
[2] *Ibid.*, art. 77.
[3] L. Aug. 10, 1871, art. 4.
[4] *Ibid.*, art. 5 ; L. April 5, 1884, art. 14.
[5] L. Aug. 10, 1871, art. 6 ; L. April 15, 1884, art. 14.
[6] L. Aug. 10, 1871, art. 17, sec. 2.
[7] *Ibid.*, art. 8.
[8] *Ibid.*, art. 9.
[9] *Ibid.*, art. 21.
[10] *Ibid.*, art. 35.
[11] *Ibid.*, art. 36.

This body meets ordinarily twice a year,[1] but may be called together on any other occasion by decree of the President of the republic or on the demand of two thirds of the members.[2] The general council elects its own officers[3] and makes its own rules,[4] with the exception that the law fixes the quorum at a majority of its members, and provides that the ayes and the noes must be called at the request of one sixth of its members, and that the president of the council decides in case of a tie vote.[5] Its meetings finally are public[6] and its members receive no salary.[7]

The powers and duties of this body relate in the main to the affairs of the department. It does, however, have a few powers relative to matters which are general in character or to those of the communes within the department. The law which fixes its powers and duties is in form an exception to the general rule adopted upon the continent for the determination of the share of the localities in the work of administration. Nowhere in it do we find a general grant of the powers of local government to the general council. On the contrary, the law enumerates the cases in which the general council may act in the domains of both local and general administration. But in the domain of local administration the enumerated powers embrace such a wide range of subjects that what is in form an exception is not so in reality. For the law puts into the hands of the general council the control of all department property, finances, and taxes, of highways except the state roads, department public works of all kinds, public charity so far as that is a branch of

---

| [1] *Ibid.*, art. 23. | [3] *Ibid.*, art. 25. | [5] *Ibid.*, art. 30. | [7] *Ibid.*, art. 75. |
| [2] *Ibid.*, art. 24. | [4] *Ibid.*, art. 26. | [6] *Ibid.*, art. 28. | |

public administration, the apportionment of the quota, which the department has to pay of the direct state taxes, among the various districts of the department, the determination of election districts, and finally gives to the general council quite a large supervision over the administration of the communes within the department.[1] It will be seen from this enumeration that, so far as the administration of affairs affecting the department interests alone is concerned, the general council has about as wide powers as if the law had simply granted to the general council, as the communes act of 1884 has granted to the communes, the general power of local government. Finally the enumeration contains instances of the grant of powers which relate not to the department administration but to the general state administration, as well as instances of supervisory powers over the administration of the communes within the department. But the general council to which these wide powers are granted has been subjected to quite an important administrative control. In one or two instances, it is true, the law has provided for a special legislative control, in that it says that if the general council wishes to exceed the limits of the taxing power which have been fixed by the general budgetary law that is passed annually, or of the borrowing power, as that is fixed by the law governing the department administration, a special law will be necessary. These are however the only instances in which the law has made express mention of any application for legislative authorization and the very mention of the fact would seem to indicate that such a practice is quite unusual in France. There are, however, many

[1] L. Aug. 10, 1871, arts. 37 and 46.

instances enumerated in the law in which the action of the general council, in order to be valid, needs the approval of the central administration. Thus where the general council desires to sell or change the use of buildings which are used for the purposes of general state administration, as *e. g.* court houses, normal schools, prefects' offices, prisons, or garrison buildings of the *gendarmerie* (police), which all belong to the department corporation, it is necessary that the resolution of the general council ordering such sale or change of use receive the approval of the central administration, which is generally given by a decree of the President of the republic.[1] Again the resolutions of the general council, deciding what the department shall pay of the expense of public works constructed by the central administration but of peculiar advantage to the department, and as to the imposition or increase by the communes of *octroi* taxes, need central administrative approval, which is usually given in the same way.[2] Finally all powers granted to the council by laws other than the law of August 10, 1871, are subject to the same central approval. While in all these cases the central administration has the right to veto the resolution of the general council on the ground that it is unwise, still the resolution of the general council is valid if the central administration does not exercise this right of veto. In certain rare cases the resolutions of the general council need, before they are valid and capable of execution, the express approval of the central administration. The most important of these is the budget. Though the general council has in a general way control over the appropriations of the

[1] L. Aug. 10, 1871, art. 48.   [2] *Ibid.*

department, still the budget may not be executed until it has been expressly approved by a decree of the President of the republic. The purpose of this provision is to offer a means of preventing the general council from neglecting to provide for the expenses which have been imposed by law upon the department, *i. e.* department charges as they would be called in the United States. If the general council should so neglect or refuse, the President of the republic has the right, when the budget is presented to him, to insert in it the necessary appropriations and to provide for the levying of a special tax if that is necessary. These obligatory expenses or department charges are those necessitated by the management of those services for which the law makes it the duty of the general council to provide. They are contained in article 60 of the law of August 10, 1871; and among them may be mentioned the provision of the necessary buildings for the officers in the department, *e. g.* the prefect, the under-prefect, the department board of education, which is a council of advice to the prefect, the garrison buildings of the *gendarmerie,* the court houses, *etc., etc.* It seems, however, that the President can make no changes in the budget other than to make provision for such expenses. Of course if the President finds on examining the budget that the general council has levied taxes or has resolved to borrow money in excess of the limits imposed by the law he may annul the decision or resolution thus violating the law, on the ground that the general council has exceeded its jurisdiction. In fact the President may annul any resolution of the general council which is in excess of its powers. But the decree of the President thus annulling the resolution of the general council is not really a veto of its act, but is simply a formal statement that it has overstepped the bounds of its competence and that its action is therefore invalid. If the ultimate decision as to the validity of the acts of the general council lay in the hands of the President of the republic this central control might degenerate into an absolute veto of all the acts of the general council. But it would seem in accordance with the general principles of the French administrative law that an appeal may be taken from the decision of the President to the highest of the administrative courts, *viz.* the council of state, which has the right to declare the act of the President null and void in case it should deem that he had declared not within its competence a decision of the general council which really was within its competence.[1] Thus the final decision as to the jurisdiction or competence of the general council is made by the administrative courts and not by the active administration itself.

From this slight review of the powers and duties of the general council and of its relation to the central administration and government it will be seen that the initiation of almost all measures affecting the purely local affairs of the department is in the hands of the general council whose decisions may, in case it exceeds the powers granted to it by the law, be annulled by the central administration, subject to the control of the administrative courts. The general council may not, however, make such use of its powers as to neglect the

---

[1] See on this point decisions of the council of state of Nov. 19, 1866, reported in Dalloz, *Récueil Périodique*, 1866, Part III., 106 ; also Aug. 8, 1872, *Ibid*, 1872, Part III., 49 ; Nov. 19, 1880, *Ibid*, 1880, Part III., 34.

duties which have been imposed upon it by the law, and where the central administration is interested, as well as the department, a power of control is given to the central administration over the acts of the general council by means of which it may annul them on the ground of their inexpediency, in which case there is no appeal to the administrative courts. The statement which is sometimes made that the central government has an absolute veto over the acts of the general council is therefore not correct. On the contrary the general council has really more control over the affairs of the department than has the county authority over the affairs of the county in the United States or even in England. The great difference between the American and the French system is that while we give very few powers to the county corporation and make it necessary for the people of the county to have continual resort to the legislature for the grant of some special power whose exercise is necessary to their welfare, but seldom resort to any administrative control over the acts of the county authority, the French prefer to grant to the department authority very wide local powers but subject their exercise to a central administrative control, in order to provide some means to prevent the general council from exceeding its powers and from acting in such a way as to prejudice the interests of the state at large.

IV.—*The district.*

Each department is divided into *arrondissements* or districts, in each of which are placed an under-prefect and a district council.[1] The under-prefect is appointed

---

[1] L. 28 *pluviôse an* VIII, art. 8.

and dismissed by the President of the republic, and, like the prefect, is a professional officer. He is the subordinate of the prefect, his main duties being to carry out in the district the orders which he may receive from the prefect, though in some cases the law grants him discretionary powers.[1] There has been some talk of abolishing this office altogether on the ground of its uselessness, but two reasons have so far prevented this from being done. One of them is that the office of under-prefect is valuable as a means of educating men for the position of prefect. The other, more of a practical political character, is that the office is valuable as a means of patronage to the central government. The council of the district is elected in the same manner as the general council of the department.[2] Its functions are, however, quite unimportant and relate only to the central administration, as the district, not being a municipal corporation,[3] has really no affairs of its own to attend to. The most important function of the council of the district is to apportion among the communes in the district the quota of the direct apportioned taxes of the central government which has been apportioned to it by the general council.[4]

Both the general council and the council of the district are regarded as councils of advice to the central government, which is often obliged by law to ask their advice on matters of general administration affecting at the same time the interests of either the department or the district, though, in accordance with the French

---

[1] *E. g.* see decree of April 13, 1861 and law of May 4, 1864.

[2] L. July 30, 1874.

[3] L. May 10, 1838.

[4] L. May 10, 1838, arts. 40, 43, 45-7.

rule to which allusion has been made, it is never obliged to follow the advice so given.[1] In addition to
giving its advice when asked, both the general council
and the council of the district have the right to express
their wishes to the central administration in regard to
matters of peculiar interest to the section which they
represent, but care is taken to prevent this power from
degenerating into a mere expression of political views,
as it is expressly provided in the law that expressions
of the general or district council on political matters
are beyond its competence, and may be declared null
and void by the central administration.[2]

V.—*The commune.*

1. *History.*—Below the department district and canton
we find the commune as the lowest administrative unit.
The commune is either rural or urban, but the French
law makes no formal distinction in organization between
the two, both being governed by the same law, *viz.* the
law of April 5, 1884. While the department is an
artificial creation of the revolutionary period, the commune is a natural growth. Before the revolution we
find that there were, as a result of social and political
conditions, two kinds of local communities in France,
viz. the urban communes and the rural communes. In
the former were an officer, called by different names
but performing for the most part executive functions,
and a deliberative council. In the rural communes,
and even in some of the cities, a general meeting of the
inhabitants was often found together with a series of
executive officers.[3] A decree of 1702 established in

[1] L. Aug. 10, 1871, art. 50 ; L. May 10, 1838, art. 4.
[2] L. Aug. 10, 1871, art. 51 ; L. May 10, 1838, art. 44.
[3] *Cf.* Dareste de la Chavanne, *op. cit.*, I., 201.

each of these rural communes an officer called a syndic, who was to act to a large extent under the supervision of the intendant of the generality or province in which the commune was situated.[1] The acts of all these authorities were subject, just before the revolution, to very strict central control, which was one of the results of the administrative centralization of the absolute monarchy. In 1789 the constituent assembly decided to efface all distinction in administrative organization between the rural and the urban districts,[2] and provided for the formation of about 44,000 communes.[3] Different experiments at organization were made in the period between 1790 and the year VIII or 1800 when the Napoleonic legislation was adopted. By this legislation there were placed in each commune a mayor and a municipal council,[4] the former attending to executive business, both that relating to the commune, which was a municipal corporation, and that affecting the state as a whole, and the latter attending simply to local business. By this Napoleonic legislation, both the mayor and the members of the municipal council were appointed and could be removed by the central administration, while the decisions of the municipal council, even though they affected simply the local affairs of the commune, were in all cases subject to the approval of the central administration.[5] Since the overthrow of the empire there has been an almost continuous tendency to decentralize this extremely centralized system. In 1831 the municipal council became elective,[6] and by a gradual process the mayor has be-

---

[1] Aucoc, *op. cit.*, I., 170.

[2] L. Dec. 22, 1789—Jan. 8, 1790, art. 7.

[3] Aucoc, *op. cit.*, I., 171.

[4] L. 28 *pluviôse, an* VIII.

[5] Ducrocq, *op. cit.*, I.,217 *et seq.*

[6] L. March 24, 1831.

come elected by the municipal council in all the communes of France.[1] But up to about 1884 no actual power of decision was given to the municipal council, whose resolutions were in most cases subject to central administrative approval.[2] The law of April 5, 1884, has made a most radical change in this respect by providing that the decisions of the municipal council are absolutely final except in those cases in which the law has specially provided for central administrative approval.[3]

2. *The mayor.*—In each commune at the present time are to be found a mayor and several deputies who are to assist him in the performance of his duties, all elected by the municipal council. In both cases the choice of the council is limited to its members. They serve for the term of the council, but may be suspended by the prefect of the department for one month, by the minister of the interior for three months, and may be removed by the President of the republic. Removal makes the person removed ineligible for the period of one year.[4] Further, the prefect has quite a large control over the mayor in that the law provides that if the mayor refuses to do an act which he is obliged by law to do, the prefect may step in and, after demand made to the mayor, proceed to do the act himself or may have the act done by a special appointee.[5] The mayor and his deputies are unsalaried and are not professional officers like the prefect. Their official expenses are to be paid however.[6]

---

[1] Boeuf, *Droit Administratif*, 276 citing L. March 28, 1882.

[2] Ducrocq, *op. cit.*, I., 219 *et seq.*

[3] Boeuf, *op. cit.*, 265.

[4] L. April 5, 1884, arts. 75–86.   [5] *Ibid.*, art. 85.   [6] *Ibid.*, art. 74.

Like the prefect, the mayor is at the same time the agent of the central administration in the commune and is the representative and the executive of the communal municipal corporation. As an officer of the central administration he is in most cases under the supervision of the prefect. Among his duties as such central officer may be mentioned his duty to keep a register of vital statistics. As the French law expresses it, he is an officer of the *état civil*. As such he also solemnizes all marriages.[1] He is also an officer of what is known as the judicial police and, as such, has the power to file informations in purely petty offences and may act as public prosecutor in the smaller places.[2] He has to publish and execute all the laws and decrees within the commune, makes up the election lists, the census tables for the recruiting of the army, publishes the assessment rolls, *etc., etc.*[3] Finally the mayor has a large power of local police. He has quite a large power of ordinance, a power which, like the similar power of the prefect, is always based upon some express provision of law. The power of ordinance granted by the statutes is, however, quite a general one. He has the right to issue such ordinances as may be necessary to maintain good order, public security and health. He has also a large power of issuing orders of individual and not general application, as *e. g.* to fix the building line for particular edifices, to grant building permits, to remove nuisances, and so on.[4] All such ordinances and orders are sanctioned by the penal code,[5] which

[1] Boeuf, *op. cit.*, 281.
[2] *Code d'Instruction Criminelle*, arts. 11, 48–50, and 53.
[3] Boeuf, *op. cit.*, 287 ; Ducrocq, *op. cit.*, I., 197.
[4] L. April 5, 1884, art. 97 ; Boeuf, *op. cit.* 289 *et seq.*
[5] Art. 471, sec. 15.

punishes the violation of all legal ordinances and orders by a fine. An instance of the control which the prefect has over the acts of the mayor when the latter is acting as an officer of the general state administration, is to be found in the case of these ordinances and orders which may be repealed by the prefect within a month after their issue.[1]

As the executive officer of the communal municipal corporation the mayor has the appointment of most of the communal officers,[2] the only important exceptions being found in the case of the local constabulary who are, to a large extent, central officers and under central control, the teachers, the forest guards, and the communal treasurer. Further the mayor is to attend to the detailed administration of all local property and is to supervise the different administrative services which are attended to by the commune. Thus in the financial administration of the commune the mayor draws up the budget of receipts and expenses of the commune, orders all expenses to be paid, has the detailed management of the revenue and property of the commune, executes its contracts and supervises its accounts and its public institutions.[3] But in all these matters it must be remembered that the mayor is simply to execute the decisions of the municipal council, which has the final determination of all matters of communal interest.

3. *The municipal council.*— The municipal council is elected by universal manhood suffrage. Electors must have resided for six months within the commune or have paid direct taxes there. Electors must be registered in order to be able to vote.[4] The rules in re-

---

[1] L. April 5, 1884, art. 95.
[2] *Ibid.*, art. 102.
19

[3] L. April 5, 1884, art. 90.
[4] L. April 5, 1884, art. 14.

gard to eligibility are similar to those in force for the general council of the department.[1] The term of office is four years.[2] The council has four ordinary sessions each year, but extraordinary sessions may be called at any time.[3] The meetings of the council are generally public. The mayor presides at all meetings of the council except when his accounts are being examined. As a rule a majority of the members constitutes a quorum. Finally the council may be suspended for a month by the prefect; and may be dissolved by the President of the republic.

The duties of the municipal council relate almost exclusively to the local affairs of the commune, their general duties being so few in number and so unimportant in character as not to deserve special notice. In the legal provisions governing the powers of the municipal council we find a good example of the continental method of regulating the participation of the localities in the work of administration. The law of 1884 (the municipal code of the present time) simply says that the municipal council shall govern by its decisions the affairs of the commune. In order, however, to prevent the municipal council from being extravagant or acting unwisely, article 68 of the law provides that in certain enumerated cases the approval of some central authority, as a general rule the prefect, shall be necessary, before the resolutions of the council are of force. In general this approval of the central administration is necessary for the sale or long lease of communal property, for the undertaking of expensive public works, for the change of use of buildings used for general ad-

---

[1] *Ibid.*, art. 31.　　　　　[2] *Ibid.*, art. 41.
[3] *Ibid.*, art. 47.

ministrative purposes, for the regulation, laying out or closing of streets, for the levy of taxes above certain limits, and for the borrowing of money beyond a certain amount, and the imposition of *octroi* taxes, *i. e.* indirect taxes on objects consumed within the cities. Finally the budget of the commune must be submitted to the central administration, which must approve it before it can be executed. The purpose of submitting the budget to the central administration is to afford it an opportunity to see if the municipal council has made appropriation for the obligatory expenses made necessary by law, and to prevent the council from being extravagant. If the budget does not provide for obligatory expenses, levies taxes or borrows money beyond certain limits, or provides for the payment of the current expenses of the commune from loans or extraordinary revenue, the central administration may make changes in the budget so as to make it conform to the provisions of law or to what the central administration regards as proper. Otherwise the central administration may make no alterations in the budget as voted by the council.[1]

Finally, in order to prevent the municipal council from overstepping the bounds of its competence as an authority for the purposes of purely local administration and from assuming functions of a central character, it is provided that the central administration may declare any act of the municipal council outside of its jurisdiction to be void. In such case the municipal council or any one interested has the right to appeal from the decision, declaring the act of the municipal council void, to the administrative courts, which thus

[1] L. April 5, 1884, art. 145.

have the power of determining finally the question of local jurisdiction.[1]

It should be added finally that the municipal council is regarded as a council of advice to the central government, which in certain cases is obliged to consult it before proceeding to act. The council may further, just as may the general council of the department, express its wishes in regard to public matters, provided it does not make use of this power to create a political disturbance.[2]

VI.—*General characteristics of the French system of local administration.*

1. *General grant of local power.*—The French law is not nearly so specialized as is the law in the United States and England governing the powers of the local authorities. Much larger powers are granted to the localities by the legislature in France than in the United States or England. Thus a French city may adopt such institutions of local concern as it may see fit without being obliged, as is so often the case in the United States, to appeal to the legislature for power. It may, in accordance with the provisions of the general law governing the powers of communes, and on account of the general grant of local administrative power to the communes, establish municipal gas-works, or operate local tramways, though no special mention is made in the law of any such powers.

2. *Central administrative control.*—On account of the large powers granted by the legislature to the French local municipal corporations it has been thought necessary to provide a central administrative control

---

[1] *Ibid.*, art. 67. [2] *Ibid.*, arts. 61 and 72.

over their actions. This central control is exercised with three objects in view. In the first place, since all the local corporations or local officers are agents for the central administrative services, the central administration has the right to force the localities or local officers to act in such a way that matters of a general character placed in their charge will not suffer by their negligence or carelessness. In the second place this central administrative control is so formed that by its means the central administration may prevent any of the local corporations from so making use of their local powers as to encroach upon what is recognized as the sphere of central administration. In order, however, to prevent the central administration from so making use of its supervisory powers as to crush out all local administration, the local corporations or persons interested may appeal from the acts of supervision of the central administration to the administrative courts, which thus have the power of delimiting finally the sphere of local administration. In the third place the central administrative control is so formed as to permit the central administration through its exercise to prevent the localities from extravagance and unwise financial administration. In this last matter the central administrative control is supplemented by a central legislative control; and it may be added that this is the only instance in the French system of a legislative control like the one exercised by the United States commonwealth legislatures through special and local legislation.

Finally it is to be noticed that the system outlined above does not apply to Paris and the Department of the Seine, or to Lyons and the Department of the

Rhone, which have a special organization rather more subject to central administrative control than the system outlined.

3. *Professional character of the local officers.*—The officers who attend to the detailed work of administration are for the most part professional in character. The only important exceptions to this rule are to be found in the case of the mayor and his deputies, who, it will be remembered, are unsalaried. As a rule the unpaid officers in the French system are simply the members of the various deliberative assemblies, such as the general council and the municipal council, whose duty is to lay down general rules for the conduct of the administration of local matters, especially the matter of local finances. The administrative officers who attend to the detailed work of administration are, for the most part, salaried, devote their whole time to the public work, and are to act in all cases where the general welfare of the country is concerned in accordance with instructions issued to them from the central administrative authorities. In many cases stringent qualifications of capacity are required. This is especially true of the municipal civil service.

CHAPTER VII.

I.—History.

1. *Conditions in 1807.*—The present form of local government in Prussia was fixed in 1807. The Prussia of the time previous to 1807 was feudal rather than modern. The collapse of feudal Prussia at the time of the French invasion in 1806 was so sudden and so complete as to prove beyond peradventure that the magnificent fabric reared with so much pains by the great Prussian kings of the eighteenth century rested on most insecure foundations.[1] The administrative system which had come down from the time of Frederick William I was bureaucratic to the last degree. The result of such a system was that the people participated hardly at all in the administration or even in the government, and naturally not only had lost all political capacity, but also had come to regard the government either with indifference or with absolute hatred. The social conditions of the Prussian people also had been such as to favor one class at the expense of the others and at the same time to impoverish the country as a whole. The distinctions of class had been so fixed as almost to divide the people into castes, and artificial barriers placed about the freedom of trade

---

[1] See *Pol. Sci. Qu.*, IV., 650.

and labor in the interest of the richer classes had prevented all classes alike from making the best use of
their opportunities.

2. *The Stein-Hardenberg Reforms.*—After the fall
of Prussia, Baron Stein was made head of the administration and during the one year of service, from which
he was finally driven by the influence of Napoleon, was
the director of the policy of Prussia and may well be
regarded as the founder of the Prussia of to-day.
Recognizing the defects of the Prussian system, he formulated and published his plan of government; and
although unable during his short term of service to
secure the adoption of this plan, he left to his successors a model of administrative reform in his great
municipal corporations act of 1808.[1]   Besides this,
Stein was able to abolish serfdom, to make it possible
for those not of noble blood to acquire and hold land,[2]
and to introduce important reforms in the general
administrative system.[3]   Stein's concrete model of an
administrative system was to be found in the English
system as then existing.[4]   But his idea of granting

[1] What Stein's ideas of government were may be seen from the famous document which the Germans have christened Stein's " political testament."   This
document was the circular which Stein sent to the officers of the administration
when he bade them farewell on the occasion of his expulsion from Prussia at
the instance of Napoleon.   The reforms which he advocated therein were : the
abolition of hereditary magistracy, very common in some parts of Prussia, and
the transfer of all judicial and police functions to officers appointed by the
king ; the formation of a national legislature ; and the establishment of not
only the right but of the duty of all property-owning classes to participate both
in the legislation and in the administration of the state.   This last principle (of
obligatory service) was realized in Stein's municipal corporations act of 1808.
Cf. Bornhak, *Geschichte des Preussischen Verwaltungsrecht*, III., 4, where
a portion of the text of the " testament " is to be found.

[2] Edict, October 9, 1807.

[3] Ordinance, December 26, 1808.

[4] Meier, *Reform der Verwaltungsorganisation*, 240

to the nobility large local powers, to be exercised under central control so as to prevent the abuse of the powers granted, was not adopted. The failure of Stein's plans brought Hardenberg to the front in 1810. Hardenberg's ideas were quite different from those of Stein. Hardenberg felt that before many privileges of local self-government could be granted to the people, the poorer classes in the community must be released from their economic dependence upon the richer classes.[1] He had the experience of the French before him and believed that the first thing to do was to establish a strongly centralized administration like the French, which should be directed by men of liberal ideas.[2] Hardenberg was not, however, able to overthrow what Stein had already established. As a part of his reforms Stein had divided the country into government districts (*Regierungsbezirke*), at the head of each of which was placed a board called the "government" (*Regierung*),[3] which attended to almost all central administrative matters that in the nature of things could be attended to in the localities. Purely local matters, *i. e.* matters recognized as belonging to the sphere of local autonomy, which were quite unimportant, were left in the charge of the cities and the rural communities, which were to act under the supervision of these "governments." Hardenberg suffered this organization to remain, but, in order to increase his influence over it, he put every two or three districts under a provincial governor who was to represent the central government in the province.[4] Below the dis-

---

[1] Bornhak, *op. cit.*, III., 6; Meier, *op. cit,,* 135, 170–172 ; and Seeley, *Life and Times of Stein, passim.*

[2] Meier, *op. cit.*, 169.

[3] Ordinance, Dec. 26, 1808.

[4] Ordinance, April 30, 1815.

trict Stein had retained a historic Prussian division, to
wit the "circle," at the head of which was the landrath, who was now made the subordinate of the "government."[1]　All of these authorities—the governor,
the "government," and the landrath—were placed
under the direction of the chancellor, which last position Hardenberg had created for himself.　Most of the
officers in this organization were salaried and professional in character.　The system was therefore, as
before, a centralized bureaucracy.　But it was better
organized than before, and it was directed by a man of
advanced liberal ideas, who made use of the vast
power he possessed to further the interests of the state
as a whole.　With this wonderfully efficient instrument great progress was made in carrying out the social
and economic reforms begun by Stein.[2]

3. *Reactionary period from 1822–1872.*—But before the reform could be completed Hardenberg died
(in 1822) and a reaction immediately set in.　The
great landholders, whose privileges had been seriously
diminished by what had been accomplished, came forward and managed to persuade the king to grant them
certain powers in the domain of purely local government.　Local legislatures were formed in which the
landholders had almost complete control[3]; and the
attempt was made later to form out of delegates from
these local legislatures a national parliament.[4]　This
attempt was frustrated by the revolution of 1848,
which was largely a protest by the commercial and
industrial classes against the monopoly of governing

---

[1] Ordinances of July 30, 1812, and July 30, 1815.

[2] *Pol. Sci. Qu.*, IV., 655.

[3] L. June 5, 1823.

[4] Patent and Ordinance of Feb. 3, 1847.

which the landholders were beginning to claim. The result of the revolution was the formation of a constitution[1] in which the suffrage was made to depend not upon the ownership of land but upon the ownership of any kind of property. At first the legislature which was formed on this basis contained a liberal majority which set to work to curtail the powers of the landowners. This led to another reaction, *viz.*, the conservative reaction of 1850–60, during which the entire power of the administration was prostituted in the interest of the Conservative party and the landholders.[2] This preying of one class upon another, which is so characteristic of the internal history of Prussia from 1822 to 1860, was largely the result of the weakness of the monarchy during that period and of the introduction of the principle of the parliamentary responsibility of the ministry into a country in which the people had not as yet learned how to govern themselves. It was only natural therefore that, when the monarchy became stronger by the accession of the late King William I, who repudiated the principle of the parliamentary responsibility of his ministers, this class tyranny should cease. The great constitutional conflict in Prussia which followed his accession to the throne (1860–4) showed the Prussian people that they had found their master, and that the Crown in a monarchial country is the natural arbiter between conflicting social classes and should protect the weak against the aggressions of the strong.

4. *Reform of 1872.*—It was seen that important changes must be made in the system of local govern-

[1] Promulgated Jan. 31, 1850.

[2] *Pol. Sci. Qu.*, IV., 656–58 ; Gneist in *Revue Générale du Droit et des Sciences Politiques*, Oct., 1886 ; Bornhak, *Geschichte, etc.*, III., 256.

ment in order to accustom the people to exercise their powers with moderation and with a regard for the interests of the minority. The necessary concrete measures were sketched by Dr. Gneist of the University of Berlin, and one of the greatest of modern public lawyers, in his little book entitled *Die Kreisordnung.* In this work Dr. Gneist referred, as had Stein before him, to the English system of local administration which they both knew so well and admired so much. After a long discussion the plans advocated by Gneist were for the most part incorporated into the law of Dec. 13, 1872, commonly known as the *Kreisordnung.* The adoption of these plans was largely due to Prince Bismarck, who believed strongly in local autonomy and self-administration, and who supported the ideas advocated by Gneist in the face of the opposition of the general public and of that of his colleagues in the ministry and the greater part of the government officials who were loth to give up any of the powers which they possessed in the organization founded by Hardenberg.[1] In addition to the *Kreisordnung* several other laws were passed in the course of the next ten years, all either carrying the reform further, or modifying details which experience had shown to be faulty.

The definite ends which this reform has had in view are :

First.   The extension of the sphere of local autonomy.

Second.   The introduction of a judicial control over the actions of administrative officers in the hope of

---

[1] As to the position and the influence of Prince Bismarck see Gneist in *Revue Générale, etc.,* Oct., 1886 ; *Preussen im Bundestag,* IV., 22, cited in *Pol. Sci. Qu.,* IV., 661.

preventing a recurrence of the prostitution of the powers of the administration in the interest of party or social faction.

Third. The introduction of a non-professional or lay element into the administration of central as well as of local matters in the hope of increasing the political capacity of the people.[1]

II.—*Provincial authorities.*

In accordance with continental ideas as to the territorial distribution of administrative functions two spheres of administrative action are recognized by the law : the one, central ; the other, local. For the purposes of the central administration which needs attention in the localities, the country is divided into administrative circumscriptions called provinces, government districts, circles, *etc.*, in which are officers under the control of the heads of the various executive departments at Berlin. For the purposes of local government certain municipal or public corporations have grown up which have their own officers and their own property separate and apart from that of the central government. At the time of the reform in many instances the boundaries of the administrative circumscriptions for the purposes of central administration were not identical with those of the various public corporations, *e. g.* the boundaries of the administrative provinces were not the same as those of the public corporations bearing the same name. In most cases, further, the authorities for the purposes of central administration were not the same as those of the public corporations. The reform of 1872 has endeavored to

---

[1] De Grais, *Handbuch der Verfassung und Verwaltung, etc.*, 1883, 51.

simplify matters. It has in the first place adopted the
old divisions, *viz.*, the provinces, districts, and circles,
but it has added a new division, *viz.*, the justice of the
peace division (*Amtsbezirk*) ; in the second place it has
in almost all instances insisted upon the coincidence of
the boundaries of the corresponding areas. Thus at
the present time in almost all cases the area of the administrative province is the same as that of the provincial corporation. In the third place the central and
local authorities within the same area have in most
cases been consolidated. In the province, however, the
attempts at such consolidation were unsuccessful.
Therefore the provincial authorities or rather the
administrative authorities in the province must be
distinguished as *Behörden der Allegemeinen Landes-
verwaltung, i. e.* as authorities for central administration, and as *Organe der Provinzialverbände, i. e.* as
authorities for local provincial administration.

Among the authorities for the general or central administration of the country are to be mentioned :

1. *The governor (Oberpräsident).*—This officer is
appointed and dismissed by the king at his pleasure.
He is a member of what is called the higher administrative service,[1] and is thus a purely professional officer.
He is the agent in the province of the central government, *i. e.* of all the executive departments at Berlin ;
the permanent representative of the ministers ; and
from his decision as such representative there is no
appeal, since the ministers are regarded as acting
through him. As such agent he must report to all the
ministers every year, and execute any orders which
they may send to him, is entrusted with considerable

[1] *Infra*, II., p. 49.

discretion of action in times of extraordinary danger from war or other causes,[1] exercises either in first or second, but in all cases in last instance very large powers of supervision over the actions of subordinate officers and authorities, as well as over the local administration of various important municipal corporations, such as the province, the circle, and certain of the larger cities,[2] and appoints the justices of the peace (*Amtsvorsteher*).[3] He attends to the administration of all business which interests the entire province or more than one government district. For example, he issues a long series of police ordinances[4]; supervises the churches[5]; transacts all business which relates to an entire army corps[6]; acts as president of a series of provincial councils or boards, such as the provincial council, the provincial school board, and the provincial board of health.[7]

2. *The provincial council.*—Up to 1875, when the late reform was introduced into the provincial administration, the governor, himself a professional officer, transacted the business of the central government in the province unchecked in the performance of his duties by the control of any popular authority. But one of the main objects sought by the reform was the introduction of a lay element into the administration

[1] Instruction of December 31, 1825 ; *cf.* Stengel, *Organisation der Preussischen Verwaltung*, 317, 318.

[2] *Allgemeine Landesverwaltungsgesetz* of July 30, 1883, sec. 10, hereafter cited as *A. L. V. G.; Kreisordnung* of 1872, sec. 177, hereafter cited as *K. O.; Zuständigkeitsgesetz* of July 26, 1880, sec. 7, hereafter cited as *Z. G.*

[3] K. O., secs. 56–58.

[4] With the consent of the provincial council, of which later. A. L. V. G., secs. 137, 139.

[5] Loening, *Deutsches Verwaltungsrecht*, p. 83, with authorities cited.

[6] *Ibid.*

[7] Instruction of 1825, sec. 3 ; A. L. V. G., sec. 10.

of affairs affecting the country as a whole. This end was attained by the formation of the provincial council. This body consists of the governor, as its president, a single councillor of a professional character, and five lay councillors, citizens of the province, *i. e.* ordinary citizens without any professional education and unsalaried. The professional councillor is appointed by the minister of the interior, must be qualified for the higher administrative service, and his term of office is practically for life. The lay members of the council are appointed by the provincial committee—a popular body—from among the citizens of the province eligible for member of the provincial diet. Their term of office is six years.[1] In the organization of this body, it will be noticed, the lay element predominates. Provision is made for professional members in the hope that by reason of their knowledge and experience the business of the council may be more wisely and more quickly transacted.

The duties of the council are of three classes. In the first place it exercises a control over the actions of the provincial governor, *e. g.* its consent is necessary for all his ordinances.[2] In the second place it acts as an instance of appeal from certain decisions of inferior authorities, such as the district committee.[3] In the third place it decides as an executive authority certain administrative matters ; *e. g.* the number, time, and duration of certain markets,[4] and questions relative to the construction of certain roads.[5] Of these duties,

[1] A. L. V. G., secs. 10–12.
[2] A. L. V. G., sec. 137 ; Z. G., sec. 51.
[3] A. L. V. G., sec. 121.
[4] Z. G., sec. 127.
[5] Stengel, *Organisation der Preussischen Verwaltung,* 435.

those of the first class are by far the most important, as it is through their performance that a popular lay control is exercised over the bureaucratic professional administration of central matters in the province.

3. *The government board and president.*—Each province is divided into from two to six government districts. At the head of each of these districts is a board called the government (*Regierung*). This is composed exclusively of professional officers, *viz.*, the president, several division chiefs, councillors, and assistants. They are all appointed by the central government at Berlin and, like the governors of the provinces, belong to the higher administrative service.

The competence of the governments originally (and at the time of the late reform) embraced all matters of administration that could be attended to at all by territorially limited authorities and in so far as special authorities had not been established to attend to them.[1] This last was not often the case. Separate authorities had indeed been established for the administration of the customs, but this was the most important instance.[2] In general all matters of central administration attended to in the localities were attended to by the governments. They were by far the most important administrative authorities in the entire Prussian system. They acted under the direction of the central authorities at Berlin or that of the representatives of the central authorities in the provinces, *viz.*, the provincial governors. Finally in addition to the actual administrative duties which they performed, they exercised a control over the various authorities of the central administration immedi-

[1] Ordinance of Dec. 26, 1808.
[2] Stengel, *Wörterbuch, etc.*, II., 972.

ately subordinated to them and over the various local public corporations.

With the introduction of the reform measures, however, the importance of the governments has somewhat decreased, owing to the establishment of other more popular authorities and to the modification in their own organization which thereby became necessary. In the "district committee" a lay authority was established in the government district[1] similar to the provincial council in the province. This innovation reduced the government so much in importance that it was felt advisable to abolish its most important division, that of the interior, which had charge of the police administration (*i. e.* the issue of police ordinances and orders) and of the supervision of the inferior authorities both of the central and of the local administration. All of these duties were assigned either to the government president, acting alone or under the control of the district committee, or to the district committee. For all other matters within the competence of the government the old organization is the same as before: *i. e.* in school, tax, and church matters the government still acts as a board of which the government president is the presiding officer.

The government president thus occupies a double position. He is either an officer with power of independent action, or he is the presiding officer of a board in which lies the real power of decision. But wherever he has independent powers of action, he is subjected to the control of the lay district committee, of which he is at the same time the president. The result is an extremely complicated organization—which, however,

---

[1] A. L. V. G., sec. 153.

answers the purposes sought by the reform. The matters left in the competence of the existing divisions of the government are matters which are not thought to be proper subjects for popular administration. The management of the domains of the state, of the central taxes and of education (*i. e.* of its pedagogical side) and the control over the churches are not regarded as subjects in which a popular control would lead to advantageous results ; but the management of police matters and the supervision of the subordinate authorities, particularly of the local corporations, are matters in which it is particularly desirable that the people should have some influence.

4. *The district committee.*—This body is formed of the government president as its presiding officer, and six councillors.[1] Two of these are professional in character, are appointed for life by the king, and must be qualified, the one for the judicial service, the other for the higher administrative service. One of these professional councillors is, at the time of his appointment, designated as the deputy of the government president in his capacity as the presiding officer of the committee ; he is called the administrative court director, and presides over the deliberations of the committee when it acts as an administrative court.[2] The other four members are lay members and are elected by the provincial committee from among the inhabitants of the district, not professional officers. It will be noticed that the character of this committee is the same as that of the provincial council. It is distinctively a lay authority, although it has a sufficient number of profes-

[1] A. L. V. G., sec. 28.   [2] *Infra*, II., p. 253.

sional members to ensure the rapid and wise discharge
of business.

While the district committee in the district sub-
serves the same purpose as the provincial council in the
province, its competence is more extended.   Its main
function is to exercise a control over the actions of the
government president, so that the administration may
be made popular in character.[1]   Thus all police ordinances, the issue of which is the chief function of the
government president when acting alone, need the
consent of the district committee.[2]   But this committee
has positive functions also.   In many cases it acts in
first instance ; *e. g.* it supervises inferior authorities
and municipal corporations, especially the cities.   It
has also an appellate jurisdiction.   This is of two kinds,
one administrative and the other judicial.   In what
cases it acts as an administrative authority, and in what
cases it acts as a judicial body, is decided by the statutes.[3]   The general principle would seem to be that
where rights of individuals are involved, the committee
acts as a judicial body.   In its double capacity of authority and court, its jurisdiction is very large ; and its
establishment has done much to weaken the importance of the " government," which was absolutely professional in character, and to establish the desired lay
control over the administration.

5.   *The provincial diet.*—Matters of purely local interest to the province—matters which the law recognizes
as falling within the domain of provincial autonomy—
are attended to by a second class of authorities, *viz.*,
the organs of the provincial municipal corporation

---

[1] Z. G., sec. 13.   [2] A. L. V. G., sec. 139.
[3] Stengel, *Organisation, etc.*, 330, 415,

(*Organe des Provinzialverbandes*). These authorities
are the direct successors of the old feudal estates of
the provinces which have come down from the middle
ages. The original Stein-Hardenberg legislation did
little to develop them; it was felt that the feudal elements were too strong in them to permit of any healthy
development. After Hardenberg's death they received
increased powers. They were so organized, however,
as to put their entire control into the hands of the
large owners of land. The main purpose of the reform movement has been so to reorganize them that
they might be entrusted with a large part of the work
which was then being done by the central administration and which was susceptible of decentralization.
The main point in this reorganization is the provision
for the representation of all classes of the people
within the province. The old system of representation was completely done away with and the present
provincial diet was established.[1] This is composed of
representatives from each of the circles into which the
province is divided, the number of representatives depending upon the population of the circles.[2] These
representatives are elected by the circle diets of the
rural circles and the municipal authorities of the urban
circles, *i. e.* cities of 25,000 or more inhabitants.[3] This
method of election assures the larger cities a fair representation in the provincial diet; and the method of
electing members of the diets of the rural circles, is
such as to guarantee to the smaller cities and the other
social interests a voice in the selection of the members
of these diets and, as a result, representation in the

[1] *Provinzial-Ordnung* of June 29, 1875, hereafter cited as P. O.
[2] P. O., secs. 9, 10.   [3] *Ibid.*, secs. 14, 15.

provincial diet also. The term of office of the members of the provincial diet is six years; and the qualifications of eligibility are German citizenship, residence in the province or the possession of landed property therein for at least a year, good moral character and solvency.[1]

The diet is called together by the Crown once in two years and as many other times as its business makes its meetings necessary.[2] The governor of the province attends to this matter for the Crown and, as the royal representative, opens its sessions and has the right to speak therein.[3]

The functions of this body relate almost exclusively to the purely local matters of the provincial administration. It decides what local services shall be carried on by the provincial corporation in addition to those which have been positively devolved upon it by law, and it raises the funds necessary for the support of the provincial administration.[4]

Its decisions, says Prof. Gneist, relate to the construction and maintenance of roads ; the granting of moneys for the construction and maintenance of other means of public communications ; agricultural improvements ; the maintenance of state alms-houses, lunatic asylums, asylums for the deaf and dumb and blind and others, artistic collections, museums and other like institutions. . . . The provincial diet votes the provincial budget, creates salaried provincial offices and deliberates upon provincial by-laws.[5]

These by-laws, it must be added, simply regulate minor points in the organization of the province which have not been already fixed by law, such as the details regarding the elections. They must be approved by

[1] *Ibid.*, sec. 17. [2] *Ibid.*, sec. 25. [3] *Ibid.*, sec. 26. [4] *Ibid.*, secs. 34-44.
[5] *Revue Générale du Droit et des Sciences Politiques*, Oct., 1886, 262.

the Crown.[1] In addition to the duties imposed upon the province by law, the diet may assume such other duties as it sees fit which are not in direct opposition to the purposes of provincial organization.[2] Finally the diet elects all the officers who attend to the local administration of the province.[3]

From this description of its duties it will be seen that the provincial diet determines largely what the character of provincial administration shall be. The law, of course, imposes certain duties upon the province which it must perform and which it may be compelled to perform, but the law does not limit its competence. On the contrary the law allows it to do almost anything which falls within the scope of what is recognized as proper for provincial administration.[4] Under the new system which imposes upon the province much of the work formerly done by the central administration, and leaves it free to do as much more purely local work as it will, the widest opportunity is given for development in accordance with particular local needs.

6. *The provincial committee.*—This is the executive authority for the local administration of the province. The number of its members varies, according to the by-laws of the different provinces, between seven and fourteen.[5] They are elected by the diet from among those citizens of the empire who are eligible to the provincial diet.[6] The term of office is six years, half of the members retiring every three years.[7] The members of this committee (and the same rule applies to the members of the provincial diet) receive no pay or

[1] P. O., sec. 119.
[2] Loening, *Deutsches Verwaltungsrecht*, 219.
[3] P. O., sec. 41.
[4] Stengel, *Organisation, etc.*, 289, note ; P. O., sec. 37.

[5] P. O., sec. 46.
[6] *Ibid.*, sec. 47.
[7] *Ibid.*, sec. 48.

salary of any kind for the performance of their duties : the province only pays their necessary expenses.[1]

The duties of this committee are to carry on the administration of the province in accordance with the general principles laid down by the provincial diet in its resolutions.[2] Its subordinate executive officer, on whom the detailed or current administration falls, is the provincial director (in some cases there is a board instead of a director), who is elected by the diet and must be approved by the king, and who is a salaried officer.[3] His position is that of a superintendent of the entire provincial civil service for purely local matters. He has no discretionary powers; the provincial committee is the discretionary executive of the province, and the director simply carries out its decisions. Service as provincial officer, it should be said, is never obligatory. The original draft of the bill which afterwards became the provincial law made this provincial organization less complicated than it now is, providing that the provincial committee should also perform the duties which have been devolved upon the provincial council; but the Conservative party in the House of Lords, whose interests were at stake, felt that this plan would not allow them sufficient independence in the management of purely provincial affairs, and insisted upon a complete separation of the general and local functions of administration in the province. The result was the formation of the separate authorities described above.[4]

Before closing this account of the administration of the province, it should be noticed that a large part of

[1] *Ibid.*, sec. 100.   [2] *Ibid.*, sec. 45.   [3] *Ibid.*, sec. 87.

[4] Stengel, *Organisation, etc.*, 150.

the revenue of the province comes from subsidies which were given by the central government to the province at the time of the reorganization of the provincial administration. The purposes for which such subsidies shall be spent are designated in the laws. In order, however, to permit the provinces to develop in accordance with their particular needs, the law provides that the provinces may raise other money by levying taxes.[1] These taxes shall consist of lump sums of money, which the circles forming parts of the province are to pay into the provincial treasury, and whose amount is to be fixed in accordance with the amount of direct taxes paid to the central government by the people residing within the circles.[2] The circle and not the individual is the taxpayer in the provincial system of finance, just as the circle and not the individual is the voter for representatives to the provincial diet. In order, however, to prevent the provincial diet from overburdening the circles, it is provided that where the province shall demand from the circle more than fifty per cent. of the amount of central taxes levied in the circle, the consent of the supervisory authority of the central government (the ministers of the interior and finance) shall be obtained.[3] The making of loans is subject to the same limitation. This is the means which has all along been adopted to restrict the actions of the provincial diet, *viz.*, a central administrative control. Thus the by-laws and resolutions which the provincial diet may adopt, filling up details in the law, often require for their validity either the approval of the Crown or that of one of the ministers.[4] Again, if any

[1] P. O., sec. 105.
[2] *Ibid.*, sec. 107.
[3] *Ibid.*, sec. 119.
[4] *Cf. supra*, p. 311.

provincial authority endeavors to do anything which is outside of its competence, the supervisory officer, *viz.*, the governor, has the right to suspend its action. Finally the Crown may dissolve the diet, and the governor may open an appropriation and levy the necessary taxes for all provincial charges for which the diet has neglected to make provision.[1] The provincial authorities may usually appeal from the decision of the supervisory authority to the superior administrative court at Berlin. The central control is thus prevented from becoming arbitrary.

III.—*The circle authorities.*

While the law recognizes, in the case of the circle as in the case of the province, that there is a sphere of local and a sphere of central administrative action which are quite distinct, it still has not seen fit to provide separate authorities for each of these different spheres of action, but on the contrary has conferred on the same authorities the right to act in both spheres. But when these authorities act in purely local matters, they are not subjected to the same strict control as when they act for the central administration. The work of the circle, further, is essentially local in character, while the work of the province affects rather the country as a whole. The law governing the organization of the circle authorities was the model on which was formed the law governing the provincial administration. There is, therefore, the same combination of professional and lay elements which has already been pointed out in the foregoing description of the provincial authorities. The only difference is that one

[1] P. O., secs. 121, and 122.

set of authorities performs all the duties in the circle which two sets of authorities perform in the province. The circle authorities are the landrath, the circle committee, the justice of the peace, and the circle diet.

1. *The Landrath.*—The landrath is the agent of the central administration, discharging in the administrative district of the circle about the same duties that are performed in the province by the governor, and in the government district by the government and the government president. He is the subordinate of the government president. He is at the same time the executive for the current local administration of the circle. In this capacity he is the subordinate of the circle committee, of which he is also president.[1] He is a professional officer, and must be qualified for the higher administrative service, and is appointed by the Crown.[2]

2. *The circle committee.*—The circle committee also is an agent as well for the central as for the local administration of the circle.[3] It occupies in the administrative district of the circle the same position that the district committee occupies in the government district, and the provincial council in the province. That is, it has certain executive functions to perform, and exercises a lay control over the actions of the professional landrath. In so far it acts as an authority of the central administration.[4] As local agent, it is the discretionary executive of the circle. It conducts the administration of the circle in accordance with the resolutions of the circle diet.[5] The circle committee is a distinctively lay authority. It is composed of the landrath, as its president, and of six members chosen

---

[1] K. O., sec. 76.　　[2] *Ibid.*, sec. 74.　　[3] *Ibid.*, sec. 130.
[4] Stengel, *Organisation, etc.*, 339, 392.　　[5] K. O., sec. 134.

by the circle diet from among the members of the circle.[1] The term of service is six years,[2] and the office is obligatory in that a fine is imposed for refusal to serve for at least half the regular term.[3] As an authority for the central administration it has under its direction the various justices of the peace. As the local executive authority of the circle it has under its direction the landrath and all other circle officers.[4]

The circle committee was modelled largely upon the English petty and special sessions of the peace. It performs in Prussia many of the duties, especially those of a police character, which its English prototype performed in England. Thus it is the general rural licensing authority, is a highway authority, and acts as the supervisory instance over the actions of the Prussian justice of the peace—which office is likewise constructed upon the English model.

3. *The justice of the peace.*—The office of justice of the peace is one of the most important established by the reform. One of the chief ends of the reform movement was to do away with the institution of hereditary magistracy, which existed especially in the eastern provinces of the kingdom, and under which the local police was administered by the large landholders. The purpose of the reform was to abolish this, almost the last relic of feudalism, and to put the local police into the hands of officers appointed by the Crown,— who, at the same time, should not be professional in character, but, like the English justices of the peace, should be chosen from society at large, should be obliged to serve, and should receive no salary for the

---

[1] *Ibid.*, sec. 131.
[2] *Ibid.*, sec. 133.
[3] *Ibid.*, sec. 8.
[4] *Ibid.*, secs. 134, 137.

discharge of these public duties. The office was to be honorary. As Dr. Gneist says:

The principal end of the law [*i. e.*, the circle law of 1872] was, after the analogy of the English justices of the peace, to attract into the service of the state the well-to-do and intelligent classes. With this end in view the territory was divided into 5658 small divisions, each of which embraced a number of manors and townships with an average population of 1500 inhabitants. In each of these divisions are a justice of the peace and a deputy, who are appointed in the name of the Crown by the governor of the province from a list drawn up and presented to him by the circle diet. . . . The duties of the justice of the peace consist principally in the administration of the police of his division. It is he who takes police measures against vagrants, administers poor relief, prevents violations of the law ; he interposes in disputes between masters and servants ; he watches over the application of the building, health, and game laws and the laws passed to preserve order in hotels and public places ; he supervises the maintenance and the police of highways. His orders are sanctioned by short terms of imprisonment ; while he can, in necessary cases, order provisional arrest without encroaching upon the ordinary jurisdiction of the criminal courts. He supervises the daily action of the executive officers of the police force and has the right to amend all acts of theirs which in his judgment are inexpedient or incorrect. . . . The justice has under his orders the mayors of the townships and the personnel of the *gendarmerie*. He himself is not put under the disciplinary power of the landrath, but under that of a sort of a *judicium parium*—the circle committee— with a right of appeal from their decision to the courts of justice.[1]

This experiment seems to have proved a success. In the ten years immediately following the introduction of the reform there was only one case of the dismissal of a justice of the peace from office for corrupt administration. Of course the personnel of the justices

[1] Gneist in *Revue Générale, etc.*, Oct., 1886, 252. See also K. O., secs. 48, 58, 59.

of the peace must to a large extent be the same as that of the old police system—that is, the larger landholders will hold the offices. But there is a great difference between an hereditary and an appointed magistracy, even when the class from which the magistrates are taken remains the same. The power of appointment possessed by the governor makes it possible to exclude from the office any person who is notoriously actuated by class motives. Further the control possessed by the circle committee, which has the right to remove a justice of the peace, and which is not composed exclusively of representatives of the landholding classes, must tend to restrain any justice of the peace from yielding too much to class feeling.

4. *Town officers.*—The only other important officers are the *Dorfschulzen* or town-mayors. Most of the political functions of local government and also most of its important economical functions are attended to by the provincial and circle authorities. The rural towns are therefore little more than organizations for the regulation of the purely prudential matters of an agricultural community ; such as common pasturage and tillage, and for the administration of a very few public services, such as the most unimportant roads, the schools, and the churches. These matters are attended to by assemblies, sometimes composed like the United States town meetings, of all the electors of the towns, sometimes formed of representatives of the electors of the towns.[1] These assemblies have the general power of controlling and regulating prudential matters of purely local interest.[2] The decisions of the assembly are enforced by executive officers—*viz.,* the village mayor

---

[1] Loening, *op. cit.,* 165.   [2] *Ibid.,* 169.

and two *Schöffen.*[1] During the old feudal days before
the reform, these offices, like the police offices, were
often hereditary. Under the new legislation the
mayors and *Schöffen* are to be elected by the town
assemblies.[2] Their choice, however, must be approved
by the landrath [3]; for the mayors, besides being the
executive officers of the towns, have the general administration of the police of the state. As police officer
the mayor has the right to order temporary arrest and
to impose small fines for the violation of his orders.[4]
Service in this office is obligatory and unpaid.[5]

Somewhat similar to the local organization of the
town is that of the manor. The manor exists only in
those portions of Prussia which have not as yet been
completely freed from the influence of the feudal
régime.[6] It is little more than a town which belongs
wholly to one person. In the manor, in addition to
the private rights which would ordinarily result from
the possession of property, the lord has certain rights
and duties of a semi-political character. Thus he acts
as mayor; but as mayor he is subject to the control of
the justice of the peace. As the justice of the peace is
now subjected to the control of the circle committee,
there is no longer the same danger as formerly that
these semi-political powers will be abused.

One of the great obstacles to the development of an
energetic and efficient local government in the towns

---

[1] *Ibid.*, 170.

[2] K. O., secs. 22–24.

[3] The landrath's veto, however, must be approved by the circle committee—
a popular authority. K. O., sec. 26.

[4] *Ibid.*, secs. 29, 30.

[5] *Ibid.*, secs. 8, 25, 28.

[6] Stengel, *Organisation, etc.*, 234.

and manors is that they are frequently of such small size that they are unable to bear the expense of the various local services, such as roads and schools. To obviate this trouble, the reform legislation permits and encourages the union of towns and manors and the transfer of their functions to the new corporation thus formed.[1] The new division formed by such a union is often coterminous with the division of the justice of the peace (the *Amtsbezirk*). When such a union is accomplished, there is provision made for an assembly for the division. This is elected by the local electors in accordance with the three-class system adopted in Prussian municipal elections.[2] It should be noted that some sort of a similar body exists in all the divisions; but it never attains the same importance in those divisions to which the duties of the communes and manors have not been transferred, since its functions in such a case are simply to control the police administration of the justice of the peace.[3]

5. *The circle diet.*—The formation and the functions of this body are of great importance, not only because of its influence in the affairs of the circle itself, but also because it elects the members of the provincial diet and because it finally raises all the provincial taxes. Before describing the formation of the circle diet, mention must be made of the fact that the principle of universal manhood suffrage has never taken root in Prussia. This is particularly true of the system of representation in the local legislatures in both the rural and the urban districts. From time immemorial repre-

---

[1] See the new Landgemeindeordnung of 1890.

[2] See Bornhak, " Local Government in Prussia," *Annals of American Academy of Political and Social Science, III.,* 403. *Cf. Infra,* p. 331.

[3] K. O., secs. 48, 50, 51, 52, 53.

sentation has been regarded as a right of property, not of men. The great difficulty has been to assign a fair representation to the different kinds of property existing in the localities. Up to the time of the late reform the owners of landed property, and especially the owners of large amounts of landed property, had been able to gain for themselves a disproportionate share in the management of local matters. This it has been the purpose of the reform to do away with, but no attempt has been made to introduce the principle of manhood suffrage.

All cities of twenty-five thousand inhabitants, it must be remembered, are excluded from the jurisdiction of the rural circles and form what are termed urban circles. As these urban circles are represented according to their population in the provincial diet, moneyed capital has its representation in the provincial diet independently of the arrangements provided for the circle diets.

In the rural circles, which are composed of the open country and of cities of less than twenty-five thousand inhabitants, the circle diet is elected by the members of the circle who possess the qualifications of local suffrage.[1] Members of the rural circle are, in the first place, all physical persons who reside within its boundaries[2]; in the second place, all physical persons who, though not residing within its boundaries, own landed property therein or pursue a stationary trade or occupation therein (these are known as the *Forensen*[3]); and in the third place, all juristic persons having their domicile within the circle, including the state if it has property in the circle.[4] All of these members of the

---

[1] K. O., sec. 7. [2] *Ibid.*, sec. 6. [3] *Ibid.*, sec. 14. [4] *Ibid.*

circle are formed into three colleges for the purpose of electing the members of the circle diet,[1] and in each of these colleges the qualifications of the electors and the effect of their votes are different.

The first college is composed of all persons, including juristic persons, who are members of the circle and who pay for their landed property a land and building tax of at least 225 marks (this sum may be raised by the provincial diet to 450 or lowered to 150 marks), or who pay a correspondingly high trade tax for a business carried on in the open country.[2] Every German citizen who falls within this category, who is *sui juris* and has not been deprived of civil honors by judicial sentence, may cast a vote. Juristic persons, women, minors, and incapables may exercise their right of suffrage through representatives.[3] This college, it will be noticed, represents the owners of large landed estates, since land will naturally form the predominant property element in the rural circles. Persons who pay a high trade tax are assimilated to the large land-owners simply in order to provide representation for the various industries which spring up in the open country.

In the second college the electing body is composed, first, of the representatives of the rural towns who have been chosen by the assemblies of such towns; second, of the owners of manors, which are assimilated to towns; and third, of those persons who pursue a trade in the circle for which they are taxed below the rate which would put them in the first college.[4] The second col-

---

[1] *Ibid.*, sec. 85.

[2] *Ibid.*, sec. 86. This is the middle rate of the highest class in the *Gewerbesteuer.*

[3] *Ibid.*, secs. 96, 97.   [4] K. O., secs. 87, 98.

lege, it will be noticed, is intended to represent the smaller owners of land, and also the smaller tradesmen, artisans, and manufacturers who otherwise would not be represented at all, since ownership of agricultural land is generally necessary to vote for members of the assemblies of the rural towns.[1] The representation given to the owners of manors is of course an anomaly. It is due to the fact that they are obliged by law to defray out of their own pockets all those expenses of the manors which, were they rural towns, would fall upon the inhabitants. But as the manors are fast disappearing this privilege is not destined to have great importance in the future.[2]

The third college is a common session of the municipal authorities of the cities within the circle.[3] It is therefore composed of the representatives of personal property or moneyed capital. This statement perhaps requires some explanation. From the social standpoint all city property, whether consisting of land, houses, or what the Anglo-American law terms personal property, is really to be regarded as personal property or capital. The owners treat it as capital, and their interests are those of the capitalistic class rather than those of the agricultural or rural land-holding classes.

The members of the circle diet to be elected by these three colleges are apportioned to the rural and city colleges according to population; except that the college of the cities, if there is more than one city in the circle, may not elect more than half of the members of the circle diet, and if there is only one city in the circle, then not more than one third. The other members of

---

[1] Loening, *op. cit.*, 165. [2] Stengel, *Organisation, etc.*, 236, note 1.
[3] K. O., sec. 88.

the circle diet—*i. e.* the number left after subtracting from the total number the number of the city college members—are to be elected in equal proportions by the other colleges ; *i. e.* the college of the large landholders and that of the small landholders each elects one half of the remainder.[1] The result of such a system of representation is to assure to all classes a share of representation on both the circle and the provincial diets.[2] The processes of election differ considerably in each college, and are of so complicated and technical a character as to offer little interest to the foreign student.[3]

The authority organized in this peculiar way has to perform for the circle as a municipal corporation about the same duties that the provincial diet has to perform for the province. That is, it lays down the general rules which shall be followed by the circle officers in their management of the circle administration ; decides what services the circle shall undertake ; and levies the taxes necessary to defray the expenses of the circle administration and to pay to the province the quota of money which the provincial diet has decided shall be paid by the circle for the maintenance of provincial institutions and administration.[4] The raising of such moneys, it may be said, is the principal function of the circle diet.[5] In the performance of this duty the circle diet does not have any very wide field of action. One of the things which the circle law was most careful to do was to take away from the circle diets the power to introduce any new taxes, because these might easily derange the system of taxation adopted for the country

[1] *Ibid.*, sec. 89.

[2] *Cf. Pol. Sci. Qu.*, V., 145.

[3] For a description of them see Stengel, *Organisation, etc.*, 244.

[4] K. O., secs. 115, 116.   [5] *Ibid.*, sec. 119.

at large. The law has obliged the circle diet to get its revenues by adding percentages to the direct central taxes.[1] There are several of these, some upon land and some upon business and some upon income, each tax thus affecting different classes of property or persons. As capital might be especially important in one circle and landed property in another, it was not felt advisable by the framers of the reform measures to fix any hard and fast rule which the circle diets must follow in fixing the rates at which each different kind of property was to be taxed for circle purposes. But at the same time it was considered unsafe to allow the circle diets perfect freedom in the fixing of such rates, from the fear that in the circles where any particular property interest was predominant the majority would be inclined to tax unfairly the property of the minority. Therefore the law has laid down limits within which the circle diets may fix the rates of the particular taxes and beyond which they may not go.[2] Under these limitations, taken together with the careful provision for a fair representation of all the different classes of property upon the circle diet, it is felt that the temptation to local tyranny through the exercise of the taxing power is to a large extent removed. As regards the total amount of taxes to be raised by any circle, the law has imposed one limitation in the interest of economical administration. It provides that if a circle diet wishes to impose a tax which is more than fifty per cent. of the entire central tax levied in the circle, it must obtain the consent of the proper supervisory authority of the central government (in this case the ministers of finance and of the interior at Berlin).[3]

[1] *Ibid.*, sec. 10. [2] *Ibid.* [3] *Ibid.*, sec. 176.

In addition to these powers of taxation, the circle diets have a series of functions to perform, some of which are imposed upon them by law, some of which they may assume voluntarily. The circle law of 1872, in sections 115 and 116, would seem to indicate that the circle diet may establish such institutions as in its judgment will benefit the circle, and which, it must be added, are among the general objects for which the circle organization has been formed.[1] For instance: it could not establish a new system of courts, since that is not a matter of local concern; but it might establish new institutions of an educational or charitable character, since they would be of particular benefit to the circle and are within the general scope of its competence. In the establishment of such new institutions, however, the diets must not overburden the circles with debts or with heavy taxes. To prevent them from so doing, the law has reserved to the central administrative authorities large powers of control. Debts not especially permitted by law may not be incurred without the approval of these authorities; nor, as has been noted, can the circle diets impose taxes beyond certain limits.[2] The question naturally arises: What is the use of two bodies with functions so similar as are those of the provincial diet and the circle diet? Why could not the work of the province as a municipal corporation be transferred to the circle, and the circle diet be allowed to attend to all the duties which are now devolved upon the province? It must, however, be remembered that the chief function of the provinces as municipal corporations is to attend to matters of a less

[1] Loening, *op. cit.*, 204 ; Stengel, *Organisation, etc.*, 25.
[2] K. O., sec. 176.

local character than those which fall within the sphere of the circles ; the object of their reorganization in their present form was to decentralize the central administration. Previous to the province law of 1875 and the dotation laws of 1873 and 1875 a series of institutions, such as asylums, were supported and administered by the central government, which, it was felt, could be better attended to nearer home. Therefore the central government gave these duties to the province. It could not well entrust them to the circle, because it was felt that the institutions in question were of too important a character to be attended to by so small a district ; that the resources of the circle, both in administrative ability and in money, would not be sufficient for the adequate performance of these duties. While the province represents the central government in these matters, the circle represents the localities, and is by far the most important of the purely local municipal corporations.

Most of the important offices in the circle which have been mentioned are honorary and unsalaried, and the acceptance of all these honorary, unsalaried offices is obligatory.[1] That is, refusal to accept office after an election or appointment is attended, where no legal excuse exists, by loss of local suffrage for from three to six years and by an increase of circle taxes of from an eighth to a quarter. Among the legal excuses are chronic sickness, the following of a business which necessitates frequent or continuous absence from home, the age of sixty years, service as honorary officer within the last three years. This system of coercion for honorary offices, says Dr. Gneist,

[1] K. O., sec. 8.

is applied without exception in the reform legislation and had before this time been applied in the municipal organization of Prussia. The people have everywhere accustomed themselves quickly to this constraint. At first it was feared that it would be impossible to find competent persons to fill a position entailing such a grave responsibility [as that of justice of the peace]. But in 1875, after the law had been put into operation, more than 5000 justices and as many deputies were found and it was necessary to fill only 183 places with salaried officers (*commissarische Amtsvorsteher*) who were temporarily appointed for those districts in which it had been impossible to find the proper persons.[1]

The purpose of the application of the principle was to cultivate a greater public spirit and political capacity among the well-to-do rural classes in the same way that such spirit and capacity had, as it was admitted, been cultivated in the municipalities through the same principle of obligatory service as developed in the municipal corporations act of 1808.

IV.— The cities.

In order to give a complete outline of the local government of Prussia it remains to speak of the municipal organization. It will be remembered that the first steps in the great reform movement of this century were made by Stein in his municipal corporations act of 1808, which served as the model for both the circle and the province laws passed so many years afterwards.[2] Stein was able to begin the great work with the cities, because, as a result of the centralization of the eighteenth century, the social conditions of the municipal population had been made comparatively equal. The strong government of Frederick William I

---

[1] *Revue Générale, etc.,* Oct., 1886, 253.

[2] For a history of the development of the Prussian and German cities up to 1808, see Leidig, *Preussisches Stadtrecht,* 2–20.

had largely freed the poorer classes from economic dependence upon the richer. Though the spirit which was breathed into the new organization was quite different from that which animated the old municipal system, the actual form of municipal government, established by the new law, was in no respect very different from that which existed before Stein began his work. The changes which he made consisted mainly in the widening of the suffrage for the city council, which still remained the important organ of the municipal government; in the new obligation which was imposed upon the citizens of the municipality to take upon themselves public duties; and in the greater degree of freedom which was allowed the cities in the management of their own affairs. Since the time of Stein, some modifications have been made in his plan—modifications which may not on the whole be called improvements. They were due mainly to the desire of the Conservative party—which, with the exception of very short periods—as during 1848-50—has until recently been in complete power—to curtail the political influence of the municipal population. These modifications have consisted mainly in the strengthening of the central control over the cities, and in the limitation of their freedom of action in the management of their own affairs. In detail, the present municipal organization is as follows:

Just as in the open country, it is recognized that there is a sphere of municipal action in which the municipality should have considerable autonomy, and that there are certain functions of administration attended to within the municipal district which interest the country as a whole, and over which the central admin-

istration should have a greater control. Just as in the
circle, again, it is believed to be better not to make a
complete separation in the authorities which are to
attend to these two different classes of duties, but to
charge the executive authorities of the city with the
performance of those duties which are of general concern. It is provided, however, that in the larger cities
the central government may, if it sees fit, put into the
hands of distinctively central organs the management
of police matters[1]; and this it has done in many cases.
In the smaller cities on the other hand, the city executive attends to these matters as well as to all other
matters which affect the country as a whole. In these
cases it is regarded as an agent of the central administration, and acts under the control of the central administrative authorities, generally the governments and
the government presidents.[2] In case the city is at the
same time an urban circle—which it will be remembered is the case in all cities having over twenty-five
thousand inhabitants,—the city executive in like
manner attends to all the duties which in the rural
circles are attended to by the landrath. In these
urban circles there is also a lay body, similar to the
circle committee, called the city committee,[3] which,
however, attends only to matters of central concern.
As this city committee consists of the burgomaster of
the city and of members chosen either from the town
executive board, or, where there is no such board,
from the town council,[4] the result is that in all cases it
is the city officers who attend to the central adminis-

[1] Law, March 11, 1850, sec. 2.
[2] *Städte-Ordnung*, May 30, 1853, sec. 56, cited hereafter as S. O., 1853.
[3] K. O., sec. 170.
[4] A. L. V. G., secs. 37, 38.

tration in the city—with the exception (already noted) of the police administration in the larger cities.

1. *City council.*—But while city officers are thus generally called upon to attend to the business of the central administration in the city, the most important functions of the municipal administration are those of a distinctively local character. The general control of this local administration is vested in the city council, which is chosen by the taxpayers of the city.[1] The method of election is peculiar: it is well adapted to keep the control of the city affairs in the hands of the wealthy classes, since the influence of a man's vote depends largely upon the amount of taxes he pays. The system is as follows: The total amount of the direct taxes paid in the city is divided into three parts. Those persons paying the highest taxes, who pay one third of the entire amount, have the right to elect one third of the members of the council. Those persons who pay the next highest taxes, and who pay another third of the entire amount, elect another third of the members of the council. All the remaining taxpayers elect the remaining third.[2]

An example taken from the city of Bonn, which has a population of about thirty-six thousand inhabitants, will show how thoroughly this method of representation throws the control of the city into the hands of the wealthy classes. Out of the total number of 3,402 electors, 162 electors elected one third of the town council, 633 elected two thirds, and the remaining third was elected by 2,607 electors. The disproportion between the classes was really much greater than the above vote indicates, for while sixty-four per cent. of

[1] S. O., 1853, sec. 35.　　　　[2] S. O., 1853, sec. 13.

the electors of the first class voted, and sixty-six per cent. of the second class, only twenty-two per cent. of the third class availed themselves of their electoral privilege. The explanation is said to be this: The vote not being secret, intimidation had been practised to such an extent that the voters of the third class preferred to stay away from the polls rather than vote for candidates who were not of their choice.[1]

The authority thus formed has the absolute control of the entire city administration. The law simply says that it shall govern by its decisions the affairs of the city.[2] In addition to deciding what branches of administration the municipality shall attend to it also elects all of the executive officers of the municipality.

2. *City executive.*—The execution of the resolutions of the town council is entrusted either to a burgomaster who has complete control of the administration in its details, or to an executive board whose members are elected by the town council. In such an executive board, a part of the members are professional in character (as, for example, the school commissioner, the corporation council, the town surveyor or commissioner of public works) and a part are purely lay officers, *i. e.* ordinary citizens who are obliged to assume office if elected, and to serve at least half the regular term of six years.[3] The same obligation to serve is imposed upon those persons who are elected to be members of the town council.[4] In case the executive authority of

---

[1] Leclerc, " La vie municipale en Prusse," *Extrait des Annales de l'École Libre des Sciences Politiques*, 13.

[2] For example, see *Städte-Ordnung der Provinz Westphalen*, March 19. 1856, sec. 35.

[3] *Ibid.*

[4] Z. G., sec. 10.

the city is vested in a such a board, the burgomaster is simply the presiding officer and has powers little greater than those possessed by the other members of the board. But the moral influence which he exercises is nevertheless so great as very largely to determine the character of the city administration.[1] He is a professional officer and receives a large salary. In filling the position of burgomaster—or, in fact, that of any of the professional officers of the executive board—the method pursued indicates the desire of the city councils to secure the best possible men. The city council of a city which needs a burgomaster, a commissioner of public works, or any such officer, advertises in the papers for the particular officer needed, stating the qualifications which are required. The council then selects from among the applicants the one who seems best fitted for the place. A large city often chooses a burgomaster who has made his reputation as a good executive officer in a smaller city.[2] As the term of office is at least twelve years, and may be for life, the positions are much sought after, and the applicants are generally well educated men who have had experience in city administration.[3] The election of these professional officers generally requires the approval of the central administration before it is of force.[4] This is considered to be necessary on account of the many duties affecting the country at large which are devolved upon the city executive. While the executive has, in the main, to carry out the resolutions of the council, it has at the same time to exercise quite a control over the actions of this body—both to keep it

[1] S. O., 1853, secs. 57, 58.   [2] Leclerc, *op. cit.*, 20.   [3] *Ibid.*, 17.
[4] S. O., 1853, sec. 33 ; Z. G., sec. 13.

within the law and to prevent it from taking unwise action. In case of conflict between the executive and the council the matter is decided by the proper supervisory authority, in this case the district committee.[1] As this is a lay authority, the professional officers of the central administration cannot now interfere in the municipal administration. A further control exercised by the central government over the municipal administration is found in the requirement of the approval of the district committee for certain resolutions of the city council before they are regarded as valid. Among the acts subjected to such control are the more important measures of the financial administration, such as the making of loans and the imposition of high taxes.[2] The rules are much the same as those already mentioned as adopted for the communal administration of the circle and the province. In fact, the control over the circle and the province was modelled on that already formed for the municipalities by the municipal corporations act of Stein as amended by later laws.

3. *City departments.*—A word must be said in regard to the organization of the city departments which attend to the detailed current administration. The municipal corporations act of 1853 provides that for these matters there may be formed permanent commissions or boards, composed either of members of the council or of members of the executive board or of these and other municipal citizens, which boards or commissions are the subordinates of the executive and have under their direction the salaried members of that

[1] S. O., 1853, sec. 56 ; Z. G., sec. 17, 1.
[2] S. O., 1853, sec. 53 ; Z. G., sec. 16, *Abs.* 3.

body.[1] The purpose of this arrangement is to call into the service of the city as many of the citizens as possible. Service on such boards is obligatory, as is the case with all unsalaried positions in the city government. Finally the same law provides that the larger cities may be sub-divided into wards, over which are to be placed ward-overseers to be elected from among the citizens by the town council.[2] These ward-overseers are the subordinates of the executive board for all matters of municipal administration. This institution has been very generally adopted in the larger cities, where it has had excellent results. The ward overseers serve as means of communication between the different districts and the executive board. If anything goes wrong in the district, there is always some one to whom complaint may be made with the assurance that the complaint will be attended to. An example of the workings of such an institution may again be taken from the city of Bonn. This city is divided into ten wards. In each of these is an overseer who, in the administration of public charity, has under him ward commissions of citizens, whose duty it is, under his direction, to examine into all cases of demand for poor-relief. So many persons are called into the municipal service of public charity that each one of them has no more than two or three families to attend to and thus knows perfectly the condition of those asking for relief.[3] This method of administering poor relief is simply the adoption in the public administrative system of the method which has been so successfully applied in this country by private associations such as the charity organization societies and the bureaus of charity.

[1] S. O., 1853, sec. 59. [2] *Ibid.*, sec. 60. [3] *Cf.* Leclerc, *op. cit.*, 57.

V.—*General characteristics of the Prussian system.*

1. *Administrative control.*—As in the French, so in the Prussian system of local government, the inter-ference of the central legislature in local affairs is infinitesimal if it exists at all. Enough of the old feudal ideas of local autonomy have remained to per-mit of the development of the principle that there is a sphere of administrative action which must be left almost entirely to the localities ; that within this sphere the legislature should not interfere at all ; that any central interference or control that may be required over this local administration should come from the administration and in the main from the lay authorities of the administration, and should be confined simply to preventing the localities from incurring too great financial burdens. Therefore the law does not, as in the United States and as it does to a certain extent in England, enumerate the powers and duties of the localities, but says simply that the local affairs of particular districts shall be governed by the decisions of local authorities in the nature of local legislatures, and that in those cases only in which the law has ex-pressly given it the power, may the central administra-tion step in to protect the localities from their own unwise action. This system is one of general grants of local power with the necessity in certain cases of central administrative—not legislative—approval or control. The benefits of such a system cannot be over-estimated. Through its adoption all the evils of local and special legislation are avoided. In place of an irresponsible legislative control, which in the United States has shown itself so incapable of preventing the extravagance of localities that in many cases the power

of the legislature to permit local action has been curtailed by the constitutions, is to be found a control exercised by responsible authorities—authorities which have a certain permanence and are well able to judge whether a given action will be really hurtful to a locality or not. At the same time the greater freedom from central interference guaranteed to the localities by this system is well calculated to encourage the growth of local pride and responsibility.

2. *Obligatory unpaid service.*—Different, however, from the French system the Prussian system of local government attempts by the adoption of the principle of unpaid obligatory service (it will be remembered that while in many cases service in the French local offices is unpaid, it is almost never obligatory) to make the local administration largely non-professional in character. This, it was felt, was peculiarly necessary in Prussia on account of the existence of a most thoroughly bureaucratic service. This idea is adopted from England, and consciously adopted from England at a time when both forms of the English system of local government are showing a tendency to abandon it.

3. *Subjection of local administration to judicial control.*—Under the system in vogue up to the time of the late reform the administration in its local as well as its central instances was almost a law unto itself. It was not only relieved from all central legislative control, but also from all central judicial control except in so far as its acts might be considered as being regulated by the principles of the private law. The experience of Prussia during the first half of this century was, however, such as to prove that if the administration

was to be satisfactory to the individual and regardful
of his rights, some sort of judicial control over it should
be established.   This, as has been stated, was one of
the main ends of the reform movement of 1872.   By
the establishment of this judicial control, [1] Prussia has
taken a great stride in advance, and may now be regarded as occupying, so far as her local administration
is concerned, a position similar to that which has for so
long a time been occupied by both England and the
United States, where the actions of the local authorities are subjected to the strictest sort of judicial control.

[1] For the details in regard to it see *infra*, II., p. 243.

INDEX.

O

COMPARATIVE ADMINISTRATIVE LAW.

TABLE OF CONTENTS.

VOLUME II. LEGAL RELATIONS.

BOOK IV. THE LAW OF OFFICERS.

CHAPTER I. OFFICES AND OFFICERS.

CHAPTER II. THE FORMATION OF THE OFFICIAL RELATION.

CHAPTER III. QUALIFICATIONS FOR OFFICE.

CHAPTER IV. THE RIGHTS OF OFFICERS.

CHAPTER V. THE DUTIES OF OFFICERS.

CHAPTER VI. TERMINATION OF THE OFFICIAL RELATION.

BOOK V. THE ADMINISTRATION IN ACTION.

CHAPTER I. DISTINCTION OF THE METHODS FROM THE DIRECTIONS OF ADMINISTRATIVE ACTION.

CHAPTER II. EXPRESSION OF THE WILL OF THE STATE.

CHAPTER III. EXECUTION OF THE WILL OF THE STATE.

CHAPTER IV. THE SOCIALISTIC ACTION OF THE ADMINISTRATION.

BOOK VI. THE CONTROL OVER THE ADMINISTRATION.

DIVISION I. THE METHODS OF CONTROL.

CHAPTER I. FORMATION OF THE CONTROL.

DIVISION II. THE JUDICIAL CONTROL.

CHAPTER I. ANALYSIS OF THE JUDICIAL CONTROL.

CHAPTER II. CONTROL OF THE CIVIL COURTS.

CHAPTER VII.   THE ADMINISTRATIVE JURISDICTION
IN GERMANY.

CHAPTER VIII. CONFLICTS OF JURISDICTION.

DIVISION III. THE LEGISLATIVE CONTROL.

CHAPTER I. HISTORY OF THE LEGISLATIVE
CONTROL.

CHAPTER II. THE POWER OF THE LEGISLATURE TO
REMEDY SPECIAL ADMINISTRATIVE ABUSES.

BOOK IV.

THE LAW OF OFFICERS.

CHAPTER I.

OFFICES AND OFFICERS.

I.—Definition.

1. *In general.*—By an office is understood a right or duty conferred or imposed by law on a person or several persons to act in the execution and application of the law.[1] By officers are meant those persons on whom an office has been conferred or imposed. The word authority is also sometimes used to designate the person or persons holding an office. It is to be noticed that an office may exist without the officer. Thus we often hear of an office being vacant. On the other hand there may be an officer who has no office. Thus an officer who has been pensioned or retired and who is not discharging official functions may be subjected to many of the duties resulting from the existence of the official relation. This is particularly true of Germany.[2]

[1] Stengel, *Lehrbuch des Deutschen Verwaltungsrecht*, 158 ; Mechem, *Law of Public Offices and Officers*, 1.

[2] *Supra*, I., p. 94.

2. *Distinction between office and employment.*—The conceptions of office and officer are conceptions of public and not of private law. The government may, however, enter into private legal relations as a result of which it may have employees as well as officers. It therefore becomes necessary to distinguish as far as may be an officer from an employee. It has been said that the term office "embraces the idea of tenure, duration, emolument, and duties."[1] It is not, however, necessary in order that a position under the government be an office that it have all of these characteristics. Thus it seems certain that the idea of emolument is not at all necessary to the conception of an office.[2] There are numerous positions which are offices and to which no salary or emolument of any sort is attached. But it does seem to be necessary, in order that a governmental position be an office, that it possess more than one of the characteristics mentioned. The mere fact that a position is under the government and concerns the public will not constitute it an office; it may be an employment. Thus one who receives no certificate of appointment, takes no oath, has no term or tenure of office, discharges no duties and exercises no powers conferred upon him directly by law, but simply performs such duties as are required of him by the persons employing him and whose responsibility is limited to them, is not an officer, and does not hold an office, although he is employed by public officers and is engaged about public work.[3] Applying these principles, deputies not obliged to take the oath required

---

[1] United States v. Hartwell, 6 Wallace, 385.

[2] See State v. Stanley, 66 N. C., 59.

[3] Olmstead v. the Mayor, *etc.*, 42 N. Y. Super., Ct. 487.

of officers, and not provided for by law, have been held
to be mere agents or employees of their principals who
may be officers.[1] But deputies provided for by law
with fixed powers and duties and giving bonds in
accordance with the law are officers, *e. g.* deputy postmasters, marshals, and sheriffs.[2] While there are
other *criteria* which may be of use in distinguishing
an office from an employment, the most important
canon of distinction is that, while an employment may
be created by contract as a result of the fact that the
government may be in some cases a subject of private
law, an office can never be created by contract, but
finds its source and its limitations in some act of
governmental power. Thus where the legislature
created by an act of legislation the position of public
printer the court held that such position was an office
and that the public printer was an officer and therefore might not assign the position[3]; but on the other
hand where the legislature provided that the public
printing was to be "contracted for," the court held
that the public printer was a contractor and not an
officer.[4] It will be noticed from these cases that the
conception of an office does not depend in any way
upon the character of the duties to be performed. It
makes no difference whether these duties carry with
them the power of compulsion or not, or whether or
not the holder of the office is permanently occupied in

[1] Kavanaugh v. State, 41 Ala., 399 ; see also U. S. v. Smith, 124 U. S., 525 ;
Throop v. Langdon, 40 Mich., 673 ; and note on page 180 of 72 American
Decisions.

[2] Dunlop v. Munroe, 7 Cranch, 242 ; U. S. v. Martin, 17 Fed. Rep., 150 ;
Eastman v. Curtis, 4 Vt., 616.

[3] Ellis v. State, 4 Ind., 1.

[4] Brown v. Turner, 70 N. C., 93 ; see also Detroit Free Press Co. v. State
Auditors, 47 Mich., 135.

the discharge of his duties, or whether or not the
duties are discretionary.[1] All that seems to be necessary is that the duties discharged be discharged in the
interest of the government, and that the right to discharge them be based on some provision of law and
not upon a contract.[2] The duties themselves may be
quite similar to or even identical in character with the
duties discharged by private persons. Thus a clerk in
an executive department of the United States or of
the commonwealths may be an officer.[3] It has been
held that even a sailmaker appointed under a warrant
under the hand of the secretary of the navy and the
seal of the department was an officer. In many
cases it is exceedingly difficult to distinguish between
an officer and an employee, the reason being that the
courts in their decisions have been influenced by some
peculiar statutory provision. Thus where statutes
have imposed criminal penalties on "officers" for the
violation of their duties the courts often give a much
narrower construction to the word officer than they do
in other cases. Take *e. g.* the case of *United States v.
Germaine.*[4] Here the court lays down the rule that
only those persons in the service of the national
government are officers who are appointed by the
President, the head of a department, or the courts, and
that all persons not so appointed are mere employees
to whom the rules affecting the official relation do not
apply.[5] This rule is not, however, to be reconciled

---

[1] State v. Salle, 41 Mo., 31 ; Carth, 479.

[2] State v. Stanley, 66 N. C., 59.

[3] *Ex parte* Smith, 2 Cranch, C. C., 693 ; U. S. v. Hartwell, 6 Wallace, 385 ;
Vaughn v. English, 8 Cal., 39.　　　　　[4] 99 U. S., 508.

[5] See also for an example of the influence which peculiar statutes have upon
the decisions of the courts the cases of United States v. Mouat, 124 U. S., 303 ;

with some of the other decisions of the Supreme Court as *e. g.* that of *United States v. Hartwell*,[1] which holds that a person whose appointment though not made by a head of a department has been approved by him, is an officer.[2] Finally it is to be noticed that the definition that has been given of the terms office and officer does not regard as officers those persons who discharge in the main what are called legislative functions, *i. e.* those persons who are members of the legislature both national and commonwealth. This is in accordance with the rule laid down by the Senate of the United States acting as a court of impeachment. In 1799 it decided that a senator was not a civil officer of the United States because he was a member of the legislature.[3] But it is to be noticed also that the action of the Senate on this point is not altogether consistent inasmuch as in January, 1864, it decided that an oath prescribed for civil officers by the act of July 2, 1862, must be taken by senators also [4]; and that the decisions of several of the courts would seem to hold that for the purpose of disqualifying for office the position of member of the legislature both national and commonwealth is an office.[5]

United States v. Hendee, *Ibid.*, 309, which hold that a paymaster's clerk who was not appointed by the head of the department and whose position was not provided for by law is not an officer for the purpose of mileage, but is one for the purpose of longevity pay ; and also the case of *Ex parte* Reed, 100 U. S., 13.

[1] *Supra*, II., p. 2.

[2] For the decisions of the courts as to the various positions under the government both national and commonwealth, see Mechem, *Law of Offices and Officers*, 12 *et seq.*

[3] See Blount's Trial.

[4] *Cyclopædia of Political Science, etc.*, *sub verbo* impeachment, II., 481.

[5] People v. Common Council, 77 N. Y., 503 ; see also Morrel v. Haines, 2 N. H., 246 ; but see Wortley v. Barrett, 63 N. C., 199, 201.

II.—Methods of organizing offices.

Official authorities differ in the way in which they are organized. Thus an authority may consist of one person or of more than one person. In the first place while one person may not do all the work of the office, while he may be assisted in the performance of his duties by many subordinates and deputies who in their turn may be officers, still all the actions of the office are to be done under his direction and on his responsibility. A system of offices founded on this principle may be called a single-headed system.[1] In the second plan of organizing an official authority the office is held by more than one person, by several persons who exercise their powers and perform their duties by means of resolutions of the entire body. In the making of these resolutions each one of the holders of the office has legally as much influence as any of the others with perhaps the exception of the president of the board, who may have the right of giving the casting vote in case of a tie vote.[2] A system in which the official authorities are organized as boards is called the collegial or board system. Each of these plans of organizing offices has its advantages and disadvantages. The single-headed system is well fitted for the discharge of duties which require energy and rapidity of action and for which it is advisable to have a fixed and well-defined responsibility; while the board system may be adopted with advantage in all those branches of administration in which carefulness of deliberation,

[1] The Germans call such a system a bureaucratic system, while the equivalent French term is *système unitaire*.

[2] See for the rules of law in the United States in regard to boards, Mechem, *op. cit.*, secs. 571–81.

regard for all sides of the case and impartial decision are particularly desired. Boards are therefore specially suited for the consideration of those matters in which a controversy between individuals involving a question of law is to be decided, *i. e.* for judicial authorities, while the single-headed system is usually the best for purely executive and administrative matters. It is, however, to be noticed that for many administrative matters the board system is to be preferred for the reasons already stated. This is particularly true of the case of the assessment of property for the purposes of taxation. For these reasons we find that seldom does any system of administrative organization adopt either one of these methods of official constitution to the exclusion of the other, but that the attempt is usually made to combine the two forms in such a way as to produce the best results. In France, however, the attempt has been made to devise one method of official constitution which will combine individual responsibility and administrative efficiency with mature deliberation and impartial decision. Here we find by the side of each of the important administrative officers who alone have the actual power of decision and alone are to assume the full responsibility for the acts of the office, a council whose advice must be asked in the more important matters within the jurisdiction of the office but whose advice need never be followed.[1]

III.—*Honorary and professional officers.*

Officers, like authorities, may be variously classified.[2] In many states there is an important distinction be-

---

[1] *Supra*, I., pp. 86, III.   [2] See Mechem, *op. cit.*, 9.

tween professional and honorary officers.[1] The first
are those officers who devote their entire time to the
discharge of public functions, have no other occupation, are indeed by law allowed to have no other
occupation, and receive a sufficiently large compensation to enable them to live without resorting to other
means. From such officers is often required by law a
professional training or more or less knowledge of the
affairs to which their official duties relate. In some states
this requirement is carried so far as to necessitate the
pursuit by the candidates for official positions of a regular course of instruction in administrative matters. A
system of administration which relies entirely or mainly
upon professional officers is termed a bureaucratic system In it we find a profession of office-holding and an
official class which attends to the administration of
public affairs. Honorary officers on the other hand do
not devote their entire time to their public duties, but
at the same time that they are holding public office
may be carrying on some other regular business and
find their main means of support in such business or
in their private means, since they receive a compensation insufficient to support them. In such a system
the office is regarded not as a means of livelihood but
as an honor, and candidates for the office are not
required to possess any particular knowledge of the
duties of the office they may desire to hold. A system
of administration which relies entirely or mainly upon
such honorary non-professional officers is called a self-
government system. In it we find no, or a very small

[1] In the United States the nearest legal distinction to this is that between
lucrative and honorary offices, the idea of professional offices being very dim.
See State v. Stanley, 66 N. C., 59 ; Hoke v. Henderson, 4 Devereux, Law N.
C., I, 21.

class of, professional officers. In it government is administered by members of society who temporarily discharge public functions. There probably never was in the history of the world an absolutely bureaucratic administrative system, though that existing in Prussia from 1720 to 1808 and that established in France in 1800 were pretty nearly completely bureaucratic. On the other hand there has seldom been seen a complete self-government system of administration, though that of England in the eighteenth century was about as near one as can well be imagined. All existing systems of administration are formed of a combination of professional and honorary officers, one of the classes predominating and giving the general tone to the system. In the United States the self-government system predominates; in Europe on the contrary the bureaucratic, especially on the continent, though England is not far behind the continent, and Prussia, and indeed Germany as a whole, has of late been trying to increase the realm of the self-government system.[1] In those countries in which the official system is most scientifically organized we find a clear distinction made between these two classes of officers. This is true of Germany where different rules govern the relations of each class of officers. In other countries, however, while the two classes of officers do really exist, no great attempt is made in the law to distinguish between them. Such for example is the case in the United States.

Each of these two systems, *viz.*, the bureaucratic and the self-government system, has its advantages. The special knowledge and training possessed by profes-

[1] *Supra*, I., p. 301.

sional officers, their generally long terms of office, and the fact that they are occupied exclusively in the management of public business make it almost certain that, when well organized, they will act more wisely and efficiently than officers who have no special knowledge of their duties, who serve for short terms, and are expected to devote only a part of their time to the public service; and make it extremely probable that the cost of such a system will, notwithstanding the fact that salaries are paid, be less than the cost of self-government administration. For these reasons the popular remedy for administrative evils is bureaucracy; and if wise, efficient, and economical administration were the only or even the main end sought in the organization of the administrative system it might be admitted without question that the popular remedy was the proper remedy. But it must never be lost sight of that good administration is only one, and that a minor, end of an administrative system. It must always be kept in mind that the prime end of all governmental systems should be the cultivation in the people of a vigorous political vitality, a patriotic loyalty and social solidarity. History shows that this end is not attained by a bureaucratic system. The experience of every state which, to carry forward pressing reforms or to secure administrative efficiency, has adopted a bureaucratic system of administration goes to prove that bureaucracy is incompatible with civil liberty. The administrative history of France and Germany under the absolute monarchy is a striking example of this fact. The conferring of most of the important administrative powers upon professional officers deprives the citizens of the state generally, of the opportunity to accustom themselves to public service and to acquire political experience; and finally destroys their ability to protect their liberties in an orderly manner. They also lose interest in the government. They regard with indifference, if not with actual hatred, a government in which they have no participation. Finally the permanent exclusion of the citizens from participation in administration encourages within them the growth of class feeling, which is one of the greatest obstacles to successful government. Seldom, if ever, being obliged to consider public questions from any but the point of view of the class to which they belong; seldom, if ever, being called upon to consider the public effects of any measure, they fail to acquire that sense of collectivism whose cultivation is so necessary. If at the same time that they are shut out from participation in administration the people are allowed to participate in legislation the result is even worse. For they carry with them into the legislative bodies the same narrow class feelings by which they are actuated in their private life. The legislature becomes the fighting ground for hostile social forces instead of being the representative of the collective interests of the whole people. A good example of the effect of a popular legislative assembly when combined with a bureaucratic administration is to be found in the administrative history of Prussia from 1822 to 1860.[1] True socialism never makes a greater mistake that when it allies itself, as it is so apt to do, with bureaucratic administration. Bureaucratic administration has thus in all governments most evil results but most particularly in

[1] See *Supra*, I., 298; *Political Science Quarterly*, IV., p. 656 *et seq.*

popular governments where the people are allowed to participate in legislation.   Its efficiency easily becomes tyranny; its economy is dearly paid for by the loss of political capacity and the growth of social faction.

What the bureaucratic system tends to destroy the self-government system tends to foster.   The participation of numerous citizens in the work of administering government not only tends to increase by the sure method of practice the political capacity of the people, but also causes them to regard the government as their own and finally brings them to consider public measures from a point of view other than that of their own social class, to consider what influence they will have on the community as a whole.   The almost complete absence of social parties in England during the sway of the self-government system is a striking example of the influence of this system of administration.   Of course reliance cannot be placed alone upon the administrative system to bring about these results.   The admonitions of religious teaching and the influences of a lofty humanitarian philosophy have their part in the work to perform,[1] but it should be recognized that the administrative system has an important influence in the conquest of human selfishness in the form of class tyranny.

There are, however, some branches of administration in which the radical defects of the system of popular non-professional officers are very marked.   The inherent weaknesses of the self-government system— its extravagance, its inefficiency, and the unwisdom of its actions—become so serious as to force the conclusion that in some branches self-government is impos-

---

[1] *Cf*. Gneist, *Das Englische Parlament*, Introduction.

sible. There are many positions in the municipal administration particularly—positions which are increasing in number with the increase of the duties of the administration—which require great technical knowledge, whose duties are so arduous as to occupy the entire time of the incumbents. Here it seems necessary to demand of the incumbents a professional training and to pay them salaries.[1] Bureaucracy is made necessary by the conditions of the case. The question is not whether we shall have a bureaucracy—for we must in the nature of things have it—but how we shall organize it so as to give it the best proportions possible and so as to avoid the evil results by which it is so generally attended. Especially must care be taken not to organize the bureaucracy on the principles which are applicable to the self-government system. If salaries are to be paid, professional knowledge and the devotion of the entire time of the officer to the work of the office should be required also, since the impossibility of such an officer's earning his living in any other way is the only reason why a salary should be paid. Long terms of office should take the place of the short terms of the self-government system. What should be a profession should not be allowed to degenerate into a trade. Finally the system should be so organized that the people from whom the governmental power comes and for whose benefit it is to be exercised, should have a control over the bureaucracy in order that the deliberate wishes of the community may have their expression in the action of the administration.

[1] *Cf.* President Eliot in the *Forum*, October, 1891, on "One Remedy for Municipal Mis-government"; Gumplowicz, *Das Oesterreichische Staatsrecht*, 179, 180.

CHAPTER II.

I.—Appointment or election.

Of the various methods of forming the official relation the two most important are appointment and election. There are, it is true, several others less important.
Thus the official relation is sometimes formed by the
drawing of lots as in the case of the jury; often other
things being equal the official relation is formed as a
result of seniority and juniority. Thus in the French
elections the two oldest and the two youngest electors
present at the opening of the polls and able to read
are the canvassers of elections.[1] In other cases office
is gained by inheritance. We find numerous examples of this method among the offices of the royal
household in England.[2] But this method is becoming
rarer and rarer as time goes by. Originally the common method of filling offices in the United States was
an executive appointment. The only exception to this
rule was to be found in the case of the town officers.
Partisan use was early made of the power of appointment in New York. Each new party that came into
power felt that it was its right to fill all offices to

---

[1] L. May 5, 1884, art. 31.
[2] Gneist, *Das Englische Verwaltungsrecht, etc.*, 1884, 167.

which appointment might be made with its own ad-
herents and to make places for them by the discharge
of existing officers.[1] This habit was not confined to
New York but afterwards made its way into the national administration and thence spread to every
one of the commonwealths. The evils resulting from
such a practice led the people very generally to change
the method of forming the official relation. Many of
the offices were made elective. The movement continued from 1825 to 1850 with the final result that
almost all the important offices were filled by popular
election both in the central commonwealth government
and in the localities. Since 1850, however, there has
been somewhat of a reaction in favor of the old method
by executive appointment, the reason being found in
the fact that the method by election did not have the
beneficial results which were expected of it. No
change in the original method of forming the official
relation was made in the national administration, not
because the same evils were not present, but because
the method of appointment being provided by the
national constitution could be changed only with very
great difficulty. In all cases where the method of appointment has been adopted the appointment is not
necessarily to be made by the administrative chief,
but in many cases by the heads of the executive departments, and in the localities by the chief local
authorities.[2]

In both France and Germany the great majority of
offices both central and local are filled by executive
appointment, the only officers of importance who are

---

[1] Gitterman, " New York Council of Appointment," *Pol. Sci. Qu.*, VII., 80.
[2] *Supra*, I., pp. 146, 243, 274.

elected being the members of the various local deliberative assemblies.[1] In England the original rule was to fill offices by appointment, but with the change in the system of local government many local authorities have become elective.[2]

The aims of these two methods of forming the official relation are quite different. The method of appointment aims at administrative harmony and efficiency. The method of election endeavors to ensure that popular control over the administration which is the fundamental principle of popular government. In order, however, that such a popular control may be exercised, the people must be in a position to judge of the merits of the respective candidates for office. They are undoubtedly in such a position in the rural districts where the feeling of neighborhood is strong. Here the people know the merits of the candidates who present themselves for local office and are in a position to make a wise choice. When we come, however, to more complex conditions such as exist, for example, in the central commonwealth administration and in the municipalities where the feeling of neighborhood is not strong, and where it will be difficult, if not impossible, for the people to know much about the merits of the different candidates, it is useless to adopt the elective method in the hope that the people will by its means be able to exercise any appreciable control over the administration. The only way in which the people may exercise such a permanent control over the administration is for them to elect only the most prominent officers of the government who are then to appoint to the subordinate offices. If a long list of

[1] *Supra*, I., pp. 84, 91, 302, 305.   [2] *Supra*, I., p. 237.

candidates is presented to the elector for his choice, if many of the offices to be filled by election are of a subordinate or unimportant character, even the most intelligent voter is apt to become confused. Other reasons than the positive merits of the candidates are apt to influence his choice, and the result of the election is apt to be in accordance with the wishes of those few persons who have the time and the inclination to busy themselves with the conduct of public affairs, rather than in accordance with the wishes of the people. The elective method thus in many cases does not secure the popular control, in order to secure which it is adopted. It not only fails of its purpose but it has one or two serious positive defects. Through its means it is often the case that men of totally opposed views on vital questions are put into office, where, in order that the administration may be efficient, it is necessary that it be harmonious. The necessity for harmony in some matters is so great that it is attained but through the crooked and devious methods known to practical politics as "deals," "dickers," and "rings." Such methods are in reality attempts to obtain the harmony which is so necessary to efficient administration ; their great fault is that through them the popular control over the administration is destroyed and the responsibility for administrative action is diffused. For these branches of administration, *i. e.* the central commonwealth administration and the municipal administration, the method of forming the official relation should be by appointment if an efficient, harmonious, and responsible administration under popular control is desired. This is the method which has been so successfully adopted in the national administration. This is also the method which has been adopted by the most recent and important municipal charters in the United States.[1]

Further the elective method of filling offices is in all instances unfitted for offices the efficient performance of whose duties requires the possession by the incumbents of large professional or technical knowledge. Such offices are those of judge, law officer, civil engineer, *etc., etc.* The requirement of the possession by the candidate of certain degrees or certificates, which are supposed to evidence the necessary qualifications, is not really sufficient. For the people even if their choice is thus confined are here again not in a position to choose wisely. Popular inclination is too apt to be swayed by other than scientific reasons. Such a method may shut out absolute ignorance from office; it will not, however, usually result in the choice of the best man for the office.

II.—The law of elections in the United States.[2]

The general rule is that the legislature may, in the absence of constitutional provision either granting or denying the power, pass reasonable regulations as to the method of holding elections.[3] In the exercise of this power the legislatures have very generally provided for the registration of voters as a necessary prerequisite to the casting of their votes. In two of the commonwealths, however, registration laws have been

---

[1] *Supra*, I., p. 210.

[2] The qualifications of voters are a matter rather of constitutional than of administrative law, and therefore will not be considered. For particulars see McCrary, *The Law of Elections*, 3d Ed., secs. 1–21.

[3] Commonwealth v. McClelland, 83 Kentucky, 686. This power is expressly granted in many of the constitutions. Stimson, *op. cit.*, sec. 235.

expressly forbidden, *viz.*, Arkansas and Texas, while in two others the provisions of the constitution are such as to render them practically nugatory. These are Pennsylvania and West Virginia, where no person may be deprived of his right to vote by reason of not having registered.[1] Such registration laws have been held to be reasonable regulations, and, as such, perfectly constitutional[2]; but a law which provides a method of voting by which it is impossible for an illiterate person to vote is not reasonable, and is therefore unconstitutional.[3] As a general thing, election regulations are directory rather than mandatory, and their violation, provided the will of the people is clearly expressed, will not invalidate the election.[4]

The general rules with regard to elections are:

1. *The election must be regular.*—Elections must always be held at the time and place appointed by the proper authority.[5] This authority may be the constitution, a statute, or an administrative act.[6] The action of the proper agency is necessary, and if the holding of the election is contingent upon the happening of some event, that event must have happened.[7]

2. *Necessity of notice.*—Notice of the time of elections does not seem to be necessary, even when expressly required by statute, except where such notice is in the nature of things necessary in order that the voter may know that an election is to take place. Its

---

[1] Stimson, *op. cit.*, sec. 236.

[2] Commonwealth v. McClelland, 83 Kentucky, 686.

[3] Rogers v. Jacobs, 11 S. W. Rep., 513.

[4] Trimmer v. Bomar, 20 S. C., 354.

[5] Mechem, *op. cit.*, sec. 170.

[6] Brodhead v. Milwaukee, 19 Wis., 624; Brewer v. Davis, 9 Humph. Tenn., 208.

[7] Stephens v. People, 89 Ill., 337.

absence will not necessarily invalidate an election, even
if it has been expressly required.   Thus the failure to
give notice of a general election, though required by
law, will not invalidate the election.[1]   But a special
election would not be regarded as valid in case no
notice of it was given.[2]   While notice of the time of
elections is not always necessary, notice of the place of
holding the election seems to be absolutely necessary ;
indeed all enactments as to the place of elections are
regarded as mandatory rather than directory.   Failure
to observe them will generally invalidate the election.[3]
It has been held, however, that in a case of an emergency
the place may be reasonably changed provided notice
is given.[4]

   3. *Method   of   voting   (ballot).*—As   a   general
thing the vote must be by ballot.[5]   The word ballot
originally meant a little ball by the casting of
which it was at first proposed that the vote should
be taken,[6] but it has come to mean in public law a
slip of paper, sometimes called a voting paper, on
which the name of the candidate to be voted for is
printed or written.   As the main object of the ballot
is a secret vote[7] the statutes regulating the ballot have
in the course of time gone more and more into detail
as to the form, appearance, and manner of folding the
ballot, each statute endeavoring to remedy some defect

---

[1] People v. Hartwell, 12 Mich., 508 ; People v. Cowles, 13 N. Y., 350.

[2] Secord v. Foutch, 44 Mich., 89 ; State v. Gloucester, 44 N. J. L., 137 ;
Mechem, *op. cit.*, sec. 176.

[3] Melvin's Case, 68 Pa. St., 333.

[4] Brodhead v. Milwaukee, 19 Wis., 624 ; Dale v. Irwin, 78 Ill., 170, 181 ;
Farrington v. Turner, 53 Mich., 27 ; Knowles v. Yeates, 31 Cal., 82.

[5] Stimson, *op. cit.*, sec. 231.

[6] Theodore W. Dwight, on " Harrington," in *Pol. Sci. Qu.*, II., 16.

[7] *Cf.* Cooley, *Constitutional Limitations*, 6th Ed., 760.

that had manifested itself, and by which the secrecy of the ballot was violated, until now the most common method of voting in the United States is by means of ballots absolutely uniform in appearance and size, having no marks upon them by means of which they may be distinguished one from the other when folded. These ballots are in many cases issued by officers of the government, and are printed at the expense of the government. A further result of the great desire for secrecy in voting is to be found in the fact that the courts in their decisions have aided the legislature, in stamping as an illegal ballot, and therefore as a ballot which may not be counted, any ballot which violates, in what at times seems only an unimportant point, the provisions of the statutes requiring secrecy.[1] The only other rule of importance as to the ballot is that requiring that it shall express clearly the intent of the voter. This rule, however, the courts do not carry so far as to throw out ballots for trifling irregularities.[2] In case the ballot is not clear on its face the best rule would seem to be that the courts may consider extrinsic evidence in explanation of it.[3] The ballots, after they have been cast, are counted by officers called canvassers, whose duties are usually ministerial in character,[4] and who, after they have once acted, have exhausted their powers and are not allowed to change their decision except as ordered by the courts.[5]

4. *What constitutes an election to office.*—As a general thing a candidate is elected to office by a plurality[6]

---

[1] Mechem, *op. cit.*, secs. 192–4.

[2] *Ibid.*, secs. 195–202.

[3] Cooley, *Constitutional Limitations*, 6th Ed., 768 ; People v. Pease, 27 N. Y., 45, 84.

[4] Mechem, *op. cit.*, sec. 208.

[5] Hadley v. Albany, 33 N. Y., 603.

[6] Stimson, *op. cit.*, sec. 232.

of the legal ballots cast, even though a majority of legal voters have not voted.[1] In the leading case of *People v. Clute* it was held, that a majority of votes cast for an ineligible candidate, if the ineligibility were not notorious, invalidated the election; that such votes were not to be regarded as merely illegal votes with the result that the candidate having the next highest number of votes would be elected. This seems to be the better rule in the United States.[2]

III.—*The law of appointment.*

The courts have sometimes attempted to hold in the United States that as the act of appointment is in its nature an essentially executive act, the exercise of the appointing power by any other than an executive or administrative authority is unconstitutional in a state whose constitution provides for the separation of powers[3]; but the difference as to the adoption in the constitutions of the various commonwealths of the principle of the separation of powers, and the different views held by the judges as to the meaning of the principle of the separation of powers when adopted have brought it about that this rule is not at all universal.[4] As to what constitutes an appointment the best rule would seem to be that it consists in the choice by the appointing power of the person appointed[5]; and is complete when the last act of the appointing power has been performed, as *e. g.* in the case where

[1] People v. Clute, 50 N. Y., 451.

[2] Mechem, *op. cit.*, sec. 206.

[3] State v. Denny, 118 Ind., 449 ; Evansville v. State, *Ibid.*, 426 ; see also State v. Kennon, 7 Ohio St., 546, 560.

[4] See Mayo v. State, 15 Md., 376 ; People v. Mahany, 13 Mich., 481 ; People v. Hurlburt, 24 Mich., 44, 63.

[5] Johnston v. Wilson, 2 N. H., 202.

the consent of some other authority than the one pro-
posing the appointment is necessary, in the grant of
the consent of that body.[1] Finally, in the absence of
any statutory provision to the contrary, the completion
of the appointment is not dependent upon the issue of
any commission, which is merely evidence of the appointment and is not the appointment itself.[2] Thus if
the commission has been issued to the wrong person
it may be revoked and a commission granted to the
proper person.[3] It is not as yet well settled in what
form the appointment is to be made, whether it must
be made in writing or whether an oral appointment
is sufficient.[4] But the power however exercised, once
exercised, is exhausted and the appointing power may
not revoke the appointment, provided of course that
the term of the appointee is not in the discretion of
the appointing officer, when of course the appointee
might be removed from office, and provided that there
has not been some mistake in the issue of the commission.[5]

IV.—*Acceptance of the office.*

While as a general thing no obligation to assume
a professional office is imposed upon its citizens by any
government,[6] it is not unfrequently the case that the
law compels the citizen to take an honorary office

[1] State v. Barbour, 53 Conn., 76 ; Marbury v. Madison, 1 Cranch, 137.

[2] *Ibid. ;* Mechem, *op. cit.*, sec. 117.

[3] Gulick v. New, 14 Ind., 93 ; State v. Capens, 37 La. Ann., 747.

[4] *Cf.* People v. Murray, 70 N. Y., 521, which holds that the appointment
must, in the absence of statutory provision to the contrary, be in writing, with
Hoke v. Field, 10 Bush, K'y., 144, which holds that it may be made orally.

[5] People v. Woodruff, 32 N. Y., 355 ; State v. Barbour, 53 Conn., 76 ; Gulick
v. New, 14 Ind., 93.

[6] *Cf.* Hinze v. People, 92 Ill., 406, in which the judge says that no man can
be compelled to assume a professional office.

whose duties are not so arduous as to require the entire time of the incumbent. This seems to have been the original rule in England, where acceptance of a municipal office might be compelled by means of the writ of mandamus,[1] and where failure to assume office might generally be punished by indictment.[2] The strictness of this rule has been somewhat relaxed in this country, where the rule has been retained. Thus where the office is in any sense obligatory, relief from the operation of the rule may be obtained by the payment of a fine, which in some cases, as *e. g.* in the case of the office of supervisor in New York, has been as high as $50. Even in these cases the law generally states that certain excuses are sufficient to relieve from service, large discretion in the matter of accepting an excuse being usually granted.

Further it has been held that the holding of one office will relieve from the obligation of accepting another.[3] Finally where acceptance of the office is not obligatory some formality indicative of the intention to assume the office seems to be necessary in order that the office may be regarded as filled.[4] Qualifying for the office is regarded as the best evidence of acceptance.[5] Refusal, and neglect to qualify will be regarded as a refusal, will operate to extinguish any right which the officer has to the office ; although mere delay will not have this effect.[6]

In France it is almost never the case that the acceptance of office is obligatory. In Germany the rule is

---

[1] Rex v. Bower, 1 B. & C., 585.

[2] See State v. Ferguson, 31 N. J. L., 107.

[3] Hartford v. Bennett, 10 Ohio St., 441.

[4] Johnston v. Wilson, 2 N. H., 202 ; Smith v. Moore, 90 Ind., 294, 306, 313.   [5] *Ibid.*   [6] Mechem, *op. cit.*, secs. 266, 433, 434.

very much the same as in the United States, but where the obligation to serve does exist, the penalty for refusal to serve is much more severe.[1] In England the old rule of obligatory service has been much modified. Much more reliance is placed on voluntaryism than formerly. There are still, however, instances of obligatory official service, as *e. g.* in the municipal service where most of the unpaid municipal offices are obligatory.[2]

V.—Officers de facto.

While it is in general true that the official relation can be formed only in one of the ways recognized by the law, and that the acts of persons who without right intrude into offices are absolutely void both as against the public and third persons, it is also a general principle of the English common law, based upon reasons of public convenience, that persons who, though not legally officers, have yet acted under color of right, *i. e.* have been declared elected or appointed or have held over in office in good faith, or whose assumption of office has been for a long time acquiesced in by the public, are regarded for many purposes as officers ; and that their acts will be given the same faith and credit as the acts of *de jure* officers. Such persons are called officers *de facto.*[3] It has, however, been held that an office must be originally established by law, *i. e.* that while there may be an officer *de facto* there can never be an office *de facto.*[4] One result of this rule as to the acts of officers *de facto* is that such acts may not, any

---

[1] *Supra*, I., p. 327. [2] *Supra*, I., p. 255.

[3] See Plymouth v. Painter, 17 Conn., 585 ; Hamlin v. Kassafer, 15 Oregon, 465 ; State v. Carroll, 38 Conn., 449 and cases cited.

[4] Norton v. Shelby Co., 118 U. S., 425, 442.

more than the acts of officers *de jure*, be impeached in a collateral proceeding to which the officer is not a party.[1] This is not, however, true of the acts of mere intruders because their acts are absolutely void.[2] Indeed the mere intrusion into an office without color of right cannot be said to result in any of the incidents of the official relation with the exception that the intruder may be forced by the government to account for moneys which he may have received.[3] While for reasons of public convenience the acts of officers *de facto* are given in collateral proceedings the same force and credit as are given to the acts of officers *de jure* this rule is not so applied as to permit an officer *de facto* to build up any claims for himself from the fact that he has assumed office. Thus he cannot recover compensation,[4] nor may he bring action in his official capacity without showing title,[5] nor may he, when sued, escape responsibility for an act which may be justified only by a valid title to the office.[6] A further result of this position of officers *de facto* is that they are liable for damages resulting from their negligence,[7] must perform all the duties connected with the office during the time they assume to hold it[8] and may be punished criminally for the commission of official crimes.[9]

[1] *Ibid. ;* People v. Hopson, 1 Denio, N. Y., 574, 579.

[2] See Conway v. City of St. Louis, 9 Mo. Appeals, 488.

[3] See U. S. v. Maurice, 2 Brock. U. S., 96.

[4] People v. Tieman, 30 Barb. N. Y., 193 ; Dolan v. the Mayor, *etc.*, 68 N. Y., 274.

[5] People v. Weber, 89 Ill., 347.

[6] Green v. Burke, 23 Wendell N. Y., 490-503 ; Riddle v. Bradford, 7 S. & R. Pa., 386, 392 ; Rodman v. Harcourt, 4 B. Mon. K'y, 224, 229 ; Patterson v. Miller, 2 Metc. K'y, 493, 496.

[7] Longacre v. State, 3 Miss., 637.

[8] Kelly v. Wimberly, 61 Miss., 548.

[9] Diggs v. State, 49 Ala., 311 ; State v. Goss, 69 Me., 22 ; see also Mechem, *op. cit.*, secs. 315-346.

CHAPTER III.

QUALIFICATIONS FOR OFFICE.

I.—Elective officers.

1. *Right to provide qualifications.*—Nowhere does the law permit any one and every one to hold offices. In all countries certain qualifications of eligibility for office are prescribed. For the power to hold office is not generally a right guaranteed by the constitution, but rather a privilege usually granted to all electors or citizens but sometimes granted to persons who are neither citizens nor electors and sometimes not to all electors or citizens, and in all cases subject to the regulation of the legislature in the absence of constitutional restriction.[1] As a general thing in the United States it is held, either as the result of a direct constitutional provision or as a result of the interpretation put by the courts upon certain general constitutional provisions, that political and religious opinions may not be made a test. Thus it has been held that it is not within the power of the legislature to provide that two members of a board of four members shall be chosen from each of the two leading political parties.[2]

[1] See Ohio v. Covington, 29 Ohio St., 102, holding that an educational qualification is proper ; Darrow v. People, 8 Col., 417, holding that a property qualification is proper ; *cf.* Barker v. People, 3 Cowen N. Y., 686.

[2] Evansville v. State, 118 Ind., 426, 435 ; People v. Hurlburt, 24 Mich., 44, 93 ; Attorney General v. Detroit Common Council, 58 Mich., 213, 215. See

2. *Usual qualifications.*—The qualifications which
have been established for elective officers are in all
countries pretty much the same. They consist for the
most part in citizenship or the right to vote,[1] the attainment of a certain age, the possession of good character,[2]
and for the majority of offices the possession of the
male sex. This is not generally the case in the United
States for school offices, and in some commonwealths,
as *e. g.* Kansas, is not the case for municipal offices.[3]
In the absence of special statutory provision as to the
eligibility of women there is no fixed and universal
rule as to the matter in the United States. In *Robinson's Case*[4] it is said that the male sex is required
where no provision as to the eligibility of women
exists, though it is admitted there is no constitutional
objection to their being made eligible by statute.[5] On
the other hand the contrary rule, *viz.*, that women are
eligible in the absence of statutory provision, seems to
be held in *In re Hall.*[6] For local officers, further, residence in the locality in which the duties of the office
are to be performed, or some equivalent therefor, is

---

also Mayor v. State, 15 Maryland, 376, 468. But see Rogers v. Buffalo, 123
N. Y., 173, which holds that a law providing that not more than two members
of a board shall belong to the same political party is perfectly proper. In
some of these cases the decision of the court was to a certain extent influenced by
the fact that it was impossible for the court to decide whether a person belonged
to one of the leading political parties.

[1] See State v. Smith, 14 Wis., 497 ; State v. Murray, 28 Wis., 96 ; State v.
Trumpf, 50 Wis., 103. But see In the matter of Ole Mosness, 39 Wis., 509,
511, where the court says that extra-territorial officers, as *e. g.* commissioners, to
take acknowledgments, need not be citizens or electors.

[2] See Mechem, *op. cit.*, secs. 77–80, particularly for the usual disqualification
resulting from conviction for crime.

[3] For a summary of the rules with regard to the eligibility of women to office
see M. Ostrogorski in the *Political Science Quarterly*, VI., 677.

[4] 131 Mass., 376, 383.

[5] See 115 Mass., 602, and Huff v. Cook, 44 Iowa, 339.

[6] 50 Conn., 131.

generally required. Finally the possession of real property is often required, particularly in the case of local offices. This last qualification is more common in Europe than in the United States.[1] In the case of offices of a technical or professional character the law usually requires that the candidate must have undergone some training or possess some degree or certificate. Thus no one but an engineer by profession may be elected to the position of state engineer and surveyor in New York.[2] Further where judges and prosecuting officers are elected by the people it is usually provided that the candidate for such positions shall be a counsellor at law of a certain number of years' standing.[3] Finally in many cases the possession of one office will disqualify for others.[4] There is not absolute agreement in the decisions as to when the qualifications required by law must exist, some decisions holding that they must exist at the time of the election[5]; others holding that it is sufficient if they are present at the beginning of the term of office, holding that the qualification is not one for election, but for holding office.[6]

II.—*Appointed officers in the United States.*

For appointed officers the qualifications differ considerably in the different countries and in many cases

---

[1] See Mechem, *op. cit.*, sec. 81, and Darrow v. People, 8 Col., 417 ; *supra*, I., p. 320.

[2] Constitution, art. v., sec. 2.

[3] See People v. May, 3 Mich., 598.

[4] See People v. Clute, 50 N. Y., 451 ; *infra*, II., p. 96.

[5] Searcy v. Grow, 15 Cal., 117, followed by the later decisions in that commonwealth ; Parker v. Smith, 3 Minn., 240 ; State v. Clark, 3 Nev., 519 ; State v. McMillen, 23 Neb., 385.

[6] State v. Murray, 28 Wis., 96 ; State v. Trumpf, 50 Wis., 103 ; Smith v. Moore, 90 Ind., 294 ; Privett v. Bickford, 26 Kan., 52. Some of the later Wisconsin cases hold to this rule only on the ground of *stare decisis*, and recognize that the other rule is the better one.

are much more stringent than are those for elective offices.

1. *General qualifications.*—The first of the general qualifications for appointment to office in the United States is the possession of citizenship or the right to vote. This does not, however, appear to be the universal rule. There is nothing in the statutes of the United States national government absolutely decisive on the point. The United States Revised Statutes which govern the form of the official oath[1] seem to presuppose that citizenship is necessary but nowhere is it expressly required. The civil-service law of 1883 does not require citizenship but general rule III[2] passed in execution of the law would seem to require citizenship for the classified service. In New York also civil-service rule 35 requires citizenship for the classified service, and in Massachusetts it would seem to be required for all positions in the service except expert positions.[3] But apart from these provisions the law does not seem to be explicit on this point; and it is well known that many positions in the diplomatic and consular services are filled by persons who are not citizens of the United States. A qualification akin to that of citizenship is that of residence. In New York and Massachusetts the rules require a residence in the commonwealth of one year for positions in the classified service.[4] In the national service there is a peculiar rule for the classified departmental service. This is[5] that appointments to the classified public service at Washington shall be apportioned among

---

[1] Secs. 1756–7.   [2] Sec. 8.   [3] Civil-Service Rule VII., 1.

[4] N. Y. Rule 35 ; Mass. Rule VII., 1, which requires it for all positions in the service with the exception of expert positions.

[5] Civil-Service Law, sec. 2, third ; Departmental Rule VII., 2.

the commonwealths, territories, and the District of Columbia in accordance with their population as fixed by the last census. This rule has been regarded by some of the best administrative officers of the government as a detriment to the service and is from the point of view of administrative science absurd in the extreme.

The next general qualification is to be found in the limits of age at which entrance into the service is allowed. The purpose of these provisions is to exclude the too young and the too old. The limits of age vary with the particular branch of the service from a minimum of sixteen for the position of junior clerk in the classified postal service to a maximum of fifty for the position of superintendent in the classified Indian service.[1] Generally, however, all persons between the ages of twenty and forty-five may enter the classified service. In New York the limits of age are fixed by the civil-service commission after consultation with the heads of departments, differences between the two being settled by the governor.[2] These vary from a minimum of eighteen for messengers to a maximum of fifty for clerical positions.[3] In the United States national, the New York service, and the Massachusetts service these limitations do not apply to persons who have been honorably discharged from the military or naval services of the United States. Such persons it is well to note are always to be preferred by the appointing officers.[4]

[1] Postal Rule II., 2 ; Indian Rule II.

[2] N. Y. Rule 24 ; *cf.* Massachusetts Rule X. which requires a certain age only for certain branches of work.

[3] See sixth report of the New York civil-service commission, 464. See also Mechem, *op. cit.*, sec. 71.

[4] U. S. L. 1883, c. 27, sec. 7 ; N. Y. L. 1884, ch. 410 ; Mass. L. 1887, ch. 437 ; *cf.* Mechem, *op. cit.*, sec. 84, especially for the decisions in construction and application of these laws.

The third general qualification is to be found in the possession of good character. The civil service laws very generally provide in addition to the usual disqualification for conviction of crime [1] that no person shall be appointed to office who habitually uses intoxicating beverages to excess, while the Massachusetts law also disqualifies all liquor sellers.[2] The rules also generally provide that no person shall be appointed in the classified service who has been guilty of a crime or of notoriously disgraceful or infamous conduct.[3] Finally it is provided in the rules generally that certificates of good moral character shall be presented at the time that the application for appointment is made, and that when such recommendations are made by public officers, especially by legislative officers, no part of such recommendation, except such as bears upon the character of the applicant, shall be considered by the appointing officer.[4]

Finally it is to be noticed that the male sex is not generally required for appointed officers. Thus it has been held or intimated that a woman may be appointed to the position of postmistress and pension agent,[5] to that of deputy clerk,[6] and to that of master in chancery.[7] Further the rules in the United States national service and in the Massachusetts service seem to presuppose that women will be appointed.[8]

---

[1] For this see Mechem, *op. cit.*, secs. 77–80.

[2] U. S. L. 1883, c. 27, sec. 8 ; Mass. L. 1884, c. 320, sec. 4.

[3] U. S. Gen. Rule IV., 2, III., 8 ; N. Y. Rule 10 ; Mass. L. 1884, c. 320, sec. 4.

[4] U. S. L. 1883, c. 27, sec. 10 ; N. Y. L. 1883, c. 354, sec. 9.

[5] *In re* Hall, 50 Conn., 131, 137.

[6] Jeffries v. Harrington, 17 Pac. Rep. (Col.), 505.

[7] Schuchardt v. People, 99 Ill., 501.

[8] U. S. Department Rule VII., 1, b ; Massachusetts Rule XI., 2.

2. *Intellectual capacity.*—The most important qualification for appointed officers is that of capacity, which
may be either physical or intellectual. Physical capacity, when required, is to be shown either by certificates of persons acquainted with the applicant or
of physicians,[1] or by examinations made either by a
physician or in the nature of tests requiring unusual
strength or agility, as *e. g.* the positions in the police
and fire services of the cities or in the national revenue
marine service. Sometime, and generally in order to
be qualified for these positions, the applicant must be
of a certain weight, a certain height, *etc., etc.*[2]

Originally there seem to have been really no legal
requirements as to intellectual capacity in the United
States for appointed officers. The earliest instance of
qualifications for capacity in the English law is said
to be found in the case of the office of the sheriff of
London. In order to be qualified for this position, the
candidate was, in a time when the arithmetical capacity
of the ordinary man was not great, obliged to count
six horse-shoes and sixty-one nails. To prove physical
capacity the candidate was obliged to cut a bundle of
sticks. While this severe test of intellectual capacity
has fallen into disuse, it is said that it is still necessary for the candidate for the office of sheriff in London
to cut the bundle of sticks which now consists of a
bundle of matches.[3] It was believed in the United
States that the officers to whom the power of appointment had been given, would of their own accord

[1] U. S. Gen. Rule III., 8 ; N. Y. Rule 10 ; Mass. Rule XII.

[2] See Massachusetts Rule X., XXII.; Comstock, *The Civil Service of the
United States,* 578 *et seq.,* 582.

[3] See Peck v. Rochester, 3 N. Y., Sup., 872, citing Hare, *Walks in London,*
N. Y. Ed., II., 272, 273.

choose the best men that they could obtain. With the growth of party government, partisan rather than administrative considerations came in many cases to govern the action of the appointing officers, both in the national and the commonwealth governments. The natural result of such a practice was a deterioration in the character of appointees; and as early as 1853 the attempt was made by Congress to prevent the appointment of absolutely incapable persons by providing that all appointees must pass an examination before they might enter the clerical service at Washington, which was divided at about the same time into classes, whence the name of classified service. This pass examination was to be conducted by officers of the departments to which the law applied. The plan was not successful when put into operation, but nothing further was done until 1870, when President Grant, in his message to Congress of that year, advocated the adoption of a system of competitive examinations. The result of the message was the passage of a law, now partly incorporated into the revised statutes, which authorized the President to prescribe such regulations for the admission of persons into the civil service of the United States as would best promote its efficiency and ascertain the fitness of each person in respect to age, health, character, knowledge, and ability for the branch of the service into which he sought to enter. For this purpose the President was authorized to appoint suitable persons to conduct the examinations which it was intended to establish. The President issued a set of rules and appointed a commission. The system of competitive examinations went into effect, and according to the statements of the highest administrative officers of the government proved eminently successful. But in 1874 Congress, in which from the first there had been considerable opposition to the system, refused to make the necessary appropriations to carry on the work of the commission, and the rules generally ceased to be enforced. The rules still continued to be applied in the New York custom-house, were later extended to the post-office, and were so successful that in 1883 the present civil-service law was passed. A law similar to it was passed in New York and Massachusetts, and the plan has been adopted in the city of Philadelphia by a Pennsylvania law of 1885.

Before entering upon the consideration of the provisions of these laws and the rules as to capacity issued by the executive in execution of them it must be noted that they are not mandatory upon either the President or the governor. They simply authorize him to appoint commissions to aid him in the work and to issue rules as to the details of the competitive or other examinations which are intended by the laws to be established. But as soon as such rules are once promulgated they become binding upon the heads of departments having the appointing power as a result of legislative enactment.[1] For since the power of appointment is in these cases based upon legislation its extent can be changed by legislation. On this account it cannot be said that the civil-service laws are unconstitutional so far as the relations of the chief executive and the ordinary heads of departments are concerned.[2]

[1] *Cf.* United States v. Perkins, 116 U. S., 483 ; see also Peck v. Rochester, 3 N. Y. Sup., 872, where the city was enjoined from paying a salary to a city official on the ground that his appointment had been made in violation of the law ; see also Rogers v. Buffalo, 2 *Ibid.*, 326.

[2] See Dorman B. Eaton's brief in the Hinckley case, *New York Times*, Sept. 28, 1885.

Where, however, the head of a department has the appointing power as a result of constitutional provision, it has been held in several decisions that the chief executive may not, even if authorized by statute, prescribe rules for appointment to the service which limit the power of appointment of such head of department by requiring that he shall select his subordinates as a result of a competitive examination.[1] The effect of these decisions has been to take away a large part of its force from the civil-service-reform movement in New York. For the superintendent of public works and the superintendent of prisons have the appointing power by grant of the constitution and appoint by far the greatest number of the administrative subordinate officers of the central government of the commonwealth of New York.[2]

The law and rules of the United States national government do not attempt to prescribe intellectual qualifications for all positions in the national service, but start out by exempting certain positions from the operation of the rules. Thus section 7 of the law provides that none of the Senate appointments shall be classified for examination except with the consent of the Senate which up to the present time has neither been asked for nor given, and that persons in the secret service of the government and laborers shall not be obliged to pass an examination in order to be appointed to positions in the service. The rest of the national

[1] People *ex. rel.* Killeen v. Angle, 109 N. Y., 564 ; People v. Durston, 6th Report of the N. Y. Civ.-Serv. Com., 231.

[2] The United States law is to be found in 27 Stats. at Large, 403, c. 27 ; the New York law is L. 1883, c. 354 ; the Massachusetts law is L. 1884, c. 320 ; and the rules and regulations of the commissions may be found in any of the reports of the commissions.

service is at the disposition of the President, who may require such intellectual or other tests for entrance into the service as he deems best. Up to the present time, however, the President has thought best to classify for examination only five branches of the service. These are, first, the "classified departmental service." The name is derived from the fact that the old classification of 1853, to which allusion has been made, has been extended practically to all subordinate positions at Washington in the eight executive departments, the civil-service commission, the department of labor, and the fish commission. In the department of agriculture are included also the employees of the weather bureau employed elsewhere than at Washington.[1] The second class is the "classified customs service," which embraces those persons similarly classified and serving under any collector, naval officer, surveyor, or appraiser in any customs district where the officials are fifty or more in number. In this class are included all appointments to which is attached a salary of $900 or over.[2] The third class is the "classified postal service," which is composed of those officers and employees in the postal service who are appointed under any postmaster of a free-delivery post-office.[3] The fourth class is the "classified railway mail service," which includes all officers and employees in the railway mail service.[4] The fifth class is the "classified Indian service," which embraces all physicians, school superintendents, and assistant superintendents, school

---

[1] Department Rules I.–IV. ; 9th Report of the United States Civil-Service Commission, 64. For an interesting article on the general subject see F. P. Powers on "The Reform of the Federal Service" in *Pol. Sci. Qu.*, vol. III., 260.

[2] Customs Rule I.   [3] Postal Rule I, sec. 2.   [4] Railway Mail Rule I.

teachers and matrons in the Indian service.[1] It is to
be noted that in all these classes the rules exempt from
the passage of examinations for appointment to the
service one private secretary for each head of an office
or bureau where such head is appointed by the President
and confirmed by the Senate, custodians of money for
whom another is responsible with certain exceptions—
i. e. those below the grade of assistant cashier or assistant teller,—disbursing officers who give bonds, deputies
and assistants not assigned to ordinary administrative
work, chief clerks and clerks of divisions, superintendents and assistant superintendents, except in the Indian
service, and persons employed exclusively in the secret
service.[2] Care is taken in the rules, it will be noticed,
to prevent an unduly wide interpretation being put by
appointing officers on the scope of these exemptions.
The result of the exemption of the chiefs of divisions
has been unfortunate. It is said that the position of
the chief of division has become rather a precarious
one and is filled now with less efficient persons than
formerly, and filled in most cases for partisan political
reasons. The demand for places has been so great and
the number of places to be distributed so small, as a
result of the enforcement of the civil-service law and
rules, that the positions of chiefs of divisions have
been used to reward political services.[3] The main
reason why these exemptions have been made is to be
found in the desire to secure perfect harmony and
confidence between the officers exempted and their

[1] Indian Rule I. ; see 7th Report of the U. S. Civil-Serv. Com., 79–89 ; 9th
Ibid., 64–70.

[2] See Departmental Rule II., sec. 3 ; Customs Rule II., sec. 5 ; Postal Rule
II., sec. 5 ; Railway Mail Rule II., sec. 5.

[3] See F. P. Powers on the " Reform of the Federal Service" in the *Pol. Sci.
Qu.*, III., 278.

superiors. It is believed that this harmony will result from a uniformity in political opinions as well as from purely personal reasons. The total number of those in the " classified services " is said to be about 43,000.[1]

Both New York and Massachusetts have followed the example set by the national government and have classified their services, both the central service and the service of the cities, for the purpose of providing tests for the ascertainment of the intellectual capacity of the candidates for office. They have further followed in the main the same principles in exempting the Senate appointments and laborers, with the one exception that Massachusetts has provided a means of forming a register of persons desiring positions as laborers, from which the appointing officers are to select laborers when wanted. It is reported very recently that such a registration of laborers has been adopted by the United States navy department for the navy yards. The classification in both commonwealths had on account of the greater heterogeneity of the services to be made on quite a different plan.[2]

For the purpose of attending to the examinations which the law intended to establish and generally of enforcing the provisions of the civil-service acts there has been established both in the national and the commonwealth service a commission of a non-partisan character to be appointed by the chief executive with the consent of the Senate or council and generally removable by him alone.[3] Under this commission is a chief examiner whose duty is, under the direction of

---

[1] 9th Rep. of the Civ.-Serv. Com., 97.

[2] For the details see the various reports of the commissions.

[3] U. S. Stats. at Large, vol. 22, c. 27, p. 403 ; N. Y. L. 1883, c. 354; Mass. L. 1884, c. 320. The Massachusetts law requires the assent of the council for the removal as well as for the appointment.

the commission, to secure uniformity and justice in the action of the various examining boards. These examining boards are to be designated from among officers in the public service, after consultation with the heads of departments, by the civil-service commission. They may hold their examinations at the capital or elsewhere. Any fraud on their part or on the part of any person in the public service in conducting the examinations is to be punished. The composition and the duties of these boards are defined in the regulations of the commissions ; and the commission will consider complaints as to the unfairness of any board and will revise the marking or grading and will order a new examination if it thinks best.[1]

In the cities in New York there are special commissions whose composition varies considerably as they are formed in accordance with the rules which the mayors of the cities have the right, subject to the approval of the commonwealth commission, to issue.[2] This power of approving the municipal rules is about the only power of control which the central commission has over the municipal service. The Massachusetts law differs from the New York law in that it puts the control of the municipal as well as that of the commonwealth service into the hands of the commonwealth commission.[3]

The examinations, to conduct which is the chief purpose of the formation of these commissions, are either pass or competitive examinations. The former, *i. e.* the pass examinations, are sometimes called standard or non-competitive examinations. They were introduced

---

[1] U. S. Reg. VI. ; N. Y. Reg. 15 ; Mass. Reg. 13.
[2] N. Y. L. 1884, c. 410, sec. 2.   [3] Mass. L. 1884, c. 320, sec. 2.

into the national administrative service in 1853 but have now for the most part been replaced by the competitive examinations. Pass examinations occur for positions under the civil-service rules only in exceptional cases. Such cases are where there has been a failure of competent persons to attend and be examined and where the subjects in which the examinations are to be held are of a technical character or require peculiar information and skill.[1] We find such pass examinations in the patent office, the state department, the pension office, the signal office, and the geological survey.[2] In addition to the places which fall under the operation of the general civil-service rules we find pass examinations held also in other branches of the service, where they have been provided by executive or departmental regulations, *e. g.* in the revenue marine service and in the United States hospital service.[3]

In the New York service these pass examinations occur more frequently than in the United States national or even in the Massachusetts service. The reason of the greater frequency was that in the opinions of the heads of the departments the competitive examinations were unsuited for many of the positions, *viz.*, expert positions[4] and the lower grades of employees.[5] Thus in the case of expert positions the appointing officer is allowed a wide discretion. He may, first, select from three persons marked highest as the result of a competitive examination; or second, he may name to the commission three or more persons for

[1] See U. S. Gen. Rule III. which makes some other less important exceptions to the rule of competitive examinations, in order to facilitate the transaction of business in the departments.

[2] See 7th Rep. U. S. Civ.-Serv. Com., 87.

[3] See Comstock, *op. cit.*, 578 and 583.

[4] N. Y. Schedule C.

[5] N. Y. Schedule D.

competitive examination; and appoint the one graded
highest in such examination; or third, he may appoint
any person who upon a pass examination shall be duly
certified to him by the commission as qualified for the
duties of the position.   This third method, *i. e.* the
pass examination pure and simple, is always used for
the lower grades of employees.[1]

The competitive examinations may be either open or
limited.   In the national service the competitive examinations are in nearly all cases open examinations, *i. e.*
open to all comers otherwise duly qualified, and in
general are written examinations.   In the national service further these open competitive examinations are
either limited or general in scope and are called copyist
examinations or clerk examinations, the former admit-
ting the applicants only to the lower grades of the
service.[2]   The subjects upon which the copyist examinations are held are orthography, penmanship, arithmetic.   The clerk examinations are on the additional
subjects of book-keeping, accounts, elements of the
English language, letter writing, elements of the
geography, history, and government of the United
States.   In addition to the copyist and clerk examinations there are what are called supplementary examinations which are held for places requiring certain
technical, professional, or scientific knowledge or acquaintance with some other language than English.[3]
The character of the open competitive examinations in
the commonwealth service is similar to that of the
national open competitive examinations.[4]   In New York

[1] N. Y. Schedule D.   See N. Y. Rules 25–28.
[2] United States Departmental Rule II.
[3] See 7th Rep. of the U. S. Civ.-Serv. Com., 39, 231.
[4] See 6th Rep. of the N. Y. Civ.-Serv. Com., 464.

in addition to the open competitive examinations there are also limited competitive examinations, *i. e.* limited to those persons who may be designated by the head of a department wishing to make the appointment.[1] But for most of the clerical service under the rules [2] the examinations are open competitive examinations.

Both the national and commonwealth civil-service laws provide that the examinations shall be practical in character and, as far as may be, shall relate to matters which will fairly test the relative fitness and capacity of the persons examined to discharge the duties of that branch of the service into which they wish to enter. On account of this provision it will be seen that in many cases the applicant will have to state in advance the branch of the service into which he wishes to enter, and that an examination which, if passed satisfactorily, will open entrance into one branch of the service, will not open to him entrance into another. This is essentially true of the New York service which is of an extremely heterogeneous character.[3]

All applicants who pass satisfactorily the open competitive examinations (seventy per cent. in both the national and New York service, sixty-five, in the Massachusetts service, in all cases an exception being made for honorably discharged sailors and soldiers of the United States [4]) are placed on an eligible list on which they may remain a year, and when a proper vacancy occurs, the commission certifies to the appointing officer a given number, *viz.*, three, standing highest on the

---

[1] See *supra*, II., p. 41. [2] N. Y. Schedule B.

[3] See 6th Rep. of the N. Y. Civ.-Serv. Com., 464 *et seq.*

[4] U. S. Dep. Rule VI., 2 and 3 ; Customs Rule III., 3 and 4 ; Postal Rule III., 3 and 4 ; Railway Mail Rule III., 3 and 4 ; Indian Rule III., 5 ; N. Y. Rule, 15 ; Mass. Rule xxviii.

list, and from these the appointing officer makes his choice. In both the national and the commonwealth service, honorably discharged sailors and soldiers of the United States are to be preferred, in some cases even to those standing higher than they, if they have been able to obtain the required minimum mark. The appointing officer has not been confined in his choice to the candidate standing highest on the list, because it was feared that this might be regarded as an unconstitutional limitation of his discretion. The United States attorney-general has held that it is not unconstitutional to confine the choice of the appointing to the four standing highest on the list of eligibility.[1] No person, it may be added, may in most cases be certified more than three times to the same appointing officer, except at the request of the appointing officer. This provision was adopted to prevent the commissions from forcing upon an appointing officer any person who was personally objectionable to him. The appointment is not yet, however, a complete one. All that the applicant has shown is a certain amount of theoretical knowledge. He is now put upon his probation, as it is called, and only at the end of the term of probation, and then only if he has shown practical aptitude for the place, is he given a permanent appointment. The term of probation is six months in the United States and Massachusetts, and three months in New York.

What has been outlined is the strict system which the laws and the rules as a whole aim to enforce. But it is to be noticed that the rules contain detailed provisions which allow the appointing officers in certain

---

[1] Opinions Attorneys-General, XIII., 516.

cases a greater discretion than would appear from this general outline. These provisions, while permitting dispensing with the rules in certain cases, are, however, intended to be framed so as to prevent such a use of the discretion given as to destroy the effect of the open competitive examination system. A further qualification provided for by section 9 of the United States civil-service law is that where two or more members of the same family are in the public service in the grades covered by the act, no other member of the same family shall be eligible for appointment to any of the said grades.

It will be noticed that in almost all cases where the American law has attempted to secure mental capacity in the positions which are to be filled by appointment, it has done so by means of a competitive examination and a term of probation. Only in a few cases, as in position of medical reviewer in the pension office,[1] where professional knowledge is necessary, is a regular training and course of study required. The result is necessarily that those persons run the best chance for preliminary appointment to most of the positions for which qualifications of capacity are required, who can " cram " the best. The disadvantage of such a method, it is attempted to overcome by providing that the examinations shall be of a practical character, and shall relate to the work of the office to which the appointment is sought; that entrance to the lower positions alone shall be obtained in this way, and finally that after the passing of the examination and the preliminary appointment, the applicant for appointment, or " probationer " as he is called, shall not be

---

[1] Comstock, *op. cit.*, 587.

considered as having a permanent appointment until he shall have proved by actual practice that he is fitted to discharge the duties of the position he desires to fill. The term of probation is, however, comparatively short, particularly in the New York service. With a term of probation so short the examinations are the most important test; and these evince theoretical rather than practical aptitude. It is on this account probably that those who have been advocating the civil-service-reform movement, as this method of filling the positions in the administrative service is popularly designated, have not attempted to extend the system beyond the lowest grades of positions. It is well that they have taken this position, for it is very doubtful if an examination is a proper method of showing capacity for places whose duties are at all discretionary in character.

III.—*Qualifications for office in France.*

1. *General qualifications.*—The qualifications necessary for appointment to office in France are fixed for the most part by executive decrees and departmental regulations but not often by law except in the case of some of the general qualifications. These general qualifications are citizenship, which is usually required for all appointive offices; a certain age which is so fixed as to ensure the entrance of candidates into the service at an early age and gradual rise by promotion to the higher grades of the service; and good character. This qualification is somewhat the same as that provided by the United States civil-service rules but a little more stringent.[1]

---

[1] See Penal Code, arts. 34, 35 ; Block, *Dictionnaire, etc.*, 974.

2. *Qualifications of capacity.*—In the purely technical and professional branches of the service the qualifications consist in passing successfully through the schools established by the government for the purpose of educating men for these branches of the service. Thus engineers must be educated at the school of bridges and roads, mining engineers at the school of mines, *etc.*, *etc.*[1] In most of the ordinary administrative services, however, great reliance is placed upon the passage of open competitive examinations. But much greater reliance is placed than in the United States on the possession by the candidate for office of a good general education which is evidenced by certain diplomas or certificates. The diplomas most commonly required are those of bachelor of letters and science, while for those positions which require a knowledge of the law the diploma of licentiate in law (about equal to the usual degree of bachelor of laws in the United States) is necessary and in some cases the highest degree in law, *viz.*, that of doctor, is required. It is to be remembered that the degrees of licentiate and doctor of laws are given only to those persons who have had a good secondary education. The degree of bachelor of letters is required for positions in the central administration of the treasury, in the department of foreign affairs and the diplomatic and consular service, and in the departments of war and agriculture. The degree of licentiate in law is necessary to obtain the position of chief of bureau in the department of justice and in the general inspection of the finances and for certain positions in the diplomatic and consular services. Where such diplomas are re-

[1] Block, *loc. cit.*

quired they must be submitted for examination at the time of application for entrance into the service when the competitive examinations supervene. All the examinations are conducted by officers in the departments into which entrance is sought and are under the supervision of the heads of the departments. There is no civil-service or examining commission. Similar examinations are held for entrance into the services of the localities.[1] Finally the French place much greater reliance than does the system in the United States upon the term of probation. The length of the term is much greater usually than in the United States, often being as long as two years, and its length often depends on the number of vacancies and the merit of the probationer. The candidate in many cases is not given any salary during the term and often has to prove to the satisfaction of the administration he has sufficient means to support himself during his novitiate.[2]

What has been said refers alone to the subordinate positions of the service. The higher positions which, as in the United States are regarded as in the main political, are not subject to any qualifications of capacity.[3] The appointing power has absolute discretion in the filling of these positions.

IV.—Qualifications for office in Germany.

1. *General qualifications.*—Among the general qualifications for offices filled by appointment in Germany are citizenship, which, however, is in many cases obtained by the appointment[4]; good character, generally

---

[1] For the details as to the French system see Métérié-Larrey, *Les Emplois Publics*, 8 *et seq.*, 15 and 83.

[2] Métérié-Larrey, *op. cit. passim.*   [3] Block, *Dictionnaire*, 975, sec. 23.

[4] De Grais, *Verfassung und Verwaltung, etc.*, 1883, 69.

more stringent than in the United States [1]; age, which varies for the different branches; and fulfilment of military service or proof that the candidate is physically unfit for military service.

2. *Qualifications of capacity.*—The qualifications of capacity differ in accordance with the two great divisions of the service, known as the higher and the subaltern service.[2] The higher service in Prussia, upon whose system the imperial system is based so that the Prussian system may be taken as a type, embraces five classes of officers, beginning with the under secretaries of state and ending with the position of inspector.[3] For the purpose of determining the qualifications necessary for appointment to the service the higher service may be divided into the general higher service and the special or technical higher service, the last of which is composed of officers such as mining engineers, *etc., etc.* The general higher service includes such positions as that of under secretary of state, heads of bureaus, provincial governors, "government presidents" and councillors, and the professional members of the important administrative authorities and courts.[4] The purpose of the required qualifications for entrance into the higher service is to bring into the service at an early age men who possess wide general culture and special knowledge of legal and political science. In detail the provisions are as follows : In the first place a good secondary education must have been had, then

---

[1] Loening, *Deutsches Verwaltungsrecht*, 120 ; Von Rönne, *Staatsrecht der Preussischen Monarchie*, 4th Ed., III., 146, note 4, referring to certain instructions issued to appointing officers in Prussia in 1817, and providing that no persons of known bad character shall be appointed to positions in the service.

[2] Von Rönne, *op. cit.*, sec. 256.

[3] De Grais, *op. cit.*, 74.　　　　　[4] See *supra*, I., pp. 304, 307.

a course of three years' study of law at some university, half of which must have been at a German university. Proof of such study must be submitted to one of the higher courts which proceeds through a commission to examine the candidate. The examination is both oral and in writing, and is upon the private and the public law, legal history, and the principles of political science. The candidate must also write an original dissertation on some legal subject, the general character of which he may select. He is allowed six weeks in which to do this work and must prove to the satisfaction of the examiners that the work is his own. The examination is held after the dissertation has been accepted ; and if the candidate is unsuccessful he will be given another opportunity to try after the expiration of six months, but if he is a second time unsuccessful he is forever shut out of the higher service. For the successful candidate the passage of the examination marks the beginning of the period of practical training. For he is at once assigned to work with some one of the higher courts. If a candidate for the judicial service, he works here for four years, if a candidate for the higher administrative service, he works for two years with the court and is then assigned to work for another two years with some administrative authority. During his connection with these authorities the law requires the presiding officer to devote his personal attention to the instruction of the *referendarius,* as the candidate is called, expressly forbids such presiding officers from making use of the *referendarii* simply to aid him in his labors, and requires that the work that is assigned to them shall be such as will best fit them for their future work. The presiding officer must keep a record of the conduct of the *referendarii* under his charge. At the end of this long period of probation the candidate, if his work has been satisfactory, is to present himself for the final examination which is known as the great state examination and which is conducted by the "Examining Commission for Higher Administrative Officers." This sits at Berlin and is under the direction of the state ministry. The examination is both oral and in writing and is on the law in force in Prussia, especially the constitutional and administrative law, and on political economy and the science of finance; and like all the examinations in the Prussian system is a pass examination. The *referendarius* who passes successfully the great state examination is then appointed to be governmental assessor, is assigned to some salaried position in the higher administrative service, and is eligible to the highest positions in the service. The only great differences between the qualifications required for the general service and those required for the special services, such *e. g.* as positions in the forest or mines administration, are that the examinations for these latter services are upon rather more technical subjects, that university study is not so commonly required, and that the period of practical training required is a longer one.[1]

The subaltern service is divided into the subaltern service proper and the subordinate service. The former embraces those positions, such as the higher clerkships, whose duties require the exercise of a certain amount of legal knowledge and the exercise of a certain amount of discretion, while the purely subordinate service includes simply the purely mechanical positions,

---

[1] For the details see Von Rönne, *op. cit.*, III., 432–451.

such as copyists, porters, and the like. Provision is made by law for the filling of most of the positions in the subordinate service with persons who are provided with military certificates. These are given to soldiers and sailors who have been invalided, or have served for twelve years in the army as non-commissioned officers. In fact the purely mechanical positions are reserved exclusively for such persons. Further one half of the positions in the subaltern service proper which do not require technical or scientific training are also reserved for persons with the military certificates, who, however, have to pass examinations where these are necessary. All other positions in the subaltern service are filled by means of the " civil supernumeriat." Entrance into the service as civil supernumerary requires the fulfilment of military duty, ability to support oneself without pay for three years, a certificate from one of the well recognized schools for secondary education such as the gymnasium *(Zeugniss der Reife für Prima)*, and an age of between eighteen and thirty years. *Referendarii* may, however, enter the subaltern service.[1] All other persons desiring to enter the subaltern service must serve a term of probation termed a novitiate and pass an examination of a practical character at its expiration.[2]

V.—Qualifications for office in England.

As a result partly of legal provisions but more of practice the English administrative service is divided into two great divisions, *viz.*, the political service and the permanent service.

1. *The political service.*—This embraces the ministers

---

[1] *Cf.* Von Rönne, *op. cit.*, III., 451-4. [2] *Ibid.*, 452.

and the parliamentary under-secretaries of state and is composed of from fifty to sixty persons who go out of office with each change of administration. The qualifications for this branch of the service are of a purely practical character. That is officers must not be too old to do their share of the work in Parliament and must in the nature of things have a good education and a sufficient knowledge of departmental routine to represent the ministry in Parliament, and finally must be tolerably sure of their seats in Parliament, of which they are members.[1]

2. *The permanent service.*—All the rest of the service has a tenure practically during good behavior, but the manner of appointment and the legal or practical qualifications for the positions in this part of the service vary greatly as a result of the fact that it is divided into many divisions. The first division to be noticed is that class of officers who are known in the English political system as "staff appointments." These consist of the permanent under-secretaries of state, commissioners, law clerks, *etc.*, *etc.* They are really the most important officers for the routine work of the departments and form the bond of union between the changing ministries and the permanent lower service. They are often spoken of as the "depositaries of official tradition," and are the indispensable advisers of the political service. While appointed generally for political reasons, there being no legal qualification generally for the positions,[2] at the same time great care is taken to obtain capable men and their terms of office are practically for life.[3] Under the present

---

[1] Gneist, *Das Englische Verwaltungsrecht, etc.*, 1884, 241. [2] Todd, *op. cit.*, I.,616.
[3] *Cf.* Gneist, *op. cit.*, 241 ; Anson, *op. cit.*, II., 199–201.

scheme of classification the higher permanent service ends with these staff appointments and clerks of the higher divisions are often promoted to these positions.[1] The second division of the permanent service is to be found in the clerks of what is known as the higher division. It is to be noted, however, that in addition to these and in distinction from them should be mentioned expert and professional positions such as clerks in the office of the solicitor of customs and in the office of criminal law accounts, appointments to such positions being the result of the passage of open competitive special examinations.[2] Positions in the higher division are quite responsible and the exercise of the duties of the office often requires the exercise of considerable discretion. Persons desiring appointment in this division first pass a preliminary test examination open to all comers between eighteen and twenty-four years of age on such elementary subjects as arithmetic, English composition, geography, and English history.[3] After passing such examination satisfactorily, they are eligible for the competitive examination which is intended to be of a character to suit young men from eighteen to twenty-three years of age trained at a good school or at one of the universities. The examination is on a small number of obligatory subjects selected by the candidate from a list prepared by the civil-service commissioners in consultation with the heads of departments. The subjects include history, literature, natural science, mathematics, mental and moral philosophy, jurisprudence, and political economy, and bear little relation to the duties of the office ap-

---

[1] Crawley, *Handbook of Competitive Examinations*, 6.
[2] See Crawley, *op. cit.*, 57 *et. seq.* and 81.　　　　[3] *Ibid.*, 45.

pointment to which is sought. The greatest weight is laid upon mathematics and natural science and the examination is intended simply to show proficiency in matters of general education. The successful candidates are placed on a list in alphabetical order and may subsequently pass on other subjects on the list, which fact is then to be noted against their names.[1] As vacancies occur the heads of departments are to select whom they wish from the list. Candidates may refuse the place offered and may notwithstanding remain a certain time on the list. After appointment in this way the candidate is put on probation for a year and if satisfactory will then be appointed permanently.[2] This method of filling the higher clerkships is regarded by many as unsatisfactory as laying too much stress on mere theoretical knowledge; and indeed the examinations are so difficult that not so many candidates present themselves as were expected.[3]

The vast body of mere clerks are to be found in what is known as the lower division. Their duties are simply to carry out intelligently the orders of their superiors. It is not the intention to permit the promotion of any such persons to the higher division.[4] The qualifications for appointment to positions in this division are practically the same, with the exception that the examinations are easier and that the appointing officer is confined in his choice to the one marked highest on the list of eligibles. The head of a department may however demand some special qualifications as *e. g.* the ability to read some foreign language. The

---

[1] *Ibid.*, 46.

[2] *Ibid.*, and Order in Council, Feb. 12, 1876, sec. 10.

[3] See *Nineteenth Century*, October, 1886.

[4] Order in Council, Feb. 12, 1876, sec. 18.

term of probation is the same, *viz.*, a year, and if the probationer is unsatisfactory in one department he may be given another trial in another department for which it is believed he is better suited. The limits of age for the lower division are from seventeen to twenty except in the case of boy clerks. These are admitted at the age of fifteen to seventeen by passing a competitive examination of a very limited character. After good service they may compete among themselves for a limited number of the clerkships in the lower divisions and those who are unsuccessful in obtaining appointment are to be dismissed from the service at the age of nineteen.[1] Finally competitive examinations are also held for the position of copyist.[2]

Finally it is to be noticed that the expenses of conducting these examinations are defrayed from fees paid by the candidates, which vary from £5 for places in the higher division to 1s. for the boy clerkships; and that the examinations are conducted as in the United States under the supervision of a civil-service commission which is appointed by the executive. As is usually the case in this country laborers are considered a legitimate element of party patronage; and no qualifications, not even registration, are required.

VI.—*Comparison of the various plans.*

If we compare the various systems which have been adopted for ensuring intellectual capacity in the incumbents of positions in the government service filled by appointment we find that Germany is the only country which has provided that the incumbents of the most responsible positions shall show any evidence of fitness

---

[1] See Crawley, *op. cit.*, 48–51.　　　　[2] *Ibid.*, 51.

except such as is to be shown by the purely practical tests
of every-day life. In Germany, office-holding, especially
in the highest positions, is regarded as a learned profession on a par with the other well recognized learned
professions and therefore it is only natural for the Germans to require of the candidates for the highest positions an education and training of the same general
grade as that which is required of the lawyer or the
physician. In England on the other hand, while no
legal requirements are laid down, the practical requirements which are in fact demanded amount to very
much the same thing, with the single exception that no
weight at all is in the higher positions (*e. g.* the staff
appointments) laid upon theoretical training. While
it is probable that persons who have passed through
the universities or who are learned in the law will
more frequently fill these positions than non-university
men still these places are open to those who have had
nothing more than the most general education. But in
England this lack of theoretical training is largely compensated for by the rule that once appointed to any of
these higher positions the incumbent will remain there
probably all his life, and also by the fact that these
positions are regarded as in the ordinary course of promotion though there is no law providing that this shall
be the case. The result is that these higher positions
are filled in England for the most part by men who are
thoroughly conversant with the duties required of them
and that a change of ministry has no perceptible effect
on the work of the administrative departments, which
goes on as before under the direction of the officers
occupying the staff appointments. In France also
somewhat the same method of filling the higher offices

has been adopted, the only difference being that perhaps considerably more emphasis than in England is laid
upon theoretical knowledge and practical administrative
experience, in that the positions in the higher service
are filled perhaps more frequently by men who have
had a legal training and by promotion from the lower
grades of the service. Here again it has not been
thought best to limit at all the discretion of the
appointing power in the filling of the highest positions. In the filling of these positions, political reasons,
undoubtedly have large influence. It must also
be noted, that the tenure of these positions is not
probably so fixed as it is in England, although the
retention of a certain proportion of each incumbent's
salary in order to form a pension fund for the payment
of official pensions[1] makes it more difficult than it
otherwise would be to make wholesale removals. As
in England and in France, so in the United States,
both in the national and the commonwealth services,
there are few legal requirements of capacity for the
higher positions. Reliance is placed almost entirely
upon the wisdom of the appointing officers who, it is
supposed, will be guided in their choice by the practical needs of the service, although political reasons
are at the same time expected to have a large influence.
One fact which makes the requirement of a knowledge of the law almost unnecessary in the American
system is the wide opportunity given in the United
States for legal instruction, which has resulted in the
fact that many if not most of the higher positions in
the government are filled by men who have been
educated in the law. It has been remarked of the

[1] *Infra*, II., p. 74.

American system of government, that it is a government of lawyers. But different from the other systems the American system has not yet, certainly so far as the higher offices are concerned, developed a permanent tenure. The class of what are deemed political offices reaches down much lower in the administrative hierarchy than in other countries. People almost expect that all positions which require the exercise of any considerable amount of discretion shall be filled with new incumbents by every incoming administration. This tendency has been rather aggravated by the laws known as the term-of-office acts,[1] which fix the term of most of the important offices in the national government at four years. The result is that while the American official has generally sufficient knowledge of the law to enable him to perform his duties with intelligence the frequent changes that are made in the higher positions make it practically impossible to keep in office many persons who are thoroughly acquainted with the details of their work. This is the weak point, from an administrative point of view, of the American system, and reform of this particular weakness seems quite hopeless so long as people have the fear, which they undoubtedly do have, of a permanent force of officials, which is associated in their minds with bureaucratic government.

The differences in the various methods of filling the lower positions of the service are not so marked in the different countries. They all agree in requiring the proof of capacity to be made by the passage of examinations. But while in England and the United States the examination and a short term of probation are the

---

[1] *Infra*, II., p. 90.

only requirements practically for most of the positions, and while the examinations bear no very close relation to the duties of the office appointment to which is sought, in France and Germany great reliance is placed upon practical work in the departments and examinations are much more closely related to the duties of the various positions, while in addition to the examinations and a long term of probation proof of a good general education is very generally required, *i. e.* the candidates for all but the absolutely mechanical positions must have had an education equal to that obtained in the first two or three years of the ordinary American college. Again the American system differs from the English system in that reliance is not placed upon these examinations on subjects of a general educational character to fill those positions whose duties are at all discretionary in character. This, it would seem, is wise, for it is just here that the examination system does not appear to work with unquestioned satisfaction. Such places should be filled by promotion from the lower grades. This the English system attempts to prevent altogether in its general prohibition of the promotion of clerks in the lower division to positions in the higher division. While unfortunately the rule in the United States does not seem to be to fill the positions of discretion by promotion from the lower positions, it is very probable that the American method, even with its present defects, is superior to the English method of attempting to fill such positions by means of examinations on such subjects as the higher mathematics and natural science. Finally the German system differs from all the others in that the examinations take place after, not before, the term of probation, in that they are pass and not competitive examinations, and in that the subjects on which they are held seem to relate very closely if not entirely to the duties of the office with which the candidate is supposed to have acquainted himself during his long term of probation. In France also it is to be noted that the examinations are much more practical in character than in England or the United States. While the present movement for the reform of the civil service has been in the main upon the lines of the preceding English reform, it is very probable that we have followed the English example about as far as we can follow it with profit, and it is doubtless either to France or Germany that we shall have to turn in our endeavors further to reform the conditions of entrance into the administrative services. We must not only do this, but also public opinion must be cultivated up to the point at which it is in England, where it will not permit wholesale changes of personnel in the higher branches of the service not wholly political in character.

CHAPTER IV.

THE RIGHTS OF OFFICERS.

I.—*Right to the office.*

The first right to be noticed is the right of the officer to exercise the powers and perform the duties connected with his office. A continuing right to the office can be spoken of only in the case of an officer whose tenure of office is independent of any administrative superior, so far as the length of term is concerned. Only those officers have a permanent right to exercise the powers and perform the duties of the office who may not be arbitrarily discharged by an administrative superior.[1] But the question of the right of an officer to his office is one which may come up at the beginning of the official relation rather than at the end. It will naturally come up more frequently in the case of elective than in the case of appointed officers, but it may come up in the case of an appointive office especially in the United States, where the term of appointed officers is so often fixed by law. For instance the appointing authority may make an appointment to an office when he believes that the

---

[1] Thus the remedy by means of which the right may be enforced, *viz.*, the *quo warranto*, may not be made use of in the case of offices of no certain duration. State v. Champlin, 2 Bailey, S. C. 220 ; Darley v. The Queen, 12 Clark & Finlay, 520, 541.

term of the incumbent has expired, while the incumbent may claim that the term has not expired and that he has a right to the office until the expiration of its term. In the case of an elective office the question as to the right may come up very frequently as the result of a dispute as to who has been elected. Everywhere this right of the officer to his office is recognized, especially in the case of elective offices ; the great difference in the different countries being as to the method by which the right is to be enforced. In England and the United States the rule has been ever since the reign of Queen Anne,[1] that the title to office is to be tried by the writ of *quo warranto,* or the information in the nature of a *quo warranto,* or its statutory substitute, by means of which the courts are to decide who are the rightful holders to offices in question, and as such entitled to exercise their powers and receive their emoluments. Further one who is clearly entitled to an office may by *mandamus* force the delivery to him of the *insignia* of office and may in like manner obtain possession of public buildings and records.[2] In the United States the appeal to the courts is generally open to any candidate for the office, to the government, and in many cases to any elector of responsibility.[3] In some of the American commonwealths special tribunals to try election cases have been established. If this is the case, recourse must be had to such tribunals and not in general to the *quo warranto.*[4] In England

[1] See 9 Anne, c. 20.

[2] People v. Kelduff, 15 Ill., 492 ; Walter v. Belding, 24 Vt., 658 ; Hooten v. McKinney, 5 Nev., 194.

[3] See Commonwealth v. Neeser, 44 Pa. St., 341 ; Commonwealth v. Swank, 79 Pa. St., 144 ; *cf.* Mechem, *op. cit.*, sec. 213.

[4] State v. Marlow, 15 Ohio St., 144 ; People v. Goodwin, 22 Mich., 496 ; see also People v. Hall, 80 N. Y., 117, and *cf.* Mechem, *op. cit.*, sec. 214.

also of late years the tendency has been to establish special tribunals to try election cases, which, however, act under the supervision and to a certain extent under the direction of the ordinary courts of law.[1] Finally in some cases in England election contests are decided by the superior authorities of the administration itself.[2] On the continent access to the ordinary courts to try the title to office is seldom allowed. It is believed such a practice would violate the fundamental principle of the independence of the administration. Generally any dispute as to the title to an office is to be tried by the administrative courts, and the right to appeal against the decision of an election bureau is given not only to the defeated candidate and to the government, but also, as is the case frequently in the United States, to any elector.[3]

II.—*Special protection.*

The second right of officers is the right to special protection offered by the criminal law. In the United States and England this protection is as a rule extended only to certain classes of officers, *viz.*, those who come in contact with the people as bearers of a direct command of a competent authority to do or not to do some particular thing. Where for the purpose of executing such commands it is necessary for such officers to use force they may do so, and not only are they relieved from responsibility for the damage which they may cause but the law has declared it to be a crime to resist them; and where an armed resistance is offered

[1] Thus see 45 and 46 Vict., c. 50, secs. 77–104.

[2] See for the poor-law union elections, Chalmers, *Local Government*, 57.

[3] For an example see the French law of July 31, 1875, governing the trial of contests relative to the general council elections.

it becomes a very serious matter for the persons who thus offer opposition. These officers are generally to be found among those who have to do with the administration of justice, the collection of revenue, and the exercise of police power. For example the United States Revised Statutes [1] declare resistance to a customs officer in the execution of his duties to be a crime punishable by fine and imprisonment, which, when the offence is aggravated by the use of a deadly weapon, may be as long as ten years. Again the penal code of New York [2] declares a person who attempts by means of any threat or violence to prevent an executive officer, *i. e.*, an executive officer in the large sense of the word,[3] from performing his duty; or a person who does actually make resistance by force or violence to any executive officer in the performance of his duty, to be guilty of a misdemeanor.[4] The offence of offering resistance to officers in the performance of their duties, it will be noticed, is a distinct offence, separate and apart from the simple offence of violating the law which the officer is attempting to enforce at the time when the resistance is offered. The latter offence is an offence against the law itself, while resistance to an officer in the performance of his duty is more in the nature of a personal matter, and the provisions of law in regard to it are intended to protect administrative officers in the discharge of their duties.[5] This protection is accorded to them only during the discharge of their duties. Assault, it would seem, might be made upon them

---

[1] Section 5447.   [2] Sections 46, 47.   [3] As defined in section 58.

[4] *Cf.* Gneist. *Das Englische Verwaltungsrecht*, 1884, 384.

[5] *Cf. In re* Neagle, 135 U. S., 1, 64–68, where it is held that the President of the United States may provide special protection for United States officers in the discharge of their duties.

after the performance of duties which were objectionable to the public and as the direct result of such performance, when such assault would be regarded as simply the assault of a private person and punishable as such.[1]

In France and Germany while the same protection is granted to public officers as is granted in England and the United States,[2] the law goes a step further and declares that all outrage and violence to public officers, either during the discharge of their duties or as a result of such duties, are punishable.[3]

III.—*Promotion.*

In the United States both in the national and the commonwealth services promotion is not usually regarded as a right. For a long time it was looked upon as a new appointment and even at the present time is largely so regarded. In both the national and the commonwealth services the civil-service laws and rules attempt to prevent the positions under the rules from being filled by the promotion of persons appointed to positions not under the rules, and to encourage the filling of some of the higher positions, in what is regarded as the subordinate service, by the appointment of persons in the lower positions,[4] who shall be advanced for other than political reasons.[5] In fact the New York

---

[1] As, *e. g.*, the assault of President Garfield by Guiteau ; but see *In re* Neagle, *supra*, II., 65.

[2] Penal Code, arts. 209–221 ; *Reichstrafgesetzbuch*, sections 112–114.

[3] Penal Code, arts. 222, 223, with the cases interpreting these articles which may be found in any one of the annotated codes. See the recent prosecution of the Archbishop of Aix for libelling the minister of public worship. *Cf.* Stengel, *Wörterbuch, etc.*, I., 141.

[4] See U. S. Law, sec. 7 ; N. Y. Rule 37.

[5] See N. Y. Rules 32 and 33.

law has formed a special schedule (E) of the higher positions under the rules, entrance to which is confined to the persons occupying positions in the lower grades.[1] Very recently also the national commission has made a tentative step in the same direction by providing rules for promotion in the New York custom-house and in certain of the departments in Washington.[2] Under these rules promotion is if possible confined to the persons in the grades immediately inferior to that to which promotion is to be made, and in the examinations for promotions which are adopted, and which are usually pass examinations, the greatest weight in the marking is laid upon office efficiency. Where such a method is adopted there is something in the nature of a right to promotion, a right which is possessed only by those in the grades immediately inferior to the grade to which the promotion is to be made. But this claim, if we may call it so, is so indefinite that it may not with propriety be called a right.

In the other countries the rules are somewhat the same as in the United States, promotion being regarded generally as a new appointment. But in many instances, within each grade there are classes to each of which a different salary is attached and transfer from one class to another within the grade is usually made as a result of seniority of service.[3] In England this method has been carried the farthest. Thus in the lower division clerkships the salary commences at £80 and rises by triennial increments of £15 to £200.[4]

---

[1] N. Y. Rule 31.

[2] 7th Report of the Commission, 74, 79 ; 9th *Ibid.*, 60–63. So also in some cases in Massachusetts, Rule xliii.

[3] For France see Block, *Dictionnaire, etc.*, 985.

[4] Order in Council, Feb. 12, 1876, cited in Crawley, *op. cit.*, 912.

IV.—Compensation.

1. *Not a contractual right.*—The fourth right of importance possessed by the official is the right to the payment of a compensation. This right is not, however, a contractual right, since the official relation is not a contractual relation. If the right to compensation exists at all it exists as the result not of a contract or by virtue of any service rendered to the government but because the law has attached the compensation to the office.[1] A person who accepts office to which no compensation is attached by law is presumed to undertake the office gratuitously[2] and cannot recover anything on the ground of an implied contract to pay what the service is worth.[3] The rule is otherwise where a person undertakes to render service to a municipal corporation at its request not as a public officer but as a private agent.[4] It has been held that such an agent may be a public officer provided that the service he renders is absolutely foreign to the office which he holds.[5]

The official relation, not being a contractual relation, and the existence of the right to compensation being dependent upon the law, we must go to the law to find if there is a salary attached to any given office. As a general rule it is true that a salary or compensation is

---

[1] Fitzsimmons v. Brooklyn, 102 N. Y., 536, 539 ; People v. Police Commissioners, 114 N. Y., 245, 247.

[2] State v. Brewer, 59 Ala., 130.

[3] Goddard v. Petersham, 136 Mass., 235 ; White v. Levant, 78 Me., 568 ; Talbot v. East Machias, 76 Me., 415 ; see also Sikes v. Hatfield, 13 Gray, Mass., 347.

[4] Lindabury v. Freeholders, 47 N. J. L., 417 ; Detroit v. Redfield, 19 Mich., 376 ; Converse v. U. S., 21 How. U. S., 463.

[5] *Ibid.*, Evans v. Trenton, 24 N. J. L., 764; but see Sedway v. Commissioners, 120 Ill., 496.

attached by law to all the positions in the national service of the United States.[1] The same rule is true of the central commonwealth service, though there are more exceptions to the rule. In the local commonwealth services it is also the rule though the exceptions become much more frequent. As a general rule the compensation is fixed by statute. In the national service this is especially true. In the statutes we find in connection with each position of any importance a statement of what is its salary. For the clerical service in the departments at Washington we find a regular classification of salaries which was made in 1853. In the commonwealths the salaries of the important positions are fixed by statute, but here more frequently than in the national service, where it is sometimes the case, the salaries are fixed by departmental regulations with the result of a great lack of uniformity in the salaries of persons doing the same kind of work in different departments. The compensation, however it may be fixed, may be changed by the authority fixing it, provided no higher law, such as the constitution when it is fixed by statute or the statutes if it is fixed by departmental regulation, prevents.[2] It may be altered, diminished, or altogether terminated during the term of office of the incumbent, and such change will not be regarded as impairing the obligation of a contract since the official relation, as has so often been said, is not a contractual relation.[3] But the act chan-

---

[1] There are a few exceptions to this rule, as *e. g.* the board of Indian commissioners, U. S. Rev. Stats., sec. 2039.

[2] Kahn v. State, 93 N. Y., 291.

[3] Butler v. Pennsylvania, 10 How. U. S., 402 ; Koratz v. Franklin Co., 76 Pa. St., 154 ; Wyandotte v. Drennan, 46 Mich., 478 ; Conner v. Mayor, 5 N. Y., 285.

ging the compensation must be clear and explicit. Thus the mere appropriation of a sum of money less than the salary does not have the effect of changing the compensation [1] unless the legislature says expressly that the new appropriation shall be full compensation.[2] It is, however, a very common provision in the United States commonwealth constitutions or statutes that the salary or compensation shall not be increased or diminished during the term of office of the incumbent.[3] If, however, the services have been rendered, a contract to pay for them at the rate fixed by law is implied, which cannot be impaired even by the legislature.[4] A further result of the fact that the official relation is not a contractual relation is that the incumbent does not lose his right to his compensation by reason of his inability, as *e. g.* from sickness, to discharge the duties of the office. So long as he holds the office he has the right to the compensation.[5] Finally if he is illegally prevented by his superiors from discharging his duties, as by an unauthorized removal, he still does not lose his claim to his compensation, and is not obliged to deduct from his salary what money he earns during the period of his absence from duty.[6]

2. *How fixed in amount.*—The amount of the salary attached to the office may be fixed or may depend on the amount of business done in the office, *i. e.*, may consist wholly or partly of fees. The latter method is very common in the consular and customs services of

---

[1] U. S. v. Langston, 118 U. S., 389; State v. Steele, 57 Tex., 200; People v. McCall, 65 How. Pr., 442.

[2] U. S. v. Fisher, 109 U. S., 143; U. S. v. Mitchell, *Ibid.*

[3] See Stimson, *American Statute Law*, sec. 214; Mechem, *op. cit.*, sec. 858; *cf.* for the compensation of the President, U. S. Const., Art. II., sec. 1, par. 7.

[4] Fisk v. Police Jury, 116 U. S., 131; Stewart v. Police Jury, *Ibid.*, 135.

[5] O'Leary v. Board of Education, 93 N. Y., 1.

[6] Fitzsimmons v. Brooklyn, 102 N.Y., 536; Andrews v. Portland, 79 Me., 484.

the national government and in the local offices in the commonwealths. The advantage of the fee system consists in the fact that the salary or compensation is paid under it by those persons who make use of the office to which the fees are attached. Its disadvantage is to be found in the fact that on account of the smallness of the fee usually required, extortion is not unfrequently practised by officers and submitted to by the public, notwithstanding the most stringent penal provisions that may be passed to prevent it. The compensation actually received is out of all proportion to the work done, and comes to be regarded rather as a reward for political service than as a compensation for work done. On this account the tendency at present is to replace fees by fixed salaries. Another method of fixing the amount of the compensation is to pay so much for each day's service rendered by the officer. This system of *per diem* allowances, as it is called, is quite common in the localities where the public business is so arranged as to require a great number of officers who shall devote only a part of their time to the public service. Still another method of fixing the amount of the salary is to be found in the national postal service, where the compensation of postmasters is, within certain limits, determined by the receipts of their offices, *i. e.*, by the number of postage stamps sold.[1]

Finally it is to be noticed that the salary or compensation of public officers is from motives of public policy not subject to garnishment or attachment.[2] Nor may a future salary generally be assigned.[3]

[1] U. S. Rev. Stats., secs. 3852–3857.

[2] See Mechem, *op. cit.*, sec. 975 ; Buchanan v. Alexander, 4 How. U. S., 20.

[3] Bliss v. Lawrence, 58 N. Y., 442 ; Beal v. McVicker, 8 Mo. App., 202 ; but see State Bank v. Hastings, 15 Wisc., 78, which held the contrary, applying to this public legal relation the rules of purely private law.

3. *How enforced.*—The claim for compensation has been spoken of as a right on the part of the officers. This description of it is not in all cases correct, or has not until quite recently been correct. Where the compensation consists of fees to be paid by third persons employing the official, the officer has an actual right to the payment of the fees as fixed by law and may retain any documents in his possession in or about which he has expended labor until the fees are paid.[1] If paid by the public, however, he cannot recover anything from a third party, even if such third party has promised to pay him.[2]

Where, however, the officer's compensation consists of a salary which is to be paid by the government it would seem that if there is no special law permitting him to sue the government, and if he cannot put his claim into such a shape as to make some one of the various municipal corporations or *quasi* municipal corporations responsible for it, he has in many cases no claim which is enforceable in a court of law. This fact is due to the principle that the government may not be sued without its consent.[3] In the national government, as a result of a special statute, officers may sue the government in the courts for their compensation.[4] In the commonwealths as yet the general rule is that officers may not sue the central government for their salaries. But it must be remembered that many of the officers who are discharging duties which affect

---

[1] Mechem, *op. cit.*, secs. 887–888 ; Baldwin v. Kansas, 81 Ala., 272 ; People v. Harlow, 29 Ill., 43 ; see also Ripley v. Gifford, 11 Iowa, 367.

[2] People v. Marble, 118 Mass., 548 ; Hatch v. Mann, 15 Wendell, N. Y., 44.

[3] *Infra*, II., p. 154.

[4] *Infra*, Patton v. U. S., 7 Ct. of Claims, 362 ; U. S. v. Langston, 118 U. S., 389.

the commonwealth at large, and who are therefore somewhat central in character, are paid by the various local corporations which are subjects of private law and may therefore be sued.[1] Finally if the duty is imposed upon any individual officer, even of the central government of the commonwealth, to pay the legal compensations of other officers, and he should refuse so to do, he might be forced to act by means of the writ of *mandamus*.[2] Thus at the present time the claim of almost every officer in the administrative system to his salary or compensation is enforceable by some sort of judicial proceedings, and may therefore be regarded as an actual right over whose existence and extent the courts and not the administration are to decide as in the case of any other private right.

Somewhat akin to the right to recover compensation is the right which all officers possess to force the payment to them of all the expenses which they have been obliged to incur in order to discharge their duties. This is true whether the expense has been incurred for the government or for an individual.[3]

In some cases pensions or superannuation allowances are included within the compensation. But in the United States this matter has received almost no attention, such allowances being found almost only in the case of certain of the judges of the national courts and in the police and fire departments of the municipalities.[4]

---

[1] *Infra*, II., p. 152.

[2] High, *Extraordinary Legal Remedies*, 2d Ed., 105 ; Turner v. Melvay, 13 Cal., 621 ; see also Nichols v. Comptroller, 4 Stew. and Port., Ala., 154.

[3] Powell v. Newbury, 19 Johns., N. Y., 284 ; Andrews v. U. S., 2 Story C.C., 202 ; U. S. v. Flanders, 112 U. S., 88.

[4] *E. g.* see N. Y. L., 1882, c. 410, secs. 303–309.

4. *Compensation in other countries.*—In the other countries the rules with regard to salaries are very much the same as here, with the exception that in Germany there are many more absolutely unpaid officers. Further the salaries are regulated in much the same manner, with the exception that in France and Germany the salary of central officers is usually composed of two quite separate portions, one of which, *viz.*, that which is regarded as the compensation for the work done being everywhere throughout the country the same for the same work, the other varying with the locality in which the office is situated in accordance with the expense of house rent. This is often called the indemnity of residence.[1] Payment of the salary may in France be enforced by appeal to the administrative courts which have sole jurisdiction over this matter,[2] in Germany by appeal to either the ordinary judicial or the administrative courts, which have concurrent jurisdiction of the matter,[3] and in England by means of the petition of right when the claim is against the central government, or by suit when against the local corporations.[4]

5. *Civil pensions.*—In all these countries, however, the compensation includes a claim to a superannuation allowance. These superannuation allowances or pensions for civil officers seem first to have been introduced into France, and the method adopted there has in its main features been adopted in both Germany and England. The most important law regulating this matter in France is the law of June 9, 1853. By this

---

[1] *E. g.* see Block, *Dictionnaire, etc.*, 978, c. xi.

[2] Laferrière, *La Juridiction Administrative*, II., 186.

[3] Schulze, *op. cit.*, I., 338.   [4] *Infra*, II. p. 154.

law the right to the pension is acquired by the attainment of sixty years of age and after thirty years of service. These limits are reduced in exceptional cases to fifty-five and twenty-five respectively. The amount of the pension is based on the average salary for the last six years of service ; one sixtieth of such average salary being granted for each year of service up to a maximum of forty-five sixtieths. Further, in order to prevent the budget from being too heavily burdened the law provides that new pensions may be granted each year only in so far as old pensions have been extinguished during the preceding year. No officer, therefore, may at any given time demand that his pension be given him even if he is sixty years of age and has served for thirty years. He must wait until an old pension has been extinguished. These pensions are paid partly out of deductions made from the salaries of officers and partly from appropriations made by the legislature. The deduction usually made is five per cent. of the salary. Finally the widow and children of a pensioner are granted certain claims also under this law. All questions relating to the pensions, *i. e.*, as to the amount, and the fulfilment of the necessary conditions for obtaining the pension are decided by the administrative courts.[1]

In Germany the main principles are the same. The only marked exception is that only ten years of service after the twenty-first year of age are required, when the pensioner would receive fifteen sixtieths of the last salary and one sixtieth for every additional year. But, as in France, the maximum pension obtainable is forty-five sixtieths and the age at which the pension is

---

[1] Laferrière, *op. cit.*, II., 190.

granted is sixty-five.[1]   Pension claims are decided by
either the ordinary judicial courts or by the administrative courts.

In England superannuation allowances are regulated
by several statutes, the most important of which is 22
Vict. c. 26 which does not, however, apply to all
branches of the service. By this law the pension is
acquired, as in Germany, by ten years of service when
ten sixtieths of the last salary are given, and rises one
sixtieth a year up to a maximum of forty sixtieths.
Sixty years of age are required, but provision is made
for dispensing with this condition in case the applicant brings evidence to the authorities, which shall
consist of a medical certificate, that he is permanently
incapacitated for the performance of his duties. The
pension claim may be enforced by mandamus.[2] A
later statute [3] provides that the pension may be
capitalized.

---

[1] See Prussian Laws, March 27, 1872 ; March 31, 1882 ; Imperial Law, March
31, 1873 ; Stengel *Wörterbuch, sub verb. Beamte, Pension.*

[2] Todd, *op. cit.*, I., 654, note and authorities cited.

[3] 34 and 35 Vict., c. 36.

CHAPTER V.

In the following treatment of the duties of officers it is not intended to discuss the various matters of official routine which are in the sphere of competence of all officers, but to refer to those general obligations which every one assumes who enters into the official relation. Before attempting to make any classification of these general obligations, it will be well to allude to a general principle of the law which is of great importance. This is that a statute which apparently confers merely a power upon an officer may be construed as imposing a duty upon him. For in many cases it is one of the duties of an officer to exercise his powers. Thus a statute which says that an officer may do a certain thing is often construed as meaning that the officer shall do the thing. The rule as to when such a statute will be construed as imposing a duty has been well laid down in the case of *Mayor v. Furze,* [1] in which it was held that a statute, conferring a power upon a municipal corporation to make and repair sewers, imposed upon such corporation the duty of repairing the sewers. Judge Nelson laid down the rule as follows : " Where a public body or officer has been clothed by statute with power to do an act which concerns the public interest or the rights of third persons, the exe-

[1] 3 Hill, N. Y., 612.

cution of the power may be insisted on as a duty, though the phraseology of the statute be permissive merely and not peremptory."[1] Finally, while in general a discretionary power may be exercised in such a manner as the officer having the discretion shall see fit, still it is generally the duty of such officer to make some exercise of his discretion.[2]

The general obligations which are imposed upon officers are of two kinds. In the first place the law states positively certain things which all officers must or must not do, and provides penalties of a criminal character for disobedience of its provisions. In the second place the very existence of the official relation makes it necessary that an officer shall or shall not do certain things or shall behave towards the public in a certain way. The first class of duties are largely negative in character and the rules of law which contain them form a sort of special criminal law for officers, in that the law imposes criminal punishment upon their violation. The second class of duties are more positive in character and form a sort of official code of ethics, which can be maintained in those countries where an official *esprit du corps* has not been developed, only by the existence of a strong disciplinary power. Where great reliance has been placed upon the *esprit du corps*, or where the disciplinary power is large, it will not be necessary to form a very large official criminal code. Where, however, this official *esprit du corps* is not to be found or where the disciplinary power is slight we find a large official criminal code.

---

[1] *Cf.* Mechem, *op. cit.*, sec. 593.

[2] Board of Police v. Grant, 17 Miss., 77 ; Hightower v. Oberbanker, 65 Iowa, 347 ; People v. Auditors, 82 N. Y., 80.

I.—Duties with a penal sanction.

1. *Common law crimes of officers.*—In the first place it may be laid down that officers even more than ordinary persons are bound to obey the law. The criminal law of almost every country regards as a crime almost every act of an officer which, if committed by an individual, would be a crime.[1] But further the criminal law of England and the United States declares any act or omission in disobedience of official duty by one who has accepted office, " when it is of public concern, to be a crime."[2] The endeavor is, however, made to distinguish between discretionary and ministerial officers. The general rule is particularly applicable, says Mr. Bishop, " where the thing required to be done is of a ministerial or other like nature, and there is reposed in the officer no discretion." In the case of officers acting with discretion the act to be punished criminally must be wilful and corrupt.[3] But it is to be noted that the law excepts the highest officers of state from this criminal common law liability for mis-feasance or non-feasance in office.[4] In these cases the control of the legislature[5] is regarded as sufficient. In some of the commonwealths this common-law liability is increased by statute so as to make the mere wilful violation of official duty without corrupt motives punishable criminally.[6]

[1] See Bishop, *Criminal Law,* II., sec. 982 ; Block, *Dictionnaire, etc.,* 981 ; Loening, *Deutsches Verwaltungsrecht,* 126.

[2] Bishop, *op. cit.,* sec. 459 ; Gneist, *Das Englische Verwaltungsrecht,* 381.

[3] People v. Coon, 15 Wendell, N. Y., 277 ; People v. Norton, 7 Barbour, N. Y., 477 ; Gneist, *op. cit.,* 381.

[4] Bishop, *op. cit.,* I., sec. 462 ; Gneist, *op. cit.,* 383.

[5] For which see *infra,* II., p. 296.

[6] So in New York. See People v. Brooks, 1 Denio, 457, construing a provision of the revised statutes.

2. *Statutory official crimes.*—Further in both England and the United States certain specific acts by certain specific officers or by officers generally are by statute expressly made punishable criminally. Thus the new civil-service laws of the United States have provided that it shall be a crime for any officer to solicit or receive assessments for the payment of party expenses from any one in the service.[1] It would be of course impossible to enumerate these criminal provisions imposing punishments upon officers for the doing of illegal acts. All that need be said about the system in the United States and England is that this method of enforcing the performance by officers of their duties has been carried further than in almost any other country, and simply for the reason that the general disciplinary powers of the higher administrative officers are rather weaker in the United States and England than elsewhere.[2]

In neither France nor Germany are the duties of officers enforced so commonly in this way. In the first place there is no common-law liability for mere mis-feasance or non-feasance in office.[3] It is to be noted also that while in France the highest officers of state are as in the United States not criminally liable before the ordinary courts, in Germany no such exception is made.[4] The method in both France and Germany is to enumerate certain acts which, when done by officers, shall be punished criminally. In many

[1] U. S. L., secs. 11–14 ; N. Y. L., secs. 11–14.

[2] M. Laferrière in his work on *La Juridiction Administrative* has called attention to this peculiarity of the American law. See I., 101.

[3] See Gneist, *Das Englische Verwaltungsrecht*, 381, note ; Loening, *Deutsches Verwaltungsrecht*, 127.

[4] Laferrière, *op. cit.*, I., 660 *et seq.* ; Bornhak, *Preussisches Verwaltungsrecht*, I., 144, sec. 24.

cases the same acts which are prohibited or commanded by the law of the United States are prohibited or commanded under similar criminal penalties by the law of both France and Germany. Thus it seems to be the general rule everywhere that, where the official oath is prescribed, as it so generally is, it is the duty, sanctioned by a criminal penalty, of the officer to take such oath before he enters upon the performance of the duties of the office. The taking of it is not, however, generally regarded as a qualification for the office, but a duty whose violation is to be punished criminally.[1] The same is true of the filing of the official bond or the deposit of security, where that is required. It is to be noticed that the rules on the continent are generally much more strict in this respect, particularly where the officer is in charge of public funds.[2] On the continent the deposit of some valuable security, either money on which the government will pay the officer interest, or the deposit of state stocks, is often required. When this is required, the government has the rights of a pledgee over the deposit, which is regarded as in the nature of collateral security.[3] In some cases the fulfilling of these formalities is expressly made something more than a mere duty, and becomes a necessary qualification in order to the filling of the office. In such cases all acts of the officer, performed before the oath is taken or the bond filed or security given, are void and of no effect. But this is rare.[4] In the second place it is very commonly

---

[1] See Mechem, *op. cit.*, secs. 255 *et seq.* ; Schulze, *Deutsches Staatsrecht*, I., 323 ; Block, *Dictionnaire*, etc., 976 *et seq.*

[2] See Mechem, *op. cit.*, secs. 263 *et seq.* ; Schulze, *loc. cit.* ; Block, *loc. cit.*

[3] Schulze, *loc. cit.* ; Block, *loc. cit.*

[4] *Cf.* Block, 20, 42, 357, 977.

provided that the attempt of an officer to extort from persons doing business with his office larger fees than are provided by law shall be regarded as a crime, *viz.,* the crime of extortion.[1] Finally it is very generally provided that the revealing of state secrets is a crime, and where this is not expressly provided such action might be regarded in some cases as treason.[2] In many countries officers may not be forced in court to testify to anything which is regarded as affecting disadvantageously the service of the country.[3]

II.—Duties of a moral character.

The second class of duties to which allusion has been made are more moral than legal in character, are largely based on executive usage, and owe their force almost entirely to the existence in the executive of a disciplinary power. Although they may in some cases be sanctioned by criminal penalties, as in the class of duties just considered, still they will never be well performed unless through the long-continued exercise of a strong disciplinary power there has grown up in the civil service an *esprit du corps* similar to that which is found in the military service and which forbids an officer to be guilty of conduct which is unbecoming an officer and a gentleman. These duties, so far as they may be classified at all, may be classified under the following heads :

1. *Obedience to orders.*—The general duty of obedience to the orders of superior officers is to be

---

[1] See for the United States, U. S. Stats. at Large, IV., 118 ; N. Y. Penal Code, sec. 557 ; for France, Penal Code, art. 160.

[2] French Penal Code, art. 80.

[3] See German Code of Civil Procedure, sec. 341 ; German Code of Criminal Procedure, sec. 53 ; Block, *op. cit.,* 981 ; *cf.* Greenleaf on *Evidence* 14th Ed., secs. 250, 251 ; Marbury v. Madison, 1 Cranch, 137.

found in all hierarchically organized administrative systems, and can in the nature of things exist only in such systems. But the different countries differ much in the responsibility which officers assume in obeying orders. In the United States, England, and in the Imperial service of Germany no officer, even where the service has been hierarchically organized, is relieved from responsibility over against third persons for violating the law or the constitution, because he has obeyed the orders of his superior[1]; and in case he disobeys orders he may be subjected to the exercise of the disciplinary power of his superior where no limit has been placed upon such power. On the continent, however, in some cases an officer who has obeyed orders is relieved from all responsibility which is to be assumed by the officer giving the orders.[2]

2. *Prompt performance of the duties connected with the office.*—This general duty differs considerably in its content in different states. But in all it means the uninterrupted performance of the duties of the office, except where leave of absence has been granted by the superior as in case of legal vacations and sickness. In some states it means also residence at the place where the office is situated.[3] In the United States, however, this would not seem to be universally or even commonly the rule. In some states also it means the devotion of the entire time of the officer to the duties of the office, *i. e.*, the officer is forbidden to engage in any other occupation.[4] In the United States and England this does not seem to be generally the rule. Of course there are a great number of offi-

[1] *Infra*, II., p. 166.
[2] Loening, *op. cit.*, 123.
[3] Stengel, *Wörterbuch*, I., 140.
[4] *Ibid.*

cers even in these countries where, in the nature of things, the duties of the office will be so absorbing that the officer will have no time to devote to any other occupation. But when this is the case, it is a practical outcome of the position rather than a legal rule. Seldom is it the rule in these countries that an officer has not the right to engage in other occupations if he can in the nature of things do so. Many of the higher officers in the United States who receive large salaries and have very responsible duties to perform are, at the same time that they are holding office, engaged in some other occupation, such, *e. g.*, as the practice of the legal profession. They in these cases simply superintend the performance of the work of their offices, leaving most of the routine work to be attended to by deputies. Our system makes it necessary to permit the higher officers, at any rate, to engage in other occupations because, on account of the legal precariousness of the official tenure and of the actually frequent changes made in the offices, it is almost impossible to demand of any man that he shall give up his entire time to his official work. Our system, when not carried too far, has also its advantages since by its means we obtain a real self-government system of administration. On the continent of Europe the rule is quite different. Office-holding is there regarded very much more as a profession to which the officer must devote his entire time.[1]

3. *Good conduct.*—The duty of good conduct, *i. e.*, courteous behavior to the public and generally orderly conduct, is a duty almost altogether of a moral character and is hardly susceptible of legal definition.

[1] *Supra*, II.; Block, *op. cit.*, 976.

Further it is dependent for its enforcement almost entirely upon the existence and the exercise of a disciplinary power. Some states, however, recognize it explicitly in their law. Thus the civil-service law of the United States national government provides that no person shall be retained in the service who habitually indulges to excess in intoxicating liquors, and most of the official codes in Germany require from officers orderly conduct—conduct such as will command the respect of the citizens. [1] This provision, although it is formulated somewhat vaguely in the law as it must necessarily be, really means something, on account of the strong *esprit du corps* among the officers of the German civil service. It is, we may say, somewhat equivalent to the duty of an officer in the military service to conduct himself in a manner becoming an officer and a gentleman. This duty of orderly conduct has of late years come in the United States and England to mean that an officer must not be guilty of offensive partisanship against the ruling party in the executive office or of taking an active part in political contests. [2] A good example of what the duty of courteous behavior to the public means and how it may be enforced may be found in an incident which occurred at Washington not many years ago. An individual who had business with one of the departments was treated with incivility by one of the clerks. Complaint was made to the superior officer and the clerk was dismissed from the service by the secretary with the remark that every man "who had business with the treasury was entitled to civil treatment, and that no employee who was un-

[1] Schulze, *op. cit.*, I., 323.
[2] See *Pol. Sci. Qu.*, III., 252 ; Todd, *op. cit.*, I., 631.

able to remember that he was a servant of the people and bound to be courteous to those whom he served need expect to be retained." [1]

III.—*Responsibility of officers for violation of duty.*

The violation of the duties which have been so briefly outlined may result in a three-fold responsibility. In the first place if an individual is damaged by the violation of his duty by an official, the official may in some cases be held liable to reimburse the injured individual to the extent of the damage which he has suffered. [2] In the second place, if the law has attached a criminal penalty to the violation of official duty the officer may be punished criminally. [3] Finally if the administration is at all centralized and if the disciplinary power is strong, as it generally is in all centralized systems of administration, the violation of official duty will lead to an administrative responsibility. In some cases, as, *e. g.*, in the United States, the disciplinary power, where it exists, consists for the most part of the power of removal. Where this is unconditional it would seem that the power to inflict lighter disciplinary penalties than removal would practically be derived from it as the offending officer would prefer to submit, for example, to the imposition of a fine rather than lose his place altogether. A disciplinary power may, however, exist where there is no absolute power of removal or where the power of removal is conditioned upon the finding of some cause when the decision of the disciplinary power as to what is cause

---

[1] See *New York Times*, Nov. 24, 1885.

[2] See for a further development of this subject *infra*, II., p. 163.

[3] See *infra*, II., p. 179.

is generally reviewable by the courts. [1] For the power may be given to a disciplinary authority to impose fines, to decree the loss of promotion, where that is provided as a claim in the nature of a right, to degrade the officer by placing him in a lower rank than that which he occupies at the time he violates his duty, to suspend him from the service and even in extreme cases to order his arrest. This sort of disciplinary power is more extended in Germany than elsewhere because of the fact that the power of removal is not generally an absolute one.[2] Although such a disciplinary power does not as a rule exist in the American administrative system, still we do find instances of it in the case of the purely professional services which have been established in some of the cities, as, *e. g.,* the fire and police forces. Thus section 272 of the present New York charter [3] provides that the board of police " shall have power, in its discretion, on conviction of a member of the police force of any legal offence or neglect of duty, or violation of the rules, or neglect or disobedience of orders, or absence without leave, or any conduct injurious to the public peace or welfare, or immoral conduct, or conduct unbecoming an officer, or other breach of discipline, to punish the offending party by reprimand, forfeiting and withholding pay for a specified time," not exceeding thirty days, or dismissal from the force.

[1] See People v. Board of Police, 72 N. Y., 415 ; State v. St. Louis, 90 Mo., 19 ; Stockwell v. Township Board, 22 Mich., 341 ; see also Kennard v. Louisiana, 92 U. S., 480.

[2] See Stengel, *Wörterbuch, etc* I., 270, *sub verbo Disciplin ;* see also for France where the power of removal is almost practically unlimited, Block, *op. cit.,* 980 *et seq.*

[3] N. Y. L. 1882, c. 410.

Each of these three kinds of responsibility, *i. e.*, the civil, criminal, and administrative, reinforces and supplements the others. Therefore, as might be expected, the extent of each kind of responsibility is not the same in different states. Where the disciplinary power is small, the criminal responsibility is very large, as is the case in the United States. Where the civil responsibility is small, as is also the case in the United States compared with some of the other countries, again we find a large criminal responsibility. Finally if the administrative responsibility is extensive it may be unnecessary to develop the other kinds of responsibility to any great extent. No hasty judgment should be drawn regarding the responsibility of officers in any one country from a consideration of only one of these various kinds of responsibility as all reinforce and supplement each other.

CHAPTER VI.

TERMINATION OF THE OFFICIAL RELATION.

The official relation is terminated in various ways. The first to be mentioned is by death. This is so simple that it hardly needs any discussion. All that need be said in regard to it is that an office held by several is not terminated or made vacant by the death of one of the incumbents[1]; that in some cases the widow or the family of the deceased officer has a claim to a pension, and that the estate of the deceased officer may be made responsible for claims against it held by the government. The official relation is thus not in all cases absolutely terminated by the death of the incumbent of the office. A more important way of terminating the official relation is by the expiration of the term of office.

I.—*Expiration of the term.*

The general rule would seem to be that the expiration of the term of the office causes the official relation to cease so far as the future is concerned. The officer has, after the expiration of his term, no duties and no authority to act, except to complete unfinished business and except in so far as the principles of law with regard to officers *de facto* may come in to modify this

[1] People v. Palmer, 52 N. Y., 84.

rule.[1]   But in order to overcome the inconveniences of such a rule it is often provided that an officer shall hold over until his successor enters upon the performance of his duties.   Where such a provision exists it is held that, so far as this is necessary to the protection of the public, the officer will be deemed to be in office even if his resignation has been accepted.[2]

In the United States the subject of the term of office has become very important on account of the practice of fixing a specified term of office for almost every governmental office.   The constitution of the United States, and the first constitution of New York provided a fixed term for very few offices.   The first change in this system of indefinite terms of offices for officers of the national government was made by the law of 1820.[3] This statute provided that all district-attorneys, collectors of the customs, naval officers and surveyors of the customs and certain other officers should be appointed for a term of four years, but should be removable at the pleasure of the removing power.   The act was retroactive in effect.   It will be noticed from an examination of the act and debates of Congress when the proposition was made several years later to repeal it, that the alleged motive in passing it was to cause the different disbursing officers of the government to feel a stronger sense of responsibility, as the formalities of a removal would not have to be gone through with in case they were not up in their accounts.[4]   It is said,

[1] People v. Tieman, 30 Barbour, N. Y., 193 ; Newman v. Beckwith, 61 N. Y., 205 ; Lawrence v. Rice, 12 Metc., Mass., 527, 533.

[2] Badger v. U. S., 93 U. S., 599, 603 : Jones v. Jefferson, 66 Tex., 576.

[3] L., May 15, 1820.

[4] See speech of Mr. Webster in the Senate, Benton's *Debates*, XII., 599, 605.

however, that the real motive in passing the act was a
partisan political one ; and that several party leaders
thought the system of arbitrary removals from office
which had unfortunately been introduced into New
York might be introduced into the national administrative system much more easily if such a law as
that of 1820 were adopted.[1] But whatever was the
motive of Congress in passing this act, which at the
time it was passed attracted little attention, it soon became apparent that its effect was the practical removal
of many officers regardless of their conduct in office
who happened not to be in sympathy with the domi-
nant political party.[2] The introduction of the principle of the removal of officers for political reasons was
believed by some of the best American statesmen to
be so disastrous that repeated attempts were made to
repeal the act of 1820, one a few years after its passage
in 1825 and one in 1836, when many prominent men in
the Senate voted for its repeal. These attempts at
repeal all failed of success ; and in the meantime the
people had become so accustomed to seeing officers,
whose term of office was limited by the law, fail of re-
appointment and replaced at the expiration of their
term by persons in sympathy with the party in power
that this principle of "rotation in office," as it began to
be called, was regarded as one of the essential features
of the American administrative system.[3] The principle was finally extended to almost all the offices in
the national government and from thence into the administrative systems of most of the commonwealths, so

---

[1] See Publications of the Civil-Service Reform Association, No. 5, p. 24 ; F.
W. Whitridge, on " Rotation in Office " in the *Pol. Sci. Qu.*, IV., 284.
[2] *Ibid.*, 286.   [3] See Benton's *Debates*, XII., 591.

that now the term of almost every administrative office
in the United States is fixed by law at a certain number of years, generally four.   Further it is generally
expected that a new administration will not reappoint
the old incumbents.[1]   The effect of these term of
office laws, as they are called, has thus been almost
altogether bad, and the alleged motive for their adoption is seen to be based on no reasonable grounds when
it is remembered that the disciplinary power of the
government at the time when they were adopted was,
as it is now, practically absolute.   The evils of the
laws have been somewhat alleviated so far as the
classified service is concerned by the introduction of
competitive examinations, since now the appointing
power may not appoint to positions in the classified
service exactly the persons it may wish to.   But on
account of the relative smallness of the classified service the evils of fixed terms of office are still very great
and the attempt is now being made to secure the repeal
of the laws which introduced the principle into the
American system.

II.—*Resignation.*

The official relation may be terminated by resignation on the part of the incumbent.   While all the cases
agree upon this principle there seems to be a difference
of opinion as to the necessity of the acceptance by the
proper person of the resignation.   Some of the cases,
basing themselves on the old English rule that governmental offices were obligatory, and seeing that the
recognition of an absolute right in the officer to resign

---

[1] As to the number of offices whose incumbents are changed by an incoming
administration, see F. P. Powers on "The Reform in the Federal Service" in
Pol. Sci. Qu., III., 267, 276.

regardless of the wishes of his superiors would result in the destruction of the obligation of office, have held that a resignation is not effective until it has been accepted.[1] Other cases have added to the old English rule the corollary that resignation has at common law absolutely no effect, that unless the statute gives the power to some one to accept a resignation, acceptance of a resignation even by an authority which is the recognized superior of the officer resigning does not have the effect of terminating the official relation.[2] Other cases, losing sight of the fact that at common law acceptance of a long series of offices was obligatory, have laid down the general rule that acceptance of a resignation from officers is never necessary.[3] If, however, the general rules laid down in these cases are not considered but only the actual decisions rendered, it will be found that the contradiction is not really so great as it seems. For almost all the cases holding that acceptance of the resignation is necessary were decided with regard to local offices which were obligatory offices in the self-government system of administration, while those cases which have held the acceptance to be unnecessary have been decided with regard to offices of the general government to which the common law rule is not regarded as applying and which take up most if not all the time and attention of the incumbent—are therefore more or less profes-

[1] Van Orsdell v. Hazard, 3 Hill, N. Y., 243 ; Hoke v. Henderson, 4 Devereux, N. C. L., 1., 25.

[2] See State v. Ferguson, 31 N. J. L., 107 ; but see Van Orsdell v. Hazard, 3 Hill, 243, which claims for the appointing power the right to accept a resignation.

[3] See People v. Porter, 6 Cal., 26 ; State v. Clark, 3 Nev., 519; Olmsted v. Dennis, 77 N. Y., 378 ; Wright v. U. S., 1. McLean, 509, 512 ; 14 Opinions Atty. General, 259.

sional in character. [1] In all cases resignation consists in the intention to relinquish the office accompanied by an absolute relinquishment. [2] Provided these facts are present it makes no difference how the resignation is made. It may be and usually is in writing, but it also may be made by parol. [3] Where the acceptance of the resignation is not regarded as necessary it has been held that the resignation is complete as soon as it is out of the power of the officer resigning to recall it. Thus the resignation has been held to be complete after it has been mailed. [4] Where, however, acceptance of the resignation is necessary the resignation is not complete until it has been received by the authority that has the right to accept it and may be withdrawn by the officer resigning at any time with the consent of the officer who has the power to accept it. [5] Finally where it is provided that an officer shall hold over until his successor enters upon the duties of the office it has been held that resignation has no effect, even if it has been accepted, as the purpose of the law is to prevent an official *interregnum.* [6] As there is no formal way prescribed for the making of a resignation so there is no formal method prescribed for its acceptance. Thus the filing without objection of the resignation in the proper office has been held to be an acceptance, [7] so also the appointment of a successor. [8] The resignation may

---

[1] See Edwards v. U. S., 103 U. S., 471.

[2] Biddle v. Willard, 10 Ind., 62, but see Blake v. U. S., 14, Ct. Cl., 462, holding that the resignation of an officer while temporarily insane is valid.

[3] Barbour v. U. S., 17 Ct. Cl., 149.

[4] State v. Clarke, 3 Nev., 519.

[5] Biddle v. Willard, 10 Ind., 62 ; but see State v. Hauss, 43 Ind., 105.

[6] Badger v. U. S., 93 U. S., 599 ; Edwards v. U. S., 103 U. S., 475 ; Thompson v. U. S., 103 U. S., 480.

[7] Pace v. People, 50 Ill., 432 ; see also Gates v. Delaware Co., 12 Iowa, 432.

[8] Edwards v. U. S., 103 U. S., 471.

never, however, be retrospective since that would permit an officer to escape official responsibilities.[1]

In France and Germany, while the general right to
resign from all offices not obligatory in character is
recognized as in England and the United States, still
certain limitations on the exercise of the right are to
be found in the laws. Thus in France the penal code[2]
punishes all officers who by a preconcerted decision
resign in order to prevent or suspend the action of
some public service; while in Germany the officer
about to resign must give three months' notice of his
intention, and the resignation is not effectual until he
has finished his work and, in case he has public
property in his charge, until his accounts have been
fully settled; and the resignation must be accepted.[3]

III.—*Loss of qualifications.*

Loss of qualifications generally entails loss of the
office. Thus the attainment of an age which by law
unfits for the office will terminate the official relation
except in so far as the doctrine of officers *de facto*
comes in to modify the rule. Also conviction for
crime, which results in the loss of the qualification of
good character, will terminate the official relation.[4]
One of the most common methods of losing the necessary qualifications is the acceptance of an incompatible
office. This is regarded as, *ipso facto*, a vacation of the
first office even if the second office is inferior to the
first[5]; and even though the title to the second office is

[1] I. First Comptroller's Decisions, 325.   [2] Article 126.

[3] Schulze, *op. cit.*, I., 341 ; for France see Block, *Dictionnaire, etc.*, 986.

[4] *E. g.*, see N. Y. L. 1892, c. 681, sec. 20.

[5] Milward v. Thatcher, 2 T. R., 81 ; I. First Comptroller's Decisions, 324
and cases cited ; Mechem, *op. cit.*, sec. 420 and cases cited.

defective the first office may not be claimed if in the meantime it has been filled.[1] The only exception to this rule is that where the incumbent of the first office has not the right to resign or where his resignation is not complete, as, *e. g.*, it has not been accepted when acceptance is necessary. Here the acceptance of the second office has no effect.[2] The incompatibility which is necessary in order to vacate the office may result from common law or from statute. The common law holds that an "inconsistency in functions of the two offices and not the mere lack of time or inability properly to perform the duties of the two offices is an incompatibility."[3] Sometimes the statutes merely declare that two offices are incompatible when the rule as stated would apply; sometimes they declare that no person shall hold at the same time two lucrative offices. Where the two offices are found in the same government, as, *e. g.*, in the commonwealth, or where the second office is held in another government over which the government laying down the rule has no jurisdiction, then the rule is that the second office is to be deemed an incompatible office, and that therefore the first office is vacated.[4]

But these incompatible offices must be clearly distinguished from forbidden offices. Here the rule is not that the first office is vacated but that it is absolutely impossible for a person to accept an office for which he is made ineligible by the fact of his holding

[1] Rex. v. Hughes, 5 B. and C., 886.

[2] Rex. v. Patterson, 4 B. and Ad., 9.

[3] See People v. Green, 58 N. Y., 295 ; Mechem, *op. cit.*, sec. 423 and cases cited.

[4] See Darley v. State, 8 Blackford, Ind., 329 ; Dickson v. People, 17 Ill., 191 ; State v. Buttz, 9 S. C., 156 ; Lucas v. Shepherd, 16 Ind., 368 ; State v. Newhouse, 29 La. Ann., 824.

another office.[1] When the law provides that no person shall hold two lucrative offices and a person holding an office over which the government laying down the prohibition has no control (as, *e. g.*, a United States post office), accepts an office over which such government has control (as, *e. g.*, a commonwealth office), then the second office is regarded as a forbidden office. The first one is therefore not vacated as in the case of an incompatible office, but the individual is deemed ineligible to the second office.[2]

Finally persistent refusal to perform the duties of the office is regarded as an abandonment of the office.[3] All cases of resignation, disqualification, or abandonment of office are decided finally by the courts.[4]

IV.—*Removal from office.*

The power may be given to an administrative officer to remove other officers whatever be the method of forming the official relation. Thus a power may be given to the chief executive to remove officers who obtained their offices by popular election. Take, *e. g.*, the case of the New York sheriff and the French mayor. Both are elected directly or indirectly by the people and yet both as a result of statute may be removed by the chief executive. Where, however, the tenure of an office is by election, or where the term of an officer is fixed by law for a certain period, it would seem to be the law in the United States that in order that the power of removal may be possessed by any

[1] People v. Clute, 50 N. Y., 451 ; see also Searcy v. Grow, 15 Cal., 117.

[2] State v. De Gress, 53 Tex., 387 ; People v. Leonard, 73 Cal., 230.

[3] Mechem, *op. cit.*, sec. 435 and cases cited.

[4] Van Orsdell v. Hazard, 3 Hill, N. Y., 243 ; Mechem, *op. cit.*, secs. 435 *et seq.*, 478 and cases cited.

other administrative officer, it must have been granted by some statute. If, however, an officer is appointed by a superior officer it would seem to be the rule, in the absence of any statute fixing the term or tenure, that the power of removal is incident to the power of appointment.[1] It is quite common in the United States for the legislature to confer upon the chief executive officer the power of removing officers whom he has not the power to appoint.[2] The power conferred in such cases may be absolute or it may be conditional. The power of removal when incident to the power of appointment is usually absolute. It is therefore absolute in the United States national government; in the common-wealths it is also usually absolute for the subordinates in the departmental services, and also for the clerical services in the localities. It is also usually absolute in both England and France, both in the central and the local services. Where conditions are imposed, they consist sometimes in the necessity of obtaining the consent of an executive council. This is frequently true of the power of the governor to remove the important "state officers."[3] In other cases, which are very frequent in the United States commonwealths, the condition consists in the fact that the removal may be for cause only. Where the cause is not particularly specified, the removing officer is generally to decide what is cause sufficient to justify his action,[4] subject, however, to the review of the courts.[5] These have held that the cause sufficient to justify a removal for cause, must be some dereliction of duty or in-

---

[1] *Ex parte* Hennen, 12 Peters, U. S., 230, 239 ; People *ex rel.* Sims v. Fire Commissioners, 73 N. Y., 437 ; Mechem, *op. cit.*, sec. 445.　　[2] *Ibid.*, sec. 447.
[3] *Supra*, I., pp. 103, 104.　　　　[4] See Dubuc v. Voss, 19 La. Ann., 210.
[5] Matter of Nichols, 6 Abbott's New Cases, N. Y., 494.

capacity or delinquency and that the mere fact that another person might perform the duties of the office better than the incumbent is not sufficient cause.[1] Sometimes the statutes granting the power of removal or fixing the tenure of an officer specify distinctly the causes for removal. If such is the case the removing officer may remove only for the causes specified in the law.[2] Ordinarily the causes which are thus specified are official misconduct, mal-administration in office, breach of good behavior, wilful neglect of duty, extortion, and habitual drunnkeness. The legislature may in the absence of constitutional provision determine what shall be sufficient to justify the exercise of the power of removal; but where the constitution provides that certain causes will justify the exercise of the power, the legislature may not add new causes.[3] Where the law provides for removal for official misconduct it is necessary to separate the character of the officer from the character of the man who holds the office. That is, misconduct must be official in character.[4] In all cases where the power of removal is conditioned upon the existence of cause it is necessary for the removing officer to give the officer to be removed an opportunity to be heard in his defence.[5] But where the removing officer has the arbitrary power of removal this is not necessary, though it may be made so by statute.[6] As a general thing the power of removal

---

[1] People v. Fire Commissioners, 73 N. Y., 437.

[2] Mechem, *op. cit.*, sec. 450 with cases cited.

[3] Mechem, *op. cit.*, sec. 457 ; Commonwealth v. Williams, 79 K'y, 42.

[4] *Ibid.* ; Commonwealth v. Hardin. Barry, K'y., 160.

[5] Dullam v. Willson, 53 Mich., 392 ; see Foster v. Kansas, 112 U. S., 201 ; Kennard v. Louisiana, 92 U. S., 480 ; Mechem, *op. cit.*, sec. 454, and cases cited.   [6] *Ex parte* Hennen, 13 Peters, 230 ; N. Y. Const., V., sec. 4.

does not include the power to suspend,[1] though it may be expressly so provided by statute.[2] The removal may be express or implied. Where the power is absolute the appointment of another person to an office with the intention of superseding the incumbent is regarded as a removal.[3] But it is said that the removal to be effectual must be brought to the notice of the officer removed.[4]

In one country, *viz.*, Germany, the rule seems to be that no officer possesses the arbitrary power of removal. Nearly all the officers are appointed for life or for fixed terms, and can be removed only as the result of a conviction of crime or of the decision of a disciplinary tribunal. The proceedings before such disciplinary tribunals have many of the characteristics of a criminal trial.[5]

V.—*Legislative action.*

It has already been pointed out that an office is not a contract. It is therefore perfectly within the power of the legislature, in the absence of some special constitutional limitation, to terminate the official relation either by abolishing the office, shortening the term, declaring the office to be vacant, or by transferring the duties of one office to another, or to increase its duties.[6]

---

[1] Gregory v. New York, 113 N. Y., 416.

[2] See New York Const., V., secs. 3 and 7 ; N. Y. L. 1875, c. 39.

[3] People v. Carrique, 2 Hill, N. Y., 93 ; Bowerback v. Morris, Wallace's Reports, C. C., 119 ; Stadler v. Detroit, 13 Mich., 346.

[4] Commonwealth v. Slifer, 25 Pa. St., 23.

[5] See Schulze, *op. cit.*, I., 342 ; Stengel, *Wörterbuch, etc., sub verbo, Beamte.*

[6] State v. Douglas, 26 Wis., 428 ; Butler v. Pa., 10 How, U. S., 402 ; Atty.-Gen. v. Squires, 14 Cal., 13 ; Bunting v. Gales, 77 N. C., 283 ; *cf.* Mechem, *op. cit.*, sec. 465.

The same is true with regard to municipal offices. The municipal authority having the power to create offices has the right to abolish them.[1] Finally the legislature often has the right to terminate the official relation by means of impeachment.[2]

[1] Augusta v. Sweeny, 44 Ga., 463 ; Ford v. Coms., 22 Pac. Rep., 278.
[2] See *infra*, II., p. 296.

BOOK V.

METHODS AND FORMS OF ADMINISTRATIVE ACTION.

CHAPTER I.

DISTINCTION OF THE METHODS FROM THE DIRECTIONS OF
ADMINISTRATIVE ACTION.

THE administration has up to this point been considered at rest. Its organization both at the centre and in the localities, the relations of the officers and authorities with each other, and the rules in regard to the official service have been treated, it is hoped, with sufficient fulness to give an adequate idea of the administrative machinery and the character of the official system. It now becomes necessary to consider the methods and forms of the action for the purpose of which the administrative system is formed.

Great care must be taken to distinguish the methods and forms of administrative action from its directions, that is, the various services which the administration may attend to in the interest of the community. While these latter vary greatly in different states, while in some the directions of administrative action may be much more numerous than in others, the forms and methods of administrative action must be everywhere essentially the same. Thus the administration may or may not attend to the telegraphic or railway services of the country. Whether it does or does not, it must in all cases make some contracts, if the government is to be conducted at all. Again the administration may or may not exercise a supervision over the press. Whether it does or does not, it must in all cases exercise a certain amount of police power.

The forms and methods of administrative action, being everywhere essentially the same, may be classified essentially in the same categories. We may go a step further. We may, on account of the uniformity in the civilization which lies at the basis of all state forms existing in or derived from western Europe, classify also the directions of administrative action in essentially the same categories. Thus everywhere we find the administration acting as the man of business of society, carrying on commercial undertakings too vast to be well managed by individual or corporate effort, or of such a nature as to produce better results to the community under governmental than under private management. In some states this kind of administrative action is much more important and extensive than in others, but everywhere we find the action of the administration, to an extent at any rate, commercial in character. Again we find the administration acting everywhere as the delegate of the sovereign and exercising powers of compulsion over those persons who are in obedience to the state ; here also we find in some states this governmental activity, as we may call it, much greater than in others, owing to the difference in the ends of government sought after in different states. Finally everywhere we find the administration acting directly in furtherance of the welfare of individuals, but neither by means of carrying on commercial undertakings nor by means of the exercise of governmental powers ; we find it, for example, collecting information, filing and authenticating documents and records, and issuing patents and charters of incorporation. But here also we find great difference in the extent of this sort of work done in different states. We may say therefore that the directions of administrative action are commercial, governmental, or directly in furtherance of the public welfare. Any detailed treatment of these directions of administrative action would result in the attempt to treat systematically of the entire field of administrative action—of the five great administrative branches which have already been distinguished, *viz.*, foreign, military, judicial, financial, and internal affairs. Such a treatment will not be undertaken here, as it is not within the scope of the present work, which must, on account of the lack of space, be confined to the presentation of the main principles of the most important administrative systems of the present time. Neither is it necessary, in order to a correct understanding of the general principles of the administrative law, to treat of these matters any further than to state the categories in which they may be placed, since the relations of the individual with the administration resulting from the action of the administration will, on account of the general conformity of the purposes of modern states, be essentially the same. But while these great fields of administrative activity and the directions of administrative action may properly be left for a work more special in its nature than the present one, while a general idea of the work of the administration is obtained when it is seen that its activity is governmental, commercial, or directly in furtherance of the public welfare; a somewhat detailed consideration of the forms and methods of administrative action must be undertaken here. For without it the whole system of remedies by which individuals are protected against a violation by the administration of the rights guaranteed to them by the constitution or statutes of the country cannot be understood. Since it is on the efficiency and adequacy of these remedies that the real value of all private rights depends, the importance of a clear understanding of the methods of administrative action can hardly be overestimated.

CHAPTER II.

The methods and forms of the action of the administration are largely dependent upon the character of the duties which the administration is called upon to perform. The character of these duties is in turn dependent upon the nature of the rules of administrative law which the administration has to apply. These rules of law are of two kinds. They either contain a complete expression of the will of the state, or so incompletely express the will of the state that some further action is necessary in order that this will may be capable of execution.

I.—*Unconditional statutes.*

Those rules of administrative law which completely express the will of the state are found in statutes, which are put into the form of unconditional commands to the people to do or to refrain from doing some particular thing and which threaten the violation of their provisions with the imposition of a penalty in the nature of a fine or of imprisonment.[1] But in no ordinary classification of the law would they be called criminal laws, nor would they generally be inserted in the penal code. Attention has already been directed[2]

---

[1] *Cf.* Gneist, *Das Englische Verwaltungsrecht*, 1884, 320 *et seq.* ; Loening, *op. cit.*, 225 *et seq.* [2] *Supra*, I., p. 16.

to the fact that criminal law does not form a special portion of the law distinct from the other portions of the law as is the administrative or the private law, but that it is a law of sanction applied to well-defined branches of the law in order to ensure the enforcement of their provisions. But while those penal provisions which are intended to protect from invasion the rights of the person and property are generally classed together in the penal code, the penal laws which are intended to ensure the enforcement of the administrative law are to be found scattered through the statute book, generally in connection with that portion of the administrative law which they are intended to protect. These statements may perhaps be made clearer by one or two examples. Take the customs administrative law. As far as possible the provisions of this law are put into the form of penal provisions. The customs administrative law says to the importer and the shipmaster that they must transact their business in a certain way, that they must do given things, as *e. g.* enter their ship and their invoices of merchandise in a certain way, also that they must refrain from doing certain things, as *e. g.* that they must not unload their ships at certain times of the day, and then it threatens them with punishment if they do not obey its provisions. The mere fact that such provisions of administrative law have penalties attached to their violation does not make them any the less administrative in character.[1] The legislature has by this means endeavored to ensure that the business of importing merchandise shall be transacted in a certain way, since, if it is transacted in this way, the duties imposed

[1] See Taylor *et al* v. U. S., 3 How., 197, 210.

upon imported merchandise will be easily collected. Again in a great many cases, which form together what is known as police law, the legislature has adopted a similar method to protect the inhabitants of the state from the happening of accidents. Thus in the larger cities the law often says that individuals must build their houses in a certain way in order to avoid the dangers of fire and ill-health resulting from careless construction and unsanitary arrangements. In order to force the individual to build his house in the way required there is a penalty attached to the violation of the provisions of such police laws. But again we would hardly insert such laws in the penal code or class them as a part of the criminal law, though it is often the case that such police laws are sanctioned by the penal code, *i. e.* violations of them are misdemeanors.[1] Another example of such rules of administrative law completely expressing the will of the state is to be found in those rules of administrative law with regard to the assessment and collection of a long series of indirect taxes. The law, as in the case of the customs administrative law, lays down the way in which all payers of indirect taxes shall transact their business and punishes the violation of its provisions with a penalty. For if the business of the payer of indirect taxes is transacted in the way provided by the law, the assessment and collection of the taxes are easy matters. Indeed it may be said that the tax assesses and collects itself where the method of payment by means of the purchase from the government of stamps, and the affixing of them to taxable articles is adopted. These are only a few examples of this method of for-

---

[1] *Cf.* Wharton, Criminal Law, 9th Ed., I., 23 and 28.

mulating the rules of administrative law. Every country strives so far as it can to put its administrative law into the form of absolute unconditional commands, since no rule of law is so easy of enforcement as a direct command whose violation is punishable. There is little chance of conflict between the administration and the individual to whom the law is to be applied, since in applying this class of the rules of administrative law the action of the administration is confined to hunting up all violations of them and to seeing that the penalties for such violations are enforced. The administration has little or no discretion to exercise, since the will of the state has been completely expressed in the law and since therefore the administration has only to execute the law.

II.—*Conditional statutes.*

But there are certain duties which the administration is called upon to perform, which it cannot perform under a system of unconditional commands. No legislature has such insight or so extended a vision as to be able itself to regulate all the details in the administrative law or to put into the form of unconditional commands, addressed to the public at large, rules which will in all cases completely or even adequately express the will of the state. All it can do is to express that will in a general way. It enacts a series of general rules of administrative law which, in distinction from the absolute unconditional commands, may be called relative or conditional commands, since they lay down the conditions and circumstances in which it will be lawful for the administration to act ; and the action of the administration in applying these conditional rules of administrative law really consists in expressing in details, which the legislature itself is unable to foresee or which, even if it can foresee, it is unable to regulate, the will of the state, the expression of which has been made only incompletely by the legislature. While the absolute unconditional commands are addressed to the people subject to the obedience of the state, the relative conditional commands are rather addressed to the administrative authorities and are instructions to them how to act in the special cases for which provision is made. The action of the administration is not therefore confined simply to the execution of the will of the state. On the contrary the administration has a large share in the expression of the will of the state in those conditions and circumstances in which the legislature, as the regulator of the administration, has said that it may express the will of the state. The administration acts in the expression of the will of the state in two ways. It either issues ordinances or general rules which fill up details not regulated in the statutes and not possible of regulation by the legislature, or it issues special orders not of general but of individual application which apply either the statute law alone or the statute law as supplemented by administrative ordinance.

1. *Administrative ordinance.*—It has already been shown [1] that ordinances may be classified as independent, supplementary, and delegated ; and that, while in monarchical governments the executive has the right of supplementary and in some cases of independent ordinance, in the United States the executive has simply the right of delegated ordinance. Official

---

[1] *Supra*, I., p. 28.

authority is based in all cases on the constitution or statutes.[1] It has also been shown that in all countries the heads of the various executive departments and the various local authorities have the right of delegated ordinance. Attention need be directed here only to the fact that while in this country the statutes of the legislature descend very much into detail, in England and especially on the continent of Europe, the legislature confines itself very much more to the enactment of general principles which it is then the duty of the executive, the heads of executive departments, or the local authorities by ordinance to carry out in their details. Thus on the continent the practice is to grant to the local authorities the local police power in the exercise of which they may enact almost any kind of ordinance whose end is to prevent the happening of harm of any kind to the people under their jurisdiction.[2] In this country, on the other hand, where the power of local ordinance is granted by the legislature the practice is to grant to some one authority the power to regulate the details with regard to some particular matter or matters. In some cases the administrative authority, which has the ordinance power, has also the right to sanction its ordinances,[3] though the tendency at the present time is for the legislature in the penal code or in some general law itself to sanction all administrative ordinances.[4] While on the continent the administrative authorities have much wider ordinance power than have the administrative authorities in the United States they are, in

---

[1] *Cf.* Mechem., *op. cit.*, secs. 501 *et seq.*

[2] *E. g.* ordinance power of French mayor, *supra*, I., p. 288.

[3] Dillon, *op. cit.*, I., 412 *et seq.*

[4] *Cf. e. g.*, the French penal code, art. 471, sec. 15.

order to prevent an abuse of their power, usually subjected to some sort of an administrative control in the exercise of this important power. Generally either the approval of some higher authority is required in order that the ordinances issued by a local authority be valid, or else as in Germany the ordinances must be issued with the concurrence of some one of the numerous popular lay authorities which have been created by the late local government reform.[1] In England also where the domain of local ordinance has of late been considerably extended, this central administrative approval is being introduced.[2] All ordinances in all countries must, in order that they shall have force, be brought by some legal means to the notice of those persons whom they will affect.[3] The means usually adopted is the same as that provided for statutes, that is, publication of some sort.

2. *Special administrative order.*—In the second place the administration aids in the expression of the will of the state by the issue of special orders of individual and not general application. It has been shown that the legislature of no state is able in all cases to declare what shall be the will of the state in such detail as to preclude the necessity of some special action on the part of the administration. Nor can administrative ordinance, and for the same reasons. Thus no general rule of any kind can declare by name what persons shall pursue those trades which require a license, or what persons or property shall pay direct taxes or the amount in money of their taxes. All that can be done

[1] *Supra*, I., pp. 304, 315.   [2] *Supra*, I., p. 260.
[3] How and Bemis, *Municipal Police Ordinances*, 352 ; Kneib v. People. 6 Hun, 238 ; State v. Hoboken, 38 N. J. L., 110 ; Baltimore v. Johnson, 62 Md., 225 ; Higley v. Bunce, 10 Conn., 436 ; Burnett v. Newark, 28 Ill., 62.

by general rule is to determine what requirements those persons who desire to pursue licensed trades shall fulfil and under what conditions and at what rate taxes shall be levied on persons and property. Of course in the case of license taxes, as *e. g.* the "special taxes" formerly levied by the United States national government on dealers in tobacco, it is possible to say that each taxpayer, *i. e.* each dealer in tobacco, shall pay a tax specific in amount. But what such a method may gain in simplicity, it loses in justice; and when it comes to any such system of taxation as property taxation, the injustice of requiring every property owner to pay the same amount of tax would be so glaring that no people would submit to it. In order that any system of property taxation shall be just, it must be proportional, *i. e.* the amount of tax which each taxpayer pays must be in proportion to the amount of property which he possesses. If this rule is adopted, as it is almost universally, before the amount of any given taxpayer's tax is ascertained, the amount of the property on which the tax is levied must be determined. The same general principle is true in the case of licensed trades. If any sort of control is to be kept over such trades, and the control of these trades is generally the reason of requiring them to be licensed, the qualifications of the person requesting the license must be ascertained before the license can be granted. Now the conditional rules of law which it is the duty of the administration to apply in all these cases simply state under what conditions licenses shall be granted and property taxed, and what rules shall be followed by the administrative authorities in the assessment of the property subject to taxation;

and in order that these conditional rules of law may
be applied, *i. e.* in order that the will of the state in
the particular conditions of some given person or piece
of property may be expressed completely so that it
may be executed, the fact of the existence of the conditions referred to in the law must be ascertained.
Furthermore the ascertainment of the existence of
these conditions is the duty of some administrative
officer, whose action in aiding in the expression of the
will of the state is absolutely necessary before that
will can be executed. The determination reached by
such an officer is an act of individual and not of general application. In this country there is no general
technical name for such an act, the name varying with
almost each kind of special act done. Thus such a
special act is called an order, a precept, a warrant, and
a decision.

There is a great variety of such special acts. Some
are in the form of commands to subordinate officers or
to individuals to do or to refrain from doing some particular thing, *e. g.* tax warrants, orders of payment,
nuisance removal and sanitary orders; some are per-
missions to individuals to carry on a given business,
e. g. licenses and authorizations; some are prohibitions
to carry on a business, *e. g.* revocation of a license or
authorization; some are acts which create a new legal
person, *e. g.* charters of incorporation; some consist of
contracts made by the administration for the government considered as a juristic person or " fiscus "; some
are decisions as to the existence of certain facts whose
ascertainment is necessary in order that the will of the
state may be completely expressed, *e. g.* assessments,
appraisements, classification of articles for duties in the

tax and customs administration; and finally some are
appointments to office or orders to individuals to serve
the government in some capacity, *e. g.* notice to serve
as juror or in the military service.

In the performance of such acts the administration
must follow a certain procedure which is laid down in
the law granting it the power to act. The law thus
says in the first place that certain acts shall be performed only by certain authorities. The authority
before acting in any of these cases must assure itself
that it is competent, for its acts will be void if it is
incompetent.[1] In the second place the content of the
act must be in accordance with the law, since every
administrative order must find its basis in the statutes
or supplementary ordinances of the administration.[2]
These statutes may state specifically, as in this country, what the administrative authorities may do, or, as
on the continent, they may lay down general norms
simply, which the administration must follow in its
discretion. In the third place the administrative act
must be performed in the way provided for in the law.
This is especially true if the method provided by law
is intended for the protection of individual rights.[3]
Sometimes the method of its performance is laid down
in the greatest detail and any failure to follow the
manner prescribed will be fatal to the validity of the
act. It is so in the case of the assessment of property
for the purposes of taxation[4]; of the destruction by
the government of the property right of the individual,

---

[1] *Cf.* Mechem, *op. cit.*, secs. 500–564, for the detailed rules of the American
law as to the competence of officers.

[2] *Cf.* Mechem, *op. cit.*, sec. 501, citing Atty.-Gen. v. Detroit Common Council, 58 Mich., 213, 219.

[3] *Cf.* Cooley, *Taxation*, 2d Ed., 280 *et seq.*   [4] *Ibid.*

as in the case of the exercise of the right of eminent domain [1] and also in the case of the contracts made by the administration for the government.[2]   The reason is that in the one case it is considered extremely important to protect individual property rights, and that in the other the government is so liable to be cheated by its officials that some method must be adopted by means of which the responsibility for every step in the making of the contract may be fixed on some person, and that the contractual powers of governmental authorities must be limited.   Further it is often the case that before a decision may be reached by the administration which has an important bearing upon private rights, opportunity must be given to all persons who are interested in the decision to raise any objections which they may desire to make to the proposed action ; and, if the authority which is to take the action is a board, that sufficient time must be given for deliberation, and that the decision which is reached finally must be made by a majority vote of all the members of the board or by a majority of a quorum of the board.   Where such formalities are provided it is, it may be said, absolutely necessary to the validity of the action of the administration that they be followed. [3]   Thus the United States courts have held that the " due process of law " required by the 14th amendment to the United States constitution for the taking of private property makes the opportunity to be heard at some stage of the proceedings a necessary formality

---

[1] Dillon, *op. cit.*, II., 706 ; Mechem, *op. cit.*, 581.

[2] Dillon, *cp. cit.*, I., 520, 543, and cases cited.   The only possible exception to this rule is in the case of *quasi* contracts, *Ibid.*, 536.

[3] *Cf.* Cooley, *op. cit.*, 287 ; Mechem, *op. cit.*, secs. 271-281.

in property tax proceedings.[1] Finally the order like the ordinance must be brought by some legal means to the knowledge of the person or persons affected by it. This is particularly true of assessments for the purpose of taxation. As a general thing this is to be done in writing or by publication, but in not a few cases a mere verbal order is sufficient, as *e. g.* in the case of an order given by a constable or peace officer to a disorderly assemblage or crowd to disperse.

Thus it is that the administration discharges a most important function in expressing in detail the will of the state, so far as that will has not been expressed completely in the statutes by the legislature. In the discharge of this function of expressing the will of the state the administration must necessarily be given a wide discretion in determining the existence of the conditions which the law requires in order that the administration shall act; and in the exercise of this discretion the administration must also necessarily come into frequent conflict with individuals. This is especially true of the whole domain of what is called police administration, where the administration endeavors to protect the individual from the happening of harm through the limitation of the right of individual action. It is seen thus that the action of the administration does not consist in mere ministerial action, in execution, that it must perforce exercise great discretion in expressing the will of the state, and that in the exercise of this discretion it has an enormous influence not only upon the welfare but also upon the sphere of free action of almost every individual in the state. But while this expression of the will of the state is one of

[1] See Santa Clara Co. v. R. R. Co., 18 Fed. Rep., 385.

the functions of the administration and has an important effect upon the character of its action, still the duty *par excellence* of the administration is not the expression but the execution of the will of the state. For whether that will has been expressed fully by the legislature or partly by it and partly by the administration it is in almost every case the administration upon which devolves the execution of that will when once completely expressed.

CHAPTER III.

I.—Means of execution.

The will of the state, whether expressed in statute, ordinance, or individual act not of general application, always contains either expressly or impliedly the command that it shall be executed. This mere command may in many cases be sufficient and in all cases would be sufficient in a perfectly well-ordered community; since individuals would, if they were perfectly patriotic and if the expressed will of the state were always just and in accordance with the law, do what they were commanded to do. But in the communities with which the administration has to deal, for some reason or other individuals will in many cases refuse to do what they are commanded to do. Some means must therefore be devised to ensure their obedience—to ensure that the will of the state be executed. The means adopted are various in kind.

1. *Imposition of penalties.*—On account of the liability of the individual to refuse to obey the command of the law, such refusal is made punishable. This is the most common means of executing the will of the state for the reason, as has been indicated, of its extreme simplicity and that it leaves little to the discre-

tion of the administration. For, as a general rule, the
penalties are to be found in the law as passed by the
legislature [1]; and such penalties are to be enforced ultimately by the ordinary courts, which are independent
of the administration and act in accordance with the
usual rules of criminal procedure. In this way the
individual is amply protected against arbitrary action
on the part of the administration. In Germany quite
frequently and in some cases in the United States,
however, the administration itself may proceed to impose the penalty without resort to the courts, and the
individual against whom the proceedings are taken has
the right to appeal to some judicial body against the
action of the administration. [2]

2. *Enforced performance of the act ordered.*—Sometimes the execution of the will of the state will not be
effected by the decree of a penalty either by the courts
or by the administration itself. In many cases the
will of the state can be executed only by the performance by the individual of a definite thing. This definite thing may often consist in the payment of a sum
of money ; or it may be absolutely necessary that the
individual with whom the administration comes in
conflict, actually himself do something which does not
consist in the payment of a sum of money.

a. *Execution of the law by the payment of a sum of
money.*—A great many of the orders of the administration, may be executed by ensuring the payment of a
sum of money. Thus the orders of the administration
to individuals to pay taxes and the like will naturally

[1] There are a few cases, especially in Germany, in which the administration
has the right of sanctioning its own ordinances and orders.

[2] Loening, *op. cit.*, 248, note 1 ; See Cooley on *Taxation*, 2d Ed., 457 ;
Parker and Worthington, *Public Health and Safety*, 103.

be executed by the payment of a sum of money and be
executed also naturally only in this way. Further it
may be possible that the act demanded of the individual by the administration can be performed by the
administration itself, whose expenses in the doing of
the act which ought to have been done by the individual at his own expense, like taxes, become an obligation of the person disobeying its order. For example
if the administration orders a landlord to make repairs
which are necessary from a sanitary point of view, and
he refuses, it is perfectly easy for the administration to
step in and do the work itself and thus found an obligation which is binding upon the individual to repay
it the expenses which it has been obliged to incur in
order to do the work. [1] Finally a similar obligation on
the part of the individual may arise from the fact
that a penalty has been incurred in the nature of a fine
for disobedience of the law or the orders of the administration itself which, as has been shown, has the right
in many cases to impose fines. [2] The methods adopted
to ensure the payment of an obligation which has
arisen in this way are usually the same as those adopted
to ensure the payment of judgments of courts. That
is, the amount due is either made a lien upon the real
property in relation to which the obligation was formed
and may be collected by its sale, or it is to be collected by the sale of the personal property of the individual from whom the obligation is due. [3]

b. *Arrest.*—But the will of the state cannot always
be executed by the payment of a sum of money. In
many cases it can be executed only by the perform-

---

[1] See N. Y. Law 1882, c. 410, secs. 630, 635.
[2] *Ibid.*, sec. 633.   [3] *Ibid.*, secs. 630, 85.

ance of a given action or the prevention of a given action. Certain things must be done or certain things must not be done in order that the will of the state may be executed. In order in these cases to compel the recalcitrant individual to act or to refrain from action he may be arrested and imprisoned. The power of arrest is found in two distinct cases in all countries. Often simple disobedience of the expressed will of the state is punished by short terms of imprisonment when the administration has the right to arrest and imprison the disobedient individual.[1] The other case in which resort is had to arrest and imprisonment, is where the individual refuses to do a thing which he has been commanded by the administration to do. This seems to be quite common in Germany, and is not unknown in the United States.[2] In such case the arrest and imprisonment are quite separate and apart from the arrest and imprisonment which the individual may have made himself liable to by his original disobedience of the law. Simple refusal to obey a competent order of the administration may be punishable by fine and imprisonment.

c. *Application of physical force.*—Finally the administration has the right to apply physical force if one of its competent orders cannot be enforced in any other way. The force may be applied to the person or to some object, and may often consist in depriving a person of some article, in shutting up some location, or in putting an end to some occupation, as *e. g.* in the

---

[1] *Ibid.*, sec. 85 ; Commonwealth v. Byrne, 20 Grattan, 165, 198, which holds that arrest decreed in accordance with law by an administrative officer in the case of non-payment of taxes is due process of law and constitutional.

[2] Stengel, *Wörterbuch, etc.*, II., 800, 801 ; Cooley, *Taxation*, 2nd Ed., 437 ; Burroughs, *Taxation*, 150.

shutting up of an illicit still and the destruction or seizure of the machinery found therein.

In all these cases, if resistance is offered to the administration or an administrative officer acting within his competence, the person offering such resistance may be arrested and punished, and ultimately the entire force of the government of the country may be called upon to overcome such resistance. Thus in the United States the mayor of a city may call out the militia[1]; the sheriff in the county may also call out the militia or the *posse comitatus;* the governor may often declare a county in a state of insurrection,[2] and on the application of the governor or of his own motion the President of the United States may call out the forces of the nation.[3] Thus every order of the administration has ultimately back of it the entire physical force of the government. But before any of the orders of the administration may be enforced, and before force may actually be applied, it is often necessary that certain formalities be complied with, which differ considerably in the different countries. This brings us to the methods of executing the will of the state after it has once been expressed completely.

II.—Methods of execution.

In general there are two methods of executing the will of the state. Either the administration may proceed of its own motion to the execution of its orders by the use of the proper means, subject to the control of the courts, which may, on the instance of the individual affected by its action, interfere to protect his

---

[1] See *e. g.* N. Y. L. 1882, c. 410, sec. 269. [2] *Supra*, I., p. 75.
[3] U. S. Rev. Stats. secs. 5297, 5298.

rights; or it is necessary for the administration to apply to the courts in the first instance to enforce its orders. The latter method is the usual one in the United States and England, although there are cases even in those countries in which the administration may proceed without having recourse to any other authority; while the former method seems to be the rule upon the continent.

1. *Judicial process.*—The reason of the adoption of the general rule in England and this country that the administration must apply to the courts to enforce its orders is largely historical. It will be remembered that at one time the justices of the peace were the most important administrative officers in the various localities both in England and in the United States. Acting singly or in pairs or in their courts of petty and special or quarter sessions the justices had a long series of really administrative duties to perform which were almost inextricably mixed up with their really judicial duties, *i. e.* with their decision of criminal cases and cases involving purely private relations.[1] It is true that all the acts of the justices were clothed in about the same formula[2]; but these may be put into three pretty distinct classes. The first class was purely judicial and took on the form of convictions or judgments made after previous hearing. The second was to be found in the orders which they issued either of their own motion or upon the proposition of an inferior officer such as a constable or overseer of the poor, where no previous hearing was given to parties who might be interested. Thus in their special sessions the

[1] *Supra*, I., p. 239.
[2] Gneist, *Das Englische Verwaltungsrecht*, 1884, 391, 392.

justices appointed parish officers and made up the jury list. In their courts of quarter sessions many of the acts performed in the exercise of their original jurisdiction, such as those relating to the financial administration of the county or the passage of by-laws, were performed of their own motion and belonged to this class of acts which were really administrative in character. In the third class may be placed those acts consisting not of decisions as to private relations or of convictions but as in the second class rather of orders in administrative matters where, however, before the order was issued a hearing was given to parties interested. Some of the acts of this class were performed by a single justice but not many; some were performed by two justices acting together, such *e. g.* as orders of removal and orders in bastardy in the poor-law administration and orders to abate nuisances in the sanitary administration; some were performed by the special sessions, as *e. g.* the decisions of differences arising between the overseers of the poor and the taxpayers in regard to tax assessments, the grant of licenses to ale-houses, the taking away of licenses, the decision of difficulties with regard to the building of roads, *etc., etc.* In all these cases the objections of interested persons were heard before the decision of the justices was made.[1] These acts were administrative in character but somewhat judicial in form, since they were performed only after the holding of some sort of a trial.

In the course of time a separation of the judicial and administrative functions was made in this country, the purely administrative powers going to new officers such as the supervisors, county commissioners, and the

[1] *Cf. Ibid.*, 266, 276-301 ; 381-4.

like, the purely judicial powers and most of the powers
whose exercise resulted in acts judicial in form going
to the justices. That is the justices retained the power
of deciding on all convictions, of giving judgments in
civil cases of a private legal character, and of issuing
almost all the orders which might be executed without
further action by any authority. The same powers
possessed by the justices after this separation of judicial
and administrative functions have since been conferred
on other courts, such as the county and similar courts,
which in this country have taken in the judicial organization the position formerly occupied by the English
courts of quarter and special sessions. The result of
this curious evolution of the justice of the peace from a
purely or almost purely administrative officer into an
almost purely judicial officer is that, since the justice or
his successors have in the course of this development
largely retained the power of ordering given things to
be done by individuals, the administration seldom has
the right to proceed to execute its orders without having first made application to a court of some sort for
the power to execute the order.

Of course it is not always necessary for the administration in England and the United States to apply to
the courts in order to enforce its orders. In certain
cases where immediate action is absolutely necessary
in order to avoid disastrous results, as in the case of
the abatement of a nuisance prejudicial to the public
health and in the case of the payment of taxes,[1] the
administration may proceed directly to enforce its
orders, and in case of resistance to the execution of the

[1] *Cf.* N. Y. L. 1882, c. 410, secs. 926–929; N. Y. L. 1885, c. 270, sec. 38;
Parker and Worthington, *op. cit.*, ch. xii.

law may, without application to the courts, apply force to overcome such resistance; and if any individual feels aggrieved by the action of the administration he may appeal to the courts and get what satisfaction he can.[1]

2. *Administrative execution.*—While application to the courts to enforce the orders of the administration is generally the rule in England and the United States, and may thus be called the English method of executing the will of the state, the direct execution of its orders by the administration is the rule on the continent. The more complete separation of administration from justice on the continent, the more important rôle assigned to the administration to play there, the greater confidence the people have in its justice, or their greater indifference to the possession by the administration of large powers, has caused them to feel that it is a matter of little consequence what authority has the power of directly executing the law. What little deprivation of individual rights they may suffer by the grant of such powers to the administration they believe is compensated for by the greater efficiency of the administration resulting from its greater powers. Where this method of direct execution of its orders by the administration has been adopted, the administration often has the right to threaten persons disobeying its orders with a penalty which it itself may enforce, and which is distinct from the penalty for the original disobedience. It may directly proceed to arrest persons and seize property, shut up buildings and destroy objects, and prevent given individuals from following

---

[1] Such summary proceedings in the case of collection of taxes are constitutional. McMillan v. Anderson, 95 U. S., 37.

certain occupations without having resort to any judicial authority. This method of executing the will of the state by the direct act of the administration itself may be called, in analogy with the action of the courts in enforcing their decrees, execution, and in distinction from their action, administrative execution. In all countries, as has been indicated, this is the method adopted to enforce the payment of direct taxes. The administration steps in and of its own accord, without the intervention of any other authority, seizes the property of the delinquent taxpayer.[1] This it is then allowed to sell, subject often to the owner's right of redemption. After deducting from the proceeds of the sale the amount due the government, it must either return the residue, if any, to the owner if he can be found or if he cannot be found, must keep such residue in trust for him. This is often the case in the United States where ordinarily administrative execution is rare.[2] This same method of administrative execution is also adopted in some countries for the enforcement of most money payments due the government,[3] but as a usual thing this is not the case in the United States[4] except in the case of the collection of taxes where the administration is regarded as peculiarly representative of the sovereign. In the other cases of sums of money due the government, either because the administration is not regarded

[1] In Germany, however, landed property can be seized only as a result of the action of a court. Stengel, *Deutsches Verwaltungsrecht*, 195.

[2] See *e. g.* N. Y. L. 1882, c. 410, secs. 926–954.

[3] So in France, Ducrocq, *op. cit.*, II., 263 *et seq.* ; Germany, Civ. Proz. Ord., secs. 708–768.

[4] But see Murray's Lessee v. Hoboken Land and Improvement Co., 18 How., U. S., 272 which holds that such a method is due process of law even in the case of debts due the government.

as so representative of the sovereign or because it is felt to be unsafe to give the administration such wide powers, the law requires that the administration shall go before a court of competent jurisdiction, present its case there, and trust to the action of the court to execute the will of the state. In the case of a contract the government is regarded as simply a juristic person having no greater rights than ordinary persons except perhaps that it may be given the position of a preferred creditor; in the case of the enforcement of a penalty the administration is regarded as simply the prosecutor, and the actual execution of the will of the state is left to the courts, which may thus, if they see fit, greatly retard the action of the administration and exercise a wide control over it.

CHAPTER IV.

THE SOCIALISTIC ACTION OF THE ADMINISTRATION.

The foregoing chapter presupposes some positive action on the part of the administration in the direction of limiting the sphere of individual liberty; action from which results a relation of antagonism between the administration and the individual, who must, however, ultimately submit to its demands. The forms and methods of action resulting from this relation of antagonism are commands and the application of force to overcome resistance. In these cases of the expression or execution of the will of the state the administration has been considered as the representative of the sovereign power, and as entering into what may be called legal relations with individuals. The powers of the administration and the forms and methods of its action in the exercise of its powers are not, however, exhausted in the enumeration which has already been given; for the function of administration is the realization of the ends of the state. The administration is to assist in widening the circle of human enjoyment and enlarging the scope of human opportunity as well as in limiting the sphere of individual liberty; is to aid man in his conflict with nature as well as order his relations with his fellow-man.[1] It must offer to the inhabitants

---

[1] *Cf.* Stengel, *Deutsches Verwaltungsrecht*, 172.

of the state means of communication, must bridge
rivers, construct highways, and carry the mails; it
must protect the coast against the action of the sea;
must keep the records of legal transactions, such as
deeds and mortgages, on whose correctness and accu-
racy depends the validity of titles to property; it must
issue patents and charters, by which new rights are
created; the administration must in fact do everything
which individuals cannot accomplish or cannot accomplish advantageously. In all of these cases it is seldom
that the administration acts as the representative of
the sovereign; seldom that it enters into hostile or
antagonistic relations with individuals, for the purpose
of its action is not here as in the class of cases
enumerated in the preceding chapters to circumscribe
the liberty of action of the individual, to make him
yield something in order to further the general well-
being; its purpose is on the contrary to offer directly to
individuals some particular advantage by which they
may profit. While in all cases the action of the administration is, or should be, intended to promote the
public welfare, it accomplishes this end in the two
classes of cases by totally different means. In the one
it acts by repression, in the other by the direct tender
of some service. The natural result is that the methods
and forms of its action will be quite different in the
different cases. In the one class, the form of its action
is a command and its enforcement, in the other it is a
rendering of a positive service to the individual upon
his initiation and his compliance with the proper pre-
liminaries. Thus the individual need only properly
direct and stamp mail matter and tender it to the administration and the administration will transmit it to

the proper address; he need only present a deed or a mortgage properly acknowledged, and on tender of the fee fixed by law the administration will record it; he need only apply for a patent for a new invention which will be given to him if he has complied with the conditions laid down in the law. The form which the action of the administration will take in these cases will be either that of contract which is usually, however, governed by peculiar rules,[1] or of a certificate or authentication which, if official in character, will be taken judicial notice of by the courts.

Further in order to perform many of these duties, as indeed to perform any other of its multifarious duties, the administration must have an acquaintance with the relations into which it enters. Sometimes the necessary acquaintance is obtained by simple observation. Simple observation is all that is necessary to determine the existence of a nuisance, the necessity of laying out a new highway, or of the construction of a bridge. But at other and most times more complicated conditions must be examined, the effect of laws and institutions must be discovered, a vast amount of information in regard to social phenomena must be obtained before the administration or even the government as a whole can wisely proceed to act. In many cases physical laws and natural forces must also be studied and information as to their workings must be collected. For though the government comes mainly into contact with human beings, it regulates their relations often only in the hope of bringing the individual into harmony with his environment; in other words it forces him to obey natural forces and laws. The government directs the

---

[1] *Supra*, I., p. 10.

mode of human life and limits the freedom of individual action, but it does this only with the desire of improving the moral and sanitary conditions of the people. In order to accomplish this duty the government must understand what conditions are provocative of evil ; what environment is favorable to the spread of disease. The necessary understanding cannot in these instances be obtained through simple observation. Resort must be had to some other means of acquiring information. Investigations must be held, testimony must be taken, experts must be heard, long series of statistics must be collected and examined. Of course these are not means exclusively used by the administration or the government. Courts hear testimony, legislatures make investigations, and statistics are gathered by private persons and associations, and are used by them to prove and disprove every imaginable proposition. The collection of information and statistics is not therefore a characteristic function of administration or even of government ; nor will the form of the action of the administration in these cases be peculiar or different from that of the action of private bodies with the single exception that the results will be more readily believed and are, not infrequently, presumed to be true in official proceedings. There is a large class of statistics, however, a certain kind of information which governmental organs alone can in the nature of things collect, partly because of the immensity of the task, partly because it is often necessary, in order to obtain such information and to collect such statistics at all, to apply force or at least to provide that the power to apply force exist, and the government is the only organization in a well ordered community to which the application of force can safely be entrusted. The organ of the government which is peculiarly fitted to perform this duty of acquiring information and collecting statistics is the active organ of the government, that is the administration. It is also the only organ properly organized for this purpose. But though it is the best fitted to perform this duty, it does not by any means confine its activity in this direction to the collection of those statistics and that information which will be of immediate use to it alone. On the contrary the administration is or should be the permanent collector of much information and most statistics which are made use of by the other departments of the government whose action, as has been shown, must be based on a wide knowledge of facts and relations, and by the people at large in their search for social and economic laws and for the causes of and remedies for existing conditions.

This kind of administrative activity, whose purpose is the direct furtherance of the social welfare, may be called socialistic in distinction from the governmental activity whose forms and methods were analyzed in the preceding chapters and in which the administration is to be seen representing the sovereign power of the state. Its forms and methods are not peculiar to governmental activity, but are in the nature of contracts, of decisions arrived at by synthetical processes. It is, however, necessary to mention them in order to convey an adequate idea of the field of administrative activity, and of the forms and methods of administrative action.

BOOK VI.

THE CONTROL OVER THE ADMINISTRA-
TION.

Division 1.—Methods of Control.

CHAPTER I.

FORMATION OF THE CONTROL.

I.—Necessity of control.

THE action of the administration, whose forms and methods have been described in the last book, is so important that it is impossible for any country possessing constitutional government to allow the administration perfectly free hand in the discharge of its duties. The public is so dependent upon the action of the administration that it is of the utmost importance that the administration shall be efficient. The administration attends to many things which it is impossible for individuals to attend to at all. If the administration does not perform its duties or performs them unwisely or inefficiently it will follow that these things will not be done at all or will be done in such a way that the results of administrative action will be of little value. Individuals also are so at the mercy of the administra-

tion that some protection must be offered to them
against the violation of their rights. The administration is often thrown into relations with the individual
citizens which must necessarily be hostile. It demands
of them sacrifices which they regard as unreasonable
or as not justified by the law of the land. Nearly
all of the expressions of the will of the state which
are to be carried out in their details and executed by
the administration cause a conflict at times between
the conception by the administration of what the
public welfare demands and the conception by the individual of the sphere of private rights guaranteed to
him by the law. If the administration had in such
cases the power of perfectly discretionary and uncontrolled action, it is to be feared that individual rights
would be violated. For the administration has back
of it the entire force of the government. Of course
it is the purpose of all administrative legislation to reduce as far as possible the realm of administrative
discretion, to lay down limits within which the administration must move. But it is impossible to do this
with such precision as efficiently to protect individual
rights. The discretion of the administration cannot
be completely taken away by legislation without causing its usefulness to be seriously impaired. Large
discretion must be given to the administration in all
states by the legislative authority, so large that some
means of controlling the administration must be devised if private rights are to be maintained.

Finally the action of the administration should be
such as will, as far as possible, promote the welfare of
society at large. There are many cases where, though
the action of the administration is not subversive of

the private rights of any particular person, it will still not be in accordance with the interests of society as a whole. Here again the discretion of the administration cannot, without diminishing greatly its powers of usefulness, be so controlled by legislation as perfectly to ensure the promotion of the public welfare. As before some other means must be devised of controlling the action of the administration more concrete in its character, more adaptable to particular cases.

For all of these reasons then it is desirable, indeed necessary, that there be formed some system of control over the action of the administration to the ends that such action be efficient, consider private rights, and promote the welfare of society at large.

II.—Interests to be regarded.

The formation of such a system of control is as difficult as it is necessary, partly on account of the variety of the interests to be regarded, partly on account of the variety and continual recurrence of the administrative acts to be controlled. Analogies from other branches of the law must be used with caution, because each of these other branches of the law has as a rule regard for only one interest, and because the acts to be controlled are not so varied in kind. Thus private law aims at the maintenance of private rights, and at the observance of the law as laid down in the books; it seldom, at any rate so far as its application is concerned, has regard for expediency. Again criminal law aims at the attainment of good social conditions, while constitutional and international law aim primarily at the efficiency of government organization and the maintenance of state integrity and power. Constitutional law does, it is true, aim also at the protection of private rights, in so far as it formulates a scheme of inviolable rights, but the remedies offered for their violation, and without which they are valueless, are to be found in the control over administrative action provided by the administrative law. If constitutional law formulates the rights, administrative law elaborates the remedies. Administrative law, on the other hand, endeavors to attain all these three ends, *viz.*, state integrity and power and efficient governmental action, the maintenance of private rights, and the attainment of good social conditions. Therefore we cannot rely on any one kind of control as in these other branches of the law. No system of private or even public actions will suffice to control the application of the administrative law and the action of the administration made necessary thereby, as it undoubtedly does suffice for the control of the application of private and criminal law. No system of administrative centralization or legislative control will suffice as in the case of international and constitutional law. On the contrary a well organized control over the application of the administrative law and over administrative action must make use of all these three methods of control, since the administrative law aims at governmental efficiency, individual liberty, and social well-being.[1]

In the formation of the control over the administration regard must be had then for the interests to be furthered by the administrative law. The first of these interests is that of governmental efficiency. Some method of control must be devised by which to force the officers of the administration to act in case they

[1] *Cf.* Gneist, *Das Englische Verwaltungsrecht*, 1884, Book II., Chap. 3, I.

neglect their duties, or to correct their action in case they act unwisely. As many cases may arise where the neglect of officials will not cause a serious violation of private rights but will simply tend to impair the efficiency of the administration, and as it is the interest of the government that its administration be efficient, this method of control should be so formed that it may be exercised by the organs of the government of their own motion and not simply at the instance of private persons.

The second interest to be regarded is the preservation of individual rights, the maintenance in its entirety of the sphere of freedom of individual action guaranteed by the law of the land. Some method of control must be devised by which the officers of the government may be prevented from encroaching upon this sphere. As this method of control is formed in the interest of the individual, it should be so formed that it may be exercised by the individual, who should be allowed to appeal to impartial tribunals from the acts of the administration which, he believes, violate the rights assured to him by the law. Such impartial tribunals are found in the courts as at present organized in all civilized countries, which in various ways may be given the power to prevent encroachment by the administration on the domain of private rights.

The third interest to be regarded by the administrative law is the social well-being. There must be some method of control devised which will force the administration in its action to keep before its mind always that it is not a law unto itself, that one of the great reasons of its existence is the promotion of the social welfare. Such a method of control should be so organized as to allow that body which primarily represents society in the government, *i. e.* the legislature, to step in and compel the administration to regard the interests of society.[1]

III.—*Kinds of control, and particularly the administrative control.*

There are thus three pretty distinct interests to be regarded and there should be three pretty distinct methods of control, each of which aims primarily at the protection and consideration of one of these three interests. These three methods of control which we find in all states in various stages of development and perfection are called, respectively, the administrative control, the judicial control, and the parliamentary or legislative control, their names being derived from the authority which exercises them.[2]

1. *The administrative control.*—We have in the first place the administrative control. This is exercised primarily in the interest of governmental efficiency, though it may be used subsidiarily in the interest of the protection of private rights and the furtherance of the public welfare. Its main endeavor is to obtain harmony in administrative action, efficiency in the service in general, and uprightness and competence in the officials. It is exercised, as its name implies, by the higher officers of the administration over the actions of their subordinates. It is thus really a sort of self-control, and its extent depends altogether upon the degree of administrative centralization present in the administrative system. It has thus been sufficiently

[1] See Gneist, *Das Englische Verwaltungsrecht*, 1884, 320 *et. seq.*
[2] *Ibid.*

treated in the discussion which has been had of the organization of the administration. Its existence must be noticed, however, in this connection, since if it is well developed it will not be necessary to develop so fully the other means of control. But where the administrative control is not developed, *i. e.* where the administration is not somewhat centralized, it will be almost useless to expect any great efficiency. Administrative efficiency may, of course, be sought in some other way, but the main means of obtaining it is through centralization and an administrative control. When analyzed, this administrative control will be found to consist of a disciplinary power,[1] and a power of supervision possessed by the higher administrative officers over the lower administrative officers. Reference to what has been said in regard to administrative organization and particularly to what has been said with regard to the relations of the central administrative authorities with the administrative authorities in the localities will show that the administrative control exists hardly at all in the United States outside of the national administration, where it is quite strong and seems to be growing stronger; that the national administration has practically no control over the administration in the various commonwealths; that the central administrative authorities in the commonwealths have little control over the localities or the administrative authorities in the localities; and that the only localities where the administrative control of the chief local authority over the other authorities is at all well developed are the cities. In England, where the condition of the administrative control was

---

[1] *Supra*, II., p. 86.

at one time very much the same as in the United States commonwealths at the present time, there has of late years been considerable change. Since 1834, and as a result of the reforms in the local government system, the administrative control has been very much strengthened, particularly that of the central over the local authorities.[1] On the continent, however, the administrative control is very highly developed. The control of the central administrative authorities over the localities and local authorities is very great, and as a result of the concentrated character of the local government system, the control of some one local authority over the other authorities in the same locality is a strong one.[2] But while in England the tendency has been since 1834 to increase the administrative control of the central authorities over the localities, on the continent the tendency has been just the other way, *i. e.* towards decentralization and local self-administration. Finally it is to be noticed that in the federal government of the German Empire, as in the federal government of the United States, the national, *i. e.* the imperial, government has no administrative control over the administration of the various members of the empire.

2. *The judicial control.*—We have in the second place the judicial control. This is exercised by the courts and primarily in the interest of the individual for the protection of his rights, but it may be made use of subsidiarily in the interest of administrative efficiency. By its means individuals may prevent the administration from violating their rights and from making any mis-application of the administrative law.

[1] *Supra*, I, pp. 259 *et seq.*   [2] *Supra*, I, pp. 266–338.

3. *The parliamentary or legislative control.*—This is exercised primarily and, it may be said, almost exclusively in the interest of the general social well-being, and is exercised by the legislature or its committees.

Every constitutional state has formed the control over its administration out of these three elements. But the strength of each of these elements in the different states varies greatly in accordance with the relative prominence of the end sought in the formation of the control, and indeed the whole body of the administrative law. In one country, as for instance in Germany, we find that the end aimed at in the administrative law and in the control over the administration is the efficiency of the government, and therefore that the administrative control is very great, *i. e.* the administration is highly centralized while the judicial control is comparatively weak; in another, as for instance in the United States, the end mainly sought is the maintenance in its integrity of the sphere of individual rights. Therefore the administration is quite decentralized and the control of the courts over it very great. As the administrative control has been sufficiently considered in what has already been written we will proceed at once to the discussion of the judicial control.

CHAPTER I.

ANALYSIS OF THE JUDICIAL CONTROL.

I.—Use of ordinary judicial institutions.

The judicial control may be largely ensured by making use of ordinary judicial machinery and by the application of the ordinary rules of law to the officers of the administration who are to be controlled. Thus the government may be regarded as a juristic person when it makes contracts or commits torts, and then considered as a subject of private rather than public law. If it is so regarded, the ordinary means of enforcing contracts and redressing wrongs in the case of private persons may be adopted in the case of the government. Again the officers of the government may be treated as private persons and apart from their official capacity; and their acts done under color of office but not in accordance with the provisions of the law may then be treated like the acts of private persons and subjected to the control of the ordinary courts. If without jurisdiction they have injured individuals they may be made responsible to such individuals in damages. Analogies may also be drawn from the criminal

law. Many of the rules of administrative law may be
put into the form of absolute unconditional commands
to the persons in the obedience of the state to do or
to refrain from doing particular things, and the violation of such rules of law may be made punishable
criminally ; the application of the penalties may be
entrusted to the ordinary courts which, before inflicting
them, will have to decide as to the criminality of the act
and will thus exercise a control over the action of the administration when it endeavors to enforce the penalties.
Further the ordinary misdemeanors of officers as well
as the violation by them of their administrative duties
may be punished in the same way. In all of these
cases the law, in order to form a judicial control over
the administration and its officers, makes use of the
ordinary judicial machinery and applies to the administration the ordinary rules of private and criminal
law. For many of the rules of administrative law such
methods of control will be sufficient, since the action
of the administration in applying them will be of such
a character that it will be subject to judicial supervision. Thus the wrongful use of governmental power
by officials to the detriment of particular individuals
will in many cases be prevented by the fear of incurring a liability for damages caused by the wrongful
act or of criminal punishment. Especially will this
method of judicial control be sufficient in the case of
all rules of administrative law which are put into the
form of absolute unconditional commands.[1] The power
which the courts have to refuse to enforce the penalties for their violation, in case the administration has
endeavored to act illegally, will preclude the possibility

[1] *Supra*, II., p. 106.

of permanent illegal administrative action. For the action of the administration in such cases consists simply in prosecuting the violation or supposed violation before the police or criminal courts which usually form a part of the ordinary judicial system. The administration has no discretion to exercise and its action neither needs nor admits of the exercise of any further control in the interest of private rights. These rights have been completely safeguarded in the first place through the complete expression of the will of the state by the legislature, and in the second place by the designation by the legislature of this means of their execution. But in certain other cases the action of the administration is not of such a character as to permit of its being brought under the control of the courts by the use of such ordinary judicial institutions and by the application to the administration of the ordinary rules of private or criminal law. In these cases it becomes necessary, in order that the judicial control shall have any value, that there be formed a special jurisdiction of some sort.

II.—*Administrative jurisdiction.*

It has been shown that it is impossible in all instances to resort to the method of putting the rules of administrative law into the form of absolute unconditional commands, that in many cases it is absolutely necessary to have recourse to conditional relative commands,[1] commands in which the legislature simply lays down the general conditions of administrative action, in which the legislature leaves to the administration the expression of the will of the state in the minor

[1] *Supra*, II., p. 109.

details, and allows it in its discretion to ascertain the existence of the conditions necessary for its action in the execution of them. Where the administration has, in order to execute these rules of administrative law, to apply to the courts (*i. e.* where the method of administrative execution has not been provided) no special judicial control is in many cases necessary though it may often be provided. For the courts, as in the case of the imposition of penalties for the violation of the absolute unconditional commands, may, when the administration applies to them for the power to put its orders into execution, refuse to grant it the power on the ground that the case before it is not one of the cases provided for in the law ; and in this way exercise a sufficient control over it. But for all cases where administrative execution is provided or where the action of the administration is not reviewable collaterally by the courts, which is usually the rule,[1] some method must be devised which will ensure that the administration shall act only in the cases and only in the way in which the law has said that it shall act. The special judicial control thus formed may be called and in most states is called an administrative jurisdiction because it is a special jurisdiction of judicial bodies over the acts of the administration.

III.—Kinds of judicial control.

The judicial control thus proves, on analysis, to be of a threefold character. In the first place it is exercised by the civil courts, first, in the power which is almost everywhere given to them to entertain suits of

---

[1] Cooley, *Taxation*, 2d Ed., 260, and cases cited.

a private legal character against or by the government or some of the public corporations within the government; and, second, in the power which in nearly all countries is given to the courts to entertain suits against officers of the administration for the damages which they may have caused by their illegal acts or the negligent performance of their duties.

In the second place the judicial control is exercised by the criminal courts, first, in the power which they have to pass upon the validity of the acts of the administration when an individual is prosecuted before them for the violation of these acts or of the law which the administration seeks to enforce; and, second, in the power which they have to punish officials for the commission of ordinary crimes or for the criminal violation of their official duties.

In the third place either there have been formed special courts, or there has been given to the ordinary courts a special jurisdiction, to hear appeals directly against the acts of the administration, *i. e.* an administrative jurisdiction. As a result of the possession of the administrative jurisdiction these courts may often annul or amend the acts of the administration which are complained of.

All systems of administration make use of these different methods of judicial control but the combinations of the different elements of which the judicial control consists, will be found different in the different countries. It will now be our purpose to ascertain what exactly is the combination, and the reasons therefor, that has been made in each of the countries whose law is being examined.

CHAPTER II.

CONTROL OF THE CIVIL COURTS.

I.—Suits by or against the government.

The power of the courts to entertain suits in contract or tort, to which the government or one of its local corporations is a party, depends upon the extent to which the government in its central or local organization is recognized as possessing corporate rights and as subject to corporate liabilities, upon how far the government is to be treated as a juristic person. As a general rule of law it may be said that the government is a juristic person so far as its power to sue is concerned,[1] but it is not fully settled in all countries that it is to be treated as a juristic person in the case that the wrong or breach of contract is committed by its officers.[2] The idea that the government cannot be sued in the ordinary courts seems to have arisen from the application of the principles of the Roman law,[3] and the adoption of the monarchical principle that the "sovereign can do no wrong." While this rule seems

---

[1] *Cf.* Dillon, *Municipal Corporations*, 4th Ed., I., 55 ; see also United States v. Maurice, 2 Brockenbrough U. S., 96, 100, 101, Opinion by Marshall, C. J. ; U. S. v. Tingey, 5 Peters, 115 ; U. S. v. Bradley, 10 Peters, 343; Dugan v. U. S., 3 Wheaton, 172.

[2] Dillon, *op. cit.*, I., 55.

[3] *Cf.* Mommsen, *Römisches Staatsrecht*, 2d Ed., I., 170, 679 ; II.. 712.

to have been at one time quite universally adopted in European states, on the continent, on account probably of the complete conception of a public corporation, it received later such modifications as to put the government in almost the same position as an ordinary corporation, it being called *fiscus*, being made a subject of private law and entering into almost all private legal relations.[1] Further in order to facilitate the action of the government as a subject of private law, in all countries, both in those following the old rule that the sovereign can do no wrong and therefore may not be sued in the courts and in those which follow the later continental rule by which the government is regarded as *fiscus* and as entering into private legal relations, many of the local organizations of the government are incorporated, are able to sue and are liable to be sued in the civil courts. On account of these facts it is necessary to consider the control of the courts over the administration in this matter of suits by or against it, from the standpoint of the individual and from that of the government, and also from the standpoint of the central government and from that of the local governmental corporations.

1. *Suits by the government against individuals.*—As far as the local corporations are concerned it may be said that they occupy as plaintiffs in a suit against individuals just about the same position that individuals occupy. In all private law suits they are in the same position as mere private corporations. Of course in many instances there are certain formalities which must be complied with by certain of these municipal corporations before they can bring the suit, and some-

[1] See Sarwey, *Das Oeffentliche Recht,* 398.

times before they can defend a suit, as *e. g.* in France where the consent of the council of the prefecture is necessary; but such limitations form rather a part of the formalities of administrative action and procedure than a part of the control of the courts over the administration. When, however, we come to the central government we find that its position as representative of the sovereign does have quite an appreciable effect in several instances on its position as plaintiff in the courts. In some cases, as has been indicated, its position as representative of the sovereign is carried so far as to permit it to enforce claims, which are liquidated in amount, against individuals without recourse to the courts at all and by means of administrative execution.[1] In such cases the only control that the courts can have over the private legal relations of the government is to be found in the possibility, which is often present, to exercise their administrative jurisdiction at the instance of some individual against the enforcement of administrative execution. And even where administrative execution has not been adopted for the enforcement of government claims, where the government has to proceed in the enforcement of its claims very much as any ordinary suitor, it often has certain privileges which are not possessed by the ordinary suitor, as *e. g.* in England by the Crown suits act, or it occupies the position of a preferred creditor, its claims taking precedence of all other claims. In case the government sues it is generally admitted that the courts, even in those countries which do not permit suit to be brought against the government directly, will make allowances in their judgment for any counter-claim or set-off proved by the indi-

[1] See Murray's Lessee v. Hoboken, *etc.*, Co., 18 How., U. S., **272**.

vidual who is defendant to the suit.[1] Use may not,
however, be made of this power to give judgment
against the government.[2]

2. *Suits against local corporations.*—As a result of
the desire to facilitate the conduct of the private legal
relations of the government many of the important
localities, into which the state is divided, are regarded
as juristic persons, and individuals may in all cases
bring suits against them in contract and often in tort.
There is, however, in the United States a distinction
made between what are known as *quasi* corporations
and full municipal corporations,[3] in accordance with
which suits in torts, except when permitted by express
statute, may not be brought against the former, inasmuch as they are agents of the central government, as
such are in the eyes of the law incapable of committing a wrong, and therefore share in the immunity
possessed by the sovereign whom they are regarded as
representing.[4] Suits in tort may, however, be brought
against the full municipal corporations since they are
formed for the peculiar advantage of the inhabitants
of the corporation and therefore may, like private
corporations, be made, in the domain of private legal
relations, subject to the rule of private law that the
superior is responsible for the acts of his agents.[5] But
it must be noticed that even full municipal corporations
are not generally responsible for damages resulting
from the execution of what are called governmental

[1] U. S. v. Macdaniel, 7 Peters, 16 ; *cf.* U. S. v. Ringgold, 8 Peters, 150, 163.

[2] U. S. v. De Groot, 5 Wall., 419 ; U. S. v. Eckford, 6 Wall., 484.

[3] See *supra*, I., p. 202.

[4] Morey v. Town of Newfane, 8 Barb., 645, 648 ; *cf.* Hill v. Boston, 122
Mass., 344. See *supra*, I., p. 173.

[5] Dillon, *Municipal Corporations*, 4th Ed., I., 45 ; Bailey v. Mayor, *etc.*,
3 Hill, N. Y., 531.

powers in contradistinction to their private powers.[1] Further, while the local corporations may thus be sued and judgment obtained against them in the usual way, it is to be noticed that such judgment is not commonly collectible in the usual way, *i. e.* by sale on execution of the property of such corporations. For such a method would interfere too much with the carrying on of the governmental powers which are generally conferred on these corporations. The usual means of enforcing a judgment against one of these local corporations is to apply to the proper authority, in case the administrative control has been adopted, then to the supervisory administrative authority, in case this is not the method, then to the courts for the exercise of their administrative jurisdiction, to force the proper local authority to insert the necessary appropriation in its budget and to provide by tax or otherwise for the payment of the judgment. The former method is the one usually adopted in France,[2] the latter is the method in the United States.[3] In Germany, however, in some places the law permits execution to issue in somewhat the usual way, the reason being probably that the localities possess as juristic persons a large amount of property which is of a purely fiscal character and is not made use of for the various administrative services carried on by the local corporations.[4] Such is the case also in some of the commonwealths of the United States.[5]

---

[1] *Ibid. ;* see also Cooley on *Taxation*, 2d Ed., 816.

[2] Boeuf, *op. cit.*, 229, citing Avis du Conseil d'État of the 12th of August, 1807.

[3] *E. g.* see N. Y. Rev. Stats. Part III., Chap. VIII., Title IV., art. fourth, secs. 102–4 ; *cf.* Dillon, *op. cit.*, II., 1028 ; Alden v. Alameda Co., 43 Cal., 270.

[4] Sarwey, *Das Oeffentliche Recht*, 300

[5] Dillon, *op. cit.*, I., 673.

3. *Suits against the central government.*—While the
rule in regard to suits against the local corporations is,
on account of the possession by the localities of juristic
personality, much the same everywhere, *viz.*, that they
may be sued in private law matters at the instance of
the individual and that suits are brought in the ordinary courts, when we come to the matter of suing the
central government we find much less similarity.   We
find that there is an English rule and a continental rule.

a. *The English rule.*—The English law, basing itself upon the principle that the sovereign can do no
wrong, and believing that when the government enters
into private legal relations the sovereign acts through
it, denies in principle to the individual the right to sue
the central government, except with its consent or in
the special way which the government may have indicated.[1]   This rule which formed a part of the common
law was introduced into this country after the formation of an independent government here,[2] although from
the beginning the sovereign has here been separated
from the government, and therefore when the government was acting it was not the case that the sovereign
was also acting.   In England, to prevent this privilege
of the government from resulting in gross injustice, the
individual was from time immemorial allowed respect-
fully to petition the Crown, which was historically
the sovereign, that right be done him.   Such a petition
was called the petition of right.[3]   It is now provided [4] that the petition of right shall be left with the

[1] Gneist, *Das Englische Verwaltungsrecht*, 1884, 375.

[2] Dillon, *op. cit.*, I., 55.

[3] It may be traced back as far as 14 Edw. III., c. 14, and perhaps even as
far as *Magna Charta.*

[4] 23 and 24 Vict., c. 34.

home secretary. It is then submitted to the Crown, which acts on the advice of the attorney-general. If he thinks that the statement of facts contained in it is sufficient to give a ground of action, he advises the Crown that it be granted and is responsible to Parliament for the advice which he gives. In case he advises that the petition be granted he writes on it the words *soit droit fait* and the petition is then heard and decided by the royal courts. By this method it will be noticed that the administration has the power to refuse the individual the right to sue the central government in the courts but must assume to Parliament the responsibility for such refusal, which fact may check arbitrary and inconsiderate action. The weak judicial control is thus in this instance reinforced by the parliamentary control. Several cases have delimited the scope of the petition of right. Among them may be mentioned that of the *Viscount Canterbury v. Attorney General*,[1] which holds that the government may not through the petition of right be made responsible for the tortious acts of its agents.[2] But it is believed that where an officer is mulcted in damages for carrying out the orders of his superior, the government is morally bound to indemnify him and is thus, morally at least, responsible for the torts which it itself commits.[3] Such a moral obligation is sometimes made a legal one in the cases of unjust enrichment by officers, as in the case of the payment by the importer on the demand of the collector of customs of more than the legal duties. Here suit may be brought by the indi-

---

[1] 1 Phillimore, 306.

[2] The same rule is adopted in Tobin v. The Queen, 16 C. B. N. S., 310.

[3] Todd, *Parliamentary Government*, 2d Ed., I., 496.

vidual against the collector, and the government is by law obliged to reimburse the collector.[1]

b. *The rule in the United States.*—In this country the method of the petition of right to the executive was felt to be inapplicable inasmuch as the executive was not historically the sovereign. The practice was for the individual to petition the legislature, which in the commonwealths had the residuary governmental power, and in all cases the power over the public purse.[2] If the petition was regarded as well founded a special appropriation bill was passed which was mandatory upon the treasury.[3] In the national government this practice has undergone considerable modification. Congress saw that it was beyond its power to make a thorough investigation of all the claims which were brought before it, that this method of settling claims practically devolved upon it a vast amount of work which was really judicial in character and for the performance of which it was unfitted. Therefore in 1855 an act was passed[4] providing a court for the investigation of claims against the United States government, based upon a law or contract. At first its decisions had no legal effect whatever, since they were drawn up in the form of a bill which was afterwards to be laid before Congress for its approval. The act was then amended so as to make the court of claims a real court whose judgments were of themselves mandatory upon the secretary of the treasury and binding upon the individual suitor and were to be paid from

[1] 39 and 40 Vict., c. 35.

[2] *Cf.* O'Hara v. State, 112 N. Y., 146 ; People v. Stephens, 71 N. Y., 527, 540, 548.

[3] Kendall v. United States, 12 Peters, 524.

[4] 10 Stats. at Large, 612.

any general appropriation for the payment of private claims. Appeal might be taken from them to the United States Supreme Court.[1] This court of claims has not, however, the same powers as an ordinary United States court. Thus it has, as a general rule, no equity jurisdiction.[2] It has also no jurisdiction over torts committed by the government,[3] although, in order to render justice, it will stretch its jurisdiction by means of the *quasi* or implied contract doctrines so as to embrace matters which bear a strong resemblance to tortious acts.[4] The jurisdiction of the court of claims is thus mainly one of suits in contract. In such suits the court may in its decision take account of any set-offs or counter-claims which the government may have against the individual bringing suit, so that the decision may result in a judgment against, instead of in favor of, the individual suing. The law organizing the court of claims also provides that the court may act as an advisory body to Congress or to the executive departments of the government in the settling of other kinds of claims.

Cases before the court of claims are conducted generally in accordance with the ordinary rules of law governing the matter of contracts between private individuals, though the procedure is somewhat different from that had before the ordinary United States courts, and though the government occupies a privi-

---

[1] 12 Stats. at Large, 865.

[2] Bonner v. U. S., 9 Wallace, 156 ; U. S. v. Jones, 131 U. S., 1.

[3] Gibbons v. U. S., 8 Wallace, 269 ; Morgan v. U. S., 14 Wallace, 31 ; Langford v. U. S., 101 U. S., 341.

[4] See 4 Ct. of Cl., 248 ; 14 *Ibid.*, 396 ; see also U. S. v. Great Falls Mfg. Co., 112 U. S., 645, where it was held that if the government took land to which it asserted no title there was an implied contract to pay for it. So also in a case of a patented invention, U. S. v. Palmer, 128 U. S., 262.

leged position. Thus the government always has the right to appeal, the individual only in specified cases. Where an excessive claim is fraudulently and wilfully made the whole claim is lost. This is true also in case false evidence is adduced. The judges also decide questions both of law and of fact; there is no jury. The procedure in the court of claims is largely in writing, for the ease of the suitors in the court who, were they obliged to appear in person, might be obliged to come or send counsel a great distance, since the court sits only at Washington.[1] The work of the court of claims has been so satisfactory and the permission to the individual to sue the government has resulted in so little inconvenience to the government that a late act of Congress has provided that individuals having claims against the government, based on a law or contract and under a certain amount, may bring suit against it in the district or circuit courts of the United States, which is then tried without a jury.[2] Finally there are one or two special courts for special classes of claims; *e. g.* court for French spoliation claims and court for private land claims.[3]

It will be noticed that by a gradual development of about thirty years we in the United States have departed from the rule that the individual cannot sue the national government, and have now practically adopted the rule in force in continental Europe. The government is conceived of as a juristic person, which may enter into private legal relations of a contractual character,

---

[1] For the procedure and the general rules governing the court see an article in the *Southern Law Review*, written by one of the justices of the court (Judge Richardson) and reprinted in vol. xvii. of the reports of the court of claims.

[2] 24 Stats. at Large, 505, 1887.

[3] L., June 20, 1888, March 3, 1890.

and is then liable to be sued in the ordinary courts. We have made this change through the medium of an advisory body to Congress, which was changed into a special court for the trial of claims against the government. But while we have thus adopted the continental rule that the government may be sued before the ordinary courts in contract we have not as yet adopted the rule that the government is ever responsible to the individual for torts committed by its officers.[1] By a special statute the government is made responsible for the judgments obtained by individual taxpayers where they have paid on the demand of the collectors of internal revenue more than the taxes required by law. Here the individual may sue the collector and the government is bound to pay the judgment.[2] This is, however, on the theory of unjust enrichment rather than tort.

In the commonwealths of the United States this development has not generally taken place. The old practice seems to obtain. The individual desiring to enforce a claim against the government must appeal to the legislature and get a special appropriation bill passed. Here as in the case of the national government the commonwealth is not responsible for the torts of its officers.[3] In some of the commonwealths, however, the first step in the development noticed in the United States government has taken place. In thirteen of the commonwealths the constitution provides that the legislature shall provide a method by which suits may be brought against the government.

[1] Gibbons v. U. S., 8 Wallace, 269 ; Langford v. U. S., 101 U. S., 341.
[2] U. S. R. S., sec. 3220.
[3] Clodfelter v. State, 86 N. C., 51 ; Lewis v. State, 96 N. Y., 71.

In five, however, this is forbidden by the constitution.[1] In others, while the constitution is silent on this point, the legislature has provided a method of suing the government. Thus in New York the legislature has provided an advisory body for the purpose of investigating claims against the government, from which appeal may be taken to the highest judicial court and which is to report its decisions to the legislature for action.[2] In other commonwealths the legislature has permitted the individual to sue the government in the ordinary courts.[3] In the commonwealths, however, the same need of the power of suing the government is not felt as in the national government. For the commonwealth system of administration is so decentralized that it may safely be said that most of the contracts made by the administration are made by some one of the local corporations which possess so many of the powers of government. Thus, notwithstanding the rule that suits may not be brought against the central government of the commonwealth, which may be subject to no exceptions, most of the contractual acts of the administration are subject to judicial control in that they may be made the subject of suits in the courts through the power of the courts to entertain suits against the local corporations.

Finally it is to be noticed that, while the government is not responsible for the tortious acts of its officers in the domain of either public or private law except in the case of the local corporations, still it seems to be recognized that it is not only in its local

---

[1] Stimson, *op. cit.*, sec. 75.

[2] N. Y. L. 1883, c. 205 ; *cf.* Dillon, *op. cit.*, I., 55, and cases cited.

[3] See Clodfelter v. State, 86 N. C., 51.

corporate organizations, including municipal corporations, but also in its central organization permitted to indemnify its officers for liability which they may incur in the *bona fide* discharge of their duties, and may raise money for that purpose.[1]

c. *The continental rule.*—On the continent the rule is that the government is liable to be sued by an individual in contract and also in tort, where the tortious act is not committed in the performance of functions of a distinctly public legal character and where the fault of the officer causing it is not purely personal to himself but consists rather in bad service, in an order badly given, not understood, or imprudently or carelessly executed.[2] Thus the government would not be held responsible for damages caused by its agents in the collection of taxes while it would be if a ship were injured by the negligence of the officers of one of its men-of-war.[3] An example of the purely personal act of one of its agents for which the government would not be responsible would be found in the case of theft by him. While the general rule as to the responsibility of the government for its contracts and torts is the same in France and Germany, the courts before which such suits should be brought are different. In France while the common law rule in the absence of statute would appear to be that the ordinary civil courts have jurisdiction, so many special statutes have, as a matter of fact, been passed giving the jurisdiction to the administrative courts that it is laid down as the

---

[1] Mechem, *op. cit.*, sec. 879 ; *cf.* Tracy v. Swartout, 10 Peters, 80.

[2] Ducrocq, *Droit Administratif*, secs. 1055 *et seq. ;* Laferrière, *La Juridiction Administrative*, II., 149 *et seq. ;* Von Rönne, *Das Staatsrecht der Preussischen Monarchie*, III., 583, 584 ; Bornhak, *Preussisches Staatsrecht*, II., 47.

[3] *Cf.* Ducrocq, *op. cit.*, II., 230, citing a decision of the Council of State.

rule that the administrative courts are alone competent to declare the government a debtor.[1] In Germany, however, it is the ordinary courts which have jurisdiction of actions both in contract and tort against the government.[2] The German rule as to the court which has jurisdiction of these cases against the government seems to be by far the more logical, since the whole responsibility of the government is based upon the theory of its juristic personality, and of its capacity to enter into private legal relations of all sorts and the consequent possibility of its being held responsible before those courts which have in their hands the application of the private law. The reason for the adoption of the French rule is largely historical and is to be found in the great desire at the time of the revolution to free the administration from the control of the ordinary courts, which had shown themselves too anxious to protect vested rights and hamper the administration in the carrying on of the necessary reforms.[3] In both France and Germany the general rules as to the responsibility of the government before the courts which have been mentioned are sometimes modified by special statutes. Thus in France the responsibility of the government for damages resulting from the carelessness of the agents of the postal and telegraph services is very much limited and the action is to be brought before the ordinary courts.[4] In Prussia the government is made responsible for the negligence of its registrars of deeds and mortgages, notwithstanding the fact that the registration of land titles

[1] Ducrocq, *loc. cit.*
[2] Von Rönne, *loc. cit.* ; Bornhak, *loc. cit.*
[3] *Infra*, II., p. 218.
[4] L., Jan. 25, 1873, art. 4.

is evidently a public legal rather than a corporate or private legal act.[1]

II.—Suits for damages against officers.

1. *The English rule.*—According to the original German law all officers of the government were subject to the law of the land in the same way as ordinary individuals, and were liable to be held responsible by the courts for their actions committed without authority of law, whenever such actions caused damage to individuals.[2] This principle seems to have been retained in England, its retention being undoubtedly aided by the character of the administrative system which was early adopted there. The English system of administration was of that kind which has been denominated the self-government system, *i. e.* a system in which the officers were absolutely non-professional in character. While in theory and on account of the early Norman centralization these officers were the officers of the Crown, still in later times they were not actually in close enough connection with the Crown nor in sufficient subordination to it to be invested with any of the attributes of irresponsibility which the law assigned to the Crown. On the contrary they were regarded simply as ordinary citizens, who for the time being were serving the government by the discharge of public functions and who after their time of service had expired would fall back again into the ranks of private citizens. The same rules were applied to them which were applied to ordinary citizens. They were not exempted in any way from the observance of the law on account of their official position. If during the period of their discharge

---

[1] L., May 5, 1872, sec. 29.   [2] Loening, *op. cit.*, 771–784.

of public functions they committed an act not justified by the law such act was regarded as *coram non judice, i. e.* as an act of a purely private and personal character for which, like any citizen, they could be held responsible before the ordinary courts.[1] The important question to be decided by the courts whenever the act of an officer came up before them was therefore the question of jurisdiction. Did the law give the officer the power to act as he had acted in the particular case or not ?

It will at once be seen what an enormous power the courts had and have through the adoption of this principle over the acts of the administration. Any act of any officer may give rise to a complaint which the courts have to decide. In deciding these complaints the courts delimit the sphere of administrative competence in all its details in that they settle what is the jurisdiction of all officers of the government. What the actual extent of this control shall be, depends, however, upon the attitude of the courts. They may pass upon every act of every officer or they may limit their power by their decisions in the interest of an efficient administration, may leave something to administrative discretion which they will not attempt to control. This has been the tendency of their decisions both in England and the United States. In both countries they have in the first place made it practically impossible to sue in damages the most important officers of state, *i. e.* the heads of executive departments in both countries and in the United States, also the President and the governors. Mr. Todd says[2]:

---

[1] Mechem, *op. cit.*, 400 *et seq.*

[2] *Parliamentary Government, etc.*, 2d Ed., I., 494, 495.

It may be stated as a general principle, that in assuming on behalf of the Crown a personal responsibility for all acts of the government, ministers are privileged to share, with the Crown, in a personal immunity from vexatious proceedings by ordinary process of law, for alleged acts of oppression, or illegality in the discharge of their official acts. . . . Whether the alleged liability arises out of contract or out of tort, or from any matter of private individual complaint against a minister of the Crown, for acts done in his official capacity, the ordinary tribunals of justice will afford him special immunity and protection.

This does not mean that in no possible case can a suit be brought against a minister, but only that the courts are very careful not to extend their control so as to hamper the administration of public business by the ministers. In the United States the rule is practically the same. Up to 1870 there was only one action brought against the head of a United States executive department,[1] and since that time I know of no other case.[2] This case, which is our only precedent, was the case of *Stokes v. Kendall*[3] and was decided adversely to the plaintiff. It is extremely interesting as showing distinctly the attitude of the courts towards this class of cases. It was preceded by the case of *Kendall v. The United States*,[4] in which the same plaintiff as in the case of *Stokes v. Kendall*, had endeavored to obtain a *mandamus* against the postmaster-general. The Supreme Court there decided that a given act was not discretionary but ministerial in character, and therefore that a *mandamus* might issue; and seven years later, when the same plaintiff brought a suit for damages against the postmaster-general, the same Supreme Court held that this same act, which it had declared in the

---

[1] See 6 Court of Claims Reports, 177, 180.
[2] *Cf.* Mechem, *op. cit.*, sec. 608.
[3] 3 How., 87.
[4] 12 Peters, 524.

other case to be ministerial, was, when a suit for damages resulting from it was brought, a discretionary act and therefore that the postmaster-general could not be held liable for damages. The immunity thus granted to the highest officers of state does not really diminish the control possessed by the courts over the administration so much as at first sight it might seem. For these high officers must come into relations with individuals generally through the medium of their subordinates, and according to the English and American system such subordinates are generally responsible for their actions and are not protected by the fact that they have acted according to instructions from their superiors.[1]

A second limitation which the courts have placed upon their control over the action of the administration, through their power to delimit its sphere of competence, is to be found in the rule, that purely ministerial officers will not be held responsible for damages where they have followed instructions which are legal on their face and contain nothing which will apprise the subordinate that they have been issued illegally, and are not within the jurisdiction of the superior who issued them.[2] The weight of authority seems to be further in favor of the rule that a ministerial officer is relieved from all responsibility for the execution of orders fair on their face, even if he is satisfied that there are illegalities lying back of them.[3] The English law has gone further than the law of the United

---

[1] Tracy v. Swartout, 10 Peters, 80.

[2] Savacool v. Boughton, 5 Wendell, N. Y., 170 ; Erskine v. Hohnbach, 14 Wallace, 613, 616 ; Cooley on *Taxation*, 2d Ed., 797, and cases cited.

[3] *Ibid.*, 798, citing Webber v. Gay, 24 Wendell, 485 ; Wilmarth v. Burt, 7 Metcalf, 257 ; Watson v. Watson, 9 Conn., 140 ; Wall v. Trumbull, 16 Mich., 228 ; Cunningham v. Mitchell, 67 Pa. St. ; see also Underwood v. Robinson, 106 Mass., 296.

States and has offered to officers, who are not ministerial in character, quite a large immunity from suits
at the hands of individuals by making their defence
very much easier.[1]

The responsibility of officers for damages before the
courts is in neither the English nor the American law
confined to the cases in which they have acted out of
their jurisdiction. In many cases officers may be held
responsible for damages arising from the non-perform-
ance or negligent performance of duties within their
jurisdiction, or from bad faith. Here the courts have
been guided in their formulation of the rules of their
control over officers, by the character both of the officer and of the duties which he has to perform and
which the court undertakes to control. Officers are
for this purpose divided by the courts into judicial,
legislative, and executive officers. In addition to these
three classes of officers there is a fourth class of officers
whose development has taken place during this century and whose duties partake of the characteristics of
those of the three other classes of officers. These officers are called administrative officers. Such are the
American supervisor and county commissioner and the
English county councillor. Of these various classes of
officers it may be said, in the first place, that purely judicial officers, *i. e.* officers that hold courts and decide
cases of criminal and private law, and legislative officers will not be held civilly responsible for damages, no
matter how gross their negligence may be, nor what
may be the character of the act giving rise to the

---

[1] See 43 Geo., II. c. 44, sec. 6, cited in Gneist, *Das Englische Verwaltungsrecht*, 1884, 378. This provides that the justices of the peace and their subordinates shall be responsible only for nominal damages except when they have
acted out of malice and without reasonable cause.

damages, provided it is within their jurisdiction.[1] The only possible exceptions to this rule are to be found in the case of the ministerial acts of *quasi*-judicial and *quasi*-legislative officers, when such officers act *quoad hoc* as administrative officers.[2] The responsibility of executive and administrative officers depends, however, largely on the character of the act which has caused the damage. If the duty, in the performance of which the act causing the damage was done, is discretionary in character, the general rule is that executive and administrative officers may not be made responsible since the courts do not like to interfere with the discretion of the administration. When, however, the duty is purely ministerial such officers may be held responsible by the courts for their negligence or mal-performance of such duty. As one judge says[3]:

The civil remedy for misconduct in office . . . depends exclusively upon the nature of the duty which has been violated. Where that is absolute, certain, and imperative, and every ministerial duty is so, the delinquent officer is bound to make full redress to every person who has suffered by such delinquency. Duties which are purely ministerial in their nature are sometimes cast upon officers whose chief functions are judicial. Where this occurs the officer, for most purposes a judge, is still civilly responsible for such misconduct. But where the duty alleged to have been violated is purely judicial a different rule prevails; for no action lies in any case for misconduct or delinquency, however gross, in the performance of judicial duties. And although the officer may not in strictness be a judge, still if his powers are discretionary to be exercised or withheld according to his own view of what is proper, they are judicial and he is exempt from all responsibility by action for the motives which influence him and the manner in which such duties are performed.

---

[1] Mechem, *op. cit.*, secs. 619, 644, with cases cited.
[2] *Ibid.*, secs. 635, 643, 647, and cases cited.
[3] See Wilson v. The Mayor, 1 Denio, N. Y., 595, 599.

There is, however, in the United States a tendency in the decisions to relax the strictness of this rule in the case of administrative officers, officers who, while not holding regular courts, exercise what are called *quasi*-judicial functions, so as to hold them responsible for bad faith and dishonest purposes notwithstanding the fact of the *quasi*-judicial and discretionary character of the duties which they perform.[1]

In respect to such cases, [says Judge Cooley] though they seem to be out of harmony with the general rule. . . . and the reasons on which it rests, yet we may perhaps safely concede that there are various duties lying along the borders between those of a ministerial and those of a judicial nature which are usually entrusted to inferior officers and in the performance of which it is highly important that they be kept as closely as possible within strict rules. If courts lean against recognizing in them full discretionary powers and hold them strictly within the limits of good faith it is probably a leaning that in most cases will be found to harmonize with public policy.[2]

2. *The Roman rule.*—While the English law, basing itself on the old German principle of the responsibility of all persons to the courts for the damages they committed unlawfully, gave the courts power to mulct officers in damages where their acts had been contrary to the law and in excess of their jurisdiction; the Roman law, starting out from the point of view of the government rather than from that of the individual, provided, in the interest of governmental efficiency, that the officers of the government could, during their term of office, be brought to account and made responsible for damages only with the consent of their

---

[1] Cooley on *Torts,* 411.
[2] *Ibid.*, 413 ; see also Pike v. Megoun, 44 Mo., 491.

superior officer.[1] The German principle of the responsibility of officers was at first adopted on the continent.[2] Soon, however, with the introduction of the Roman law, came the Roman principle of official irresponsibility.[3] In the Holy Roman Empire the powers of the imperial courts diminished so much as a result of the decay of the empire that it was impossible to enforce the responsibility of the various territorial lords, to the most important of whom a legal exemption from responsibility to the imperial courts was given by the grant of the *privilegium de non appellando.* The result was that at the time of the Reformation the monarchs and princes on the continent with all their agents were uncontrolled by the courts, which no longer had the power to hold them responsible for the damages which they might illegally inflict upon individuals.

The reason of the adoption among German peoples of this rule of law which seems so regardless of private rights is to be found in the needs of the administration at the time that it was adopted. The struggle with feudalism was at its height and it was the private rights of the feudal lords, or what they chose to consider as their private rights, which were most liable to violation on the part of the princes of the continent. Now the imperial courts in Germany and the royal courts in France were held by judges who were independent in tenure over against the Emperor, any given prince, or the King—in Germany because the judges were chosen by the estates, in France because the judgeships in the ordinary courts were bought and

[1] Mommsen, *Römisches Staatsrecht*, 2d Ed., I., 170, 629 ; II., 712.

[2] Loening, *Deutsches Verwaltungsrecht*, 771.

[3] *Ibid.* Parey, ; *Verwaltungsrecht*, I., 4, citing De Tocqueville, *L'Ancien Régime et la Révolution*, chap. 4.

sold and treated as private property. The retention of the principle of the responsibility of the royal and princely officers to the ordinary courts would therefore have effectually prevented the kings and princes from destroying the feudal system with all its abuses and pretended vested rights and would have made impossible the development of the national state upon the continent. In England the condition of things was quite different. There the officers of the royal courts were the paid servants of the King and subject to his disciplinary power.[1] They did not possess a tenure independent of the Crown till 1701, when the act of settlement provided that they should be removed only on the address of both houses of Parliament. The desire of the absolute monarchy to reduce the nobility to submission and to do away with feudalism was thus the cause of the adoption on the continent of the Roman principle that the officers of the government might be sued by the individual only after the consent of their superior had been obtained. In France this consent was to be given by the Council of the King which, before granting such consent, determined the question of jurisdiction, *i. e.* whether the officer had acted contrary to the law ; and the suits had to be brought before special courts over whose organization the King had full power.[2]

The effect of the French revolution on the position of governmental officers was at first simply to increase their irresponsibility. Since the time of the revolution the position of officers in France has undergone a somewhat different development from that of officers in

---

[1] *Infra*, II., p. 193.
[2] See Laferrière, *La Juridiction Administrative*, I., 584, note 1.

Germany, though Germany has been influenced by what has been done in France. It will be necessary therefore to treat these countries separately.

a. *The modification of the Roman rule in France.*— The desire of the leaders of the revolution to carry on the reform work of the monarchy was so great[1] and their distrust of the courts on account of their attempts to protect the privileged classes in the latter days of the monarchy was so widespread[2] that little desire was felt of subjecting the administration, which was to carry on the reforms of the new era that had just dawned, to the control of the courts. Accordingly we find incorporated into article 75 of the constitution of the 22d of *frimaire an* VIII (1800), from which year date almost all of the permanent administrative results of the revolution, the principle which had come down to the absolute monarchy from the Roman law, *viz.*, that no individual could bring suit in the courts against an administrative officer until the Council of State, an administrative council, had decided that the officer had acted outside of his jurisdiction, and had given its consent to the bringing of the suit. In case such consent was given the suit was to be brought in the ordinary courts. But after the reforms of the revolutionary period had been completed this principle had outlasted its usefulness and remained only a menace to private rights. For use of it was made to destroy almost all fear in the minds of the officers of the administration that they would suffer pecuniary loss for violating their duties; and an important sanction for administrative integrity was lost. Article 75 was deemed by some of the best French public lawyers to

[1] See *supra*, I., p. 270.　　　　[2] See *infra*, II., p. 218.

be unnecessary for the maintenance of the principle of the separation of powers and of its corollary, the independence of the administration, which are deemed so important by the French law.[1] As a result of the abuse of this principle by the government of the second empire, the French people decided to tear it out of their public law root and branch. Therefore after the overthrow of the government of the empire one of the first acts of the new government of the national defence was to repeal article 75 and all provisions of law depending upon it or of like import.[2] At first it was thought that this gave the ordinary courts the power to entertain suits in damages against officers, not only for purely personal acts, such as negligence, but also for acts done by them in connection with their duties but outside their jurisdiction; that the courts had as a result of the repeal of article 75 the same power as the courts in the United States have to delimit the sphere of administrative competence. But the principles of the separation of powers and the independence of the administration were too firmly imbedded in the French law to permit of their being shaken by the mere repeal of the necessity of obtaining the consent of the Council of State as a prerequisite to the bringing of suits against the officers of the government. And the Tribunal of Conflicts,[3] when called upon to decide what was the effect of the repeal of article 75, held that the competence of the courts was not enlarged by its repeal in such a way as to give them the power to decide upon the legality of an

---

[1] *Cf.* Dareste, *La Justice Administrative en France*, 520 ; Aucoc, *op. cit.*, I., 676.

[2] Decree of Sept. 19, 1870.

[3] As to the nature of this body, see *infra*, II., p. 258.

act of an administrative officer, since such a construction would practically destroy the independence of the administration.[1] That is the ordinary courts are not yet competent to determine the jurisdiction of an administrative officer. They may, however, mulct an officer in damages where he has done an act of a purely personal character clearly out of his jurisdiction, by which an individual has suffered. Of course the courts have in the first instance to pass upon the question of jurisdiction, but if they make any attempt to encroach upon the sphere of the administration, the conflict, as it is called, is raised and the case is removed into the Tribunal of Conflicts, which thus has the power of preventing the ordinary courts from making such use of their power to hold an officer responsible in damages for his purely personal acts, as to decide the question of the legality of administrative acts.[2] The exact powers of the French courts may probably be best explained by a citation of several cases. It has been held that, when an officer has clearly gone out of his way and has slandered another person, even though the slander was committed by the officer while in the discharge of his functions ; or when he has been negligent in the discharge of his duties ; or when he has been guilty of a clear abuse of power, he may be held responsible by the ordinary courts in damages. In accordance with these principles a commissary of police was declared liable for slander who had in open court addressed a former magistrate and said that the court was extremely fortunate in being rid of such a magistrate ; an engineer who made mistakes in his calculations with the result that the con-

---

[1] *Arrêt* 26 *juillet,* 1873, *affaire Pélétier.*   [2] *Infra,* II., p. 259.

struction which he was erecting fell down and injured several persons, was held responsible for the damages which his negligence caused ; an officer who, to protect a building of the state from the nuisance of stray dogs, deliberately enticed a dog to come near it and killed it by giving it poisoned meat was held responsible for the damage he caused. On the other hand a prefect who shut up a factory while acting in accordance with instructions issued by one of the ministers in order to execute a law, could not be held responsible before the ordinary courts even though his act was not legal. The difference between these cases will at once be seen, though it is impossible to state it with the exactness of a mathematical formula.[1]

It will be noticed that the French rule as to the responsibility of officials before the courts for damages caused by their illegal acts is at the same time narrower and broader than the English and American rule. It is narrower in that the ordinary courts are not allowed to decide finally the question of the jurisdiction of the administration which is so important with us; it is broader in that any purely personal act of the officer may be a ground for damages whether it was done in the performance of a discretionary duty or a ministerial duty.

A word must be said as to the position of the ministers. It seems to be the opinion of the best writers that they occupy a more protected position than do other officers. The same rule applies to them as to other officers so far as regards the acts which cannot be considered as purely personal in character. The courts may not delimit the sphere of their competence or determine their

---

[1] Laferrière, *La Juridiction Administrative*, I., 595, *et seq.*

jurisdiction. But, further, the principle of parliamentary responsibility is believed to cover in great measure
their purely personal acts, for which they may be held
responsible by the courts, only with the consent of the
house of the legislature to which has been given by
the constitution the right of impeachment.[1]

b. *Modifications of the Roman rule in Germany.*—
After the breaking up of the empire in 1806 the only
judicial control that could in the nature of things be
exercised over the officers of the government was to be
exercised by the courts of the different states, which
came into being as a result of the dissolution of the
empire. These courts were held by judges who, owing
to the permanent tenure of all the officers of the government, had a practical independence of the administration. The old German rule as to the responsibility
of the officers of the administration to the courts[2] was
felt to be inconsistent with the needs of an administration able to cope with the problems presented in this
century. It was feared that the administration would
be unable to perform its work. Therefore the old
Roman principle was reintroduced into Germany, or at
any rate into Prussia, which may be taken as a type,
and it was provided that no individual might sue an
officer of the administration before the consent of an
administrative body called a competence court had been
given.[3] As in France the responsibility of officers for
damages was not in theory destroyed but the bring-

[1] Laferrière, *La Juridiction Administrative*, I., 610.

[2] This was, it will be remembered, that they were responsible for damages
resulting from every violation of their duties and for negligence in their discharge as well as for the positive overstepping of their jurisdiction. (Gneist,
Das Englische Verwaltungsrecht, 1884, I., 379, note.) This rule resulted in a
wider responsibility than that asserted by the English rule, which relieved officers
from responsibility for negligence in the performance of a discretionary act within
their jurisdiction.   [3] Prussian Law, Feb. 13, 1854.

ing of a suit was simply made more difficult. But, as
in France, the way in which the law was applied did
not give satisfaction ; and when the present empire was
founded the attempt was made to do away with the evils
which experience had shown were connected with the
adoption of such a method of protecting the independence of the administration. The law of Jan. 27, 1877,
which organized the imperial judicial system, provided
that the body whose consent was necessary before the
suit could be brought, should be judicial in character,
i. e., either the highest administrative court, if there
were one in the particular member of the empire, or if
there were none, then the imperial court at Leipsic.
In other words the preliminary question of the jurisdiction of the officer is to be decided by a body judicial
in character and completely independent of the administration. The result of this development is that the
responsibility of German officials to individuals for the
damages they may have committed either through a
violation of the law or through their negligent action
is broader than in any other of the countries whose law
is being considered. The old German principle has,
notwithstanding the temporary adoption of the principles of the Roman law, retained a greater influence in
the land of its birth than in any of the other countries ;
and this method of judicial control over the administration is really the most important means by which the
ordinary courts may force administrative officers to
obey the law and act efficiently and justly.[1] It is, however, to be noticed that on account of the separate decision of the preliminary question of jurisdiction the
exercise of this control of the civil courts is more
difficult than in either England or the United States.

[1] *Cf.* Bornhak, *Preussisches Verwaltungsrecht,* II., 42, *et seq.*

CHAPTER III.

I.—*Power of the police courts.*

The control which the criminal courts may exercise over the administration is exercised in two ways. In the first place these courts may be allowed, and in most systems of administration are allowed, to decide actions brought by the administration against individuals, either for violation of those rules of administrative law which have been put into the form of simple absolute unconditional commands, including the ordinances of the administrative authorities, and whose violation has been by law made punishable criminally, or for unlawful resistance to officers discharging their duties. In all such cases the criminal courts have the right to refuse to punish the person prosecuted, on the ground that the administration has exceeded its powers and has acted without jurisdiction. They thus delimit the sphere of administrative action and competence and force the administration to keep within the bounds set by law. The law of all countries is in theory the same in this respect. But in England and the United States the power of the criminal courts is rather greater than on the continent, on account of the fact that so many of the rules of the administrative law of those countries

have been put into the form of simple absolute unconditional commands.

II.—*Power of the criminal courts to punish officials. Method of prosecution.*

The second way in which the control of the criminal
courts is exercised over the administration is by deciding criminal prosecutions brought not against individuals
but against officials to punish them for the criminal violation of their duties. The extent and efficacy of this
method of control depend, in the first place, on the content of the criminal law, *i. e.* on the extent to which the
violation of official duty is punishable criminally, and, in
the second place, on the method of prosecution.[1] For
while the content of the criminal law may be such as
to provide for a large control over the administration,
if the method of prosecution give the administration a
large discretion as to when the control shall be exercised,—if the courts or individuals have little power of
initiating and carrying on a prosecution against an
officer—the control of the criminal courts may amount
virtually to nothing.

There are two methods of conducting prosecutions,
the one through a private prosecutor, the other through
a public prosecutor. So far as the control of the criminal
courts aims at the protection of private rights the
system of private prosecution will undoubtedly produce
the best results; so far as that control aims at the efficiency of the administration, as it must to a certain
extent in all countries and as it does particularly in the
United States, the system of public prosecution is
capable of greater efficiency, since it is certain that

[1] For the content of the criminal law see *supra*, II., p. 79.

private prosecutors usually initiate prosecutions only in those cases where their private rights have been violated.

1. *Private prosecutor.*—As the English system of criminal procedure was formed with the special purpose of offering protection to private rights, it is only natural that we should find that it has always made provision for a private prosecutor and, indeed, has mainly relied on this method of prosecution. Even the law which within quite recent years has made provision for public prosecutors[1] still permits the private prosecutor also to act. It guarantees no monopoly of the power of prosecution to the administration. In order, however, to ensure the bringing of prosecutions the English law has always regarded the power of prosecution, which was guaranteed by the system to individuals, as a duty which the courts could enforce by binding over the individual complainant to prosecute. The action of the public prosecutor in England is simply subsidiary and is generally made use of for those cases where the incentive to private prosecution is not strong. The usual method of prosecution is complaint of the individual to a committing magistrate who makes a preliminary examination of the prisoner and sends the case up to the grand jury. This body then proceeds by indictment. It is not, however, confined in its action to such cases, but may proceed of its own motion in regard to matters of which it has personal knowledge. Sometimes also it is proper for individuals to make their complaint direct to the grand jury, but in some instances in the United States this has been held to be improper.[2] Public prosecutors are permitted to

---

[1] The Director of Prosecutions Act of 1879, 42 and 43 Vict., c. 22.

[2] Thus *cf.* McCullough v. Commonwealth, 67 Pa. St. 30.

proceed of their own motion by means of criminal information. This power is, however, made use of against officers only in case they have acted from corrupt motives, or have been guilty of manifest acts of oppression and wilful abuse of power. This power is usually exercised by the officers of the Crown such as the attorney general or the solicitor general, and not so much by the directors of public prosecutions, whose main duty is to conduct the prosecutions after they have once been initiated.[1] The further power is given to the public prosecutors to quash a prosecution by entering a *nolle prosequi*. This power does not, however, put the control of prosecutions into the hands of public prosecutors. For they act under the control of Parliament and public opinion ; and the entering of a *nolle prosequi* is no bar to another indictment.[2]

2. *The United States district attorney.*—The basis of the American system of prosecution is the same. It has, however, received important modifications owing to the very general introduction of public prosecutors, *i. e.* the district attornies or similar officers, who are to be found in nearly all the commonwealths as well as in the national administration. As the establishment of this office was due very largely to the desire to prevent inconsiderate prosecutions, great discretion is given by the decisions of the courts to the district attornies in the initiation of prosecutions, although a monopoly of such power is not given to them. That is, the individual is still permitted to make his complaint before a committing magistrate, when the grand

---

[1] See Gneist, *Das Englische Verwaltungsrecht*, 1884, 383.
[2] *Cf.* U. S. v. Shoemaker, 2 McLean, 114.

jury will act in very much the same way as in the old English method. Some of the cases, however, would seem to indicate that the individual has no longer the right to go before the grand jury and make his complaint directly to them.[1] This power has been replaced by the power given to the public prosecutor to present cases himself to the grand jury. As in all cases the management of the case before the grand jury is largely in the hands of the public prosecutor, the result is that for the punishment of almost all crimes which the officers of the administration may commit, the action of the public prosecutor has become a practical necessity.[2] This is particularly true because of the fact that the conduct of the prosecution, after it has once been initiated, is largely, indeed almost entirely, in the hands of the public prosecutor. Some of the cases on this point go so far as to intimate that the participation of other counsel than the public prosecutor in a prosecution for crime is absolutely forbidden[3]; while others declare that though other counsel, *i. e.* counsel representing some private individual interested, may be admitted, their admission is a privilege which may be granted or refused by the district attorney and not a right which the individual may demand by application to the courts.[4] All these cases are decided as a result of the application of the principle that the prisoner is to be protected from malicious prosecution

[1] McCullough v. Commonwealth, 67 Pa. St., 30 ; Fout v. State, 3 Haywood, Tenn., 98 ; Commonwealth v. Simons, 7 Philadelphia, 167.

[2] *Ibid.;* Peacock v. State, 42 Ind., 393 ; Hite v. State, 9 Yerger, Tenn., 198 ; see also Wharton, *Criminal Pleading and Practice,* sec. 354.

[3] See People v. Hurst, 41 Mich., 328.

[4] Commonwealth v. Williams, 9 Cushing, Mass., 582 ; Commonwealth v. Knapp, 10 Pickering, Mass., 477 ; Commonwealth v. King, 8 Gray, Mass., 501.

on the part of the individual, and that, therefore, the public prosecutor has a monopoly either of initiating or of conducting the prosecution.[1] There seems to be no case which directly answers the question whether the courts, in case a district attorney refused without reason to bring a prosecution against an officer of the government, might appoint an attorney to conduct such prosecution. This has, however, been provided in some cases by statute.[2] Thus a statute in Pennsylvania provides that if the district attorney shall neglect or refuse to prosecute in due form of law any criminal charge regularly returned to him or to the court of the proper county or if, in case of the admission of the counsel of a private prosecutor, the district attorney shall differ with him as to the conduct of the proceedings, the court on the petition of the private prosecutor may direct the private counsel of the prosecutor to conduct the entire proceeding. Further it is to be noticed that, as a rule, the public prosecutors have the right to quash a prosecution by the entering of a *nolle prosequi*. Some of the cases hold that the action of the public prosecutor in so doing is subject to the control or consent of the court,[3] but most of the cases insist upon the necessity of this consent only after a jury has been empanelled, their reason being to protect private rights, *i. e.* the rights of the prisoner. For as had been said, a *nolle prosequi* is no bar to another indictment. They seldom seem to require the consent of the court in order to

[1] See also Gonzales v. State, 26 Texas, 197, which seems to recognize in the courts a power for "special reasons," which are not indicated, to appoint counsel for the prosecution of suits ; *cf.* Wharton, *op. cit.*, sec. 555.

[2] See Pa. L., March 12, 1868.

[3] State v. Moody, 69 N. C., 529 ; Statham v. State, 41 Ga., 507.

prevent the public prosecutor from rendering an indictment or other prosecution nugatory.[1] In some
cases, however, the power of the public prosecutors to
enter a *nolle prosequi* has been taken away altogether
by statute, and the indictment may be quashed only
as a result of the action of the court on a motion to
dismiss made by the public prosecutor.[2]

This method of prosecution tends of course to relax
very greatly the control over the administration exercised by the criminal courts. For the public prosecutor,
in whose hands is practically the power both to initiate
and conduct prosecutions against officers of the administration, is, whatever be the method of organizing the
system, in more or less close affiliation with the administration and is liable to over-estimate the importance
of administrative independence even to the detriment
of private rights and in some cases of administrative
efficiency. We have had in our administrative history too many instances of the refusal on the part of
the district attorney to proceed with the prosecution
of public officers, or of such negligence on his part in
conducting a prosecution which he has been forced by
public opinion to initiate, that officers guilty of official
and other crimes have been able to escape responsibility for their actions, altogether. The " pigeon-holing "
of indictments has become altogether too common in
the case of officers or of persons in close relation with
the administration. The danger is undoubtedly greater

---

[1] See U. S. v. Shoemaker, 2 McLean, 114 ; U. S. v. Stowell, 2 Curtis C. C.,
153 ; State v. I. S. S., I. Tyler, Vt., 178 ; Commonwealth v. Tuck, 20 Pickering, Mass., 356 ; Commonwealth v. Briggs, 7 Pickering, 716, 179 ; *Ex parte*
Donaldson, 44 Mo., 149 ; State v. McKee, 1 Bailey, 651 ; State v. Kreps, 8
Alabama, 951.

[2] See *e. g.* N. Y. Code of Criminal Procedure, secs. 668–671.

when the public prosecutor is dependent in his tenure of office and in his action upon the administration than it is where he is elected by the people; but even in this latter case his party affiliations are so strong as often to preclude the probability of an energetic prosecution of official criminals. One way of organizing the prosecuting force, which would remedy these defects, would be to have the public prosecutor appointed and dismissed by the courts, or at least to provide, as has been done in Pennsylvania, that, in case of the neglect of the public prosecutor, the courts may appoint attornies to conduct the prosecution.

In the system of public prosecution adopted in the national administration all public prosecutors are appointed by the President with the consent of the Senate and dismissed by the President alone. As the President is, as has been shown,[1] the head of the national administration, the administration has it in its power practically to prevent the efficient conduct of any prosecution against any officer of the administration. It may further prevent the filing of any information against officers of the administration, though it cannot prevent the finding of an indictment. For the Revised Statutes provide that a circuit or district judge may in his discretion order a *venire facias* to issue, by which a grand jury will be summoned. This body may then find an indictment,[2] which it will be the duty of the district attorney to prosecute.[3] But as the district attorney commonly has charge of the proceedings before the grand jury, will conduct the case after it has been initiated, and has the power to enter

[1] *Supra*, I., p. 69. [2] U. S. R. S., sec. 810.
[3] *Ibid.*, sec. 771.

a *nolle prosequi* practically in his discretion [1] his negligence or unwillingness to act, or that of the administration which he represents and upon which he is dependent, may often render very difficult, if not absolutely impossible, a conviction of an official of the national administration for a criminal violation of his duty. Finally it is said that the President may order the entering of a *nolle prosequi* at any stage of criminal proceedings.[2] In the commonwealths, however, the public prosecutors are usually elected by the people of the counties and the danger is not so great, though even here it is a real one on account of the party affiliations of the public prosecutors which must necessarily have a great influence on their action.

3. *Public prosecutor.* — While England is the home of private prosecution, which also lies at the basis of the system in the United States, France is the originator of the modern institution of public prosecution. Originally founded in France with the purpose of merely supplementing the activity of the private prosecutor, which the old Teutonic law provided, the office of public prosecutor has in France completely replaced the private prosecutor, who no longer exists. The code of criminal procedure provides [3] that the public prosecutor alone has the right to initiate criminal proceedings. During the period of the absolute monarchy the public prosecutors were appointed by the King, who thus had in his hands the control of all prosecutions against officers of the administration. After the revolution, during the short period of decentralization, the least important of these public prose-

---

[1] U. S. v. Stowell, 2 Curtis, C. C., 153.
[2] 5 Opinions Att'y Gen'l, 729.
[3] Art. 1.

cutors were elected by the people. But in 1800 [1] the election of public prosecutors was done away with, and appointment became the rule. Now all public prosecutors, with the exception of the mayor, who, it will be remembered, may be removed by the President of the republic, and who is the public prosecutor in the most unimportant districts for police offences, are appointed and removed by the President of the republic. They all act under the direction and control of the minister of justice. They are also to a small extent under the control of the courts to which they are attached. The courts may thus send orders to them, supervise their acts, and see that these are regular. The actual disciplinary power which the courts have over them would, however, seem to be quite small. Indeed the only cases in which the law says that the public prosecutors must act, seem to be where the complaining parties initiate civil proceedings against officers at the same time that they endeavor to get the public prosecutors to initiate criminal proceedings, as may be done under the French law. In such cases the judges must send on the criminal complaint to the public prosecutors who, it is said, are bound to act.[2] The effect of such a method of prosecution upon the control of the criminal courts over the administration is to put almost completely into the hands of the central administration the decision as to when it shall be exercised. The control of the criminal courts in France over the administration amounts therefore to very little; in time of political excitement it would be impossible to make use of it at all.

---

[1] Constitution of 22 *frimaire, an* VIII, art. 53.

[2] Block, *Dictionaire de la Politique*, II., 317, *sub verbo Ministère public.*

The old German method of criminal prosecution gave to the criminal courts an almost complete control over all criminal proceedings. The procedure before the courts was an inquisitorial procedure as a rule,—a procedure in accordance with which the courts were the prosecutors and were set in motion by the complaint of any individual who had been injured by the commission of a crime. The criminal courts, thus having the whole matter of criminal prosecutions in their hands, and being in their tenure practically independent of the administration, offered to the individual as complete a remedy against the illegal and criminal action of the administration as could well be desired or devised. The position of the criminal courts was so strong that they could, and indeed more than once did defy the prohibitions of the executive to hear criminal complaints against officers of the administration.[1] In Prussia, however, during this century French institutions were copied in this respect as in so many others. Soon after the revolution of 1848 a royal ordinance [2] took away from the courts all power of criminal prosecution and gave it to the public prosecutors who were then provided and who were placed completely under the control of the ministry. This ordinance thus destroyed all responsibility of the officers of the administration before the courts for criminal actions, and permitted the ministry to violate with impunity the rights of individuals by allowing officials to go scot free who had under its direction violated the law. This condition of things was aggravated by the law of Feb. 23, 1854, which did so much to weaken the civil responsibility of officials.[3] This law provided

---

[1] Gneist, *Das Englische Verwaltungsrecht*, 1884, 383, note.
[2] Of date Jan. 2, 1849. [3] *Supra*, II., p. 176.

that before even the public prosecutor could initiate criminal proceedings against officers of the administration, the competence court at Berlin, which was practically under the control of the ministry, should first decide that there was a proper case for criminal prosecution, a "*zur Strafverfolgung geeigneter Fall.*" The abuse which was made of this power was so marked—it resulted in destroying all control possessed by the criminal courts over the administration—that after the empire was established it was provided : First, that the preliminary decision necessary before an officer of the administration can be prosecuted criminally [1] shall be confined to the question whether such officer has violated his duties, and shall be rendered by a really independent body of a judicial character, *i. e.* either by the Imperial Court at Leipsic or by the highest administrative court, if there is any, whose members must be independent in tenure of the administration ; and second, that, while the public prosecutors are still in principle to retain their monopoly of criminal prosecution where this is provided by local statute, still in case they refuse to act, the courts may on the proposition of an interested party initiate the proceedings and appoint an attorney to conduct them. [2] The result is that while the formalities to be complied with before a suit may be brought against an officer of the administration, are in some districts rather formidable, the courts and not the administration have in their hands the initiation and the conduct of such proceedings.

---

[1] It is to be noted that many of the members of the empire do not require such a preliminary decision, though Prussia does.

[2] Code of Criminal Procedure, secs. 169–175 ; *Cf.* Gneist, *loc. cit.* This seems to be somewhat the same method which was adopted in Pennsylvania by L. March 12, 1868, *supra*, II., p. 183.

CHAPTER IV.

I.—Characteristics of the administrative jurisdiction in general.

The direct judicial control over the administration which has so far been considered, has been found in the remedies offered to individuals against officers to obtain satisfaction for the commission of an illegal act. It has been seen how careful the law in most countries is to limit both the civil and the criminal responsibility of officials in order to protect them from vexatious suits. It often requires practically an absolute overstepping of their jurisdiction or corruption where they have acted within it, in order to found the responsibility, as in England and the United States, or where it has acknowledged such a responsibility in a wider form, as in France and Germany, it has been very careful to make sure that the courts will make moderate use of their power to determine the question of jurisdiction; in all cases makes it much more difficult to sue officers of the government than to sue ordinary private persons; and all but denies any responsibility of the government for the tortious acts of its officers. But even were this method of judicial control more easily exercised than it is, it would be found in many

cases to be ineffectual. A civil suit for damages
against an official may be an altogether inadequate
remedy, because damages will not in some cases be an
adequate means of relief, and because, even if they
were, the official sued may not be the possessor of
enough property to satisfy a judgment. Again, the
successful prosecution of a criminal suit against an
officer may have value in tempering the future conduct
of officials but does not result in any actual improvement of the condition of the individual whose rights
have been violated. In both cases a right may have
been violated and adequate satisfaction has not been
made. Therefore, were the remedies which have been
mentioned the only means which the courts had to
control the actions of the administration in the interest
of private rights, the judicial control over the administration would be quite incomplete. Some means must
be provided by which the courts may directly control
the acts of the administration. It may be of vital importance to the individual or to the public that a thing
be done which the law says shall be done. It is not
just to tell an individual that he must wait until his
right has been violated and then sue the proper official
for damages, or even prosecute him criminally. The
individual desires a definite thing done by the administration which the law says shall be done. Again it
may be of vital importance that an officer be prevented
from doing an act which he threatens to do, or that
a decision which is regarded as unfair or illegal be
reviewed and annulled or amended. Here, for the
same reason as before, it is not right to force the individual to rely on his power to sue the officer in damages or prosecute him criminally.

In all these cases, if individual rights are to be adequately protected against the administration, some method of judicial control must be devised in addition to those already mentioned. Some means must be offered of reaching the acts and not the persons of the officers of the administration. The various remedies which the law offers against the acts of the administration form what may be called the administrative jurisdiction. For through the application of these remedies the courts take cognizance and jurisdiction of administrative acts. Such a jurisdiction may be formed in two ways. It may be granted to the ordinary courts, or special courts may be formed for its exercise. The former method is that which has been adopted in England and the United States. The latter is that which has been adopted very generally on the continent of Europe.

II.—*History of the English method.*

1. *History to the beginning of the eighteenth century.* —The English administrative jurisdiction, whose main principles have been adopted in the United States, is simply an outgrowth of the original system of administrative control. The Norman political system made no distinction between governmental authorities. All powers of government were consolidated in the hands of the Crown. First to be differentiated was the legislative authority, the Parliament. But for a long time after the differentiation of Parliament there was almost no legal distinction between the position of the officers for the administration of justice and that of the officers for the administration of government. Indeed most important officers discharged functions in both branches,

and all alike were regarded as merely the servants of the Crown. Some, it is true, were engaged mainly in the application of the private law, others were engaged mainly in the application of the public and administrative law. But all were officers of the Crown, which directly or indirectly could remove them all from office and could dictate to them what should be the decision of the cases which were brought before them.[1] To the officers of one of the courts, *viz.*, the court of king's bench, which was regarded as occupying a superior position because the Crown by a fiction of the law was supposed always to be present in it,[2] was given a supervisory power over all other authorities.[3] If any one was aggrieved by an act of a subordinate officer of the Crown he had the right to appeal to the Crown, who was the fountain of justice,[4] and such an appeal went to the court of king's bench. At first it seems to have gone to the *Curia Regis* or King's Council, before the development of the court of king's bench.[5] Indeed, after the development of the king's bench, when with the usual habits of judges the members of this court became very technical in their application of the law, appeals went in many cases directly to the Crown and were attended to generally by the chancellor or the council. For the King at the time of the formation of the court of king's bench specially reserved to himself

[1] Gneist, *English Constitutional History*, I., 391 ; High, *Extraordinary Legal Remedies*, 2d Ed., 5. As to the influence of the Crown over the decisions of the judges even, witness the famous case of John Hampden in the court of the Exchequer.

[2] See as to the origin of this fiction Stubbs' *Constitutional History*, I., 487, 601, II., 266 ; *cf.* Blackstone's *Commentaries*, III., 41.

[3] Gneist, *Const. Hist.*, I., 386, citing Bracton.

[4] See Stubbs' *op. cit.*, II., 254 ; Palgrave, *King's Council*, 61.

[5] 1 Ryleys' *Pleadings*, 534 ; *Abbreviatio Placitorum*, 21.

the decision of particularly difficult cases.[1] From these reserved judicial powers grew up the court of chancery as well as other courts.[2] In answer to such appeals the court of king's bench issued in the name of the Crown certain writs directed to the officer whose decision was complained of, and so formed as to afford the desired relief. Though these writs were originally issued from the office of the chancellor,[3] the court soon obtained the right to issue them directly.[4] These writs were named from the most prominent words in them—words which largely expressed the purpose of the writ. Thus, if anyone appealed to the Crown to force a recalcitrant officer to do something which the law of the land commanded the officer to do, the writ which was issued in answer to the appeal was called the writ of *mandamus*.[5] But at the same time that the court of king's bench was developing these special remedies, which became known as extraordinary legal remedies or prerogative writs, the chancellor, the keeper of the King's conscience, was, through the exercise of the reserved judicial powers of the King, also developing a series of special remedies called equitable remedies, the most important of which, from the point of view of administrative law, was the bill of injunction. Originally, however, the injunction does not seem to have been made use of commonly against officers. While most of the writs issued by the royal courts were issued to

---

[1] Stubbs, *op. cit.*, I., 487.

[2] *Ibid.*, 601–603.

[3] Palgrave, *op. cit.*, 8.

[4] Gneist, *Const. Hist.*, I., 394 ; Palgrave, *op. cit.*, 16, 17 ; Reeves, *History of the English Law*, II., 394, 507, 605.

[5] The word " mandamus " was applied originally to all the commands of the King, but was later confined to the writ issued by the court of king's bench.— High, *Extraordinary Legal Remedies*, 5.

litigants upon proper demand *de cursu,* and were
known as writs *ex debito justitiœ,* the writs by means
of which the court of king's bench exercised its supervisory powers over the other authorities do not seem
to have become, in early times at any rate, writs of
right, writs *ex debito justitiœ,* but were issued only in
extraordinary cases when some gross injustice was
done. They were known, therefore, as "prerogative
writs." The same was practically true of the equitable
remedies, and particularly of the bill of injunction.
Further on the return to these writs, generally only
questions of law were considered. They were made
use of simply to keep the lower authorities within the
bounds of the law, and could not be used, after the
practice in regard to them became crystallized, to review any question of fact or of expediency. It therefore became necessary to develop some further remedy,
unless the lower authorities were to be permitted to
decide such questions free from all control. Such a
method was found in the power which was granted to
the individual to appeal to the Privy Council. Such
appeals the council might hear as a result of the fact
that the King granted to a division of it, *viz.,* the star
chamber a portion of his reserved judicial powers.
This body acted as the administrative superior of the
royal authorities in the localities, and on appeal to it
questions of fact and expediency, as well as of law,
could be considered.[1] Formed in the time of Henry
VII to control the nobility, who had grown turbulent
during the wars of the Roses, it served at first to protect the weaker classes of the community against the

---

[1] Blackstone, *op. cit.,* IV., 266 ; Palgrave, *op. cit.,* 57–61, 101–108 ; Stubbs,
op. cit., I., 603.

arbitrariness of the administrative authorities, which were largely chosen from the nobility[1]; but it was later, *viz.*, under the Stuarts, used in such a way that it was abolished on the occasion of the revolution in 1640.[2] In order to offer an appeal similar to the one which disappeared on the occasion of its abolition, it was provided in a series of statutes that the court of quarter sessions of the justices of the peace, which had been theretofore mainly an administrative authority for the purpose of county administration, could hear and decide appeals from those decisions of the justices of the peace, acting singly or in petty and special sessions, which affected property and the right of personal liberty.[3] There was thus formed for the decision of questions of fact and expediency, as well as of law, an administrative court in each county, which came finally to have a very wide power of control over the acts of subordinate administrative officers. Its members further would certainly have special knowledge of the law they had to apply and of the conditions of administrative action, since they were engaged in other capacities as administrative officers.

Further the commission of the justices of the peace enjoined upon them in difficult cases to take the advice of the royal courts. This came finally to be done by "stating a case" which was agreed upon by the justices and the parties before them, and which was then submitted to the royal courts, and finally decided by them.[4] In consequence of these facts, one of the writs which were originally issued by the court of king's bench,

---

[1] *Supra*, I., pp. 164, 196. [2] 11 Car., I., c. 10.

[3] See Smith, *Practice at Quarter Sessions*, London, 1882, title, Appeals ; Gneist, *Das Englische Verwaltungsrecht*, 1884, 397.

[4] Smith, *op. cit.*, 518.

viz., the *certiorari,* lost much of its earlier importance in England; and we find that statute after statute was passed which prohibited its use as a means of appealing from the acts of administrative officers.[1]

But up to the coming to the throne of the Orange-Stuarts in 1689, all officers, whether judges or administrative officers, held their office at the will of the Crown. There was no judicial tenure as there was at the time in both France and Germany. In this fact, and in the existence in the Crown of reserved judicial powers, are probably to be found the reasons why the Crown permitted such a control over the administration to be given to the courts. For the Crown could exercise at any time a strong personal influence over the judges of the courts; and if it was found that the administration of the law was becoming so technical as to hamper the action of the administration, the Crown could at any time exercise its reserved powers and transfer any matter to a newly created and more pliable authority.[2]

In 1701, however, all this was changed. The act of settlement made the judges independent of the royal power, and the whole tendency of English development was to make the justices of the peace actually, though not legally independent of the Crown. An attempt by Lord Somers during the reign of William III to coerce, through the power of dismissal from office, numerous justices of the peace raised such a storm of opposition that no later ministry has dared to make use of such a power.[3]

---

[1] Gneist, *Das Englische Verwaltungsrecht,* 1884, 406.

[2] This was actually done in several instances, as has been shown. *Cf.* Palgrave, *op. cit.,* 57–61.　　　　　　　　　　[3] *Supra,* I., p. 236.

At the same time that the tenure of the judges and the justices became independent of the Crown their administrative jurisdiction remained essentially the same, with the result that the control which might before have been regarded as merely a part of the administrative control became absolutely judicial in character, *i. e.* was exercised by authorities independent of the administration which was to be controlled.

2. *History in the United States.*—Such was the condition of the English administrative jurisdiction at the time the American colonies were founded. At first, indeed, the American judges, like the English judges of the same period, were both in tenure and action under the control of the executive which they were to control, but soon their tenure was assured both against the executive and the legislature, so that from a very early time the higher courts exercised a really judicial control over the actions of the administration. The justices of the peace did not, however, at first become independent of the administration in tenure. And this was probably the reason why our courts of quarter sessions were not able to develop any very large administrative jurisdiction. The appointment early in our history of other officers for purely administrative purposes relegated the justices to the position of inferior judicial officers who have a police jurisdiction and a minor civil private law jurisdiction. They were left very few administrative duties to perform. Notwithstanding the fact that the justices of the peace in the United States later on obtained a tenure independent of the administration, in that they became generally elected by the people for a fixed term of office, they never got anything like the same administrative juris-

diction that was given to their English brothers. It is true that in special instances we find appeals from the decisions of administrative officers allowed to the courts of the justices or their successors, the county courts. Especially is this true in some of the southern commonwealths and in Pennsylvania. But it may safely be said that there has never been, and is not now in the United States any at all important administrative jurisdiction except such as is to be found in the writs which the higher courts, as a result of their being the heirs of the English court of king's bench, have the right to issue. We have lost an important part of the English administrative jurisdiction—particularly important because by its means a host of questions of fact and of expediency could be reviewed on appeal. With us such questions are decided finally by the administration, with the result that a most precious means of protecting individual rights has been lost.

CHAPTER V.

I.—At common law.

1. *The special remedies.*—The most important of the
special remedies developed by the royal courts were
five in number, each one corresponding to a particular
need which experience had shown to exist. They were
the *mandamus*, to force the administration to do what
it had illegally refused to do; the prohibition or the
injunction, to prevent the administration from proceeding to act where it ought not to act; the *certiorari*, to
review a decision already made by the administration,
to the end that such decision might be annulled or
amended; the *habeas corpus ad subjiciendum*, to bring
the matter of an arrest up before the courts, so that the
person arrested might be set at liberty in case the administration had acted illegally; and the *quo warranto*,
to prevent the usurpation of a royal franchise or privilege. This was later so shaped as to be made use of
to decide the question, who was rightfully entitled to
an office of trust and profit. Logically there was no
need for the development of these last two remedies,
as the same result might be reached through the use of

one of the other remedies.[1] But the questions of illegal arrest and imprisonment and the usurpation of franchise or office were believed to be so important that as a matter of fact special remedies were developed for these matters. What was originally a somewhat informal complaint on the part of the individual that injustice had been done, became finally, as in the case of all the writs issued by the royal courts, a demand for the issue of a special remedy or writ such as the courts had fallen into the habit of issuing. It was but a short step under such conditions for the courts to hold that the demand for a special remedy did not justify the court in issuing any other writ than the one demanded. While the appeal to the court might be made against any act of the administration and the administrative jurisdiction was not enumerated in the sense that a special statutory authorization was necessary in each case of its exercise, the remedies which could be asked for in particular cases were gradually enumerated in the decisions of the courts. A simple complaint of the denial of justice was finally insufficient.[2] The decisions of the courts have thus become quite technical in their character and hold that a writ which may be properly made use of for one purpose may not be made use of for another. Thus the

[1] Thus in New York the *habeas corpus* has as a result of the provisions of the Code of Civil Procedure been somewhat replaced by the *certiorari* to inquire into the cause of detention. Sec. 2015 ; *cf.* Church, Habeas Corpus, 330 *et seq.*

[2] Viner's *Abridgement*, 2d Ed., xv., 185, citing Barnwell's Chancery Rep., 377, *anno* 1740, where the plaintiff asked for a bill in chancery and was told to ask for a *mandamus ;* also p. 200, citing Queen v. Hungerford, 11 Mod. Rep., 142, where *quo warranto* was asked for and the applicant was told he could have a *mandamus*. See also p. 206, citing 12 Mod. 196 ; and p. 208, citing 11 Mod., 254.

mandamus is not the proper writ to try the title to office.[1] Neither the *mandamus* nor the injunction is the proper remedy to review the decision of a subordinate administrative authority; this is to be done by the *certiorari*.[2] It has therefore become necessary for the applicant for the exercise of the administrative jurisdiction of the higher courts to make it certain, before he applies for the issue of any particular writ, that he is asking for the proper remedy. For if he does not he will be non-suited.

2. *Prerogative character of the writs.*—In the second place, owing to the fact that these writs were developed as a result of the exercise of the reserved judicial powers of the Crown they have never become writs *ex debito justitiæ*, that is the individual may not have them merely for the asking, as is the case with the writs beginning ordinary actions. The courts may refuse in their discretion to issue them.[3] From a very early time, however, on account of the importance of maintaining in its integrity the right of personal liberty, the *habeas corpus* has been regarded as a writ *ex debito justitiæ i. e.* to be issued on probable cause shown[4]; and the *Habeas Corpus* act,[5] provided that the judges should issue it under a penalty for refusal. With this exception the rule was that these writs were, as the law expressed it, prerogative in character. The tendency of the more modern decisions as well as of the statutes passed on this

[1] People v. Corporation of New York, 3 Johnson's Cases, 79.

[2] Mowers v. Smedley *et al.*, 6 Johnson's Chancery, 27 ; People v. Police Commissioners, 43 Howard's Pr., 385.

[3] See Viner, *op. cit. sub verbo Certiorari*, iv., p. 345, citing 8 Mod., 331 ; also King v. Barker, 1 Wm. Blackstone, 352.

[4] Church, *op. cit.*, 94 *et seq*.

[5] 31 Car. II., cap 2, X. ; Church, *op. cit.*, 109.

subject has in both countries been to assimilate these writs more and more to ordinary actions which have no prerogative character at all. This tendency has been more marked in the United States than in England.[1] In some cases too the writs have been abolished altogether and ordinary actions substituted for them. This is true in New York of the *quo warranto*, and the information in the nature of a *quo warranto* which soon took its place. Here, however, the individual before the action can be brought must get the attorney general to move, who, it would seem, has the monopoly of the action; and it has been held that the courts may not force the attorney general to bring such action.[2] Even in England, where the writs are regarded as more prerogative in character than here, the modifications in the procedure adopted of late years have resulted in a practically greater freedom and ease in obtaining the writs. Indeed in some cases, as the result of statutory provision, they have become really little more than ordinary actions.

But notwithstanding the limitation of their prerogative character the courts, even of the United States, have large discretion in granting or refusing the application for the issue of most of the writs. In some cases the preliminary decision refusing the issue of the writ is not appealable even[3]; and in no case will they issue them where there is any other adequate remedy.[4]

[1] High, *Extraordinary Legal Remedies, passim ; cf.* Commonwealth v. Denison, 24 Howard, U. S., 66.

[2] Code of Civil Procedure, secs. 1948, 1893 ; People v. Fairchild, 67 N. Y., 834.

[3] See People v. Stillwell, 19 N. Y., 531 ; People v. Commissioners, 82 N. Y., 506 ; People v. Hill, 53 N. Y., 547.

[4] Rex v. Water Works, 1 N. & P., 48 ; People v. Board of Apportionment, 64 N. Y., 627 ; People v. Betts, 55 N. Y., 660 ; High, *Injunctions*, 3d Ed., sec. 28.

What is an adequate remedy is to be decided by the courts. They have held that a suit for damages against an official is not an adequate remedy,[1] but have intimated, at any rate, that a suit for damages against a municipal corporation, where damages were in the nature of things a perfectly competent means of relief, is an adequate remedy.[2] They have also held that the remedy by indictment of an officer was not an adequate remedy.[3]

3. *The purpose of the writs.*—The purpose of the writs is twofold. In the first place, they are issued mainly with the intention of protecting private rights; in the second place, some of them may be made use of also for the purpose of the maintenance of the law regardless of the fact whether in the particular case a private right is attacked or not. Thus in the case of the *certiorari* it has been held that this writ may not be made use of simply for the maintenance of the law, that no one may apply for it unless he has some particular interest in its issue which is greater than that possessed by the ordinary citizen.[4] The courts have, however, held with regard to the *quo warranto* that it may be issued on the demand of a citizen of responsibility[5]; and the better rule would seem to be that in

[1] People v. Green, 58 N. Y., 295.

[2] Buck v. City of Lockport, 6 Lansing, 251.

[3] Queen v. Eastern Counties R'y Co., 10 Ad. & El., 531 ; King v. Severn & Wye R'y Co., 2 Barn. & Ald., 644 ; People v. Mayor of N. Y., 10 Wendell, 395 ; *In re* Trenton Water Power Co., Spencer, N. J., 659 ; Fremont v. Crippen, 10 Cal., 211 ; see also Mechem, *Law of Public Officers*, sec. 941, note 3.

[4] People v. Leavitt, 41 Mich., 470; People v. Walter, 68 N. Y., 403; People v. Phillips, 67 N. Y., 582 ; State v. Lamberton, 37 Minn., 362 ; Granville v. County Commissioners, 97 Mass., 193.

[5] Commonwealth v. Neeser, 44 Pa. St., 341 ; State v. Kammer, 42 N. J. L., 435 ; Commonwealth v. Commissioners, 1 S. & R., 380; State v. Martin, 46 Conn., 479.

matters of public concern any citizen or taxpayer may apply for the *mandamus.*[1] Further in the proper cases the officers of the administration may apply to the courts to force by these writs inferior officers to perform their duties.[2] Finally as a result of the *Habeas Corpus* act passed in the reign of Charles II any one may apply for the writ of *habeas corpus* whether he has any particular interest or not, that is, whether his own private rights are involved or not.[3] This rule has been very generally adopted into the law of the United States and is undoubtedly due to the necessity of affording as complete a protection as possible to the right of personal liberty, to the necessity of the maintenance of the law on this subject.

4. *Questions considered on the writs.*—As a general rule the courts may not on these writs consider or review the questions of fact or expediency which have been decided by the administrative authorities. This is one of the most important general principles affecting the use of the writs and lies at the basis of nearly all the cases.[4] The principle is applicable whatever be the rank or character of the officer who is to be controlled. Be he never so humble if he have discretion that discretion he is to exercise free from any control; be he never so influential he must act in accordance

[1] People v. Collins, 19 Wendell, 56 ; People v. Halsey, 37 N. Y., 344 ; see also People v. Common Council of Buffalo, 38 Hun N. Y., 637.

[2] People v. Canal Board, 55 N. Y., 390 ; People v. Trustees, 54 Barb. N. Y., 480 ; Attorney General v. Boston, 123 Mass., 460; Wellington *et al.* Petitioners, 16 Pickering, Mass., 87, 105.

[3] 31 Car. II., cap. 2, X. ; Church, *op. cit.*, 93.

[4] Rex v. Chichester, 2 El. & El., 209 ; King v. Justices, 4 Dow. & Ry., 735 ; United States v. Seaman, 17 Howard, U. S., 225; Gaines v. Thompson, 7 Wallace, 347 ; People v. Commissioners, 30 N. Y., 72 ; Burch v. Hardwicke, 23 Grattan, Va., 51. An important exception is made in the case of the *habeas corpus*, see Church, *op. cit.*, c. xiii.

with the law. Thus the decision by a board of local highway commissioners as to the route to be taken by a highway may not be reviewed by the courts,[1] while the refusal of the United States secretary of the interior to issue a patent for lands after all questions of discretion had been decided in favor of the applicant has been held to be the violation of a ministerial duty and may be overcome by application to the court.[2] This rule is, however, subject to one or two exceptions. The questions of fact which have been decided by an administrative authority in deciding as to the title to office may be reviewed by the courts on either *mandamus* or *quo warranto.*[3] Further the courts will not permit administrative officers so to make use of their discretion as to make a decision which is absolutely unsupported by the evidence but will on *certiorari* quash such decision.[4] Again the courts hold that where a statute provides that an officer may be removed from office for cause only, they have the right to control the discretion of the removing officer in deciding what is cause.[5] The courts, it is true, do not ground their decisions on any desire to control the discretion of administrative officers, but on the proposition that the question, what is cause, is not a question of discretion but a question of law. But this does not alter the fact that, as a result of these

[1] People v. Collins, 19 Wendell, 56.

[2] United States v. Schurz, 102 U. S., 378. See also People v. Beach, 19 Hun, N. Y., 259.

[3] State v. Garesche, 65 Missouri, 480 ; People v. Pease, 27 N. Y., 45.

[4] People v. Board of Police, 39 N. Y., 506 ; People *ex rel.* Hogan v. French ; People *ex rel.* McAleer v. French, 119 N. Y., 493, 502.

[5] People v. Board of Police, 72 N. Y., 415 ; People v. Board of Fire Commissioners, 73 N. Y., 437 ; State v. St. Louis, 90 Mo., 19 ; Stockwell v. Township Board, 22 Mich., 341 ; see also Kennard v. Louisiana, 92 U. S., 480.

decisions, the courts do exercise a control over the discretion of administrative officers—and that too upon a
point where many think that it is necessary that the
administration should possess full and unlimited discretion. Finally in several instances special statutes
have been passed which expressly give to the courts a
control over the discretion of the administration. Thus
the present customs administrative act gives to the circuit courts of the United States the power on a sort of
statutory *certiorari* to reverse or amend the decisions
even of fact of the board of general appraisers as to
classification of articles for duty under the tariff acts.[1]
Thus also the legislature of New York has provided[2]
that if the commissioners of excise in the larger cities
refuse arbitrarily to issue a license for the retail sale of
liquor to be drank on the premises, the party who has
thus been refused a license may appeal to the courts
for the issue of a *mandamus* to the commissioners to
grant the license. Thus also the legislature of the
same commonwealth has provided[3] that in case any
person is aggrieved by the decision of the assessors as
to the value of his property for the purposes of taxation, he may have a *certiorari* on which the courts may
reverse or amend the decision of the assessors on the
ground both of illegality and of unfairness or dispro-
portionality.[4]

Finally for political reasons the courts have very
generally laid down the rule that they will not exer-

[1] U. S. Laws of 1889–90, c. 407, sec. 15. Here it is probably a remedy *ex
debito justitiæ*.

[2] L. 1886, c. 496.

[3] L. 1880, c. 269.

[4] See also New York Code of Civil Procedure, sec. 2140, which provides that
the court in deciding on the writ of *certiorari* may consider the weight of the
evidence.

cise their administrative jurisdiction where it brings them into actual conflict with the chief executive.[1] The rule is clear as to the President of the United States, but is not so clear as to the governors of the various commonwealths.[2] Most of the cases where the *mandamus* has been issued to the governor have been friendly suits where the governor has not objected to the jurisdiction; indeed one of them holds expressly that the court will issue the writ of *mandamus* to the governor if he does not object.[3] Where, however, the courts may issue the writs without coming into direct conflict with the executive they seem to have no objection to issuing them, even if they will be forced to annul the acts of the executive.[4] Thus they have issued a *habeas corpus* to consider the validity of an act of the governor in the extradition of a fugitive from justice, and have decided that such act was not in accordance with the law.[5] In the case of *Ex parte Merryman,* a case of *habeas corpus,* however, the writ absolutely failed of its purpose because the officer to whom it was issued was supported in his action by the President, and the court refused to take any further step on account of the danger of a conflict with the executive. Some of the commonwealths have endea-

---

[1] State of Mississippi v. Johnson, 4 Wall., 475 ; Grier v. Taylor, 4 McCord, 206 ; People v. Hill, 13 N. Y. Supplement, 186 ; *New York Law Journal,* April 13, 1891 ; affirmed on different grounds in 126 N. Y.. 497 ; High, *Extraordinary Legal Remedies,* 2d Ed., sec. 118 and cases cited.

[2] As to the *mandamus* see Cotton v. Ellis, 7 Jones, N. C. 545 ; State v. Chase, 5 Ohio St., 528.

[3] People v. Bissell, 19 Ill., 229. As to the *quo warranto* see Attorney General v. Barstow, 4 Wis., 567.

[4] See People v. Platt, 50 Hun, 454.

[5] People v. Curtis, 50 N. Y., 321 ; People v. Brady, 56 N. Y., 182 ; see also *Ex parte* Merryman, Taney, 246, 9 *American Law Register,* 524 ; *Ex parte* Field, 5 Blatchford, 63.

vored to extend this exemption from the operation of the administrative jurisdiction of the courts to the heads of departments. But this is not the best rule either in the United States or England, and is in conflict with the decisions of the United States Supreme Court.[1]

5. *Distinction between legal and equitable remedies.* —Besides these general rules which are applicable to all the remedies by which the administrative jurisdiction of the courts is governed there are a number of special rules with regard to each one of the remedies. Thus there is quite a distinction between the extraordinary legal and the equitable remedies. While the former are almost always issued where the act of the administration is absolutely illegal in character, the latter may be issued only in those cases where the applicant for the remedy can bring his case under one of the recognized heads of equitable jurisdiction, such as that the act complained of is a breach of trust, will result in irreparable mischief to real property or will lead to a multiplicity of suits.[2] Further if we compare the injunction with the prohibition, whose purposes are largely the same, we find that the injunction appears to be, in the United States at any rate, the popular remedy. Although legally the courts have about the same discretion as to the issue of both of these remedies, as a matter of fact they seem to issue the injunction much more easily than the prohibition, and indeed in some of the commonwealths make use of the pre-

---

[1] See U. S. v. Schurz, 102 U. S., 378. There is also conflict on this point in the English decisions. See Queen v. Lords, etc., 4 Ad. & El., 286 ; Same v. Same, 4 Eng. Rep., 277 ; Same v. Same, L. R., 7 Q. B., 387 ; *cf.* Gneist, *Das Englische Verwaltungsrecht*, 1884, 712.

[2] Green v. Mumford, 5 R. I., 472, 475 ; Dow v. Chicago, 11 Wall., 108 ; Hilliard, *Injunctions*, 3d Ed., 486.

liminary injunction with such freedom as in many cases to paralyze almost completely the action of the administration. This is unfortunately the case in New York. Here police officers have in several instances been by the injunction restrained from preventing palpable violations of the law.[1] In England, however, the injunction seems rarely to be made use of as a means of preventing administrative action. Gneist does not even mention it as one of the remedies in his description of the administrative jurisdiction of the English courts, but speaks of prohibition only[2]; and a search through the English digests reveals very few cases of the use of the injunction against administrative officers.[3]

6. *Administrative jurisdiction of the United States federal courts.*—In the case of the commonwealth courts the general rule is that the administrative jurisdiction is possessed by all those courts which have inherited the jurisdiction of the court of king's bench —and most courts of general common law jurisdiction have inherited such jurisdiction. This rule prevents courts with a mere appellate jurisdiction from exercising the administrative jurisdiction[4]; and results also in the fact that the equitable remedies may be issued only by courts possessing equity jurisdiction. The administrative jurisdiction of the United States federal courts is not however governed by these general prin-

---

[1] A good collection of these cases was made in an editorial of the New York *Times* of April 23, 1886.

[2] *Das Englische Verwaltungsrecht,* 1884, 404.

[3] That it is used now and then may be seen from the cases of Ellis v. Earl Grey, 1 Simon, 214 ; and 1 Vesey Sr., 188.

[4] Morgan v. Register, Hardin, 609 ; State v. Biddle, 36 Ind., 138 ; State v. Ashley, 1 Ark., 513 ; Memphis v. Halsey, 12 Heiskell, Tenn., 210 ; see also Perry v. Shepherd, 78 N. C., 83.

ciples, but is so fixed in detail by the constitution and the statutes that it becomes necessary to have reference to these and to the decisions made in interpretation of them in order to understand what exactly is the jurisdiction of these courts. It has been held in a series of decisions that the United States courts generally have no power to issue the *mandamus* or *certiorari* except to aid an already acquired jurisdiction : the Supreme Court, because the constitution does not include this power within the original jurisdiction given to that court [1]; the circuit courts and the district courts, because such power has not been granted to them by the judiciary act.[2] The supreme court of the District of Columbia may, however, as a result of the fact that it has inherited for the territory of the District of Columbia the jurisdiction of the court of king's bench, issue the *mandamus*,[3] and probably as a result of the application of the same principle the writ of *certiorari* also. It is to be noted, however, that the recent customs administrative act gives the power to the circuit courts to issue a sort of statutory *certiorari* to the boards of general appraisers in customs matters.[4] Where, however, it is necessary to issue such writs in order to enforce a jurisdiction already in other ways acquired, they may issue the *mandamus*, and as a result of the application of the same principle the *certiorari*.[5] In

---

[1] Marbury v. Madison, 1 Cranch, 137 ; *In re* Kaine, 14 Howard, 103 ; *Ex parte* Vallandigham, 1 Wallace, 243 ; U. S. v. Young, 94 U. S. 258, 259.

[2] McIntire v. Wood, 7 Cranch, 504 ; U. S. v. Smallwood, 1 Chicago Legal News, 321 ; *Ex parte* Van Orden, 3 Blatchford, 167 ; Patterson v. U. S., 2 Wheaton, 221.

[3] Kendall v. U. S., 12 Peters, 524.

[4] *Supra*, II., p. 207.

[5] Lansing v. County Treasurer, 1 Dillon, 522 ; see also Rees v. City of Watertown, 19 Wall. 107.

some of the cases laying down this rule a *mandamus* was issued by a circuit court to a municipal corporation to compel it to provide for the payment of a judgment obtained in the court against such corporation. Further as a result of the provisions of the United States constitution the Supreme Court, it would seem, has such power in cases where a commonwealth, or a foreign diplomatic or consular officer is a party.[1] The rules are about the same with regard to the prohibition. The Supreme Court has no right to issue a prohibition except in admiralty matters [2]; and it is very doubtful whether the circuit courts may issue a prohibition at all.[3] The rules are, however, more liberal with regard to the injunction, the *habeas corpus*, and the *quo warranto*. The power to issue the *habeas corpus* even to the administrative authorities of the commonwealths is given to all the United States courts, except the Supreme Court.[4] They have also the right to issue the *quo warranto* when the question at issue concerns the denial of the right to vote on account of race, color, or previous condition of servitude for any officer other than presidential elector and legislative officers, or concerns the disqualification for office resulting from the violation of official oath, by engaging in insurrection or rebellion against the United States or giving aid and comfort to its enemies.[5] The Supreme Court may not issue the injunction except to aid an already acquired jurisdiction and except in cases where a commonwealth, or a

[1] Const., Art. III., sec. 2, par. 3.

[2] U. S. Rev. Stats., sec. 688 ; U. S. v. Peters, 3 Dallas, 121 ; *Ex parte* Christy, 3 Howard, 292 ; *Ex parte* Insurance Co., 118 U. S., 61.

[3] U. S. Rev. Stats., sec. 716 ; *In re* Binninger, 7 Blatchford, 159.

[4] U. S. Rev. Stats., secs. 751–766 ; *Ex parte* Barry, 2 How. 65.

[5] Amendment 14, sec. 3 ; U. S. Rev. Stats., sec. 563, pars. 13 and 14.

foreign diplomatic or consular officer is a party.[1] The
other United States courts have a large power, except
in tax cases, to offer the equitable remedies in proper
cases against the action of both national and commonwealth officers though they are pretty careful in their
issue of the injunction.[2]

These rules apply as well to the issue of these remedies against commonwealth officers as to their issue
against the officers of the United States government.
If they have not an already acquired jurisdiction in the
cases where this is necessary, they may not issue the
writs. If they have they may.[3] On the other hand
the courts of the commonwealths may never exercise
their administrative jurisdiction in order to control the
actions of the officers of the national government. For
the United States courts have exclusive jurisdiction
generally of all cases arising under the constitution
and laws of the United States.[4] The result is that the
officers of the national government are not nearly
so subject to the administrative jurisdiction of the
courts as are the commonwealth officers. But this
control is not nearly so necessary as in the commonwealth administration. For the administrative control
is so strong in the United States administrative system that the mistakes of subordinate administrative
officers are quite easily corrected on appeal[5]; and if on
such appeal the aggrieved individual is not able to ob-

---

[1] U. S. Const., Art. III., sec. 2, par. 3.

[2] U. S. Rev. Stats., sec. 629, par. 2.

[3] *Supra*, II., p. 211 ; Graham v. Norton, 15 Wallace, 247 ; Commonwealth v.
Dennison, 24 Howard, 66.

[4] U. S. Const., Art. III., sec. 2, p. 1 ; Brewer v. Kidd, 23 Mich., 440 ; Able-
man v. Booth and U. S. v. Booth, 21 How., 506 ; Tarble's Case, 13 Wall.,
397.

[5] Butterworth v. U. S., 112 U. S., 50, 57.

tain satisfaction he in all cases has the right of applying to the supreme court of the District of Columbia, which has the common law administrative jurisdiction for the territory of the District of Columbia, where all the heads of departments are to be found ; and appeal may be taken from this court to the Supreme Court of the United States.

II.—*Special and statutory administrative jurisdiction of the lower courts.*

The special and technical character of the common law administrative jurisdiction of the courts has made it seem advisable in certain rather exceptional cases, where no one of the writs affords the proper relief, to provide by statute for special appeals, generally to the lower courts, from the decisions of administrative officers, when either questions of law alone or questions of both law and fact may be considered.

1. *Appellate jurisdiction of courts of quarter sessions or county courts.*—It has been shown that, after the abolition of the court of star chamber, which served as an appellate court on questions of both law and fact for the decisions of the subordinate English administrative officers, it was provided in a series of statutes that appeals should thereafter be taken to the court of quarter sessions of the county, which was composed of the justices of the peace of the county. This sort of administrative jurisdiction differs considerably from that of the royal courts, which has been considered. In the first place, the remedy is a general one—a simple appeal against the act complained of—while the jurisdiction is enumerated. In the royal courts it will be remembered that the converse is true, *i. e.* the remedies

are special in character and the jurisdiction is general. No one can appeal to the quarter sessions from an order or decision unless a statute specially permits an appeal to be taken in the class of cases of which the one at bar is one.[1] In the second place, the appeal may be and is usually taken on questions of fact. If questions of law are raised the proper courts to appeal to are the royal courts, to which appeal goes by special case or special writs.[2] In the third place, the general conditions under which the appeal may be taken are that the party appealing must be immediately aggrieved by the act complained of, not consequentially but immediately aggrieved. Thus the mapping out of a road is not an immediate grievance.[3] Officers of the localities may as private individuals appeal in the interest of their locality.[4] In the fourth place, while this sort of administrative jurisdiction is enumerated in the statutes still the statutes have been based on general principles in allowing these appeals. These are that the appeal is only granted where the rights of personal liberty and private property are involved.[5]

While in the United States the statutes granting a power of appealing from the decisions of the administrative officers to the courts of quarter sessions or county courts, which have largely taken their place, are not nearly so numerous, still we do find not a few instances of them. Thus in New York any one interested may appeal to the county court from the decision of the superintendent of the poor as to the settlement of a poor person.[6] An instance of a similar power of appeal, though in this case the appeal does not go to

[1] Rex v. Hanson, 4 B. & Ald., 521. [3] Rex v. Middlesex JJ., 1 Chitty Rep., 366.
[2] Still v. Brennan, 41 L. J. M. C., 85. [4] Rex v. Colbeck, 11 Ad. & El., 161.
[5] Gneist, *Das Englische Verwaltungsrecht*, 1884, 397.   [6] L. 1872, c. 38.

the county court, is the power given to any individual, who has been refused a patent for an invention by the commissioner of patents, to appeal from this decision to the supreme court of the District of Columbia.[1]

2. *Special case.*—A most notable example of these attempts to supplement the administrative jurisdiction of the higher courts is to be found in the English habit of stating a special case. This habit, as has been indicated,[2] originated in a clause in the commission of the justices of the peace which enjoined upon them to ask the advice of the royal judges in cases where they were in doubt. These special cases are mostly statements of facts, are made up in both the quarter and the special sessions, and go up to the higher courts which decide the matter for the justices. At first the decision of the royal courts was only consultative in character, the justices not being bound by it, but the judicature act of 1873 has made the decision, it is believed, binding upon the justices and mandatory.[3] The courts have all alone encouraged the sending up of these special cases which have almost replaced the *certiorari.*[4] As a general rule the allowance of a special case is in the discretion of the justices.[5] On a special case the courts do not, as a rule, interfere with the discretion of the justices.[6] The special case, while not common in the United States, is not unknown to the American law.

[1] U. S. Rev. Stats., sec. 4911. This is in place of the administrative appeal to the head of department ; Butterworth v. U. S., 112 U. S., 50, 57.

[2] *Supra*, II., p. 196.

[3] Wallsall v. Ry. Co., 48 L. J. M. C., 65.

[4] Gneist, *Das Englische Verwaltungsrecht*, 1884, 407 ; Smith, *Practice at Quarter Sessions*, 518–520.

[5] *Ex parte* Jarvin, 9 Dowl. P. C. 120. But see Smith, *op. cit.*, 521.

[6] Rex v. Ry, Co., 43 L. J. M. C., 57 ; Rex v. Kent, JJ., 41 J. P., 263.

CHAPTER VI.

I.—History.

In France, as has been said, the administrative jurisdiction has been given to special courts. France may be said to have founded the modern system of special administrative courts. Even before the revolution France possessed special administrative courts. Some of these were independent of the active administration, and had been established simply as a result of the application of the economic principle of the division of labor. Such *e. g.* were the court of moneys and the chamber of accounts. But by the side of these tribunals there grew up in the 17th century new authorities completely dependent upon the active administration, and purposely made dependent upon it in order that the administration might have perfect freedom of action in its endeavor to perform the greater tasks imposed upon it as a result of the great increase of the powers of the Crown.[1] While in England as late as 1701 the ordinary courts were under the control of the Crown, and there was consequently no need, in order to make the administration independent in action, of forming special administrative courts, in France the

[1] Aucoc, *op. cit.*, I., 396, 397.

ordinary judicial bodies were quite independent of the Crown. The chief judicial bodies in France before 1789 were the parliaments, and their members were independent of the Crown as a result of the fact that the position of member of parliament was venal and bought and sold as property. The powers of these parliaments were never clearly defined, and in the general confusion of the time as to the distribution of the three great so-called powers of government, the parliaments often tried to assume a control over the actions of the administration. When Louis XVI came to the throne in 1774, it was seen that great reforms in the administration of the government and in the social conditions of the people must be undertaken. For this purpose the King chose Turgot as one of his ministers. The reforms which Turgot endeavored to introduce did not meet with the approval of the privileged classes. As the parliaments were composed of members of the privileged classes they opposed these reforms, refused to register the various edicts issued by the King,[1] encroached upon the royal power by themselves issuing decrees, and tried to hinder the action of the royal officers by issuing commands to them and citing them to appear before the parliaments to answer complaints made against them.[2] When the liberal elements obtained control of the Constituent Assembly, this action of the parliaments was remembered and the principle already enunciated by Montesquieu that the three so-called powers of government must be entrusted to different and independent authorities, was incorporated in the celebrated " declaration of the rights of

---

[1] Such *e. g.* was their action as to the edict abolishing the *corvée* or enforced labor of the peasants on public works. [2] Aucoc, *op. cit.*, I., 17, 52.

man and of the citizen."[1] The administrative authorities were made completely independent of the judiciary,[2] and judges were forbidden under pain of forfeiting their positions to interfere in any way whatever with the acts of the officers of the administration or to cite them before them for the performance of their duties.[3] For said the Constituent Assembly :

> The constitution will be equally violated, if the judiciary may meddle with administrative matters and trouble administrative officers in the discharge of their duties. . . . Every act of the courts of justice which purports to oppose or arrest the action of the administration being unconstitutional, shall be void and of no effect.[4]

Thus the desire of the absolute monarchy to free the administration from all judicial control was realized by the revolution. This is the origin of the great principle of the independence of the administration which permeates all French law. Its adoption in modern times is due in great part to the fact that the ordinary judicial tribunals had hampered the administration in its work of reform in the 17th and 18th centuries, which they were able to do as a result of their position of independence over against the Crown.

In order, however, to offer the individual some remedy against the decisions of the subordinate officers of the administration, there was formed a most extended system of appeals from the subordinate to the higher administrative authorities. This it was easy to form in France on account of the formation after the revolution of a most centralized system of administra-

---

[1] Art. xvi.

[2] L., Dec. 22, 1789–Jan. 8, 1790, sec. iii., art. 7.

[3] L., Aug. 16–24, 1790, title ii., art. 15.

[4] Instructions to the law last cited, *Lois et Actes du Gouvernement,* I., 98.

tion.[1] Care was soon taken to give the power to decide the most important of these appeals to authorities not immediately connected with the active administration.[2] The active administration thus ceased to be at the same time party and judge. The plan was so successful, that the jurisdiction of the most important of these administrative tribunals, as they were called, has been gradually extended until this administrative jurisdiction is now really more extensive than that possessed by the ordinary judicial courts in the English and American system.

II.—Reasons for the retention of the system.

1. *Need of special courts.*—While this method of judicial control over the administration was adopted largely as a result of peculiar local conditions, it has been retained for purely practical reasons. In the first place the special character of the matters which are embraced within the administrative jurisdiction requires, it is believed, for their satisfactory treatment special knowledge, which judges who devote most of their time to the consideration of questions of private law cannot be expected to possess. Different habits of thought and a practical knowledge of administrative law, to be obtained for the most part by direct contact with active administrative work, are regarded by the advocates of special administrative courts as essential. It is believed that these qualities are essential not only to the government but also to the individual. French experience has shown in those few

---

[1] See *e. g.* L., Sept. 7-11, 1790, which provided for appeals in tax matters, and L., Dec. 14, 1789, arts. 55 and 60, cited in Aucoc, I., 399, 400.

[2] L. 28 *pluviôse an* VIII (1800), art. 14.

instances where the decisions of the ordinary judicial courts and those of the administrative courts relative to private rights are capable of comparison, that the decisions of the administrative courts have been more favorable to private rights than those of the judicial courts. The tendency of the ordinary private law judge when confronted with an administrative question is to apply to it the rules of private law, which often lead him into errors and result in too great technicality.

2. *Need of an inexpensive and informal procedure.*— A further reason for the retention of the special administrative courts is the desirability of an inexpensive and informal procedure such as is not to be found in the ordinary procedure of the civil courts. In case of a conflict between the administration and the individual the contestants are not on a par as in an ordinary suit is usually the case ; and it is desirable, as far as may be, to encourage individuals to bring suits against the officers of the administration in order to prevent an over-zealousness on the part of the administration to the detriment of private rights.[1]

III.— The general characteristics of the French system.

1. *Administrative courts, courts of enumerated jurisdiction.*—The general rule is the same now that it was at the time of the Constituent Assembly, *viz.*, that the decision of all conflicts between the administration and individuals, and the interpretation of all administrative acts are reserved to the active administration. The ordinary courts are forbidden to interfere in any way with administrative action, even to interpret an

[1] *Cf.* Aucoc, I., 401-8.

administrative act of individual application which comes before them collaterally. This can be done only by the administration.[1] There are, however, exceptions to this rule. Thus the ordinary courts have as a result of special statutory provision the entire control of the matter of expropriation or the exercise of the right of eminent domain.[2] Again arrests made by the administration are under the control of the ordinary courts as a result of the penal code.[3]

On the other hand, as a result of the grant to the ordinary judicial courts of the application of the private and the criminal law, the general rule is that the courts have control of all contracts made by the administration and the entire police jurisdiction. This general rule is subject to several exceptions. Thus all contracts made by the central or local administration relative to public works and to public lands and all contracts of the central administration relative to the public domain and for material or supplies of personal property are put into the jurisdiction of the administrative courts. Further certain of the administrative courts have a certain amount of police jurisdiction, but not much.[4] But the usual rule is that the administration has the jurisdiction of all administrative acts and of administrative acts alone. In certain cases, however, which have been growing more and more numerous during this century, the statute law states specifically that the decision of complaints against certain classes of administrative acts shall be made not by the active administration, but by bodies called administrative courts, which are in large part unconnected with

---

[1] Aucoc, I., 424. [2] L., May 3, 1841. [3] Arts. 119 and 120.
[4] Simonet, *Droit Public Administratif*, 157, and laws cited.

it. Each of these bodies has to decide in the particular cases provided in the statutes. The result is that the administrative courts are courts of enumerated jurisdiction. The particular grants of jurisdiction are, however, so numerous that, though in theory courts of enumerated jurisdiction, the important administrative courts are practically courts of general jurisdiction. This is true of the Council of State and the councils of the prefecture.

2. *Judges not independent of the administration.*— The judges of the administrative courts do not possess the same independent tenure that is possessed by the judges of the ordinary courts. They are all appointed and may at any time be removed by the President of the republic. This is undoubtedly a great theoretical objection to the French system,[1] but in practice their weakness of tenure over against the administration does not appear to have had any appreciable influence on their decisions. As has been shown, where it is possible to compare the decisions of these courts with those of the ordinary courts it is found that the decisions of the administrative courts have as a general thing shown more regard and consideration for private rights than those of the ordinary courts, whose judges have a fixed tenure of office. The reason why this precarious tenure has been retained in the French system, notwithstanding the advances that have been made in other directions during this century in the development of these administrative courts, is that it is believed necessary, in order that the administrative judges may have the necessary knowledge of administrative affairs, that they be continually engaged in

---

[1] *Cf.* Dicey, *The Law of the Constitution*, 3d Ed., 312.

active administrative work. Therefore the administrative courts are at the same time administrative councils, which are being continually called upon to advise the administration ; and it is felt in a country like France, where the belief in the necessity of administrative centralization is so strong, that it would be unwise to relax the usual administrative control over the members of the administrative councils. This argument, however, seems to have really little weight. Of course the desirability of the possession by the administrative judges of special administrative knowledge cannot be gainsaid. The success of the English courts of quarter sessions is too great to permit the proposition to be questioned. But to attain this result it does not seem necessary that administrative judges shall be dependent upon the administration. The tenure of the English justices of the peace, though in theory not protected against the administration, is in reality protected, inasmuch as any ministry which should attempt to dismiss them from office for reasons other than absolute corruption would have to assume a most grave responsibility before Parliament.[1] Again, as will be shown later, the tenure of the judges of the administrative courts which have been lately formed in Prussia is made the same, as far as its independence is concerned, as that of the ordinary judges. It is possible in other ways to ensure that the administrative judges will have the necessary special knowledge of administrative affairs.

3. *Judges professional in character.*—The character of all the judges of the most important administrative courts is professional. That is, they all must have had a certain theoretical or practical administrative

---

[1] *Supra*, II., p. 197.

training, must be learned in the law; they receive a large salary also, and are not permitted to have any other occupation or profession. In most of the important administrative courts there is in addition to the judges a representative of the government. Such officer differs very much from an ordinary advocate. He is rather an *amicus curiæ* whose duty is to advise the court on difficult points, and to endeavor as far as possible to see that justice and right are done even to the detriment of the particular claim which the government may be making at the time.[1] This is not simply his theoretical position. Nothing is more common than to see such officer actually advocating the views which have been set forth by the individual who is protesting against some particular administrative act.

4. *Great freedom of appeal.*—In the administrative courts there is an almost unlimited power of appealing from the decisions of the lower courts to the higher court. On these appeals questions both of law and fact may be reviewed. There are very few of the courts which decide at the same time in first and last instance on questions of fact and none but the supreme court, the Council of State, which so decides on questions of law. This power of appeal is not limited by the amount in question. It is possible to go up to the Council of State in order to claim a reduction of a few *centimes* on a personal property tax for example. The French have felt this is necessary in order to check the too great zeal of subordinate officers. For when the contest is between the government and the individual the consequence of the commission of injustice cannot be measured by the amount at stake. The

---

[1] Aucoc, *op. cit.*, I., 415.

power of appeal has further been increased by the provision that in certain matters of especial importance costs are done away with altogether or are very largely reduced in amount, while the procedure has purposely been made very simple. It is to a large extent in writing, and is of a somewhat inquisitorial character. That is, the judges are not confined in their consideration of the case to what is laid before them, but may take such measures as they see fit to get at the truth. To a very large extent, the necessary action of a plaintiff in a suit in an administrative court consists simply in laying his complaint before the court which then attends to the rest.[1]

IV.—*Nature of the remedies.*

1. *The general jurisdiction of the administrative courts.*—The general jurisdiction of the administrative courts, the jurisdiction which all the courts possess over those matters which have been assigned to them by law, what the French call the *contentieux administratif*, has been worked out by the administrative courts themselves in their decisions, although the actual administrative matters over which they have this jurisdiction are designated in the statutes. This general jurisdiction consists in deciding complaints made by individuals against those non-political acts of the administrative authorities of special and not general application, whose immediate effect is to violate the rights of individuals acquired by virtue of some statute, ordinance, or a contract. Almost every word of this definition is essential.

In the first place it is to be noticed that the act must

[1] *Cf.* Aucoc, *op. cit.*, I., 411–423.

be non-political in character in order that the administrative courts may hear complaints against it. What
is a political act it is difficult to say. The legislature
has not defined it. In order therefore to determine
what is such a political act we must have recourse to
the decisions of the administrative courts themselves.
These have held that acts are political in character
which are performed by the President in carrying on
the relations of the executive with the other governmental authorities and which relate to the carrying on
of war, of diplomatic relations, and to domestic peace
and tranquillity.[1] The only acts of this class which
need special notice are those which relate to the domestic peace and tranquillity. The tendency of the
decisions of the administrative courts has, it must be
admitted, been to relieve the administration from all
judicial control for acts which have been extremely
arbitrary in character and very restrictive of private
rights, where by such acts the administration was
attempting to ensure domestic peace and tranquillity.
The decisions have held that in time of public disturbance measures taken by the administration to prevent
the publication of a journal which the administration
alleged was inflaming the passions of the people,
measures which resulted in the complete destruction
of the plant of the journal, were of a political character
and were not subject to the control of the administrative courts.[2] The tendency of these decisions is not
regarded favorably by several of the French writers.[3]

In the second place in order to give the administra-

---

[1] Laferrière, *La Juridiction Administrative*, II., 32.

[2] *Con. d'État, Arrêts* of Feb. 26, 1857 ; May 9, 1867, cited in Ducrocq, *op. cit.*, sec. 64 ; *cf.* Aucoc, I., 441 *et seq.*

[3] *Cf.* Simonet, *Droit Public, etc.*, 155.

tive courts jurisdiction the act complained of must be of special and individual and not of general application, *i. e.* it cannot be an ordinance.[1] There is a special remedy against ordinances which will be alluded to later.

In the third place the act must have for its immediate, not its indirect and ultimate, effect, the violation of a right. Thus a prefect authorizes a commune to sell or close up a road which he and it regard as useless. A private individual may think that the particular road belonged to him; he cannot on that account, however, appeal to the administrative courts against the prefect's decision. For his right is not violated until the commune actually attempts to sell the road. Then and only then may he appeal.[2] This it will be noticed is similar to the English distinction, is the matter of appeals to the court of quarter sessions between immediate and consequential grievances. Further it must be noticed in this connection that the act must actually violate a right and must not be simply contrary to the interest of the individual complaining. This distinction between the violation of a right and the failure to consider an interest may be made plain by an example. The French law forbids any citizen to change his name without the authorization of the President. No person is considered as having a right to change his name, and in refusing to authorize a change of name the President violates no right. Therefore no one can appeal from the decision of the President, refusing the necessary authorization,

---

[1] Ducrocq, I., sec. 247.
[2] *Arrêt du Con. d'État*, Jan. 24, 1851 ; *Affaire Dénizet*, cited in Aucoc, I., 432.

to the administrative courts. But in case such a decision of the President does authorize a change of name, the right of a third person may be violated, since a family name is considered by the French law to be in the nature of a property right. Therefore an appeal is allowed to an interested third person from the decision of the President permitting an individual to assume the family name of the interested third party.[1] What is a right and what is an interest have been worked out in the decisions of the administrative courts. While this is the general rule exceptions have been made in particular cases by statute, but they are not important.

2. *Appeal to the Council of State for excess of powers.* —A second remedy is offered in the power granted to any individual to appeal to the Council of State against any act, not of a political character, of any administrative authority, on the ground that such authority has, in the performance of the act complained of, exceeded its powers or violated the law. This appeal is permitted even if the act complained of is of general application and even if it does not violate a right. This remedy, like the *contentieux administratif*, was worked out by the administrative courts, but has been given recently the sanction of statute, the law of May 24, 1872, providing [2] that the " Council of State decides finally on all demands to annul for excess of powers acts of administrative authorities." In what now does an excess of powers consist? When do we find a violation of the law? The decisions of the Council of State hold that there is an excess of powers : when an

---

[1] Ducrocq, *op. cit.*, I., 234, citing *Arrêt du Con. d'État*, Aug. 16, 1862.
[2] Art. 9.

administrative authority encroaches upon the competence of some other authority, whether that other
authority be the legislative authority, a judicial authority, or another administrative authority [1]; when
an administrative authority does not follow the formalities laid down in the law as necessary [2]; and when
an administrative authority, even when acting within
its competence and following the necessary formalities,
uses its discretionary power for purposes other than
those for which the power was granted.[3] The following case will give a good example of this last kind of
excess of powers. It is almost as famous in the French
law as the ship-money case of John Hampden is in the
English law, or the case of the miller of *Sans-Souci* is
in the law of Prussia. The French law gives to the
prefect the right to regulate the movement of carriages
about railway stations in the interest of public order,
i. e. the police power. In order to obtain regular communications between the railway station at Fontainebleau and the city itself, the railway company entered
into negotiations with an owner of carriages to meet
all trains. This man demanded a monopoly. At the
request of the company the prefect issued an ordinance
which forbade all carriages but those of the contractor
to enter the court of the railway station. The proprietor of a hotel in Fontainebleau, who had been in
the habit of sending an omnibus to meet travellers at
the station, sent an omnibus as before and was prosecuted for it. He appealed to the Council of State, on
the ground that the prefect had made use of the police
power to grant a monopoly, and the Council of State
annulled the ordinance. This case is interesting for

[1] For example see Aucoc, *op. cit.*, I., 466.　　[2] *Ibid.*　　[3] *Ibid.*, 467.

several reasons. First it gives a good idea of what the French call a *détournement du pouvoir*, in the second place it shows that the remedy of appeal for excess of powers may be made use of against an act of general application, *i. e.* an ordinance. In the third place it illustrates the great regard which the administrative courts have for private rights—a regard which is greater than that of the ordinary judicial courts. For the ordinance of the prefect in question was a penal ordinance, and therefore, in accordance with the general principles of the French law, was to be enforced by prosecution before the police courts, from which appeal might be taken to the highest of the ordinary courts. Now before appealing to the Council of State the hotel proprietor in this case had been prosecuted and condemned to pay the penalty affixed to the ordinance, although the police courts had the right to refuse to enforce the ordinance on the ground that it was not legally made. On appeal to the Court of Cassation, the highest of the ordinary courts, this judgment had been affirmed, and it was only after exhausting the jurisdiction of the ordinary courts that the hotel proprietor decided to avail himself of his appeal to the Council of State which, as has been said, overturned the ordinance, notwithstanding that the highest judicial court had decided that it was legal.[1]

The interpretation of the words "acts of administrative authorities " contained in the law of 1872 is equally as broad as that given to the phrase " excess of powers." These words are held by the decisions of the Council

---

[1] See *Arrêts du Con. d'État,* Feb. 25, 1864, *affaire Lesbats,* June 7, 1865, *Arrêts de la Cour de Cassation,* Dec. 6, 1862 ; Aug. 25, 1864, cited in *Bulletin de la Société de Législation Comparée,* 1872-3, 229 ; *cf.* Aucoc, *op. cit.,* I., 467.

of State to mean every act of every administrative authority, with the exception of political acts; and of late years the tendency of the decisions has been to take jurisdiction of many political acts in extreme cases.[1]

The remedy of appeal for excess of powers differs considerably in its character and its effects from the *contentieux administratif*. While as a result of the exercise of the *contentieux administratif* the administrative courts may review and amend the decision complained of, even if this involves the consideration of questions of fact and expediency, the Council of State may, when appeal is made to it on the ground of excess of powers, simply annul the act complained of and may not amend it or substitute another decision for the one appealed from, and will necessarily consider questions of law almost alone. The remedy is therefore much like the *certiorari* at common law. It also discharges somewhat the same function as the prohibition or injunction. For while the mere appeal to the Council of State is not suspensive, *i. e.* does not prevent the official whose act is complained of from going on and enforcing it, the Council of State may, if it sees fit, declare that the appeal in the particular case shall have suspensive effect, or may transmit the papers in the case to the proper minister and call his attention to the demand of the plaintiff that the appeal shall be suspensive. The minister may then order all administrative proceedings to be stopped.[2] This is practically equivalent to a temporary injunction. The other administrative courts do not seem to have power to declare that an appeal to them shall prevent the

---

[1] Ducrocq, *op. cit.*, I., sec. 252 ; Aucoc, *op. cit.*, I., sec. 300.
[2] Laferrière, *op. cit.*, I., 289, 290.

officer whose act is complained of from acting. But as in practically all cases, where an absolutely illegal act is complained of, the appeal against it goes to the Council of State on the ground of excess of powers, the power possessed by the Council of State is amply sufficient to protect individual rights. Finally it is to be noticed that France is the only country, whose laws are under consideration, which permits such a remedy to be made use of against the acts of the highest officers of state, including even the chief executive. The fact that the members of the Council of State are dependent in tenure upon the President of course will tend to prevent an immoderate use of their power.

V.—*The administrative courts.*

1. *General administrative courts. The councils of the prefecture.*—While the councils of the prefecture may be called general administrative courts, they are not courts of general jurisdiction. But the statutes conferring jurisdiction upon them are so numerous that they have a much wider jurisdiction than any of the other lower administrative courts, and, in point of fact, do have jurisdiction over almost all important conflicts that arise between the administration in its lower instances and the individual. These councils are composed of three or four councillors and the prefect, as president, who, in point of fact, seldom presides, and the secretary-general of the prefecture, who acts as the representative of the government. The councillors, who are the real judges, are appointed, and may be removed by the President of the republic. To be appointed as councillor the applicant must be twenty-

five years of age, and have either a theoretical or a practical knowledge of administrative matters. That is, he must be a licentiate in law, a degree which corresponds somewhat to an American degree of bachelor of laws, which admits to practice at the bar and is a university degree given by the faculty of law, or he must have served ten years in the judicial or administrative service, or for ten years have been a member of a general council of one of the departments. The functions of councillor of the prefecture are salaried, and are by law incompatible with the pursuit of any other occupation or profession.[1] The position is thus strictly a professional one.

The council of the prefecture is not only an administrative court, but is also an administrative council, and as such has to advise the prefect often in his administration and has in certain cases the absolute power of decision.[2] It is in this way that the French make it certain that the councillors of the prefecture shall be in daily contact with the workings of the active administration, and will therefore be able to decide with understanding the various matters which come up before them when they are organized as a court.

The jurisdiction of the council is of three kinds. In the first place it has the general administrative jurisdiction, *i. e.* the *contentieux* of a long series of matters. These are the direct taxes and taxes assimilated to the direct taxes; certain special questions of fact in connection with the indirect taxes, though indirect taxes as a whole, are for special reasons in the jurisdiction of the ordinary judicial courts; questions relative to the administrative control over the communes and the in-

---

[1] L. June 21, 1865.   [2] *Supra*, I., p. 274.

stitutions which the French call public establishments, *i. e. quasi* public corporations ; questions relative to communal elections and a series of miscellaneous matters which are not susceptible of classification, but which embrace a great many important administrative acts.[1]

In the second place the councils of the prefecture have a large original jurisdiction over the contracts and torts made and committed by the administration relative to the public works of both the central and local administration, to the public domain of the state, and the contracts for material and supplies of the central administration.[2]

In the third place the council of the prefecture has a large police jurisdiction of violations of police ordinances relative to the main roads, the draining of marshes and quarries.[3] This is an exception to the general rule which is that the entire police jurisdiction is given to the ordinary courts. The reason for the exception is to be found in the desire to give the administration great freedom of action. This purpose of the law has been incompletely attained. For the decisions of these councils and of the Council of State, particularly in regard to violations of the highway regulations, are here again more favorable to private rights than those of the ordinary courts, which have jurisdiction of the violations of the regulations relative to the lesser roads.[4]

Finally the councils of the prefecture act as boards of audit for the account of officers of *quasi* public corporations and of the less important communes.[5]

---

[1] Aucoc, *op. cit.*, I., 495 ; Laferrière, *op. cit.*, I., 317–321.
[2] Aucoc, *op. cit.*, I., 503–512.   [3] *Ibid.*, 515.
[4] Ducrocq, II., sec. 859.   [5] Aucoc, I., 517.

In most of these cases the councils of the prefecture decide finally but there is always an appeal from their decision not only of questions of law but also of questions of fact.

2. *Special administrative courts.*—The most important of the special administrative courts, *i. e.* those courts formed for the decision of only one or two kinds of questions, are the educational courts and the councils of revision.

a. *Educational courts.*—There are two grades of these : first, the departmental council and the academic council; and second, the superior council. These are all composed largely of *ex officio* members and particularly of persons engaged in the work of education and of members of the various recognized churches.[1] Like the other administrative courts they are also administrative councils, and as such are to advise the officers of the educational administration, and have quite a control over the pedagogical part of primary, secondary, and superior education. As administrative courts the departmental and academic councils hear complaints made by teachers against the acts of educational officers in the primary and secondary branches respectively. Thus *e. g.* if the prefect should revoke a teacher's certificate, without which he may not teach in either a public or a private school, such teacher may appeal to the departmental council or the academic council, according as he is a primary or secondary teacher. The academic council has also jurisdiction of all similar complaints that may arise in the superior as well as the secondary educational administration. The

[1] See for details, Simonet, *op. cit.*, citing L., June 14, 1854 ; L., Feb. 27, 1880, art. 9 ; and 1.

superior council has, as a council of advice, to give its opinion when asked on all matters connected with the subject of education, and as an administrative court to hear appeals from the departmental council as to matters relating to primary education, and from the academic council as to matters relating to secondary and superior education. As a court it has appellate jurisdiction alone, and its decisions as to questions of fact are final, but in case such decisions exceed its powers or violate a law appeal for excess of powers may be taken to the Council of State.

b. *The councils of revision.*—The councils of revision are governed by the law of July 27, 1872, and were formed for the purpose of deciding complaints which may arise as a result of the conscript laws. They are composed of both military and civil members, though the actual control is in the hands of the civil members. The prefect is the president. The civil elements are representatives of the general council, the council of the prefecture, the departmental commission, and of the councils of the *arondissements* of the departments over which the council of revision has jurisdiction. It moves about from canton to canton in the department, and revises the drawing of the lots which decide who shall serve in the army where there are a greater number of candidates for the army than are required, and decides on all cases of exemption from service in time of peace. Its decisions are generally final as to questions of fact, but may be appealed from to the Council of State on the ground of excess of powers and violation of the law.

In addition to these bodies there are also certain other commissions which are sometimes regarded as administrative courts, such as the commissions of moneys and the commissions for levying assessments for local improvements.

3. *The supreme administrative court. The Council of State.*—The organization of this body has already been described and it has already been pointed out that it is the most important administrative council in the French system and, as such, advises the President of the republic and the various ministers.[1] It has also been pointed out that it is divided up into sections, four of which are administrative sections and are to advise the government in purely administrative matters, but that the fifth section is the judicial section whose duty is to do a large part of the work devolved upon the council in its capacity of administrative court. This judicial section is called the *section du contentieux* and is composed of five councillors of state and a certain number of commissioners (*maîtres des requêtes*) and auditors. It decides alone all less important matters and for all the more important matters makes the preliminary examination, though in these cases the actual decision is made by the whole council which is then said to be acting *au contentieux*. The law of May 24, 1872, has given the council acting as an administrative court an absolute power of decision.

Its general administrative jurisdiction, *i. e.* the *contentieux administratif*, is both original and appellate. Its original jurisdiction may be said to be general, as an appeal may be taken to it from any decision of the President of the republic or of the ministers which violates a right ; and it has the right to interpret all acts of the chief executive and the ministers which are

[1] *Supra*, I.. p. 108.

administrative in character. In certain cases though not often, it has original jurisdiction of complaints against the action of the prefects.[1]

Further its appellate jurisdiction consists in the hearing of appeals from the decisions of the councils of the prefectures and of most of the special courts; and on such appeals it may review questions of fact and of expediency as well as of law.[2]

Finally the Council of State acts as a court of *cassation*, as a result of its jurisdiction of appeals for excess of powers and violation of the law.[3] Here the decision of the Council of State simply affirms or reverses the decision of the body whose act is complained of. It may not, as it may in the exercise of its ordinary apellate jurisdiction, substitute its decision for that of the authority from whose action appeal has been taken.[4]

[1] Aucoc, *op. cit.*, I., 588.
[2] *Ibid.*, 591.
[3] *Supra*, II., p. 229.
[4] Aucoc, *op. cit.*, I., 591.

CHAPTER VII.

THE ADMINISTRATIVE JURISDICTION IN GERMANY.

I.—History.

1. *From 1806 to the formation of the empire.*—
When the old German kingdom and Holy Roman
Empire was broken up in 1806 the administrative
jurisdiction of the royal-imperial courts was completely
destroyed and individuals were left at the mercy of the
separate states which then came into being.   The
imperial administrative jurisdiction over the acts of the
officers of the most important members of the empire
was not very great as a result of the *privilegium de
non appellando* which was possessed by most of them and
in accordance with which appeals to the imperial courts
against the acts of officers in these sections were not
allowed.[1]   The separate German states were very generally guided in their regulation of the relations of the
courts and the administration by the new principle of
the separation of powers which had been so fully developed by the French revolution.   This had for its
corollary, it will be remembered, the complete independence of the administration over against the courts,
which were to be confined to the decision of private

---

[1] Meyer, *Deutsches Verwaltungsrecht*, I., 29 ; *cf.* Gneist, *Der Rechtsstaat*,
cap. v.; *Das Englische Verwaltungsrecht*, I., 423, *exc.*

and criminal law cases. That is all complaints against the action of the administration, so far as they did not come within the domain of the private or the criminal law, were in Germany as in France to be decided by the administration itself; and perfect freedom of appeal from the decisions of the subordinate authorities to the higher authorities was provided. This condition of things did not, however, lead at first to great arbitrariness of action on the part of the administration. For the administrative authorities in their higher instances were so organized as to ensure to the individual almost the same guaranties of impartial action as were to be found in the courts.[1] They were organized for the most part as boards whose members had a tenure similar to that of the judges, *i. e.* practically during good behavior. When, however, the absolute monarchy was changed into the constitutional monarchy as a result of the revolution of 1848 all this was changed. The highest administrative authorities, the ministers, became partisans rather than the representatives of an impartial crown. The administrative organization became more single-headed in form and was more completely subordinated to the ministers.[2] The administration thus became an instrument which might be made use of by the political party which happened to be in power in the legislature to further its own ends; and as all of the great political parties were essentially social parties the danger became very great of the partisan application of the administrative law in the interest of some particular social class. In Prussia this was actually the case during the reactionary period

[1] Meyer, *Deutsches Verwaltungsrecht*, I., 32.
[2] *Supra*, I., p. 299; II., p. 188.

from 1850–60.[1] The conservative party which was the landholding interest, *i. e.* the nobility, got control of the administration and prostituted it in the interest of their own social class and to the detriment of other social classes. German publicists saw that some change must be made,—that some judicial control over the administration must be provided. The great question was how should this judicial control be formed? Should it be given to the ordinary courts or should there be formed special courts after the model of the French courts which by this time had shown themselves to be efficient protectors of individual rights? Prussia, where the condition of things was the worst, was the first to answer this question and answered it by granting in 1861 to the ordinary courts a control over certain administrative acts connected with the tax administration.[2] It is, however, to be noticed that a Prussian ordinance of as early a date as 1808 and another of May 11, 1842, had taken steps in this direction by permitting appeal to the courts in the case of police orders on the ground that they were absolutely contrary to law. Further, in case the law recognized an obligation on the part of the government to indemnify an individual for an invasion of his property rights the courts were permitted to decide as to the necessity and the amount of the indemnity. At about the same time Baden declared in favor of special administrative courts.[3] The progress of the reform in Prussia, however, was interrupted by the serious internal and external questions which presented themselves for

---

[1] *Supra*, I., p. 299.

[2] L. May 24, 1861 ; *cf.* Meyer, *Deutsches Verwaltungsrecht,* I., 31, *et seq.*

[3] See L. Oct. 5, 1863, cited in Meyer, *Deutsches Verwaltungsrecht,* I., 33.

solution and it was not till after the wars with Austria and France had been fought that the question was again taken up. It is therefore with the formation of the empire that the problem was definitely solved.

2. *Since the formation of the empire.*—As a result of imperial legislation the following is the condition of things : The imperial law organizing the courts maintains in theory the independence of the administration in its former extent,[1] but it and other laws have given to the courts in a few special instances a control over the administration,[2] while as a result of the general principle of German law which is in many cases formally expressed in the imperial statutes,[3] the courts control all private legal acts of the administration, *i. e.* when acting as fiscus it makes contracts or commits torts.[4] Other imperial laws also have provided in special instances for special administrative courts. The imperial legislation, however, leaves everything else to be regulated by the legislation of the separate members of the empire, simply providing that questions of competence between the administration and the courts shall be decided by a body in which the courts shall have a fair representation.[5]

II.—The general characteristics of the German system.

1. *General canons of distinction.*—In the first place the action of the administration when acting as a public power is in theory both in the empire and in the separate members of the empire free from all judicial con-

[1] L. Jan. 27, 1877, art. 13.

[2] Loening, *op. cit.*, 787 ; Laferrière, *La Juridiction Administrative*, I., 37.

[3] As *e. g.* in the statute putting in force the code of civil procedure, secs. 4 and 5.　　　[4] *Supra*, II., p. 162.　　　[5] L. Jan. 27, 1877, sec. 17.

trol both from that of the ordinary courts and from that of the administrative courts except where the law has specifically laid down that it should be subjected to control. In the second place the particular cases where the administration is subjected to judicial control are of two kinds ; either it is subjected to the control of the ordinary courts or it is subjected to the control of special administrative courts.

2. *The administrative jurisdiction of the ordinary courts.*—Individual liberty is protected as in France against attack on the part of the administration by the code of criminal procedure which makes it certain that a person who has been arrested may be able to have his case brought up at once before the ordinary courts for decision as to the legality of his detention.[1]

Again in most cases where power has been given to the administration to decide in first instance private law cases, as *e. g.* where police authorities are given, as is usually the case, the power to decide conflicts arising between innkeepers and their guests as to charges, appeals may be taken to the ordinary courts.[2]

Further in most cases where the law recognizes that the government is bound to pay an individual an indemnity for an invasion of his property rights, as *e. g.* in the case of the exercise of the right of eminent domain, the ordinary courts are to decide the amount of the indemnity but may not usually consider the question whether the administration was acting legally ; the latter question is to be decided by the administration or the administrative courts as the case may be.[3]

---

[1] Stengel, *Wörterbuch des Deutsches Verwaltungsrecht, sub verbo Verhaftung*, citing arts. 114, 132, 341 of the code of criminal procedure.

[2] Sarwey, *Das Oeffentliche Recht, etc.*, 625. [3] *Ibid.*, 633 *et seq.*

Still further, where the law permits administrative execution [1] in the enforcement of money payments due the government, appeal may be taken to the courts if such administrative execution is directed towards real rights—*dingliche rechte.*[2]

Finally in Prussia it is provided that the individual may appeal to the ordinary courts against the acts of the administration in tax and police matters, *i. e.* he may allege that the tax is already paid, or that he is relieved in some way from the payment, or that, as the result of some special statute or privilege, he is not liable to do the thing ordered by the police authority.[3]

III.—*The administrative courts in Germany.*

These are to be found both in the empire and in its separate members. In the empire these administrative courts, though comparatively numerous, have a very limited jurisdiction, being confined, each of them, to the decision of a certain class of cases. In most instances they act at the same time as administrative authorities, this being the method adopted of making it certain that the members of the courts have the necessary special knowledge, and in one or two cases appeal goes from their decisions to the imperial court at Leipsic.

1. *Imperial courts.*—These are :

a. *The imperial poor-law board (Bundesamt für Heimathswesen).*—This tribunal decides all conflicts arising between the poor-law unions of different members of the empire relative to the duty of offering

---

[1] *Supra*, II., p. 127.

[2] *Ibid.*, citing law introducing code of civil procedure, sec. 4.

[3] Stengel, *Wörterbuch, sub verbo Rechtsweg* for this and for the provisions of a similar character, contained in the laws of the other members of the empire.

public charity to poor persons.[1] Its competence does not extend over Bavaria and Alsace-Lorraine, whose inhabitants are, from the standpoint of the poor-law, to be treated as foreigners. The separate members of the empire may by local statute provide that the final decision of conflicts between their own poor-law unions may be made by this authority. This has been done in Prussia, Hesse, and several others.[2]

b. *Imperial fortress belt commission.*—This body was organized by the law of December 21, 1871, and decides on appeal conflicts between the individual and the administration relative to the imposition of restrictions on real property within a certain distance of fortresses. It is to be noticed, however, that in accordance with the general principle already noted, all conflicts relative to the amount of the indemnity to be paid to the individual are to be settled by the ordinary courts.[3]

c. *Imperial railway court (Verstärkte Eisenbahnamt).* —This was organized by the law of June 27, 1873, and decides conflicts between the railway commission and the various railways when the railways claim that the commission has acted contrary to the law. In case of such an appeal certain judicial officers are added to the commission, which then takes on the name of the railway court, and is to act quite independently of the administration, which presents the case to it.

d. *Imperial patent office.*—This was organized by the law of May 25, 1877, and not only issues patents, but annuls and revokes them. In these last cases appeal goes to the imperial court at Leipsic.[4]

---

[1] L. June 6, 1870, sec. 42.

[2] See De Grais, *Verfassung und Verwaltung.*, *etc.*, 311, note 20.

[3] See Meyer, *Deutsches Verwaltungsrecht*, II., 163.   [4] *Cf. ibid.*, I., 425.

e. *The disciplinary court and chambers.*—These bodies decide as to the removal of officers in the imperial administration, and the imposition upon them of disciplinary penalties.[1]

f. *The imperial superior marine office.*—This was organized by the law of July 27, 1877, and decides complaints against the decisions of the marine officers, either taking away licences from pilots and ship officers or refusing to prosecute them on the complaint of the marine commissioners.

The position of the members of the poor-law board seems to be more assured than that of the members of the other bodies. It is similar to that of the judges of the ordinary courts. The members of the other courts are for the most part merely administrative officers. But it must be remembered that all administrative officers have practically a tenure during good behavior and can be removed in the absence of criminal acts only as a result of a disciplinary procedure before the disciplinary courts. Therefore wherever the law says that these officers are to act independently of the administration, which is usually the case, they are not subject to the directions of the administration. For refusal to obey the commands of the administration would not probably be regarded as a case for the exercise of the disciplinary power. These courts are all of them thus practically independent of the administration. Their organization, which is often peculiar, and their jurisdiction are fixed in the laws organizing them.[2]

---

[1] *Supra*, II., p. 87.

[2] The details may be found in the laws which have been cited, or in Meyer, *Deutsches Verwaltungsrecht*, under the appropriate heading.

2. *The Prussian administrative courts.*—In the separate members of the German Empire the administrative courts are differently formed and possess a varied jurisdiction. The most completely organized courts and the courts which possess the widest jurisdiction are those of Prussia to which our future consideration will be confined.

a. *The jurisdiction of the Prussian administrative courts.*—Though the jurisdiction of the Prussian administrative courts has been modelled in large part on the jurisdiction of the French administrative courts, there are several points of essential difference. In the first place their jurisdiction does not include any of the decisions of the ministers which are not subjected as a rule to any administrative jurisdiction at all ; nor does it as a general thing include the decisions of any of the officers of the central administration except in so far as they relate to the administration of internal affairs and to the purely local taxes. The control of the central taxes is in the hands of the central administration alone ; for no special exception has been made in this case as has been made in the case of local taxes. In the second place it may be laid down as a general rule that no appeal to the administrative courts is open to the individual against the general acts of the administration, *i. e.* ordinances.[1] The appeal may be taken only from a special administrative act not of general application. Nevertheless on the appeal from a special act of the administration, performed in order to enforce an ordinance, the administrative courts may consider collaterally the question of the validity of the

---

[1] Stengel, *Organisation, etc.,* 458. There is no remedy in the Prussian system similar to the French appeal to the Council of State for excess of powers.

ordinance and may refuse to enforce the special act on the ground that the ordinance which it is issued to enforce is illegal.[1]

There are two general rules governing the right of appeal to the administrative courts against the special acts of the administration.

In the first place only those acts may be appealed from whose tendency is to violate private rights. As a result, however, of the enumerated jurisdiction of the administrative courts a provision of law must give the right to appeal even when a private right is violated. The special cases enumerated in the statutes are so numerous that almost every individual right, subject to the limitations mentioned above, is protected by an appeal to the administrative courts. The only exception to the rule that the existence of a special provision of law is necessary in order that recourse to the administrative courts may be had is in the case of the acts of the administration relating to what are called police matters, *i. e.* resulting from the exercise of the police power. Here the law distinctly says that the individual may appeal from the police orders of the administration on the ground that his rights are violated thereby, because the police authorities have not applied the law or have made a wrongful application of it on the ground that the conditions are not present, which by the law are necessary in order that the police authorities may act.[2] As these police orders constitute by far the larger number of the acts of the administration in the administration of internal affairs, and as this rule permits the administrative courts to review the decisions of the administration not only on ques-

[1] *Ibid.*   [2] *Ibid.*, 491.

tions of law but also on questions of fact, *i. e.* they are
to determine whether the conditions made necessary by
law for the action of the police authorities are present,
it will be noticed that the control of the administrative
courts over the administration of internal affairs is
quite an extended one. Further, not only may individual persons appeal to the administrative courts, but
also public corporations may appeal to these courts
against the decisions of the supervisory authorities
made in the exercise of the central administrative control over public corporations and their officers. Thus
if the supervisory authority should insert an appropriation in the budget of a city for the payment of an
expense which it regarded as obligatory, but which the
municipal authorities did not regard as obligatory, the
municipality might appeal from the decision of the
supervisory authority to the administrative courts.

While the general rule is that the appeal to the
administrative courts is open only in case of the violation of a private right, in a few cases it is permitted
simply in the interest of the maintenance of the law.
This is so *e. g.* in the case of elections. Here not only
a defeated candidate but also any elector may appeal
to the administrative courts against the decision of the
election officers on the ground that it has violated
the law.[1]

Finally in all cases where an appeal is made to the
administrative courts the appeal is made in the same
form, *i. e.* in the form of a complaint that injustice has
been done. Like the appeal to the English quarter
sessions the remedy is general though the jurisdiction
of the courts is enumerated. As a general thing the

[1] Stengel, *Organisation, etc.*, 493.

appeal to the administrative court has a suspensive effect, and is therefore similar to the injunction in English law. But if the execution of the act complained of may not in the judgment of the administration be suspended without harm to the public weal, it may be executed notwithstanding the pendency of the suit. In no case, however, may the administration decree the arrest of a person until the case has been decided in its favor by an administrative court or until after the time provided for appeal to the administrative court has elapsed.[1]

b. *The organization of the Prussian administrative courts.*—The Prussian administrative courts may, like the French, be divided into courts of first instance, and appellate courts. For a large class of cases, however, there are three instances. For the appellate courts for some cases, are courts of first instance for others. What shall be the court of first instance in a given case is determined largely by the grade in the administrative hierarchy of the authority whose act is complained of.

The Prussians, like the French, and indeed like the English in the formation of the appellate jurisdiction of the courts of quarter sessions, have recognized the importance of having their administrative judges learned in the administrative law and have adopted practically the same method to attain the desired end. That is the judges in most cases are in other capacities engaged in the work of active administration. The only exception to this rule is to be found in the case

---

[1] *Ibid.*, 520 ; citing L. July 30, 1883, secs. 53, 133. This of course refers only to the decree of executive arrest as a means of executing the law. *Supra*, II., p. 121.

of the highest administrative court. In all cases, different from the French administrative judges and more like the English justices of the peace, the Prussian administrative judges are independent in tenure over against the active administration. Further in the lower instances the Prussian administrative judges, like the English justices of the peace, are laymen and are unpaid. The judges of the highest court are, however, professional lawyers and are salaried and are not engaged in active administrative work.

In detail the Prussian administrative courts are as follows :

First, the circle committee in the rural districts and the city committee in the city circles. These bodies have at the same time active administrative work to perform.[1] The circle committee is composed of the Landrath, who, it will be remembered, is the representative of the central administration in the rural circles and the executive of the circle as a local municipal corporation and is appointed by the Crown,[2] and of six members elected by the circle diet from among the inhabitants of the circle.[3] As these six members represent the lay non-professional element which is unsalaried, all professional officers of the administration are ineligible. In the city circles (*i. e.* cities of over 25,000 inhabitants) the city committee is composed of the burgomaster as president, and of four municipal citizens chosen by the city executive.[4] The president and one at least of the members must be qualified for the judicial or higher administrative courts. The jurisdiction of this, the lowest of the administrative

---

[1] *Supra*, I., pp. 315, 330.
[2] *Supra*, I., p. 315.
[3] *Kreisordnung*, sec. 181.
[4] L. July 30, 1883, secs. 37, 38.

courts, as enumerated in the statutes, embraces all cases which arise between communes relative to their boundaries and to the apportionment of common charges such as for roads and schools, local taxes, common enjoyment of public institutions and communal property ; complaints relative to the enjoyment or loss of membership in the commune or smaller city ; appeals in regard to communal elections, difficulties relative to the civil service, *i. e.* the imposition of disciplinary penalties on the non-professional officers ; appeals made by the local authorities from the decisions of the supervisory officers ; difficulties relative to the quartering of soldiers and military requisitions in time of peace ; various difficulties relative to the police of highways, waterways, building, commerce, industry, and hunting ; complaints against the action in local police matters of all local police authorities.[1]

Such in general is the jurisdiction of the circle and city committee, but in all these cases if the administrative authority from which appeal is taken is an important one the appeal even in these matters goes, not to the circle or city committee, but to the next highest court, the district committee. Thus in the matter of police appeals, if the action complained of has been taken by an authority of a city of over 10,000 inhabitants the competent administrative court is not the circle or city committee but the district committee.

Second, the district committee. This, like the circle committee, is an authority for the active administration but its territorial jurisdiction is much larger, extending

---

[1] Stengel, *Organisation, etc.*, 404 ; *cf.* Laferrière, *La Juridiction Administrative*, I., 47.

over the entire governmental district, which corresponds somewhat to the American county. It is however differently organized as an administrative authority and as an administrative court. In the first capacity the government president, the representative of the central administration in the district, is president, in the second capacity it is presided over by the administrative court director who is appointed by the Crown and is to be one of the two professional members provided by the law. These two professional members are to be appointed by the Crown for life and must possess, one, the qualifications for the judicial service, the other, the qualifications for the higher administrative service. In addition to the two professional members there are four lay members who are appointed by the provincial committee from among the inhabitants of the district.[1] The district committee has, as administrative court, original and appellate jurisdiction. It has appellate jurisdiction of the decisions of the circle and city committees and has original jurisdiction over the affairs of the rural circles and the cities of over 10,000 inhabitants similar to that which the circle committees has over the affairs of the communes and the less important cities.[2] The whole question of jurisdiction is settled by the competence law of 1883 which goes into the most minute details and settles not only the question whether appeal may be taken to an administrative court (*Verwaltungsklage*), or whether it is to go to an administrative authority (*Verwaltungsbeschwerde*), but also determines to what court the appeal, when allowed, is to go.

[1] L. July 30, 1883, secs. 27, 28, *supra*, I., p. 307.
[2] Stengel, *Organisation, etc.*, 424 ; Laferrière, *op. cit.*, I., 49.

Third, the superior administrative court. This court sits at Berlin, and is the highest administrative tribunal. It is composed of judges who must be at least thirty years of age and are appointed by the Crown on the presentation of the state ministry. Half the judges must possess the qualifications necessary for the judicial service, the other half must be qualified for the higher administrative service.[1] It is divided, in order to facilitate the transaction of business, into sections or senates,[2] but in order to keep its decisions uniform, it is provided that, if any senate desires to depart from the decision of any other senate or from that of the general assembly of the court, the matter in question must be decided by the general assembly.[3] This court acts as a court of appeal, as a court of cassation, and in a few instances as a court of original jurisdiction. It acts as a court of appeal from the decisions of the district committee when it often acts as a court of third instance. Its jurisdiction as a court of cassation can with difficulty be distinguished from its jurisdiction as a court of appeal, the only difference being that when it acts as a court of cassation it does not as a usual thing decide questions of fact and simply quashes or affirms the decision of the court appealed from whereas when it acts as a court of appeal it may decide questions of fact and may substitute its decision for that appealed from. As a court of original jurisdiction it decides as a rule simply complaints against the decisions of the highest of the officers in the localities, *viz.*, the governors of the provinces and the " governments " and the " government " presidents in the districts. When it acts in these particular capacities is decided

[1] L. July 3, 1875, secs. 17, 18.   [2] *Ibid.*, sec. 20.   [3] Sec. 29.

by statute which descends into the most minute details.[1]

Finally, the procedure in all of these administrative courts is generally oral, and the sessions are public, but this may be changed by consent. The procedure is also somewhat inquisitorial in character, but in the main controversial.[2]

It will be noticed that the general system of administrative courts in Prussia is based on the French plan, but care has been taken to avoid the appearance of dependence on the active administration, which is regarded by some writers as so serious a defect in the French system, as taking away in fact from the French administrative tribunals the characteristics of judicial bodies. The Prussians have also laid great stress on the non-professional character of the administrative judges, in imitation of the English courts of quarter sessions. The similarity to the English method is not accidental, but is due to the influence of that great student of English public law, Professor Gneist of the University of Berlin, to whose exertions was largely due the organization of the system, and who insisted on the dominance of the non-professional elements in courts whose duty it was to control so professional an administration as is the Prussian.

[1] *Cf.* Stengel, *Organisation, etc.*, 438 ; Laferrière, *op. cit.*, I., 50.
[2] Stengel, *Organisation, etc.*, 508 *et seq.*

CHAPTER VIII.

CONFLICTS OF JURISDICTION.

Our examination of the administrative jurisdiction in the various countries coming under consideration has shown that England and the United States have given this jurisdiction in first or in last instance to the ordinary courts, while France and Germany have with some exceptions put it into the hands of special administrative courts. While in England and the United States the possession by the ordinary courts of the administrative jurisdiction has resulted in the formation of a series of more or less special remedies and a very technical procedure,[1] the existence of special courts in France and Germany has brought about the possibility and indeed the probability of conflicts of jurisdiction between the two classes of courts, or between the ordinary judicial courts and the administration. Either the judicial courts attempt to encroach upon the competence of the administration or the administrative courts, and *vice versa*, when we have a positive conflict; or they both refuse to take jurisdiction on the ground that they are incompetent, when we have a negative conflict. It is necessary to provide

---

[1] An example of the technicality of the procedure may be found in the Virginia coupon cases, lately decided by the United States Supreme Court. See Poindexter v. Greenhow, 114 U. S., 270 ; Hartman v. Greenhow, 102 U. S., 672 ; Antoni v. Greenhow, 107 U. S., 769.

some means of settling these conflicts. This means has been provided in both countries which have given the administrative jurisdiction to special courts or to the administration itself. In France the Tribunal of Conflicts has been formed for the purpose of settling these conflicts; in Germany either a similar tribunal, known as a competence court, has been established, or else the power to settle these conflicts has been given to the ordinary judges. Where special conflict courts have been formed, the principle upon which they have been formed is essentially the same, that is that they shall be composed of an equal number of judges of the ordinary courts and of administrative judges. The law organizing the French Tribunal of Conflicts is that of May 24, 1872; that relative to this matter in Germany is the law organizing the courts of January 27, 1877, sec. 17, developed in its details in Prussia by Ordinance of August 1, 1879. This law provides in the first place that all conflicts of jurisdiction between the courts and the imperial administrative officers shall be settled by the ordinary courts themselves[1]; and in the second place permits the separate members of the empire to give the imperial courts the power to decide conflicts arising between the courts and administrative officers, but permits them at the same time to form special conflict courts. But if they avail themselves of the latter privilege the special courts provided must be so organized that one half of their members shall be at the same time members of the higher imperial courts, while the other half must be appointed for life. The only exception to this general principle in force in both France and Germany as to the equal

---

[1] *Cf.* Stengel, *Organisation, etc.*, 557.

representation in the conflict courts of both the judicial and administrative elements is in the fact that the president of the French Tribunal of Conflicts is the minister of justice. The administration would thus seem to have the casting vote in France. But it must be remembered that the minister of justice is almost as liable to declare in favor of the jurisdiction of the ordinary courts as in favor of that of the administration, since his duties connect him much more closely with the ordinary courts than with the administrative courts or the administration.

The method of raising the conflict as it is called or as we would say in America, of removing the cause, is in both countries practically the same. But it is arranged primarily to prevent the ordinary courts from encroaching on the power of the administration; and this is only natural since the whole system of special administrative courts is largely based upon the principle of the independence of the administration from the control of the ordinary courts. Thus in both France and Germany the power to remove the cause is given to an administrative officer only; and he is, in case a court is in his opinion attempting to encroach upon the competence of the administration,[1] to notify the court of the opinion of the administration. If the court believes the claim of the administration is well founded it will stop its action in the case, if it does not it opposes such claim and the question goes up directly to the conflict court for decision. In the German imperial administration no conflict can be raised, but the courts, *i. e.* the ordinary courts, decide the matter along with

[1] In France the prefect, Boeuf, *Droit Administratif*, 546; in Germany the provincial or district officers, Loening, *op. cit.*, 792, note 4.

other jurisdictional questions and in the same manner.[1] In those cases in which the conflict may be raised the notification by the administration of the removal of the cause suspends all proceedings before the ordinary courts until the decision of the conflict court is made.[2] In France one means has been provided of preventing the administrative courts from encroaching upon the jurisdiction of the ordinary courts. The ministers have the right to remove any matter before the Council of State, which they believe belongs before the ordinary courts, into the Tribunal of Conflicts, if the Council of State on demand refuses to declare itself incompetent.[3] It must be noted that the exercise of such a check on the administrative courts is in the hands of the administration and not in those of the judiciary. The minister of justice has, however, the same right in this respect as the other ministers.

In case of negative conflicts the individual concerned is to bring the matter before the court of conflicts where that exists.[4] In France, however, an interested minister and particularly the minister of justice may bring the matter before the Tribunal of Conflicts.[5] In the case of the positive conflict it is provided in the interest of vested rights, that the cause must be removed, in Germany before judgment,[6] in France before final judgment, in the ordinary courts.[7]

The existence of these conflicts is one of the greatest disadvantages of the system of special administrative courts. It is a greater disadvantage probably than the

[1] Stengel, *Organisation, etc.,* 597.

[2] Boeuf, *Droit Administratif,* 549 ; Loening, *op. cit.,* 793.

[3] Boeuf, *op. cit.,* 550, citing L. May 24, 1872, art. 26.

[4] Boeuf, *op. cit.,* 554 ; Loening, *op. cit.,* 793.   [6] L. Jan. 27, 1877, art. 17.

[5] Boeuf, *op. cit.,* 554.   [7] Boeuf, *op. cit.,* 546.

special character of the remedies and the technical character of the procedure in the administrative jurisdiction of the ordinary English and American courts. For in the case of a positive conflict the decision of a private law case may be greatly delayed, while in the case of a negative conflict an individual may be obliged to apply to both classes of courts and to the conflict court before he knows which court is the proper one. Cases have occurred in France in which a suitor has gone through all the ordinary courts up to the Court of Cassation only to be told that the ordinary courts are incompetent, has then applied to the administrative courts and finally obtained the decision of the highest one of these, the Council of State, only to be told here also that the administrative courts were incompetent and has then been obliged to appeal to the Tribunal of Conflicts and after all the trouble and expense necessitated by this long litigation is only in the position of suitor beginning litigation with a knowledge of the court which has jurisdiction of his case. Of course much of this trouble is avoided in the administrative system of the German Empire where, as in the United States, in the matter of the jurisdiction of the United States and commonwealth courts, the supreme judicial court has the final power of decision. But while this method is of course of great advantage to the suitor it must be remembered that by it the independence of the administration, which is one of the main reasons for providing special administrative courts, is not so well assured.

Division III.—The Legislative Control.

CHAPTER I.

HISTORY OF THE LEGISLATIVE CONTROL.

The history of the legislative or parliamentary control must be studied in the history of English institutions, since England developed the modern legislative body. In the historical sketch which has been given of the English administrative organization [1] it was seen that there was gradually developed by the side of the absolute Norman king a body composed at first of the *meliores terræ* and finally of the representatives of the entire population of the kingdom. One of the most important functions of this body, the Parliament, was from the earliest times to redress grievances. Even so late as the latter part of the middle ages much of the time of Parliament was taken up in the discharge of this function. The grievances which the Parliament sought to redress not only were notable abuses in the government but were found in the most minute details of the government. Indeed at first, the main means of controlling the administration, not only in the interest of society at large but also in that of individual rights, was to be found

---

[1] *Supra*, I., pp. 98, 122.

in this parliamentary control. As a result of the government of the Stuart kings two facts, however, became apparent. The first was that the party conflicts which are so apt to arise in Parliament made it an improper authority for the exercise of such an extended control; the second was that the parliamentary control was altogether insufficient for the protection of individual rights against an arbitrary and corrupted administration. These defects in the system of control over the administration were remedied by increasing the independence of the local organs and of the courts, and the consequent increase of the judicial control over the administration.[1] The parliamentary or legislative control was in this way reduced to the position of a subsidiary but at the same time a necessary control.[2] The general redress of grievances was therefore made by the courts and Parliament redressed only grievances of an extraordinary character. Petitions for redress of grievances from this time on took on the character more of propositions *de lege ferenda.* At the same time Parliament began to increase its control over the administration in other directions. Thus it began to specify in its appropriation acts the purposes for which money might be spent by the administration. The spending of money had been before 1676 altogether an affair of the royal prerogative with which the Parliament had not interfered. But it was led to assume this power as a result of the wasteful administration of the kings,[3] and as a result of the fact that through this power it could exercise a very efficient control over the general policy of the execu-

---

[1] Gneist, *Das Englische Verwaltungsrecht,* 1884, 345.
[2] Gneist, *loc. cit.*   [3] *Infra,* II., p. 280.

tive. Further in order that this power might be of any value it was necessary for the Parliament to assure itself in some way that the administration had conformed in its actions to the provisions of the appropriation acts. It therefore, somewhat later, began to examine the accounts of the administration. Again while the Parliament still retained its former power of impeaching the ministers of the Crown in case of their continued and wilful disobedience of the resolutions of Parliament and violation of the law of the land, it added very much to its powers of control by insisting that the ministers of the Crown should be such persons as could obtain and retain the confidence of Parliament. The result of the development of this principle of the responsibility of the ministers led to a further increase of the control of the Parliament, which is not capable of exact juristic determination, and which has practically resulted in the abandonment of the power of impeachment.

The formerly all embracing parliamentary control has been reduced thus practically to the exercise of three powers which are largely subsidiary to the other methods of control. These three powers are: first, the power to remedy special abuses in the interest of the social well-being by entertaining propositions *de lege ferenda* and by investigating the conduct of the administration; second, the power of controlling the general policy of the administration through the voting of the appropriations and the examination of the accounts of the administration after the execution of the budget in order to see whether the provisions of the appropriation acts have been observed; and third, in the extraordinary power of impeachment, to be made use of only when all else fails to bring the administration within the bounds of the law. This power is supplemented by the principle of the responsibility of the ministers to Parliament, and is largely replaced in actual practice by that principle.

Such was the form of the parliamentary or legislative control in England at the time the general English system of constitutional government was introduced into the governmental system of constitutional states, which have generally adopted it, subject, however, to those modifications made necessary by their peculiar constitutional system.

CHAPTER II.

The exercise of this power may result from petitions
which have been sent to the legislature by individuals.
For almost all constitutions guarantee to the individual
the right to address petitions to the government, and
the legislature is the place where most of such petitions
go. The legislature may further act of its own motion
as it is generally on the watch for administrative
abuses. The means of exercising this control are the
passing of resolutions condemnatory of the administration, the putting of questions or interpellations to the
administration, and, in case satisfactory answer is not
made by the administration, the undertaking on the
part of the legislature, through committees appointed
by it, of investigations which may have in view either
the unearthing of abuses which have been suspected or
obtaining information *de lege ferenda*. The extent and
influence of the power in all these cases of its exercise
depends very largely upon the character of the relations of the executive and the legislature as fixed by
the constitution. If in the special political system the
executive power is independent of the legislature such
control loses all its sanction, except in so far as it may
be used for the purpose of legislative reform (*de lege*

ferenda). But on this account alone the legislatures of all states, even of those where the executive is independent of the legislature, have large powers of control over the administration. For the legislature through the passage of laws may circumscribe the action of the administration so far as discretionary powers are not guaranteed to it by the constitution, which is not often the case. In those countries, however, where the executive is dependent upon the legislature, this control has a most powerful sanction. For the action of the legislature may result in an expression of its lack of confidence in the ministry, which is then bound to step out and give place to a ministry whose conduct will satisfy the legislature. From this point of view the countries under consideration may be divided into two classes. In the first will be found the United States and Germany, not only in their central but also in their commonwealth organizations; in the second class are to be placed England and France.

I.—Where the administration is independent of the legislature (United States and Germany).

In the United States and Germany this control is exercised in all the ways which have been mentioned. In Germany it is, however, more efficient than in the United States. For, though the administration is independent of the legislature in tenure, it is customary for the highest administrative officers, *i. e.* the ministers, to be present at the sessions of the legislature. Being present they are naturally forced to answer questions put to them. This obligation seems to be simply a moral one, their refusal to answer or their unsatisfactory answer leading to no legal or political results. Still the mere fact that officers of the administration are present and practically have to answer questions put to them has an important moral effect in making them conduct their offices properly. This method of exercising a control over the administration by the legislature is called on the continent interpellation. In the United States such a method of control is not even so important as it is in Germany for the simple reason that the officers of the administration are never present at the sessions of the legislature; and therefore there is no opportunity for the legislature to question them personally, although, as the result of resolutions passed by either house of the legislature, questions may be put which the administration may answer or not as it sees fit. In neither Germany nor in the United States do resolutions condemnatory of the administration have any political or legal effect, though in both countries the legislature has the right to pass such resolutions. Further their moral effect does not seem to be very great.

All the control that the legislature can exercise over the administration in the United States and Germany other than the moral one just alluded to is to be found in the powers of the standing committees of the legislature and of the special investigating committees which from time to time may be appointed. In the United States there is usually one such standing committee for each administrative department. The main function of such standing committees is to scrutinize carefully the way in which the business of the particular department is transacted. The special committees are formed for the purpose of investigating some particular abuse in the administration whose existence is alleged

by individuals or has come to the notice of the legislature. Real authority such committees do not have,
except where the legislature may have the power of
removal. Their action can result simply in new
legislation. Further their power of obtaining information either from the officers of the administration or from private individuals is often not a great
one. This is true, particularly of the committees
of the national Congress. For quite a time it was
supposed that, as a result of a decision of the United
States Supreme Court,[1] Congress and its committees
had full power to punish witnesses for contempt who
refused to answer questions put to them ; but the same
tribunal in a more recent case has limited very greatly
this power. It has decided[2] that a congressional committee had no power to punish a witness for contempt
in refusing to answer questions in regard to matters
over which Congress had no jurisdiction; and, while
the Supreme Court expressly refused to decide whether
Congress had the power to force a witness to testify
in cases where it desired information for its use in
legislation, it seems to indicate in its opinion that Congress has no such power. Nothing, however, prevents
Congress or its committees from gathering testimony
from willing witnesses. When we come to the commonwealths it is not so easy to say exactly what is the
power of the legislature in this respect. It is easily
conceivable that the legislatures of the commonwealths
might have this power although it is not possessed by
the national Congress. For there is no principle of our
constitutional law which is clearer than that, while

[1] Anderson v. Dunn, 6 Wheaton, 204.
[2] Kilbourn v. Thompson, 103 U. S., 168.

Congress is an authority of enumerated powers, the legislatures of the commonwealths may do anything which they have not been expressly forbidden to do by the constitution.[1] And seldom do we find in the commonwealth constitutions any provisions which clearly take away any such power from the commonwealth legislatures. Indeed in the constitutions of twenty-four of the commonwealths[2] such power of punishing for contempt would seem to be granted. The constitutions of several of the commonwealths provide that the legislature shall have "all other powers necessary for the legislature of a free state."[3] The constitution of Massachusetts has been so interpreted by the supreme court of the commonwealth as to give a committee, appointed for the simple purpose of investigation, the power to punish witnesses for contempt.[4] Finally in the case of those commonwealths whose constitutions contain no provision as to this point we have several cases which throw light on the subject. Most of these cases are in the courts of New York, which has exercised this power more frequently than the other commonwealths. Here it has been decided that the legislature or its committees, to which it has delegated the power of investigation either by statute or by resolution, have the power to punish for contempt.[5] The latest case on the point[6] imposes an apparent limitation

---

[1] See Bank of Chenango v. Brown, 26 N. Y., 467, 469 ; People v. Dayton, 55 N. Y., 380.

[2] Alabama, Arkansas. Colorado, Connecticut, Delaware, Florida, Illinois, Indiana, Iowa, Louisiana, Maine, Maryland, Massachusetts, Minnesota, Missouri, Nebraska, Nevada, New Hampshire, Oregon, Pennsylvania, South Carolina, Tennessee, Texas, and West Virginia. See F. W. Whitridge on "Legislative Inquests," in *Pol. Sci. Qu.*, I., 84, 89.

[3] *Ibid.*, 89.   [4] Burnham v. Morrissey, 14 Gray, 226.

[5] People v. Learned, 5 Hun, 626 ; see also Wilckens v. Willet, I. Keyes, 521, 525.   [6] People *ex rel.* McDonald v. Keeler, 99 N. Y., 463.

on this power in that it says that the legislature or one
of its committees may only punish for contempt witnesses who refuse to answer questions put with the
desire of obtaining information for the future legislative action of the legislature; but, as it at the same
time admits that the court cannot judge of the intention of the legislature, all that the legislature has to do
in order to bring itself under the rule stated in this
case is to declare in the resolution appointing the committee that it desires such information.[1]   But even if
the legislature does not possess this power, still as a
matter of fact the officers of the administration will
usually comply with the summons of an investigating
committee of the legislature, and will answer all reasonable questions put to them since "desiring legislation and always desiring money [they have] strong
motives for keeping on good terms with those who
control legislation and the purse."[2]   It would seem
that the German law recognizes as belonging to the
legislature a similar control over the administration
through the appointment of investigating committees.[3]

*II.—Where the administration is dependent upon the legislature
(France and England).*

When we come to consider those states whose political system recognizes that the administration is dependent upon the legislature we find that this kind of control
of the legislature over the administration is very much
greater.   Since the administration must keep the con-

---

[1] See also the case of *Ex parte* Dalton, 44 Ohio St., 142, which holds that the
legislature may punish for contempt in election cases.

[2] Bryce, *American Commonwealth*, I., 154.

[3] Stengel, *Deutsches Verwaltungsrecht*, 204.

fidence of the legislature it must, in the nature of things, defend its policy when it is attacked and, since the legislature may at any time force the ministry out of office, it may investigate and censure the administration at such times and in such manner as it sees fit. Indeed the sanction of the control is so great that the control itself will amount in actual practice to just about what the legislature sees fit to make it. If the legislature does not impose bounds upon its control it may through its exercise practically take the place of the administration or reduce the administration to such a weak position that it will be all but impossible for it to transact properly the business in theory assigned to it. This the legislature has done in France. Interpellations, addresses, questions as to its policy and censures of the action of the administration have been so frequent that the French acting executive has been completely terrorized and paralyzed; and the control which the legislature possesses and which, in order that the government may be well conducted, should be used with moderation, it has made use of to deprive the administration of almost all discretion and practically to concentrate in the legislature many administrative functions. The existence of such a control presupposes that the ministers will guide the legislature, that they will have its confidence, which shall not be withdrawn for trivial reasons. The ministry in such a political system serves or should serve the purpose of the standing committees of those legislatures in which the ministry is not represented. Where this is not the case, as it is not the case in France, the ministry and the administration become the servants rather than the guides of the legislature and naturally become so anxious to win the approval of the legislature that they are unable wisely to conduct the government. If this legislative control is not to degenerate into the performance by the legislature of administrative functions it is necessary that the legislature limit its exercise of this method of control. This is exactly what the legislature has done in England. There the ministry are not the servants of the Parliament but on the contrary are their guides, the great standing committee of the Parliament which is to direct all its business subject to the necessity of getting the general approval of the Parliament on its policy taken as a whole. This matter of the parliamentary control in England is treated very fully by Mr. Todd in his *Parliamentary Government in England.*[1] He lays it down as the general rule that Parliament is designed for counsel and not for rule,[2] for advice and not for administration. On the authority of May it is said that "its power is exercised indirectly."[3] Since the passage of the reform bill of 1867, however, the House of Commons has shown a disposition to encroach more and more upon the sphere of government. It regards any matter as the proper object for its censure. Resolution after resolution is proposed with the object of expressing the disapproval of Parliament of some particular administrative practice or measure[4]; and if the result of such a resolution is the disapproval of Parliament, according to May "ministers must conform to its opinion or forfeit its confidence." Many of the precedents cited by Mr. Todd go, however, to show that Parliament does not always in unimportant matters,

[1] 2d Ed., I., Chapters vii.–xii. [2] *Ibid.,* I., 414. [3] *Ibid.,* 421.
[4] See precedents cited by Mr. Todd, *op. cit.,* I., 422.

even in case of its disapproval, go so far as to force the ministry to resign or even to conform to its views. The concrete result depends very largely upon the character of the individual case. It may be laid down as a general rule that Parliament may not, as a result of this control, proceed to give orders to any of the subordinate officers of the government, as this is regarded as actual administration rather than control.[1]

Of late years it has become a common practice for Parliament to appoint what are known as select committees for the purpose both of acquiring information with a view to legislation and of examining into the constitution and management of the various departments.[2] Such committees are appointed either at the suggestion or with the approval of the government. But both parties are represented on them though the party in the majority in the house itself is given the majority. After taking evidence from every available source, and it would seem that such committees have the power to punish for contempt the refusal to answer questions,[3] the committee reports to Parliament, generally embodying in its report practical suggestions which are submitted for the consideration of the government.[4] It is usual to leave to the administration the initiation of the necessary measures.[5] Finally as a result of its powers of control and investigation Parliament may demand the presentation by the administration of papers and documents, though the rule generally is that Parliament will not require the government to bring forward any papers which in its opinion should be kept secret for political reasons.[6]

---

[1] Todd, *op. cit.*, I., 421. [2] *Ibid.*, I., 428.
[3] May, *Parliamentary Law and Practice*, 73, 74. [4] Todd, *op. cit.*, I., 432.
[5] See precedents, *Ibid.* [6] *Ibid.*, I., 439 *et seq.*

CHAPTER III.

Through its control over the finances the legislature exercises a control over the general policy of the administration. For the conduct of the entire administration is closely connected with the amount of money which may be spent. The control over the finances is to be found in three powers: first, in the power any given legislature has to fix the amount of money which is to be spent by the administration for the coming budgetary period; second, in the power it has to fix the purposes for which money has to be spent; and third, in the power it must have, if the second power is to amount to anything, to ascertain, after the expenditure of the money, whether the administration has acted in accordance with the provisions of law fixing the amount to be spent and the purposes for which money is to be spent.

I.—*Control over receipts.*

The legislative control over the finances in its modern form was, like the other methods of legislative control, developed by England. Originally the only way in which the English Parliament endeavored to control the financial administration was by fixing the amount of money which could be raised by the Crown by means of imposing taxes upon the people. The Parliament did not attempt to control the amount of money which could be spent nor the purposes for which it should be spent.[1] This was also true of the early American colonial government.[2] The later development has reversed this condition of things. At the present time most of the receipts, *i. e.* taxes, are fixed by permanent law. No given Parliament has much to do with receipts. For its action is no longer necessary in order that the receipts shall come in. So long as the law establishing the taxes is not repealed, which will require the combined action of both houses of Parliament, the administration may go on collecting the taxes regardless of Parliament, providing it acts in accordance with existing law.[3] This principle has been introduced into the United States. Thus in the national government the customs duties and the internal revenue taxes, from which two sources most of the revenue of the national government is obtained, are both fixed in amount by permanent law in that the rates which may be levied are so fixed. The amount of money which is received from these sources is independent of the action of any particular Congress and depends rather upon the business and prosperity of the country. If the houses of Congress take no action on these matters the duties are still levied. This is true also of the other receipts of the national government, such for example as tonnage dues and the receipts of the post office and from the sale of public

[1] Cox, *Institutions of the English Government,* 199.

[2] *Supra,* I., p. 53.

[3] Gneist, *Das Englische Verwaltungsrecht,* 1884, I., 431 ; II., 715. At the present time almost the only tax which is fixed in amount by each Parliament is the income tax.

lands. A given Congress has generally therefore nothing to say as to the amount of the receipts of the government. In order to change it in any way either the two houses and the President must agree or the two houses of Congress must act by a sufficiently large majority to overcome the veto of the President.

The same rule is generally true of the receipts in Germany with the exception of those of the imperial government. Some imperial receipts are indeed fixed by permanent law, as *e. g.* the receipts from the post office. But these receipts constitute a very small part of the total receipts of the empire. The greater part is to be found in the matricular contributions which the separate members of the empire have to pay into the imperial treasury and whose amount is settled largely in accordance with the population of the particular member. The separate members are allowed to collect in accordance with imperial laws taxes on imports, *i. e.* customs duties, and on objects of domestic consumption and manufacture, *i. e.* internal revenue, in order to pay such matricular contributions. The actual amount of these contributions is to be fixed annually by the imperial legislature.[1] Therefore the larger part of the receipts is under the control of each imperial legislature and if one of the houses of the legislature fails to act or if both houses fail to agree, while the taxes might still be levied in the particular members of the Empire the receipts from them would not be at the disposition of the imperial administration. In the separate members of the German Empire, however, we find as a rule the receipts independent of the yearly action of the legislature. Thus in Prussia, the consti-

---

[1] Imperial Constitution, Art. 70.

tution provides [1] that the taxes as fixed by law shall continue to be collected until the law fixing them has been amended or repealed which, it will be remembered, may not be done without the consent of the Crown, the chief of the administration.

In France the action of each legislature each year seems to be necessary in order that the receipts may come in, and thus each legislature has almost complete control over the receipts. It was thought by the French constitution-makers that they were introducing into their public law the principles of the English law when they adopted this rule. But they knew the English law only from such works as those of De Lolme and Benjamin Constant. These writers, particularly Constant, obtained their knowledge of English public law almost entirely from Blackstone, who fails to lay the stress he should on the principles which are back of the law, but which are still of great importance.[2] As Blackstone speaks of taxes being imposed only with the consent of the legislature, and lays great stress upon the powers of Parliament to withhold supplies, it was only natural for French publicists to believe that the taxes were completely in the control of each particular Parliament, and that if there were not a common action of both houses it would be impossible for the Crown to obtain supplies. Therefore in their new constitutions the French adopted in its extreme form the principle that taxes must be voted annually by the legislature. It is true that such taxes as the customs duties are fixed, as regards their rate,

[1] Art. 109.
[2] See Gneist, *Das Englische Verwaltungsrecht*, I., 433, note ; *Ibid.*, *Gesetz und Budget*, 85.

by a permanent law. But in accordance with the theory, it is at the same time provided that, in order that even such rates be collectible by the administration, annual action or authorization by the legislature is necessary; and it is an actual crime upon the part of any administrative officer to collect a tax which has not been so authorized.[1] Finally the ordinary courts are to decide whether a tax which the administration attempts to collect is legal.[2]

We find similar instances of the annual vote of taxes by the legislature in some of the American commonwealths. Indeed this seems originally to have been all but the universal rule as a result of the kind of tax which was adopted. This was the general property tax, and the way in which it was levied was to ascertain the amount of money to be spent, and then apportion it out among the counties of the commonwealth. This of course necessitated action by the legislature at each of its sessions. But with the recent changes in the tax system the control each legislature has over the receipts has been considerably lessened. For many of the taxes are now fixed as to rate by permanent law, *e. g.* the corporation tax and the inheritance taxes, and the action of any particular legislature is no longer necessary to their collection.

II.—*Control over expenses.*

It has already been pointed out that the English Parliament originally contented itself in the exercise of its control over the financial administration with fixing the amount of the supplies obtained from taxa-

[1] See Constitutional Law, Feb. 24, 1875 ; Penal Code, art. 174 ; Ducrocq, *Droit Administratif*, I., 544. [2] Ducrocq, *loc. cit.*

tion which were to be placed at the disposition of the Crown. It did not attempt in any way to exercise a control over the disposal by the Crown of the money in its control, regarding the spending of money once raised as peculiarly a part of the royal prerogative. But the abuses of the financial administration particularly by the Stuart kings led the Parliament to begin soon after the restoration, *viz.*, in 1676, regularly to designate the purposes for which the money should be spent, by the insertion in the grant of what was known as an " appropriation clause." [1] This clause not only designated the purposes for which money was to be spent but also forbade the Crown to make any other use of the money granted than that expressed in the clause.[2] It must be remembered, however, that this clause at first affected only the extraordinary revenue of the Crown, *i. e.* the revenue coming from taxation, and was also of a very general character. But with the gradual enormous increase of the extraordinary revenue and at the same time the decrease not only in importance but also in actual amount of the ordinary revenue (*i. e.* the revenue from the royal domains, *etc.*) the legislature got into its hands the control of most of the expenses of the government as well as that of the receipts which at this time had not become permanent. The result was a very unstable condition of the finances. This, it was felt, weakened the power of the state particularly since, as a result of the foreign policy of England during the reign of William III, a large debt had

---

[1] Cox, *Institutions of the English Government*, 199. Cox cites here much earlier instances of such appropriation clauses but says they were of rare occurrence.

[2] In 1680 Sir Edward Seymour, the Treasurer, was impeached for not observing such clauses. *Ibid.*, 200, note (a), citing 8 State Trials, 127.

grown up. This instability was remedied in the following way: In the first place the receipts were made stable by establishing the taxes by permanent law instead of making the action of each Parliament necessary in order that they might flow into the treasury. Further all the revenues were to be paid into what were called the funds, *viz.*, the General Fund, the South Sea Fund, the Aggregate Fund which were later consolidated in the Consolidated Fund.[1] In the second place in order to insure the stability of certain at any rate of the expenses it was provided that such expenses should be paid out of these funds as a result of a permanent law. Such was particularly the case with the interest on the public debt which, it was felt, should not be dependent on the annual action of the Parliament.[2] When the special funds were consolidated into the Consolidated Fund these expenses became chargeable upon the Consolidated Fund. Two further facts contributed to increase the stability of the expenses. The ordinary revenue of the Crown was not controlled by Parliament; and from it were defrayed quite a number of expenses such as the salaries of the judges and of ambassadors. Further, the revenues from customs and inland revenues were for a long time reported net. That is, the expenses of their collection were defrayed from the receipts and the balance only was paid into the Consolidated Fund.[3] This arrangement was, however, felt by Parliament to give it too little control over the expenses, so it was finally provided that the ordinary revenue of the Crown should like

[1] 27 Geo. III., c. 13.
[2] See 3 Geo. I., c. 7 ; Gneist, *Das Englische Verwaltungsrecht*, 1884, 686.
[3] Gneist, *op. cit.*, 688.

the extraordinary revenue be paid into the Consolidated Fund, and that the expenses which had been defrayed from it, as *e. g.* the salaries of the judges and of ambassadors and the civil list of the Crown, should thereafter be paid out of the Consolidated Fund as a result of permanent law.[1] This is regarded as somewhat in the nature of a contract between the Crown and Parliament, and is renewed regularly at the accession of each ruler. The civil list of the Crown is, it is said, just about equal to the revenues transferred to the fund in this way.[2] Further within almost the last generation it has been provided that the receipts from customs and internal revenue shall be reported by the Crown to Parliament in gross and paid into the fund in gross. Parliament has thus obtained control of the expenses of collection and administration inasmuch as they are not to be paid out of the fund in accordance with permanent law.[3] The result of this arrangement is that the Crown presents each year to Parliament estimates for the following expenses which are in the control of each Parliament; Army estimates, Navy estimates, Miscellaneous Civil Service estimates, and Revenue Department estimates which are divided up into about 200 appropriations.[4] These are the only expenses of the government over which Parliament exercises an annual control. It does not therefore exercise an annual control over the civil list of the Crown, the expenses of the public debt, or the salaries of judges or ambassadors, but does over the army and navy estimates. The reason why the army and navy

[1] See I. Geo. III., c. 3.

[2] The fund is now regulated in its main features by 17 and 18 Vict., c. 94.

[3] Gneist, *op. cit.*, 688.

[4] Gneist, *op. cit.*, 691, 692, citing Parl. Papers, 1880, xlv., xlvi.

estimates are voted every year is to be found in the experience of the people under the reigns of the Stuarts and during the Commonwealth when the army was used to oppress them. Again the geographical position of England is such as not to make it absolutely necessary that the strength of the army shall be independent of the chance of an agreement of both houses of Parliament. It is to be noted that, notwithstanding the fact that Parliament has, as has been shown, quite a large control over the expenses of the government, it has always been very careful not to interfere very much with the estimates as presented by the Crown. It has never refused to approve the estimates as a whole, but has usually contented itself with making minor changes in them. It is felt that the refusal to vote the estimates would tend too much to cripple the administration ; and the principles of ministerial responsibility to Parliament have brought about the recognition of the fact that a sensible alteration of the estimates as brought in by the administration is equivalent to the expression of a lack of confidence in it and will in almost all cases be followed by the dissolution of Parliament or the resignation of the ministers.[1] It is further to be noted that the position of the ministers as the great standing committee of Parliament, which is to examine, before it is presented, every important measure and is to guide the deliberations of Parliament, has brought about the adoption of the rule that no appropriation of any importance is to be made except on the proposition of the Crown, *i. e.* the administration. It may happen in isolated cases that the house will address the Crown to the effect that certain

---

[1] Gneist, *op. cit.*, 723.

appropriations be made, but it is not customary for appropriations of any importance to originate otherwise than with the Crown. This is now fixed by a standing order of the House of Commons.[1] Finally it has been decided as a result of long practice that the control of Parliament over the appropriations shall not be so made use of as to compel the administration to take action which it believes is unwise. That is Parliament may not tack to an appropriation bill any clause or provision foreign to it. Whenever such an attempt has been made by the House of Commons the House of Lords has regularly thrown out the objectionable bill.[2]

In the United States a somewhat similar method of insuring the stability of certain of the expenses has been adopted. As has been shown the receipts are permanent. The statutes of Congress have also provided for quite a number of appropriations which are based upon permanent law. The growth of the national debt made the Congress feel the same fear that had been felt before in England as to the effect on the public credit of the country of the dependence of interest and sinking fund payments on congressional action. There was therefore adopted a system of what were called permanent annual appropriations established by permanent law which should be sufficient authorization to the administration to make the necessary payments without any special action on the part of the Congress. Among these permanent annual appropriations are to be mentioned, in addition to the debt payments, the expense of collecting the customs

---

[1] Standing Order of June 25, 1852, cited in Cox., *op. cit.*, 192.

[2] Gneist, *op. cit.*, 727, citing Amos, *English Constitution*, 73.

duties, the salaries of judicial officers, and the expense of purchasing a certain amount of silver each year in the endeavor to keep up the price of silver and to bring about ultimately the adoption of the complete bimetallic standard. This last permanent annual appropriation may be evidenced as a striking example of the importance of these permanent appropriations to those who are interested in the stability of a certain expense. Finally as a result of the decisions of the Supreme Court[1] the fixing of salaries by permanent law, which is often the case, is regarded much as a permanent annual appropriation. For the officer whose salary is thus fixed may sue the government for it. The salaries would thus have to be paid regardless of the action of Congress unless such action was by a majority sufficient to override the President's veto. This decision of the Supreme Court has vastly increased the independence of the administration.[2] It is indeed true that the act organizing the Court of Claims provides that judgments against the United States shall be paid out of the appropriation for private claims; but in time of conflict between the Congress and the President it is very probable that the President would conduct the government and would have salaries paid without annual appropriations, and be able to do so successfully. The result of these permanent annual appropriations is that more than half of the current expenses of the government, exclusive of pensions and salaries, are beyond the reach of any particular Congress. That is, it is not necessary in

[1] U. S. v. Langston, 118 U. S., 389.

[2] See also Antoni v. Greenhow, 107 U. S., 769, in which it is said that the declaration by the legislature that money shall be spent is an appropriation by law.

order that these expenses be paid that there be any action on the part of Congress at all. The failure of Congress to act or to agree with the President will not affect the action of the administration in the carrying on of the government through the payment of a large part of the expenses. The particular expenses of the government which are under the control of each Congress are, those of the army, the navy, and of the other branches of the administration with the exception of the customs. Congress has never, as has the English House of Commons, divested itself of the right to make appropriations other than those proposed by the administration. Indeed in practice many of the most unwise appropriations of the national government are made on the proposition of Congress and not on that of the administration. Congress further always makes use of its undoubted right to cut down or amend in some way the estimates sent in by the administration. It has also attempted, by tacking to appropriations provisions objectionable to the administration, to force their acceptance by it, under a threat of a refusal of the estimates, but the determined stand recently made by one of the Presidents and the absolute impossibility of refusing important appropriations to the administration have finally convinced the Congress that this is not a proper use of its control over the finances.

When we come to the control of the commonwealth legislatures over the expenses we find such a variety of systems that it is impossible to say what is the general rule. In some commonwealths we find that the amount of the appropriations is fixed almost altogether by the administration in accordance with general and permanent laws over which a given legislature has practically little control[1]; and it has been held that without any special appropriation the payment of salaries fixed by permanent law may be enforced by *mandamus.*[2] In other and indeed in most cases most of the appropriations are made annually or biennially by the legislature.[3] In all the commonwealths the legislature has the power to make appropriations other than those proposed by the administration if the administration is to submit estimates to the legislature. Generally also the legislature, where such estimates are submitted to it, has the right to cut them down and often exercises this power. But as a result of the very general power of the governor to veto items in appropriation bills[4] the legislature may not force the administration to take action not approved by it as a result of tacking such a provision to an appropriation bill.

In France the legislature has just as complete a control over the expenses as over the receipts. It may also and does as a matter of fact, make appropriations, estimates for which are not presented by the administration, to the great detriment of the budget, and has the right, which it not unfrequently exercises, to cut down the estimates as presented.[5]

The exact control which the legislature has over the

---

[1] The courts seem to regard this practice as perfectly proper. See People v. Supervisors, 17 Hill N. Y., 195 ; John J. Townsend, trustee, v. Mayor, *etc.*, 77 N. Y., 542.

[2] Nichols v. Comptroller, 4 Stew. and Port. Ala., 154.

[3] In some cases this is required by the Constitution, Stimson, *op. cit.*, p. 320 B. This is so in Arkansas, Kansas, Louisiana, Missouri, Ohio, and Texas.

[4] *Supra*, I., p. 75.

[5] Ducrocq, *op. cit.*, I., 533–544. *Cf.* also Leroy Beaulieu, *Science des Finances*, chapter on *Le Vote du Budget.*

expenses in the German Empire does not seem to have been fixed. There is even at the present time a struggle going on between the believers in what is known as French liberalism and those who feel that the existence of a strong administration requires that a large part of the expenses should be independent of the yearly action of the legislature. So far the result is that while some of the expenses are based on permanent law and while others are fixed for a term of years, by far the larger part of the expenses are in the control of the legislature whose annual action is necessary in order that they be paid. It must, however, be remembered that a large part of the expenses of the imperial administration are defrayed by the members of the empire. Such is the case *e. g.* with the expenses of collecting the customs duties and the internal revenue. For the separate members of the empire pay, in their matricular contributions only the net income of these taxes.[1] Among the expenses of the imperial government which have been fixed by permanent law are the interest on the imperial debt, the expenses of all institutions and authorities which owe their establishment to permanent law, *i. e.* the salaries of all officers having permanent positions, since judgments against the treasury obtained in the ordinary courts by them for their salaries have to be paid.[2] The main expense which is fixed for a term of years is the expense of the army, one of the largest items of the imperial budget. The German practice on this matter has varied considerably. But the latest settlement of the question would seem to be that the expenses of the army shall be fixed for a period of seven years. The reason why it has seemed

[1] Meyer, *Deutsches Staatsrecht*, 546.　　　[2] Meyer, *op. cit.*, 549.

necessary to give to the army expenses a more permanent character than is possessed by most of the expenses of the administration, while most of the countries, which have adopted most fully the idea of permanent appropriations, have left the legislature a large control over the army expenses, is to be found in the geographical position of the German Empire. Germany has almost no natural boundaries to the east and west and on both of these frontiers lie hostile states ready to take any advantage of the least symptom of weakness. A strong administration of military affairs is therefore absolutely necessary. This is accomplished by this arrangement, which is known as the *septennate.* For during the periods for which the estimates are voted the legislature has practically no control over the military administration. The privilege granted to the presiding state of the empire, *viz.*, Prussia, which means practically the Emperor, to veto any proposition amending the laws regarding the army, gives the Emperor the power to prevent the repeal or amendment of the septennate.[1]

In the separate members of the empire the rules with regard to the control of the legislature over the appropriations are about the same as those in force in the empire. Among the permanent expenses are to be mentioned the matricular contributions (at least over these the legislature of the particular member of the empire has no control), the civil list of the prince, and all payments to be made as a result of the application of the rules of private law inasmuch as they may be enforced by the judgments of the courts.[2]

An interesting question which arises in this connec-

---

[1] See Imperial Constitution, Art. 7.   [2] Meyer, *op. cit.*, 538.

tion is what is the power of the administration with regard to the payment of unforeseen expenses which arise after the voting of the appropriations and which must be made when the legislature is not in session. France and England are about the only countries that attempt to regulate this matter by law. In France it is provided that[1] the President of the republic may, in case the legislature is not in session, enlarge the amount of any given appropriation, though it expressly forbids him to open an absolutely new appropriation. This is to be done by a decree issued after taking counsel with the Council of State and must be submitted to the legislature at the opening of its next session. England has provided a series of funds, *viz.*, the civil contingencies fund and the treasury chest fund to which the government may have recourse.[2] But it is said that the administration is " strictly accountable to Parliament for all such transactions and the advances so made out of these funds must be replaced out of moneys voted by Parliament for that purpose."[3] Further in England unexpended balances of appropriations are largely at the disposition of the administration. As the heads of the administration, the ministers, are always responsible to the Parliament, such a power is not susceptible of great abuse.[4]

In the other states the rule generally is that any modification made by the administration in the appropriations so as to increase the amount appropriated is made at the peril of the administration. Circumstances arise also even in states, like England and France, which make some provision for the payment of unfore-

---

[1] L. Dec. 14, 1879.

[2] Todd, *op. cit.*, I., 730.

[3] *Ibid.*

[4] *Ibid.*, 759.

seen expenses, when, in order that the government may go on, the appropriations must be exceeded. Such cases are not susceptible of juristic treatment. The fact simply presents itself to the administration that in order that the government may go on the law must be broken. As it is more important that the government shall go on than that the law shall be observed, the universal practice is for the administration, whether it is republican or monarchical, to break the law and then come before the legislature for an indemnity. The question is a purely political one and the action of the administration will be judged in accordance with the facts of the particular case. But it is seldom that the legislature will be unreasonable. Where the administration is dependent in tenure on the legislature the case can never be a serious one. For the result of the disapproval of the legislature will finally be the overthrow of the ministry. Where, however, the administration is independent of the legislature a more serious case may arise—a case which must be settled not by law but by politics. Similar instances of conflict may arise in case the legislature refuses to grant the appropriations. But these are as before political rather than legal questions.

III.—*Examination of accounts.*

In order that the control which the legislature possesses over the administration through its control over the receipts and expenses may be of any value it is necessary that it have the further power of examining the accounts of the administration after the execution of the budget. In this way and in this way alone can it satisfy itself that its directions relative to the receipts and expenses have been observed. All constitutions grant some such power to the legislature ; and the usual rule is that the legislature makes use of some authority independent of the administration to aid it in the examination which it makes. This is the case in France, England, and Germany. In France it is the Court of Accounts, whose members though appointed by the President are irremovable, which examines the accounts of all administrative officers having charge of public money and property, and which thus acquires a large knowledge of the methods of action of the administration in the execution of the provisions of the budget and reports its findings to the legislature.[1] In Germany both in the empire and in Prussia a similarly organized body with a similar name discharges similar functions.[2] These bodies both in France and Germany really also exercise a judicial control over most of the actions of the administration relative to the finances. In England the comptroller and auditor general, who has the judicial tenure, examines the accounts of the officers of the administration (thus having a judicial control) and has the further power of preventing the unauthorized expenditure of money. He is also called upon to report to Parliament the results of his investigations and to aid it in its endeavor to ascertain how far the administration has observed the provisions of the appropriation acts.[3] In the United States, however, the legislature acts in its investigations unaided by any other authority. Great care is taken both by

[1] Boeuf, *Droit Administratif*, 84–102.
[2] Meyer, *Deutsches Staatsrecht*, 540, 551.
[3] Todd, *Parliamentary Government in England*, II., 569.

the national constitution and by the statutes of Congress to ensure the full publicity of the accounts of the administration, some of whose departments have to report directly to the legislature while the secretary of the treasury has to report to it in full the entire receipts and expenditures of the preceding year.[1] The rules of the House of Representatives have usually provided [2] that such accounts shall go to the speaker of the house and be submitted by him to the house for reference.   They are then to be referred [3] to one of the eight standing committees on expenditure which shall examine them together with the manner of keeping them, the economy, justness, and correctness of the expenditures, their conformity with appropriation laws, the proper application of public moneys, the security of the government against unjust and extravagant demands, retrenchment, the enforcement of the payment of moneys due the United States, the economy and accountability of public officers, the reduction or increase of pay of officers, and the abolishment of useless offices.   Each of the eight standing committees on the expenditures of the departments has one or more of these subjects within its purview and after making the necessary examinations is to report to the house.   What the legislature will do in case of unauthorized expenditures or of failure to observe the provisions of the budget, the laws and the rules do not say ; and it is not the habit of the house to pass any law or resolution settling and affirming the actions of the administration in case they are in conformity with the appropriation acts and releasing the officers of the government having

[1] Const., Art. I., sec. 9, par. 7 ; U. S. R. S., secs. 260, 261, 266, and 267.
[2] See rule 42.   [3] Rule 11, sec. 32.

control of the execution of the budget from all further responsibility for it. In England the action of the House of Commons is very similar. There is a committee of acounts which is to pursue the same kind of investigations, but which is aided in its work by the comptroller and auditor general.[1] The effect of their investigations is about the same. That is, it does not seem to be the habit of the house to take any formal action as to the release of the officers of the administration from responsibility for the execution of the budget. But in case any serious irregularities were discovered which the house felt it could not, with justice to itself, allow to pass unnoticed, the remedy would, in accordance with the general principles, be the passage of a vote of censure or of lack of confidence in the administration which might ultimately lead to the overthrow of the ministry. In France, and Germany, however, the result of the investigations of the legislatures into the conformity of the actions of the administration with the provisions of the budget always results in the passage of a law, which, if nothing serious is discovered involving the administration, releases the officers controlling the administration from all responsibility for the execution of the budget.[2] In France, however, this law comes so long after the execution of the budget that it really does not amount to much. Indeed the investigation by the legislature of the accounts of the administrations supervenes so long after the execution of the budget that there is plenty of time in the peculiar conditions of French politics for the existence of several separate ministries

[1] Gneist, *Das Englische Verwaltungsrecht,* 1884, 731.
[2] Ducrocq, *Droit Administratif,* I., 423 ; Meyer, *op. cit.,* 539.

before the examination is undertaken of the accounts of any particular budgetary year. If, however, it happens that the ministry whose accounts are being examined is in office at the time of the examination the result of the discovery of any unauthorized expenditures might be its fall. There is further a criminal responsibility which might be enforced before the courts even if the ministry were out of office for collecting any unauthorized taxes.[1] In Germany it is difficult to see what would be the result of the discovery by the legislature of a serious lack of conformity of the actions of the administration with the provisions of the budget. As the principle of parliamentary responsibility has not been adopted the result would certainly not be the retirement of the ministry so long as it was backed by the Emperor or the prince. Again though the constitution of both the empire and of Prussia would seem to recognize some responsibility of the ministers this principle has not been sufficiently developed to permit of their being impeached. Indeed the Prussian constitution was put to the test in this very matter in the great constitutional conflict over the army appropriations in 1860–64 and the result showed that this legislative control over the finances was of no value in a case of real conflict between the administration and the legislature.

[1] *Supra*, II., p. 278.

CHAPTER IV.

IMPEACHMENT.

This like the other methods of legislative control is derived from England. The method of impeachment seems to have been necessary in England because the English law did not allow a civil or criminal suit to be brought against the highest officers of state except with extreme difficulty. It was thus developed mainly to fill up a gap in the judicial control. A further reason for its development is to be found in the impossibility of obtaining a conviction of the great nobles before the ordinary courts [1] and in the necessity of some means of legislative control in the days when the principle of the parliamentary responsibility of the ministers had not been developed.[2] Since its development in England it has been adopted to some extent in almost all constitutional countries, and in some cases is made use of against not only the ministers but also all civil officers of the government.

The ordinary English method of impeachment was formed in analogy with the ordinary criminal procedure, the House of Commons taking the part of the grand jury and thus bringing forward the impeach-

[1] Blackstone, *Commentaries*, IV., 360.
[2] For its history see Cox, *Institutions of the English Government*, 229 *et seq.*, 468.

ment or indictment, the House of Lords acting as the court.[1] The grounds for impeachment were originally abuse of office from corrupt, partial, or oppressive motives, violation of the law, and treason, which was usually defined by the court of impeachment to suit itself, and depended very much upon its feeling towards the accused,[2] but later came to include, especially during the reigns of the Stuarts, offences political in nature.[3] The punishment originally was death, banishment, fine, or imprisonment in the discretion of the court of impeachment. Soon after this method was developed there grew up the habit of exercising this control through the ordinary process of legislation, *i. e.* by the passage of a bill of attainder in accordance with which no fair trial was granted the person attainted. This seems to have originated with the Tudors and was quite frequently employed during the constitutional struggle of the seventeenth century.[4] This method has, however, in practice been abandoned as it was grossly unjust. Parliament still of course has the power to pass a bill of attainder if it wishes to, although in the United States such action by Congress is forbidden by the national constitution.[5] The method of impeachment even, has with the development of the principle of the Parliamentary responsibility of the ministers, rather fallen into disuse, the last case being that of Warren Hastings, which occurred about the end of the last century. The other methods of legislative control are so complete that it is difficult to see in what cases it could be applied with advantage. The

---

[1] *Ibid.*, 229, 470, 471.

[2] Gneist, *Das Englische Verwaltungsrecht* (1884), 436.

[3] *Ibid.*   [4] Cox, *op. cit.*, 235, 465.

[5] Art. I., sec. 9, p. 3, sec. 10.

power still remains in Parliament and may be made use of in an extreme case where all other means of control fail to bring the administration to an observance of the laws or customs of the land.

This method of impeachment has been adopted in the United States both in the national and in the commonwealth governments. The national constitution provides that the House of Representatives shall have the sole power to impeach the President, vice-president and all civil officers of the United States [1]; that the Senate shall, with the chief justice of the United States as presiding officer in case the President is impeached, have the sole power to try impeachments and shall convict only as a result of a two-thirds vote of the members present [2]; and that the punishment in case of conviction shall be removal from office and disqualification to hold any office of honor, trust, or profit under the United States in the future, with the impossibility of pardon, but that the person so convicted shall be liable to indictment, trial, judgment, and punishment according to law.[3] The causes of impeachment are [4] treason, bribery, and other high crimes and misdemeanors. There have been two views as to the meaning of this phrase. One is that the only cause for impeachment is a crime, *i. e.* an act for which a person may be indicted and punished in accordance with the law; the other assigns a much wider meaning to the phrase and claims that the phrase was purposely left vague at the time of the formation of the constitution so that it might by construction be made to include political offences. The cases in which the article in

[1] Art. I., sec. 2, p. 5 ; art. II., sec. 4.   [2] Art I., sec. 3, p. 6.
[3] Art. I., sec. 3, p. 7.   [4] Art. III., sec. 4.

the constitution relative to the causes of impeachment has been construed are few in number and some of them have been decided for jurisdictional reasons and are therefore of little value in throwing light on the meaning of the article. Thus the first case, *viz.*, that of Senator Blount, decided that a Senator of the United States could not be impeached inasmuch as he was not a civil officer of the United States in the meaning of the constitution, while the last case, *viz.*, that of a cabinet officer was decided largely on the ground that, as such officer had resigned and his resignation had been accepted by the President, he was not subject to the jurisdiction of the impeachment court. The only cases in which the person impeached has been convicted are those of Judge Pickering, who was convicted of offences distinctly not political; Judge Humphreys, who was convicted of treason in the beginning of the war, his treasonable acts being the making of a speech in favor of secession and acceptance of the office of judge in the southern confederacy. On the other hand Judge Chase, who was impeached for " highly indecent and extra judicial " reflections upon the government of the United States made to a grand jury during the time when the alien and sedition laws were in force; President Johnson, who was impeached for a political offence which had been made a high crime and misdemeanor by act of Congress; and Judge Peck, who was impeached for arbitary conduct in committing for contempt of court an attorney who had published a criticism of one of his opinions, were all of them acquitted.[1] It would seem therefore that the phrase "high crimes

[1] See *Cyclopedia of Political Science, etc., sub verbo* Impeachment. Article by Alexander Johnston.

and misdemeanors " does not include political matters. This is largely due to the fact of the large majority which is required for conviction in the court of impeachment. For in the case of an impeachment for an act of a political character party feelings will be arrayed against each other, and in the state of political parties in the United States it will be very unusual for any party to have such complete control of the court of impeachments as to be able to get the requisite two-thirds majority.

The constitutions of most of the commonwealths recognize the right in the legislature to impeach and convict the officers of the government but the provisions differ somewhat in their details. One constitution, *viz.*, that of Oregon, expressly forbids impeachment. The majority of the constitutions provide for the impeachment of all civil officers. Some expressly refer to the governor.[1] The cause for impeachment in most of the constitutions is crime, but some provide that immorality, official corruption, or misconduct and even incompetence, incapacity, or neglect of official duty, and favoritism will be sufficient cause.[2] All the commonwealths in which provision is made for impeachment, with the exception of Nebraska, provide that the lower house of the legislature is to initiate the impeachment generally as a result of a majority vote. In Nebraska the impeachment is to be initiated by the legislature in joint assembly of the two houses. In all but two commonwealths the impeachment is to be tried by the senate, a vote by two-thirds of whose members or two-thirds of whose members present, being usually

[1] Stimson, *American Statute Law,* 63.
[2] So in Louisiana, West Virgina, Virginia, and Florida. See *Ibid.,* 64.

necessary for conviction. In New York, however, the judges of the court of appeals, the highest court, are joined with the senate and together with it form the court of impeachment, while in Nebraska the supreme court is the court of impeachment.[1] The effect of conviction is in almost all cases removal from office and in most cases also disqualification to hold office. But generally persons impeached may be at the same time indicted and punished in the usual way.[2]

In France as in England the adoption of the principle of the parliamentary responsibility of the ministers has made impeachment almost unnecessary. Still one of the constitutional laws[3] provides that the President, who is responsible to the legislature only for treason,[4] may be impeached only by the Chamber of Deputies and can be judged only by the Senate, and that the ministers, who are individually responsible to the legislature for their personal acts and solidly responsible for their general policy,[5] may be impeached for crimes committed in the exercise of their functions and tried in the same way. Finally the President may constitute the Senate into a high court of justice to judge all attempts against the safety of the state.[6]

While the responsibility of the ministers in Prussia and of the chancellor in the empire is recognized in the constitutions of both Prussia and the German Empire no law has been passed by either government which regulates the matter sufficiently in detail to permit an impeachment trial.[7] In most of the other members of the empire, however, provision is made

[1] *Ibid.*   [2] *Ibid.*, p. 65.
[3] L. July 16, 1875, art. 12.   [4] L. Feb. 25, 1875, art. 6.
[5] L. Feb. 25, 1875, art. 6.   [6] L. July 16, 1875, art. 12.
[7] Meyer, *Deutsches Staatsrecht*, 476 ; 480,481.

for impeachment. As a general thing only ministers may be impeached as in France. The causes for impeachment are generally the commission of crimes and the violation of the constitution. The impeachment is, where there are two houses, undertaken by either house of the legislature or by a concurrent resolution of the two houses. The court is either the highest judicial court or a special court composed for the most part, of judges, one half of whom are chosen by the prince, one half by the legislature. Punishment on conviction is generally as in the United States, removal from office and disqualification for office in the future.[1]

[1] *Ibid.*, 474 *et seq.*

LIST OF AUTHORITIES.

ABBREVIATIO PLACITORUM, II. 193.

ADAMS, H. C., *Public Debts*, I. 10.

ALLINSON AND PENROSE, *City Government of Philadelphia*, in Johns Hopkins University Studies in Historical and Political Science, V. 1–73 : I. 207, 209, 210, 216.

ALLINSON AND PENROSE, *Philadelphia*, I. 197, 201, 204, 211, 212, 214–216, 218.

AMOS, *English Constitution*, II. 284.

ANSON, SIR WILLIAM, *The Law and Custom of the Constitution*, I. 98–100, 124–126, 143, 163, 239, 245 ; II. 53.

ARNOLD, *Municipal Corporations*, 3d Ed., I. 255.

ASH, MARK, *Consolidation Act*, I. 200.

AUCOC, *Conférences sur l'Administration et le Droit Administratif*, I. 35, 50, 85, 88, 107, 108, 111, 112, 148, 150, 154, 159, 268, 271–275, 286 ; II. 217, 218, 221, 222, 225, 226, 230–232, 235, 239.

BENTON, *Abridgment of the Debates in Congress*, II. 90, 91.

BENTON, *Thirty Years' View*, I. 130.

BEVERLY, *History of Virginia*, I. 58.

BISHOP, *Criminal Law*, II. 79.

BLACK, *The History of the Municipal Ownership of Land on Manhattan Island*, in Studies in History, Economics, and Public Law, edited by the University Faculty of Political Science of Columbia College, I. 3 : I. 200, 201.

BLACKSTONE, *Commentaries*, II. 193, 195, 296.

BLOCK, M., *Dictionnaire de l'Administration française*, I. 148, 273, 274 ; II. 46–48, 67, 74, 79, 81, 82, 84, 87, 95.

BLOCK, *Dictionnaire de la Politique*, II. 187.

BOEUF, *Droit Administratif*, I. 8, 16, 85, 87, 88, 110, 132, 155, 157, 158, 287, 288 ; II. 153, 259, 260, 292.

BORNHAK, *Geschichte des Preussischen Verwaltungsrecht*, I. 296, 297.

BORNHAK, *Local Government in Prussia*, in Annals of American Academy of Political and Social Science, III. 403 : I. 320.

BORNHAK, *Preussisches Staatsrecht*, I. 92, 115, 141 ; II. 161, 162.

BORNHAK, *Preussisches Verwaltungsrecht*, II. 80, 177.

BRODHEAD, *History of New York*, I. 167, 169.

BRYCE, JAMES, *The American Commonwealth*, I. 52, 104, 203, 207, 208, 213, 218 ; II. 271.

BURGESS, *Political Science and Comparative Constitutional Law*, I. 3, 13, 39, 84, 93, 97, 98, 99.

BURROUGHS, *Taxation*, II. 122.

BUSBEE, J. M., *City Government of Boston*, in Johns Hopkins University Studies in Historical and Political Science, V. 73-135 : I. 199-201, 207-214, 216.

CAMPBELL, *History of Virginia*, I. 58.

CHALMERS, *Local Government*, I. 246-252, 258, 260, 262 ; II. 64.

CHURCH, *Habeas Corpus*, II. 201, 202, 205.

CLARK, *Debates of the Convention of 1821*, I. 77.

COCKER, *Civil Government in Michigan*, I. 183, 185.

COMSTOCK, *The Civil Service of the United States*, II. 33, 41, 45.

CONKLING, *Executive Power*, I. 61.

COOLEY, *Constitutional Limitations*, I. 24. ; II. 20, 21.

COOLEY, *Taxation*, 2d Ed., I. 12, 13, 18, 230 ; II. 115, 116, 120, 122, 147, 153, 166.

COOLEY, *Torts*, II. 169.

COX, *Institutions of the English Government*, I. 129 ; II. 276, 280, 296, 297.

CRAIK, *The State and Education*, I. 258.

CRAWLEY, *Handbook of Competitive Examinations*, II. 54-56, 67.

DARESTE, *La Justice Administrative en France*, II. 173.

DARESTE DE LA CHAVANNE, *Histoire de l'Administration en France*, I. 269, 285.

DE FRANQUEVILLE, *Le Gouvernement et le Parlement Britanniques*, I. 112, 264.

DE GRAIS, *Handbuch der Verfassung und Verwaltung, etc.*, I. 155, 301 ; II. 48, 49, 246.

DÉTHAN, *L'Organisation des Conseils Généraux*, I. 268, 269, 271, 275.

DE TOCQUEVILLE, *L'Ancien Régime et la Révolution*, II. 170.

DICEY, A. V., *The Law of the Constitution*, I. 6, 112, 155 ; II. 223.

DILLON, *Municipal Corporations*, I. 24, 43, 173, 175, 188, 197, 202-204, 206, 207, 209, 213, 214, 219, 223 ; II. 111, 116, 149, 152-154, 156.

DOCUMENTS RELATING TO THE COLONIAL HISTORY OF NEW YORK, I. 53, 54, 166.

DUCROCQ, *Traité du Droit Administratif*, I. 35, 85, 271, 286-288 ; II. 128, 161, 162, 228, 229, 232, 279, 287, 294.

DUNNING, W. A., *The Constitution in Civil War*, in Political Science Quarterly, III. 454 : I. 32, 121.

DWIGHT, T. W., *Harrington*, in Political Science Quarterly, II. 16 : II. 20.

ELIOT, PRESIDENT, *One Remedy for Municipal Misgovernment*, in The Forum, Oct., 1891, I. 217 ; II. 13.

ELLIOT'S DEBATES, I. 52.

ELMES, WEBSTER, *Executive Departments*, I. 64.

FISHER, S. P., *Suspension of Habeas Corpus*, in Political Science Quarterly, III. 163 : I. 63.

FOWLE, *The Poor Law*, I. 237.

GITTERMAN, *The Council of Appointment*, in Political Science Quarterly, VII. 80 : I. 54 ; II. 15.

GNEIST, *Constitutional History of England*, II. 193, 194.

GNEIST, *Das Englische Parlament, etc.*, II. 12.

GNEIST, *Das Englische Verwaltungsrecht*, 1884, I. 28, 98, 124, 125, 144, 149, 154, 236 ; II. 14, 53, 65, 79, 80, 106, 124, 125, 138, 140, 154, 167, 181, 188, 189, 196, 197, 209, 210, 215, 216, 240, 263, 276, 278, 281–284, 294, 297.

GNEIST, *Der Rechtsstaat*, I. 31 ; II. 240.

GNEIST, *Die Kreisordnung*, I. 300.

GNEIST, *Gesetz und Budget*, II. 278.

GNEIST, *Les Réformes locales en Prusse*, in Revue Générale du Droit et des Sciences Politiques, Oct., 1886, I. 299, 300, 310, 317, 328.

GNEIST, *Selfgovernment, Communalverfassung und Verwaltungsgerichte*, I. 162, 193, 198, 248–250.

GNEIST, *Verwaltung, Justiz, und Rechtsweg*, I. 92.

GOODNOW, *Local Government in England*, in Political Science Quarterly, II. 638 : I. 162.

GOODNOW, *Local Government in Prussia*, in Political Science Quarterly, IV. 260 : I. 295, 297, 299, 324 ; II. 11.

GOSS, JOHN D., *The History of Tariff Administration in the United States* in Studies in History, Economics, and Public Law, edited by the University Faculty of Political Science of Columbia College, I. No. 2 : I. 45, 153.

GREENLEAF, *Evidence*, II. 82.

GUGGENHEIMER, *The Development of Executive Departments*, in Jameson, Essays in the Constitutional History of the United States, I. 128.

GUMPLOWICZ, *Das Oesterreichische Staatsrecht*, I. 16, 129 ; II. 13.

HAMMOND, J. B., *History of Political Parties in the State of New York*, I. 79.

HARE, *Walks in London*, II. 33.

HERBERT AND JENKIN, *The Councillor's Handbook*, I. 242, 244, 251.

HIGH, *Extraordinary Legal Remedies*, I. 82 ; II. 73, 193, 194, 203.

HIGH, *Injunctions*, II. 203.

HILLIARD, *Injunctions*, II. 209.

HOLLAND, *Elements of Jurisprudence*, I. 7.

HOW AND BEMIS, *Municipal Police Ordinances*, II. 112.

HOWARD, *Introduction to the Local Constitutional History of the United States*, Book III. Chapters I. and II. *passim*, I. 165 *et seq.*

HOWE, W. W., *Municipal History of New Orleans*, Johns Hopkins University, Studies in Historical and Political Science, VII. 71–155 : I. 209, 210.

INSTITUTES OF JUSTINIAN, I. 15.

JOHNSTON, A. R., *On Impeachment*, in Lalor's Cyclopædia of Political Science, etc., II. 481 : II. 5, 299.

KENT, *Commentary on the Charter of the City of New York*, I. 200, 201.

KIDD, BENJAMIN, *The Civil Service as a Profession*, in Nineteenth Century, October, 1886, XX. 491 : II. 55.

KIRCHENHEIM, *Einführung in das Verwaltungsrecht,* I. 1. 4, 10, 11, 15, 20.

LAFERRIÈRE, *La Juridiction Administrative,* II. 74, 75, 80, 161, 171, 175, 176, 227, 232, 235, 243, 253, 254, 256.

LECLERC, *La Vie municipale en Prusse,* Extrait des Annales de l'École libre des Sciences Politiques, I. 332, 335.

LEIDIG, *Preussisches Stadtrecht,* I. 328.

LEROY-BEAULIEU, *La Science des Finances,* II. 287.

LIGHTWOOD, *The Nature of Positive Law,* I. 7, 16.

LOENING, *Deutsches Verwaltungsrecht,* I. 114, 115, 132, 141, 146, 148, 158, 303, 311, 318 ; II. 49, 79, 80, 83, 106, 120, 163, 170, 242, 260.

LOW, SETH, *Municipal Government,* in Bryce, American Commonwealth, I. 630 : I. 215, 224.

MACAULAY, *History of England,* I. 126.

MACKAY, Ae. J. G., *The Science of Politics, its Methods and its Use,* in the Juridical Review, II. 1 : I. 7.

MAY, *Parliamentary Law and Practice,* II. 274.

MCCRARY, *The Law of Elections,* 3d Ed., II. 18.

MECHEM, *Law of Officers,* I. 149, II. 1, 5-7, 19-24, 26, 28, 29, 31, 32, 63, 70-72, 81, 95-100, 110, 115, 116, 161, 164, 165, 168, 204.

MEIER, *Reform der Verwaltungsorganisation,* I. 296, 297.

MÉTÉRIÉ-LARREY, *Les Emplois Publics,* II. 48.

MEYER, *Deutsches Staatsrecht,* I. 89-91, 95, 114, 116, 117, 140, 148 ; II. 288-290, 292, 301, 302.

MEYER, *Deutsches Verwaltungsrecht,* I. 45 ; II. 240-242, 246, 247.

MILLER, *The Constitution,* I. 24.

MOMMSEN, *Römisches Staatsrecht,* II. 149, 170.

MONTESQUIEU, *Esprit des Lois,* I. 20, 27.

MOREHOUSE, *Supervisor's Manual,* I. 181, 183.

OPINIONS OF ATTORNIES GENERAL, *passim.*

OSTROGORSKI, M., *Woman Suffrage in Local Government,* in Political Science Quarterly, VI. 677 : II. 28.

PALGRAVE, *King's Council,* II. 193-195, 197.

PAREY, *Verwaltungsrecht,* II. 170.

PARKER AND WORTHINGTON, *Public Health and Safety,* II. 120, 126

PENROSE, see Allinson and Penrose.

POORE, *Charters and Constitutions,* I. 53, 57.

POWERS, F. P., *Railroad Indemnity Lands,* in Political Science Quarterly, IV. 452 : I. 69.

POWERS, F. P., *The Reform of the Federal Service,* in Political Science Quarterly, III. 260 : II. 37, 38, 85, 92.

PREUSSEN IM BUNDESTAG, I. 300.

PROBYN, *Local Government and Taxation in the United Kingdom,* I. 240, 248, 256, 257.

REEVES, *History of the English Law,* II. 194.

RICHARDSON, *The Court of Claims,* in Southern Law Review, reprinted in volume XVII. of Ct. of Cl. Reports : II. 158.

ROBINSON, J. H., *Original Features in the United States Constitution*, in Annals of American Academy of Political and Social Science, I. 222 : I. 52.

RÜTTIMAN, *Das Nord-Amerikanische Bundesstaatsrecht*, I. 52, 69, 105, 130.

RYLEY, *Pleadings*, II. 193.

SARWEY, *Allgemeines Verwaltungsrecht*, I. 11, 21, 26–28, 31, 32.

SARWEY, *Das Oeffentliche Recht*, II. 150, 153, 244.

SCHULZE, *Deutsches Staatrecht*, I. 89–92, 129, 132, 140, 142, 148 ; II. 74, 81, 95, 100.

SEELEY, J. R. *Life and Times of Stein*, I. 297.

SHAW, ALBERT, *Municipal Government in Great Britain*, in Political Science Quarterly, IV. 199 : I. 255.

SIMONET, *Droit Public Administratif*, II. 227, 236.

SMITH, *Practice at Quarter Sessions*, I. 239 ; II. 196, 216.

SMITH, MUNROE, *State, Statute, and Common Law*, in Political Science Quarterly, III. 147 : I. 40.

SNOW, MARSHALL W., *City Government of St. Louis*, in Johns Hopkins University Studies in Historical and Political Science, V. 135–155 : I. 204, 209, 213, 216, 218.

STENGEL, *Lehrbuch des Deutschen Verwaltungsrecht*, I. 1, 4, 121, 154, 158 ; II. 1, 128, 271.

STENGEL, *Organisation der Preussischen Verwaltung*, I. 41, 114, 268, 303, 304, 308, 311, 312, 315, 319, 323, 324, 326 ; II. 248–251, 253–256, 258.

STENGEL, *Wörterbuch des Deutschen Verwaltungsrecht*, I. 115, 305 ; II. 66, 76, 83, 87, 100, 122, 244, 245.

STEPHEN AND MILLER, *The County Council Compendium*, I. 242, 245.

STIMSON, *American Statute Law*, I. 7, 27, 74–76, 78–80, 102, 103, 135, 179, 227 ; II. 18–21, 70, 160, 287, 300, 301.

STONE, *Practice of Justices of the Peace at Petty and Special Sessions*, 9th Ed. I. 239, 241.

STUBBS, *Constitutional History of England*, I. 97, 122, 123, 162, 163 ; II. 193–195.

TODD, ALPHEUS, *Parliamentary Government in England*, I. 98–101, 129, 132, 143, 148, 150 ; II. 53, 76, 85, 155, 273, 274, 290, 292.

VINER, *Abridgment*, II. 201, 202.

VON RÖNNE, *Staatsrecht der Preussischen Monarchie*, II. 49, 51, 52, 161, 162.

WHARTON, *Criminal Law*, I. 18 ; II. 108.

WHARTON, *Criminal Pleading and Practice*, II. 182, 183.

WHITRIDGE, F. W., *Rotation in Office*, in the Political Science Quarterly, IV. 284 : II. 91.

WHITRIDGE, F. W., *Legislative Inquests*, in Political Science Quarterly, I. 84 : II. 270.

WIGRAM, *The Justices' Note-Book*, I. 239, 240.

WOOD, *History of Long Island*, I. 169.

WORTHINGTON, see Parker and Worthington.

ZORN, *Das Reichsstaatsrecht*, I. 16, 93–96, 116–119, 129, 140.

INDEX.